T0213738

# Lecture Notes in Artificial Intelligence    10162

Subseries of Lecture Notes in Computer Science

LNAI Series Editors

Randy Goebel
 *University of Alberta, Edmonton, Canada*
Yuzuru Tanaka
 *Hokkaido University, Sapporo, Japan*
Wolfgang Wahlster
 *DFKI and Saarland University, Saarbrücken, Germany*

LNAI Founding Series Editor

Joerg Siekmann
 *DFKI and Saarland University, Saarbrücken, Germany*

More information about this series at http://www.springer.com/series/1244

Jaap van den Herik · Joaquim Filipe (Eds.)

# Agents and Artificial Intelligence

8th International Conference, ICAART 2016
Rome, Italy, February 24–26, 2016
Revised Selected Papers

 Springer

*Editors*
Jaap van den Herik
Leiden University
Leiden
The Netherlands

Joaquim Filipe
Polytechnic Institute of Setúbal/INSTICC
Setúbal
Portugal

ISSN 0302-9743          ISSN 1611-3349 (electronic)
Lecture Notes in Artificial Intelligence
ISBN 978-3-319-53353-7          ISBN 978-3-319-53354-4 (eBook)
DOI 10.1007/978-3-319-53354-4

Library of Congress Control Number: 2017930646

LNCS Sublibrary: SL7 – Artificial Intelligence

© Springer International Publishing AG 2017
This work is subject to copyright. All rights are reserved by the Publisher, whether the whole or part of the material is concerned, specifically the rights of translation, reprinting, reuse of illustrations, recitation, broadcasting, reproduction on microfilms or in any other physical way, and transmission or information storage and retrieval, electronic adaptation, computer software, or by similar or dissimilar methodology now known or hereafter developed.
The use of general descriptive names, registered names, trademarks, service marks, etc. in this publication does not imply, even in the absence of a specific statement, that such names are exempt from the relevant protective laws and regulations and therefore free for general use.
The publisher, the authors and the editors are safe to assume that the advice and information in this book are believed to be true and accurate at the date of publication. Neither the publisher nor the authors or the editors give a warranty, express or implied, with respect to the material contained herein or for any errors or omissions that may have been made. The publisher remains neutral with regard to jurisdictional claims in published maps and institutional affiliations.

Printed on acid-free paper

This Springer imprint is published by Springer Nature
The registered company is Springer International Publishing AG
The registered company address is: Gewerbestrasse 11, 6330 Cham, Switzerland

# Preface

The present book includes extended and revised versions of a set of selected papers from the 8th International Conference on Agents and Artificial Intelligence (ICAART 2016), held in Rome, Italy, during February 24–26, 2016.

ICAART 2016 received 149 paper submissions from 39 countries, of which 12% are included in this book.

The papers were selected by the event chairs and their selection is based on a number of criteria that include the classifications and comments provided by the Program Committee members, the session chairs' assessment, and also the program chairs' global view of all papers included in the technical program. The authors of selected papers were then invited to submit a revised and extended version of their papers having at least 30% innovative material.

The purpose of the International Conference on Agents and Artificial Intelligence is to bring together researchers, engineers, and practitioners interested in the theory and applications in the areas of agents and artificial intelligence. The conference has two related tracks, covering both applications and current research work. One track focuses on agents, multi-agent systems and software platforms, agile management, distributed problem solving and distributed AI in general. The other track focuses mainly on artificial intelligence, knowledge representation, planning, learning, scheduling, perception, data mining, data science, reactive AI systems, and evolutionary computing and other topics related to intelligent systems and computational intelligence.

The papers included in this volume address a number of open research trends in agents and artificial intelligence. In an innovative manner the authors highlight the trends in intelligent multi-agent systems natural language processing, soft computing, and knowledge representation. In one way or another, all papers are related to knowledge representation.

In the intelligent multi-agent systems area we have included a set of five papers focusing on aspects related to team formation and planning. The topics addressed are: "Adaptive Team Formation in Changing Environments," "Multi-Agent Coalition Formation in Self-Interested Environments," and "Discrete Multi-Agent Plan Recognition: Recognizing Teams, Goals, and Plans from Action Sequences"; two additional papers in this area address more reflective issues, namely: "From Reviews to Arguments and from Arguments Back to Reviewers' Behavior," and "Model Checking Approaches to Branch-and-Bound Optimization of a Flow Production System." Finally, one paper discusses issues related to the interaction with virtual agents: Perception of Masculinity and Femininity of Agent's Appearance and Self-adaptors.

The area of natural language processing is approached from several perspectives by a set of four papers. Two of them are related to "Spatial and Temporal Understanding with Modelling the Directionality of Attention During Spatial Language Comprehension," and "Integrating Graded Knowledge and Temporal Change in a Modal Fragment of OWL"; two other papers are related to text understanding, namely: "Natural

Language Argumentation for Text Exploration," and "Advanced User Interfaces for Semantic Annotation of Complex Relations in Text."

Three papers focus on soft computing by discussing uncertainty representation, neural nets, and fuzzy systems. They are: "Enhancing Visual Clustering Using Adaptive Moving Self-Organizing Maps (AMSOM)," "An Automatic Approach for Generation of Fuzzy Membership Functions," and "Enhancing Support Vector Decoders by Integrating an Uncertainty Model." Finally, we have included in this book a set of papers that address knowledge representation, related to decision support and machine learning: "Qualitative Possibilistic Decisions," "Detecting Hidden Objects," and "Improving Cascade Classifier Precision"; two additional papers in this area use the Semantic Web principles to address issues such as privacy or context-based recommendations, namely: "Keeping Secrets in EL+ Knowledge Bases" and "An Agent-based Architecture for Personalized Recommendations."

We would like to thank all the authors for their contributions and to express our gratitude to the reviewers who helped ensure the quality of this publication.

February 2016

Jaap van den Herik
Joaquim Filipe

# Organization

## Conference Chair

Joaquim Filipe      Polytechnic Institute of Setúbal/INSTICC, Portugal

## Program Chair

Jaap van den Herik      Leiden University, The Netherlands

## Program Committee

| | |
|---|---|
| Giovanni Acampora | University of Naples Federico II, Italy |
| Jose Aguilar | Universidad de Los Andes, Venezuela |
| Varol Akman | Bilkent University, Turkey |
| Isabel Machado Alexandre | Instituto Universitário de Lisboa (ISCTE-IUL) and Instituto de Telecomunicações, Portugal |
| Vicki Allan | Utah State University, USA |
| Klaus-Dieter Althoff | German Research Center for Artificial Intelligence/ University of Hildesheim, Germany |
| Francisco Martínez Álvarez | Pablo de Olavide University of Seville, Spain |
| Frédéric Amblard | IRIT - Université Toulouse 1 Capitole, France |
| Cesar Analide | University of Minho, Portugal |
| Andreas S. Andreou | Cyprus University of Technology, Cyprus |
| Diana Arellano | Filmakademie Baden-Württemberg, Germany |
| Tsz-Chiu Au | Ulsan National Institute of Science and Technology, Republic of Korea |
| Jean-Michel Auberlet | IFSTTAR (French Institute of Science and Technology for Transport, Development and Networks), France |
| Snorre Aunet | Norwegian University of Science and Technology, Norway |
| Kerstin Bach | Norwegian University of Science and Technology, Norway |
| Florence Bannay | IRIT, Toulouse University, France |
| Federico Barber | Universidad Politécnica de Valencia, Spain |
| Kamel Barkaoui | Cedric-CNAM, France |
| John Barnden | University of Birmingham, UK |
| Roman Barták | Charles University in Prague, Czech Republic |
| Teresa M.A. Basile | Università degli Studi di Bari, Italy |
| Sebastián Basterrech | National Supercomputing Center, Technical University of Ostrava, Czech Republic |

| | |
|---|---|
| Nabil Belacel | National Research Council Canada, Canada |
| Christoph Benzmüller | Freie Universität Berlin, Germany |
| Carole Bernon | University of Paul Sabatier, Toulouse III, France |
| El Hassan Bezzazi | Faculté Droit Lille, France |
| Ludovico Boratto | Eurecat, Spain |
| Marco Botta | Università degli Studi di Torino, Italy |
| Djamel Bouchaffra | Centre de Développement des Technologies Avancées (CDTA), Algeria |
| Noury Bouraqadi | Ecole Des Mines De Douai, France |
| Ramón F. Brena | Tecnológico De Monterrey, Campus Monterrey, Mexico |
| Paolo Bresciani | Fondazione Bruno Kessler, Italy |
| Stefano Bromuri | University of Applied Sciences Western Switzerland, Switzerland |
| Mark Burgin | University of California, USA |
| Aleksander Byrski | AGH University of Science and Technology, Poland |
| Giacomo Cabri | Università di Modena e Reggio Emilia, Italy |
| Patrice Caire | University of Luxembourg, Luxembourg |
| Silvia Calegari | Università Degli Studi Di Milano Bicocca, Italy |
| David Camacho | Universidad Autónoma de Madrid, Spain |
| Rui Camacho | Faculdade de Engenharia da Universidade do Porto, Portugal |
| Valérie Camps | IRIT, Université Paul Sabatier, France |
| Amilcar Cardoso | University of Coimbra, Portugal |
| John Cartlidge | University of Nottingham in Ningbo China, China |
| Ana Casali | Universidad Nacional de Rosario (UNR) and CIFASIS, Argentina |
| Cristiano Castelfranchi | Institute of Cognitive Sciences and Technologies, National Research Council, Italy |
| Patrick De Causmaecker | Katholieke Universiteit Leuven, Belgium |
| Amedeo Cesta | CNR, Consiglio Nazionale delle Ricerche, Italy |
| Wen-Chung Chang | National Taipei University of Technology, Taiwan |
| Mu-Song Chen | Da-Yeh University, Taiwan |
| Adam Cheyer | SRI International, USA |
| Anders Lyhne Christensen | Instituto Superior das Ciências do Trabalho e da Empresa, Portugal |
| Robin Cohen | University of Waterloo, Canada |
| Carlo Combi | Università degli Studi di Verona, Italy |
| Gabriella Cortellessa | ISTC-CNR, Italy |
| Paulo Cortez | University of Minho, Portugal |
| Massimo Cossentino | National Research Council, Italy |
| Matteo Cristani | University of Verona, Italy |
| Darryl N. Davis | University of Hull, UK |
| Andreas Dengel | German Research Center for Artificial Intelligence (DFKI GmbH), Germany |
| Enrico Denti | Alma Mater Studiorum, Università di Bologna, Italy |
| Ioan Despi | UNE, Australia |

| | |
|---|---|
| Dragan Doder | University of Luxembourg, Luxembourg |
| Agostino Dovier | Università degli Studi di Udine, Italy |
| Marek J. Druzdzel | University of Pittsburgh, USA |
| Béatrice Duval | LERIA, France |
| Michael Dyer | University of California Los Angeles, USA |
| Stefan Edelkamp | Universität Bremen, Germany |
| Thomas Eiter | Technische Universität Wien, Austria |
| Fabrício Enembreck | Pontifical Catholic University of Paraná, Brazil |
| Floriana Esposito | Università degli Studi di Bari, Italy |
| Maria Fasli | University of Essex, UK |
| Christophe Feltus | Luxembourg Institute of Science and Technology, Luxembourg |
| Stefano Ferilli | University of Bari, Italy |
| Alberto Fernández | University Rey Juan Carlos, Spain |
| Vladimir J. Filipovic | Belgrade University, Serbia |
| Klaus Fischer | German Research Center for Artificial Intelligence DFKI GmbH, Germany |
| Roberto Flores | Christopher Newport University, USA |
| Agostino Forestiero | ICAR-CNR, Italy |
| Claude Frasson | University of Montreal, Canada |
| Muhammad Marwan Muhammad Fuad | Aarhus University, Denmark |
| Naoki Fukuta | Shizuoka University, Japan |
| Sarah Alice Gaggl | Technische Universität Dresden, Germany |
| Catherine Garbay | CNRS, France |
| Leonardo Garrido | Tecnológico de Monterrey, Campus Monterrey, Mexico |
| Alfredo Garro | Università della Calabria, Italy |
| Max Gath | Center for Computing and Communication Technologies, Universität Bremen, Germany |
| Benoit Gaudou | University of Toulouse 1 Capitole, France |
| Andrey Gavrilov | Novosibirsk State Technical University, Russian Federation |
| Jean-Pierre Georgé | University of Toulouse, IRIT, France |
| Maria Gini | University of Minnesota, USA |
| Adrian Giurca | Brandenburgische Technische Universität Cottbus, Germany |
| Herman Gomes | Federal University of Campina Grande, Brazil |
| Madhu Goyal | University of Technology, Sydney, Australia |
| Perry Groot | Radboud University Nijmegen, The Netherlands |
| Sven Groppe | University of Lübeck, Germany |
| James Harland | RMIT University, Australia |
| Hisashi Hayashi | Toshiba Corporation, Japan |
| Pedro Rangel Henriques | University of Minho, Portugal |
| Jaap van den Herik | Leiden University, The Netherlands |
| Hanno Hildmann | Universidad Carlos III de Madrid, Spain |
| Rolf Hoffmann | Darmstadt University of Technology, Germany |

| Wladyslaw Homenda | Warsaw University of Technology, Poland |
| Wei-Chiang Hong | Oriental Institute of Technology, Taiwan |
| Mark Hoogendoorn | Vrije Universiteit Amsterdam, The Netherlands |
| Ales Horak | Masaryk University, Czech Republic |
| Jomi Fred Hübner | Federal University of Santa Catarina, Brazil |
| Marc-Philippe Huget | University of Savoie Mont-Blanc, France |
| Luke Hunsberger | Vassar College, USA |
| Dieter Hutter | German Research Centre for Artificial Intelligence, Germany |
| Carlos Iglesias | Universidad Politécnica de Madrid, Spain |
| Hiroyuki Iida | JAIST, Japan |
| Thomas Ioerger | Texas A&M University, USA |
| Luis Iribarne | University of Almería, Spain |
| Sherif Ishak | Louisiana State University and A&M College, USA |
| Michael Jenkin | York University, Canada |
| Janusz Kacprzyk | Polish Academy of Sciences, Poland |
| Ozgur Kafali | North Carolina State University, USA |
| Geylani Kardas | Ege University International Computer Institute, Turkey |
| Petros Kefalas | CITY College, International Faculty of the University of Sheffield, Greece |
| Graham Kendall | University of Nottingham Malaysia Campus, Malaysia |
| Gabriele Kern-Isberner | TU Dortmund University, Germany |
| Sung-Dong Kim | Hansung University, Republic of Korea |
| Stefan Kirn | University of Hohenheim, Germany |
| Fernando Koch | Samsung Research Institute, Brazil |
| Ah-Lian Kor | Leeds Beckett University, UK |
| John Korah | Illinois Institute of Technology, USA |
| Hristo Koshutanski | Universidad de Málaga, Spain |
| Andrew Koster | Samsung, Brazil |
| Igor Kotenko | St. Petersburg Institute for Informatics and Automation of the Russian Academy of Sciences (SPIIRAS), Russian Federation |
| Pavel Kral | University of West Bohemia, Czech Republic |
| Uirá Kulesza | Federal University of Rio Grande do Norte (UFRN), Brazil |
| Amruth N. Kumar | Ramapo College of New Jersey, USA |
| Yau-Hwang Kuo | National Cheng Kung University, Taiwan |
| Cat Kutay | UTS, Australia |
| Mila Kwiatkowska | Thompson Rivers University, Canada |
| Jérôme Lang | Université Paris-Dauphine, France |
| Ramoni Lasisi | Virginia Military Institute, USA |
| Letizia Leonardi | Università di Modena e Reggio Emilia, Italy |
| Renato Levy | Intelligent Automation, Inc., USA |
| Churn-Jung Liau | Academia Sinica, Taiwan |
| Francesca Alessandra Lisi | Università degli Studi di Bari Aldo Moro, Italy |
| Chao-Lin Liu | National Chengchi University, Taiwan |

| Weiru Liu | Queen's University Belfast, UK |
| Faraón Llorens-Largo | Universidad de Alicante, Spain |
| Stephane Loiseau | LERIA, University of Angers, France |
| António Lopes | University Institute of Lisbon, Portugal |
| Noel Lopes | IPG, Portugal |
| Manuel López-Ibáñez | University of Manchester, UK |
| Emiliano Lorini | IRIT - CNRS, France |
| Adolfo Lozano-Tello | Universidad de Extremadura, Spain |
| Bernd Ludwig | University of Regensburg, Germany |
| Daniela Lopéz De Luise | CIIS Lab, Argentina |
| José Machado | Centro ALGORITMI, University of Minho, Portugal |
| Lorenzo Magnani | Università degli Studi di Pavia, Italy |
| Letizia Marchegiani | Oxford University, UK |
| Elisa Marengo | Free University of Bozen-Bolzano, Italy |
| Goreti Marreiros | Polytechnic Institute of Porto, Portugal |
| Nicola Di Mauro | Università di Bari, Italy |
| Miguel Angel Mayosky | National University of La Plata, Argentina |
| Fiona McNeill | Heriot-Watt University, UK |
| Paola Mello | Università di Bologna, Italy |
| Eduardo Mena | University of Zaragoza, Spain |
| Benito Mendoza | CUNY, New York City College of Technology, USA |
| Emanuela Merelli | University of Camerino, Italy |
| Daniel Merkle | University of Southern Denmark, Denmark |
| Marjan Mernik | University of Maribor, Slovenia |
| Elena Messina | National Institute of Standards and Technology, USA |
| Bernd Meyer | Monash University, Australia |
| John-Jules Meyer | Utrecht University, The Netherlands |
| Ambra Molesini | Alma Mater Studiorum, Università di Bologna, Italy |
| Raul Monroy | Tec de Monterrey in Mexico, Mexico |
| José Moreira | Universidade de Aveiro, Portugal |
| Pedro Moreira | Escola Superior de Tecnologia e Gestão, Instituto Politécnico de Viana do Castelo, Portugal |
| Maxime Morge | University of Lille, France |
| Bernard Moulin | Université Laval, Canada |
| Conor Muldoon | University College Dublin, Ireland |
| Konstantinos Nikolopoulos | Bangor University, UK |
| Jens Nimis | Hochschule Karlsruhe, Technik und Wirtschaft, Germany |
| Farid Nouioua | LSIS UMR 7296 du CNRS, Aix-Marseille University, France |
| Luis Nunes | Instituto Universitário de Lisboa (ISCTE-IUL) and Instituto de Telecomunicações (IT), Portugal |
| Andreas Oberweis | Karlsruhe Institute of Technology (KIT), Germany |
| Michel Occello | Université Pierre-Mendès-France, France |
| Dimitri Ognibene | Universitat Pompeu Fabra, Spain |
| Haldur Õim | University of Tartu, Estonia |

| Sancho Oliveira | Instituto Universitário de Lisboa (ISCTE-IUL), Portugal |
| Andrea Omicini | Alma Mater Studiorum, Università di Bologna, Italy |
| Stanislaw Osowski | Warsaw University of Technology, Poland |
| Nandan Parameswaran | University of New South Wales, Australia |
| Antonio Gonzalez Pardo | Universidad Autonoma de Madrid, Spain |
| Andrew Parkes | University of Nottingham, UK |
| Krzysztof Patan | University of Zielona Gora, Poland |
| Manuel G. Penedo | University of A Coruña, Spain |
| Célia da Costa Pereira | Université de Nice Sophia Antipolis, France |
| Wim Peters | University of Sheffield, UK |
| Tuan Pham | University of Aizu, Japan |
| Gauthier Picard | Hubert Curien CNRS Laboratory, France |
| Aske Plaat | Tilburg University, The Netherlands |
| Agostino Poggi | University of Parma, Italy |
| Filipe Portela | Centro ALGORITMI, University of Minho, Portugal |
| Riccardo Rasconi | National Research Council of Italy, Italy |
| Marcello Restelli | Politecnico Di Milano, Italy |
| Lluís Ribas-Xirgo | Universitat Autònoma de Barcelona, Spain |
| Patrizia Ribino | ICAR- CNR, Italy |
| Alessandro Ricci | Alma Mater Studiorum - Università di Bologna, Italy |
| Eva Onaindía de la Rivaherrera | Universitat Politécnica de Valencia, Spain |
| Fátima Rodrigues | Instituto Superior de Engenharia do Porto (ISEP/IPP), Portugal |
| Daniel Rodriguez | University of Alcalá, Spain |
| Andrea Roli | Università di Bologna, Italy |
| Javier Carbó Rubiera | Universidad Carlos III de Madrid, Spain |
| Alvaro Rubio-Largo | University of Extremadura, Spain |
| Ruben Ruiz | Universidad Politécnica de Valencia, Spain |
| Luca Sabatucci | National Research Council, Italy |
| Fariba Sadri | Imperial College London, UK |
| Lorenza Saitta | Università degli Studi del Piemonte Orientale Amedeo Avogadro, Italy |
| Francesco Santini | Università di Perugia, Italy |
| Jorge Gomez Sanz | Universidad Complutense de Madrid, Spain |
| Fabio Sartori | Università degli Studi di Milano Bicocca, Italy |
| Christoph Schommer | University Luxembourg, Campus Kirchberg, Luxembourg |
| Johan Schubert | Swedish Defence Research Agency, Sweden |
| Valeria Seidita | University of Palermo, Italy |
| Leticia María Seijas | University of Buenos Aires, Argentina |
| Ivan Serina | University of Brescia, Italy |
| Emilio Serrano | Universidad Politécnica de Madrid, Spain |
| Mohammad Shojafar | University Sapienza of Rome, Italy |
| Danielle Rousy Dias da Silva | UFPB, Brazil |

| | |
|---|---|
| Flavio S. Correa Da Silva | University of Sao Paulo, Brazil |
| Viviane Silva | IBM Research, Brazil |
| Ricardo Silveira | Universidade Federal de Santa Catarina, Brazil |
| David Sislak | Czech Technical University in Prague, Agent Technology Center, Czech Republic |
| Alexander Smirnov | SPIIRAS, Russian Federation |
| Marina V. Sokolova | Instituto de Investigación en Informática de Albacete, Spain |
| Margarita Sordo | Harvard Medical School, USA |
| Armando J. Sousa | Universidade do Porto, Portugal |
| Bernd Steinbach | Freiberg University of Mining and Technology, Germany |
| Oliviero Stock | Fondazione Bruno Kessler, Italy |
| Emmanuelle Grislin-Le Strugeon | LAMIH, Université de Valenciennes, France |
| Thomas Stützle | Université Libre de Bruxelles, Belgium |
| Toshiharu Sugawara | Waseda University, Japan |
| Vijayan Sugumaran | Oakland University, USA |
| Boontawee Suntisrivaraporn | Sirindhorn International Institute of Technology, Thailand |
| Pavel Surynek | National Institute of Advanced Industrial Science and Technology (AIST), Japan |
| Yasuhiro Suzuki | Graduate School of Information Science, Nagoya University, Japan |
| Ryszard Tadeusiewicz | AGH University of Science and Technology, Poland |
| Nick Taylor | Heriot-Watt University, UK |
| Mark Terwilliger | University of North Alabama, USA |
| Jan Tozicka | CTU in Prague, Czech Republic |
| Thomas Tran | University of Ottawa, Canada |
| Franco Turini | KDD Lab, University of Pisa, Italy |
| Paulo Urbano | Faculdade de Ciências da Universidade de Lisboa, Portugal |
| Marco Valtorta | University of South Carolina, USA |
| Eloisa Vargiu | EURECAT, Spain |
| Srdjan Vesic | CNRS, France |
| Serena Villata | CNRS, France |
| Marin Vlada | University of Bucharest, Romania |
| George Vouros | University of Piraeus, Greece |
| Yves Wautelet | KU Leuven, Belgium |
| Stephan Weiss | Alpen-Adria-Universität Klagenfurt, Austria |
| Jianshu Weng | HP Labs Singapore, Singapore |
| Cees Witteveen | Delft University of Technology, The Netherlands |
| T.N. Wong | The University of Hong Kong, Hong Kong, SAR China |
| Bozena Wozna-Szczesniak | Jan Dlugosz University, Poland |
| Ning Xiong | Mälardalen University, Sweden |

Feiyu Xu                    Deutsches Forschungszentrum für Künstliche Intelligenz
                             (DFKI), Germany
Bruno Zanuttini            GREYC, Normandie Université, UNICAEN,
                             CNRS UMR 6072, ENSICAEN, France
Pascale Zaraté             Université Toulouse 1 Capitole, France
Haibin Zhu                 Nipissing University, Canada
Jean-Daniel Zucker         UMI UMMISCO, France
Alejandro Zunino           ISISTAN, Universidad Nacional del Centro de la Provincia
                             de Buenos Aires, Argentina

## Additional Reviewers

Viktor Ayzenshtadt         University of Hildesheim/DFKI, Germany
Xenofon Fafoutis           University of Bristol, UK
Stefano Ferilli            University of Bari, Italy
Bruno Fernandes            Universidade de Pernambuco, Brazil
Carmelo Bastos Filho       University of Pernambuco, Brazil
Sebastian Palacio          DFKI GmbH, Germany
Andrea Pazienza            University of Bari, Italy
Pascal Reuss               University of Hildesheim, Germany
Andrea Tundis              University of Calabria, Italy
Alessandro Umbrico         Università degli studi Roma Tre, Italy
Autilia Vitiello           University of Salerno, Italy
Roberto Yus                University of Zaragoza, Spain

## Invited Speakers

Katia Sycara               Carnegie Mellon University, USA
Tom Heskes                 Radboud University Nijmegen, The Netherlands
Jérôme Lang                Université Paris-Dauphine, France
Jaime Sichman              University of São Paulo, Brazil
Eric Postma                Tilburg University, The Netherlands

# Contents

# Agents

# Perception of Masculinity and Femininity of Agent's Appearance and Self-adaptors

Tomoko Koda[1(✉)], Takuto Ishioh[1], Takafumi Watanabe[2], and Yoshihiko Kubo[2]

[1] Graduate School of Information Science and Technology,
Osaka Institute of Technology, Osaka, Japan
tomoko.koda@oit.ac.jp, mlm16a03@st.oit.ac.jp
[2] Department of Information Science and Technology,
Osaka Institute of Technology, Osaka, Japan

**Abstract.** This paper reports how our perception of virtual agents differ by the combination of the gender of their appearances and gestures. We examined how we perceive masculinity and femininity of agents and how our perception of agent's gender affect our impression of the agent. Human-human interactions among Japanese undergraduate students were analyzed with respect to usage of gender-specific self-adaptors in a pre-experiment. Based on the results, a male and a female agent were animated to show these extracted self-adaptors. Evaluation of the interactions with the agents that exhibit self-adaptors typically exhibited by Japanese human male and female indicated that there are cross gender interactions between participants' gender and agents' gender. Male participants showed more favorable impressions on agents that display feminine self-adaptors than masculine ones performed by the female agent, while female participants showed rigorous impressions toward feminine self-adaptors. Although the obtained results were limited to one culture and narrow age range, these results implies there is a possibility that the combination of male appearance and masculine gestures is "safer" in order to facilitate neutral impressions and avoid any cross gender interactions made by the gender of human users. Designers of virtual agents should consider gender of appearance and gesture animations of virtual agents, and make them customizable according to the user's gender and preferences.

**Keywords:** Conversational agents · Intelligent virtual agents · IVA · Gesture · Self-adaptors · Non-verbal behavior · Gender · Evaluation

## 1 Introduction

Intelligent virtual agents (IVAs) that interact face-to-face with humans are beginning to spread to general users, and IVA research is being actively pursued. IVAs require both verbal and nonverbal communication abilities. Among those non-verbal communications, Ekman classifies gestures into five categories: emblems, illustrators, affect displays, adapters, and regulators [1]. Self-adaptors are non-signaling gestures that are not

© Springer International Publishing AG 2017
J. van den Herik and J. Filipe (Eds.): ICAART 2016, LNAI 10162, pp. 3–18, 2017.
DOI: 10.1007/978-3-319-53354-4_1

intended to convey a particular meaning [2]. They are exhibited as hand movements where one part of the body is applied to another part of the body, such as picking one's nose, scratching one's head and face, moistening the lips, or tapping the foot. Many self-adaptors are considered taboo in public, and individuals with low emotional stability perform more self-adaptors, and the number of self-adaptors increases with psychological discomfort or anxiety [2–4]. According to Caso et al. self-adaptor gestures were used more often when telling the truth than when lying [5].

Because self-adaptors have low message content and are low in relevancy to the contents of conversations, they are believed to be actions that are easily ignored during a conversation. Thus, there has not been much IVA research done on self-adaptors, compared with nonverbal communication with high message content, such as facial expressions and gazes. Among few research that has dealt with an IVA with self-adaptors, Neff et al. reported that an agent performing self-adaptors (repetitive quick motion with a combination of scratching its face and head, touching its body, and rubbing its head, etc.), was perceived as having low emotional stability. Although showing emotional unstableness might not be appropriate in some social interactions, their finding suggests the importance of self-adaptors in conveying a personality of an agent [6].

However, self-adaptors are not always the sign of emotional unstableness or stress. Blacking states self-adaptors also occur in casual conversations, where conversants are very relaxed [7]. Chartrand and Bargh have shown that mimicry of particular types of self-adaptors (i.e., foot tapping and face scratching) can cause the mimicked person to perceive an interaction as more positive, and may lead to form rapport between the conversants [8].

We focus on these "relaxed" self-adaptors performed in a casual conversation in this study. If those relaxed self-adaptors occur with a conversant that one feels friendliness, one can be induced to feel friendliness toward a conversant that displays self-adaptors. We apply this to the case of agent conversant, and hypothesize that users can be induced to feel friendliness toward the agent by adding self-adaptors to the body motions of an agent, and conducted two experiments.

The first experiment evaluated continuous interactions between an agent that exhibits self-adaptors and without [9]. The results showed the agent that exhibited relaxed self-adaptors was more likely to prevent any deterioration in the perceived friendliness of the agent than the agent without self-adaptors. However, when we consider evaluators social skills, there is a dichotomy on the impression on the agents between users with high social skills (HSS hereafter) and those with low skills (LSS hereafter). Social skills are defined as "skills that are instrumental in conducting smooth personal communication" [10]. People with HSS are able to read nonverbal behaviors of their conversants and tend to use a great amount of nonverbal behaviors themselves in order to makes smooth interactions. We focused on this characteristic of social skills and considered that it could have the same effect when applied to non-verbal behavior of an agent. The results of the first experiment indicated people with HSS harbour a higher perceived friendliness with agents that exhibited relaxed self-adaptors than people with LSS. Moreover, HSS's friendliness feeling toward the agent with self-adaptors increased over time, while LSS felt higher friendliness toward the agent that does not exhibit self-adaptors. The dichotomy between the use's social skills suggests that it is possible to continually improve users' sense of friendliness toward IVAs by combining the presence of self-adaptors with the user's level of social skills during continued interactions with agents.

The second experiment evaluated interactions with agents that exhibit either relaxed self-adaptors or stressful self-adaptors in a desert survival task [11]. The results indicated that the exhibiting of any types of self-adaptors in interactions that exchange serious opinions, such as a desert survival task, caused deterioration in the agents perceived friendliness and empathy, although such deterioration does not occur during a casual conversation with the agent displays self-adaptors. This results suggests that users unconsciously expect agents to behave in a manner that is appropriate to the topic of conversation as we do with humans. Thus non-verbal behaviors of agents should adapt to the conversational topics. Taken together with the results of previous research, the results shows that it will be necessary to make the non-verbal behavior of an agent, at least, self-adaptors, adapt to the social skills of the other person in an interaction, and to the conversational content.

This paper reports a result of our consecutive experiment of self-adaptors that deals with gender issues. As Cassell points out in [12, 13], considering gender effect is essential for successful and comfortable human-computer interaction, so as for human-agent interaction.

## 2   Related Research on Gender and Virtual Agents

Social psychology studies have indicated gender stereotypes and roles. Men are regarded as more dominant, influential and more effective leaders than women, while women are submissive, supportive, and better listeners than men [14, 15]. Commercially used virtual agents mainly serve as virtual assistant chatbots to help online users. They are often represented as female due to the above gender stereotypes, i.e., Aetna's virtual online assistant Ann (Fig. 1(a)[1]), IKEA's virtual assistant Anna (Fig. 1(b)[2]), and Alaska Airline's virtual assistant Jenn (Fig. 1(c)[3]).

However, it is still an open question whether female appearance is adequate for any virtual agent applications and domains. Zanbaka et al. examined the role of gender in an application where virtual agents act as persuasive speakers, and found cross gender interactions between the agents' gender and the participants' gender. The male participants were more persuaded by the female agent than the male agent, and female participants are more persuaded by the male agent than the female agent [16].

Our two previous experiments used a female agent only and did not consider the effects of appearance of the agent's gender. Moreover, as some self-adaptors are gender-specific [17], i.e., "crossing arms" self-adaptors are more frequently found in

---

[1] https://member.aetna.com/AskAnn/agent.aspx.

[2] https://twitter.com/IKEA_jp_Anna.

[3] https://www.alaskaair.com/content/about-us/site-info/ask-jenn.aspx.

(a) Aetna's virtual online assistant Ann

(b) IKEA's virtual assistant Anna

(c) Alaska Airline's virtual assistant Jenn

**Fig. 1.** Female virtual agents used for commercial purpose.

males, and "covering mouth" self-adaptors are mostly found in Japanese females, we need to consider gender of the agent, gender-specific self-adaptors, and gender of participants.

Hence, we evaluate the impression of the agents with male/female appearance and masculine/feminine self-adaptors in this experiment in order to examine whether cross gender effects similar to [16] can be found in our experimental settings. We hypothesize that (1) when the agent's gender, and gender of the gender-specific self-adaptors are consistent, participants feel higher naturalness. (2) Male participants have better impression toward the agent with female appearance and feminine self-adaptors, while female participants have better impression on the agent with male appearance and masculine self-adaptors", and conduct an experiment.

## 3    Video Analysis of Self-adaptors and Implementation of Agent Animation

### 3.1    Video Analysis of Self-adaptors

We conducted a pre-experiment in order to examine when and what kind of self-adaptors are performed, and whether/what kind of gender-specific self-adaptors are found during a casual conversation between friends in a Japanese university. We invited ten pairs (5 male pairs and 5 female pairs) who are friends for more than three years (they are university students who study together) to record their free conversation for 20 min.

The video analysis were made in terms of the body parts touched, frequency of each self-adaptors, and number of participants who performed each self-adaptors during the conversation for all 20 participants. Total of 587 self-adaptors were identified during the 20 min recordings of the 10 male participants. Total of 617 self-adaptors were identified during the 20 min recordings of the 10 female participants. Figures 2 and 3 show the body parts touched by the male and female participants

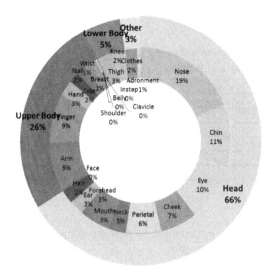

**Fig. 2.** Ratio of body parts touched by the male participants.

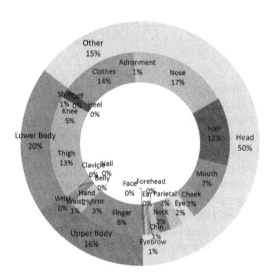

**Fig. 3.** Ratio of body parts touched by the female participants.

respectively. The most frequently touched body part by the Japanese male participants is head (66%), followed by upper body (26%). The most frequently touched body part by the Japanese female participants is head (50%), followed by upper body (16%). Table 1 shows the top five types of self-adaptors performed most frequently and most participants (how and which body parts were touched, how many times for each self-adaptor, and by how many people for each self-adaptor) by the male participants and Table 2 by the female participants.

**Table 1.** Number of self-adaptors performed by male participants in video recordings (left: number of times, right: number of people).

| Male participants | | n=587 | Male participants | | n=10 |
|---|---|---|---|---|---|
| Order | Self-adaptor | Frequency | Order | Self-adaptor | Number of participants |
| 1 | touching nose | 61 | 1 | scratching head | 9 |
| 2 | toucing chin | 55 | 2 | touching nose | 9 |
| 3 | scratching head | 35 | 3 | scratching forehead | 6 |
| 4 | touching cheek | 30 | 4 | touching chin | 6 |
| 5 | scratching nose | 29 | 5 | scratching neck | 6 |

**Table 2.** Number of self-adaptors performed by female participants in video recordings (left: number of times, right: number of people).

| Female participants | | n=617 | Female participants | | n=10 |
|---|---|---|---|---|---|
| Order | Self-adapator | Frequency | Order | Self-adaptor | Number of participants |
| 1 | Touching nose | 66 | 1 | Touching mouth | 8 |
| 2 | Stroking hair | 49 | 2 | Touching nose | 7 |
| 3 | Touhcing sleeves | 40 | 3 | Stroking hair | 6 |
| 4 | Toucing mouth | 38 | 4 | Touching bangs | 6 |
| 5 | Touching fingers | 31 | 5 | Scratching nose | 6 |

We identified the following gender-specific self-adaptors from the recordings of the conversations among Japanese university students. There are three types of self-adaptors occurred most frequently in most male participants: "touching nose", "touching chin," and "scratching head." We call these self-adaptors as "masculine self-adaptors" hereafter. The most frequent self-adaptors performed by most female participants are "touching nose", "stroking hair", and "touching mouth (covering mouth)". We call these self-adaptors as "feminine self-adaptors" hereafter. Figure 4 shows typical masculine self-adaptors seen in the video recordings performed by Japanese male students, and Fig. 5 shows those by Japanese female students.

We implement those masculine/feminine self-adaptors to our conversational agents for the experiment. In terms of the timing of self-adaptors, 50% occurred at the beginning of the utterances in the video recordings.

**Fig. 4.** Male participants perform three masculine self-adaptors (from left: "touching chin," "scratching head," and "touching nose".

**Fig. 5.** Female participants perform three feminine self-adaptors (from left: "touching nose", "stroking hair", and "touching lips (covering mouth)".

## 3.2 Agent Character and Animation Implementation

The agent characters (male and female) and animation of the six types of self-adaptors were created using Poser[4]. Figures 6 and 7 show the agents carrying out the three masculine self-adaptors and three feminine self-adaptors respectively. We created the following four types of animations in order to examine the combination of gender of the character and self-adaptors; "male agent performs masculine self-adaptors", "male

**Fig. 6.** Male agent performs three masculine self-adaptors (from left: "touching chin," "scratching head," and "touching nose".

---

[4] http://poser.smithmicro.com/poser.html.

**Fig. 7.** Female agent performs three feminine self-adaptors (from left: "touching nose", "stroking hair", and "touching lips (covering mouth)".

agent performs feminine self-adaptors", "female agent performs masculine self-adaptors", "female agent performs feminine self-adaptors."

We found no literature that explicitly described the form of the movement (e.g., how the nose has been touched, in which way, by which part of the hand etc.), we mimicked the form of the movements of the participants in the video recordings. We adjust the timing of the animation of self-adaptors at the beginning of the agent's utterances as found in the video recordings.

Besides these self-adaptors, we created animations of the agent making gestures of "greeting" and "placing its hand against its chest." These gestures were carried out by the agent at appropriate times in accordance to the content of the conversation regardless of experimental conditions in order not to let self-adaptors stand out during a conversation with the agent.

## 4 Experiment

### 4.1 Experimental System

The agent's conversation system was developed in C++ using Microsoft Visual Studio 2008. The agent's voices were synthesized as male and female voice using the Japanese voice synthesis package AITalk[5]. Conversation scenarios, composed of questions from the agent and response choices, were created beforehand, and animation of the agent that reflected the conversational scenario was created. Figure 8 shows the experiment system components. By connecting animated sequences in accordance of the content of the user's responses, the system realized a pseudo-conversation with the user. The conversation system has two states. The first state was the agent speech state, in which an animated sequence of the agent uttering speech and asking questions to the user was shown. The other state was the standby for user selection state, in which the user chose a response from options displayed on the screen above the agent. In response to the user's response input from a keyboard, animated agent movie that followed the conversation scenario was played back in the speech state.

---

[5] http://www.ai-j.jp/.

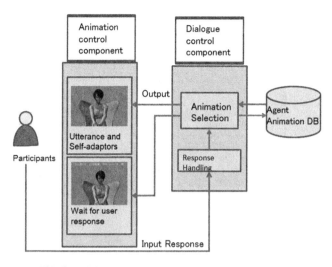

**Fig. 8.** Dialogue and agent animation control system.

## 4.2    Experimental Procedure

The interactions with the agents were presented as pseudo conversations as follows: (1) the agent always asks a question to the participant. (2) Possible answers were displayed on the screen and the participant selects one answer from the selection from a keyboard. (3) The agent makes remarks based on the user's answer and asks the next question. The contents of the conversations were casual (the route to school, residential area, and favorite food, etc.). The reason we adopted the pseudo-conversation method was to eliminate the effect of the accuracy of speech recognition of the users' spoken answers, which would otherwise be used, on the participants' impression of the agent.

The participants in the experiment were 29 Japanese undergraduate students (19 male and 10 female), aged 20–23 years, who did not participate in the video recording pre-experiment. The experiment is conducted as 3 × 2 factorial design. The experimental conditions are participants' gender (male/female), agent's gender (male/female), gender of self-adaptor (male/female). Each participant interacted with all four types of agents (male agent performing masculine self-adaptors, male agent performing feminine self-adaptors, female agent performing masculine self-adaptors, female agent performing feminine self-adaptors) randomly assigned to them. Thus, there are four conversation sessions with different combination of the agent and self-adaptor for each participant. The conversational topics are different for each interaction and the topics are randomized. Each agent performed three all gender specific self-adaptors in any interaction and the gestures of "greeting" and "placing its hand against its chest."

After each interaction, the participants rated their impressions on the agent using a semantic differential method on a scale from 1 to 6. A total of 27 pairs of adjectives, consisting of the 20 pairs from the Adjective Check List (ACL) for Interpersonal Cognition for Japanese [10] and seven original pairs (concerning the agent's

**Table 3.** Four factors and adjectives for interpersonal impressions.

| | | Factor | | | | | | |
|---|---|---|---|---|---|---|---|---|
| | | 1 | 2 | 3 | 4 | 5 | 6 | 7 |
| Tolerance | Short-tempered – Calm | .921 | -.029 | -.118 | -.054 | -.120 | -.054 | .100 |
| | Narrow-minded – Broad-minded | .782 | -.049 | -.072 | -.135 | -.080 | .070 | .011 |
| | Unkind – Kind | .700 | .223 | .060 | -.001 | -.079 | .148 | -.011 |
| | Rough – Soft | .644 | -.149 | .195 | -.074 | .064 | .061 | .219 |
| | Unsoficated – Sofisticated | .571 | -.047 | .440 | -.033 | .064 | -.033 | -.057 |
| | Annoying – Quiet | .413 | -.040 | .332 | -.137 | .322 | -.082 | -.073 |
| | Unpleasant – Pleasant | .343 | .247 | .101 | .108 | .250 | .249 | -.076 |
| Sociability | Inert – Active | -.039 | .833 | .064 | .022 | .029 | .126 | -.117 |
| | Gloomy – Cheerful | -.105 | .714 | .333 | .153 | -.228 | -.162 | .067 |
| | Unconfident – Confident | -.058 | .678 | -.082 | -.064 | .067 | -.095 | .204 |
| | Unsocial – Social | .151 | .548 | -.087 | .089 | -.016 | .118 | .009 |
| | Servile – Grand | .004 | .452 | -.317 | -.116 | .211 | -.090 | .314 |
| | Unshy – Shy | -.004 | -.385 | .313 | .064 | .213 | -.033 | .243 |
| Gender | Hateful – Lovable | -.063 | .306 | .766 | .347 | .055 | -.020 | .100 |
| | Masculine – Feminine | .005 | .146 | .758 | -.399 | .003 | .135 | .254 |
| | Tough – Delicate | .088 | -.297 | .645 | .124 | -.096 | -.132 | -.148 |
| | Immature – Mature | .247 | .162 | -.407 | .224 | .222 | -.044 | -.189 |
| Naturalness | Unnatural – Natural | -.076 | .137 | -.088 | .656 | .077 | .073 | -.031 |
| | Unhumanlike – Humanlike | -.141 | .020 | .005 | .628 | -.094 | .029 | .078 |
| | Unreasonable – Reasonable | -.110 | -.055 | -.069 | .105 | .668 | .215 | .202 |
| | Incautious – Cautious | .250 | .058 | .035 | -.180 | .613 | .028 | -.132 |
| | Passive – Positive | .246 | .042 | -.249 | .322 | -.491 | .037 | .247 |
| | Impertinent – Pertinent | .335 | -.305 | -.076 | .228 | .361 | -.014 | .109 |
| | Hard-hearted – Soft-hearted | .064 | -.005 | .001 | .069 | .138 | .879 | -.088 |
| | Irresponsible – Responsible | .332 | .152 | -.119 | .127 | .231 | -.344 | .166 |
| | Hostile – Amicable | .141 | .146 | .159 | -.027 | .012 | -.160 | .610 |
| | Unfriendly – Friendly | .021 | -.098 | .149 | .262 | -.007 | .280 | .544 |

"humanness," "naturalness," "annoyingness", and "masculinity" etc.), were used for evaluation. The list of adjectives is shown in Table 3 in Sect. 5. At the end of the experiment, a post-experiment survey was conducted in order to evaluate the participants' subjective impression of overall qualities of the agents, such as the naturalness of their movements and synthesized voice and whether they have noticed the difference of gestures.

## 5    Results

### 5.1    Results of Factorial Analysis

Factor analysis (FA hereafter) was conducted on the agent's impression ratings obtained from the experiment in order to extract the factors that composes our interpersonal impressions toward the agents. The results of FA using the principal factor method extracted four factors (shown in Table 3). The First factor is named as "Tolerance factor" (composed of adjectives such as calm, broad-minded, kind, soft, and sophisticated), the second as "Sociability factor" (composed of adjectives such as active, cheerful, confident, and social), the third as "Gender factor" (composed of adjectives such as lovable, feminine, and delicate), and the forth as "Naturalness factor" (composed of adjectives such as natural and humanlike).

Cronbach's coefficients alpha for the factors are 0.84 for "Tolerance factor", 0.79 for "Sociability factor", 0.67 for "Gender factor", and 0.62 for "Naturalness factor", which show high enough internal consistency of the extracted factors. The result of the factorial analysis indicates when the participants perceive the agents interpersonally and rate their impressions, these four factors have large effects. Thus we will use the factors and factorial scores for later analysis to evaluate the gender effects.

## 5.2    Analysis of Tolerance Factor and Sociability Factor

We performed three-way ANOVA (repeated measures) with factors "participant gender", "agent gender", and "gender of self-adaptor". The dependent variables are total factorial score of each factor.

The result showed there are no main effects of participants' gender, agent's gender, and gender of self-adaptor on "Tolerance factor" and "Sociability factor". There are significant second-order interactions in the "Tolerance factor" ($p \leq 0.05$) between participants' gender and agents' gender. Figure 9 shows the tolerance factor score of each condition. The male participants rated the female agent performing feminine self-adaptors significantly higher than the same agent performing masculine self-adaptors (F: 4.58, $p \leq 0.05$). While the female participants showed tendency for higher rating to the female agent performing masculine self-adaptors (F: 2.55, $p = 0.122$). There are no difference in the tolerance factors when the participants evaluated the male agent. While to the case of the female agent, the tolerance scores were higher when the female agent performs different gender's self-adaptors from the participants' gender. There are no significant main effects nor second-order interactions found in the "Sociability factor" (shown in Fig. 10).

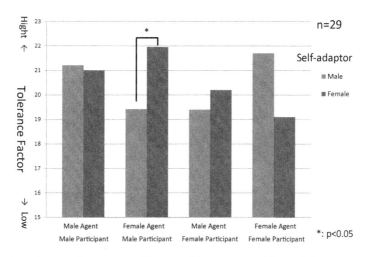

**Fig. 9.** Tolerance factor score of four conditions compared by participants' gender.

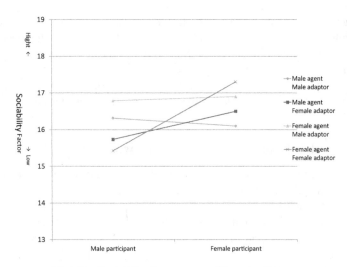

**Fig. 10.** Sociability factor score of four conditions.

## 5.3 Analysis of Gender Factor

We performed three-way ANOVA for total factorial scores of gender factor. Figure 11 shows gender factor scores of four conditions. The main effect of agent's gender on gender factor is found ($p \leq 0.01$). Significant second-order interactions are not seen in gender factor. These results mean the agents' appearance made significant differences in impression of gender. The male agent were perceived as more masculine than the female agent regardless of the gender of self-adaptors, and the female agent were perceived as more feminine than the male agent regardless of the gender of the self-adaptors by both gender of participants.

However, when we focus on the gender factor score of the female agent, a significant difference in participants' gender was found. As shown in Fig. 12, in the case

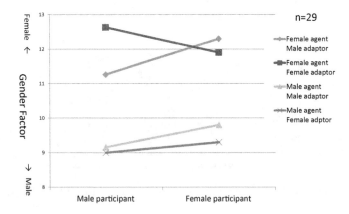

**Fig. 11.** Gender factor scores of four conditions compared by participants' gender.

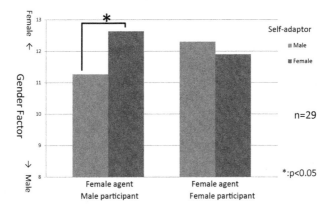

**Fig. 12.** Gender factor scores of female agent conditions compared by participants' gender.

of the female agent, the male participants perceived significant higher femininity to the female agent performing feminine self-adaptor (F: 4.88, $p < 0.05$) than the same agent performing masculine ones. While the female participants showed no difference in the gender scores of the same agent conditions. It should be noted that only one female participant (out of 29) noticed the difference of each condition and identified masculine and feminine self-adaptors.

## 5.4    Analysis of Naturalness Factor

We performed three-way ANOVA for total factorial scores of "Naturalness factor". Figure 13 shows naturalness factor scores of four conditions. There are no significant main effects nor second-order interactions found in the naturalness factor. This means the participants perceived agents with all conditions as equally natural.

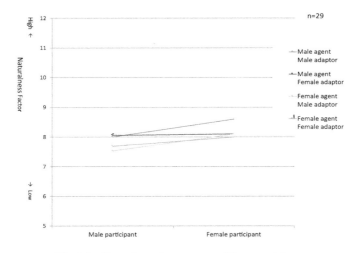

**Fig. 13.** Naturalness factor score of four conditions.

# 6  Discussion and Future Directions

The above results showed we did not find deterioration in the perceived naturalness of agents when the agents' appearance and gender of self-adaptors don't match. Thus, our hypothesis 1 "when the participant's gender, agent's gender, and gender of the gender-specific self-adaptors are consistent, participants feel higher naturalness than any other combinations" was not supported.

In the case of the female agent, there are interactions between the participants' gender and gender of self-adaptors in the tolerance factor. Specifically, the female participants had lower impression on the feminine self-adaptors performed by the female agent. Thus, our hypothesis 2 "Male participants have better impression toward the agent with female appearance and feminine self-adaptors, while female participants have better impression on the agent with male appearance and masculine self-adaptors" was not fully supported. We will discuss why the hypothesis was not supported below.

When the participants evaluate the impression of the agents used in the experiment, the four factors forms the overall impression of the agent, namely, tolerance, sociability, gender, and naturalness. The analysis of gender factor showed the participants of both gender correctly perceived the gender of the agent. Only male participants perceived the feminine self-adaptors performed by the female agent as most feminine, while such correct perception did not occur in the case of the female participants, nor of the male agent, and the masculine self-adaptors. On the other hand, all agents in four conditions are perceived as equally natural even when the gender of the agent and the gender of self-adaptors don't match. In terms of perceived tolerance, the female agent's performing the feminine self-adaptors resulted in opposite impressions between the male and female participants. The male participants perceived the female agent performing feminine self-adaptors as most tolerant, while the female participants rated the same condition as least tolerant in all conditions. Such cross gender interaction was not found in the case of the male agent with both self-adaptors (masculine/feminine).

The results suggest interesting cross gender interactions in perceiving the feminine self-adaptors. The Japanese male participants are in favor of the feminine self-adaptors, while the Japanese female participants have rigorous impression on them when they are performed by the female agent, without noticing the difference as all conditions are rated as equally natural. This suggest there is a dichotomy between participants' gender in the perception of combination of self-adaptor and agent's gender. Thus the hypothesis 2 is partially supported only to the case of the female agent.

This research is still at a starting phase, thus has several limitations. Firstly, we need to conduct more fine grained study on the self-adaptor in human-human interactions. Extraction of self-adaptors was made from the video recordings of only 20 participants, who are undergraduate students in Japan. The evaluations of self-adaptor performing agents were made by 29 Japanese undergraduate students (different subjects from those who were videotaped). Given the enormous inter-subjective variability in gesture use, we need to conduct close observations on the form and movements of self-adaptors with larger samples with wider age range and cultures.

Secondly, although we compared only masculine/feminine self-adaptors in this experiment, we need to compare impressions with non-self-adaptor condition in order to evaluate the masculinity and femininity of the self-adaptors solely.

Thirdly, the result of this study is limited to the virtual agents used in our experiment and may not generalize to other types of virtual agents. Further research should use wider variety of virtual agent appearances.

Finally, future work should also consider cultural diversity in expressing and perceiving self-adaptors. There are culturally-defined preferences in bodily expressions [18–21] and in facial expressions [22, 23], and allowance level of expressing non-verbal behavior are culture-dependent. Japanese male tend to perform self-adaptors around their nose and chin more frequently than other cultures by observation, and Japanese female tend to cover their mouth while talking, which is considered as typical Japanese female self-adaptor. We will investigate culture specific self-adaptors from video recordings of human-human interactions from other cultures. Furthermore, we will implement them with agents, and conduct a cross-cultural evaluation study.

## 7 Conclusion

The contributions of this study are: (1) identified gender specific self-adaptors in Japanese male and female university students, (2) suggested significant cross gender interactions between the gender of agents and the participants' gender in the case of the female agent. Our evaluation of the interactions between the agents that exhibit self-adaptors typically exhibited by Japanese male and female indicated that there is a dichotomy on the impression on the agent between participants' gender. Japanese male participants showed more favorable impressions on agents that display feminine self-adaptors than masculine ones performed by the female agent, while Japanese female participants showed rigorous impressions toward feminine self-adaptors.

Although we need to investigate our perception of agents with wider variety of agent's appearances, gestures, and cultures, the result implies the combination of male appearance and masculine gestures might be "safer" in order to facilitate neutral impressions and avoid any cross gender interactions made by the gender of human users. Designers of virtual agents should consider gender of appearance and gesture animations of virtual agents, and make them customizable according to the user's gender, preferences, social skills, conversational content, and cultures. We could make use of the advantage of virtual agents that they are flexible to customize to make them suit various conditions.

**Acknowledgement.** This research is partially supported by KAKENHI, a Grant-in-Aid for Scientific Research (C) 26330236) (2014–2016) from the Japan Society for the Promotion of Science.

## References

1. Ekman, P.: Three classes of nonverbal behavior. In: Aspects of Nonverbal Communication. Swets and Zeitlinger (1980)
2. Waxer, P.: Nonverbal cues for anxiety: an examination of emotional leakage. J. Abnorm. Psychol. **86**(3), 306–314 (1988)

3. Ekman, P., Friesen, W.V.: Hand movements. J. Commun. **22**, 353–374 (1972)
4. Argyle, M.: Bodily Communication. Taylor & Francis, Milton Park (1988)
5. Caso, L., Maricchiolo, F., Bonaiuto, M., Vrij, A., Mann, S.: The impact of deception and suspicion on different hand movements. J. Nonverbal Behav. **30**(1), 1–19 (2006)
6. Neff, M., Toothman, N., Bowmani, R., Fox Tree, J.E., Walker, M.A.: Don't scratch! Self-adaptors reflect emotional stability. In: Vilhjálmsson, H.H., Kopp, S., Marsella, S., Thórisson, Kristinn, R. (eds.) IVA 2011. LNCS (LNAI), vol. 6895, pp. 398–411. Springer, Heidelberg (2011). doi:10.1007/978-3-642-23974-8_43
7. Blacking, J.: The Anthropology of the Body. Academic Press, Cambridge (1977)
8. Chartrand, T.L., Bargh, J.A.: The chameleon effect: the perception–behavior link and social interaction. J. Pers. Soc. Psychol. **76**, 893–910 (1999)
9. Koda, T., Higashino, H.: Importance of considering user's social skills in human-agent interactions. In: Proceedings of ICAART 2014, pp. 115–122 (2014)
10. Hayashi, T.: The measurement of individual differences in interpersonal cognitive structure. Exp. Soc. Psychol. **22**, 1–9 (1982). (in Japanese)
11. Koda, T., Mori, Y.: Effects of an agent's displaying self-adaptors during a serious conversation. In: Bickmore, T., Marsella, S., Sidner, C. (eds.) IVA 2014. LNCS (LNAI), vol. 8637, pp. 240–249. Springer, Heidelberg (2014). doi:10.1007/978-3-319-09767-1_31
12. Cassell, J., Jenkins, H.: From Barbie to Mortal Kombat: Gender and Computer Games. MIT Press, Cambridge (2000)
13. Cassell, J.: Genderizing HCI. In: Jacko, J., Sears, A. (eds.) The Handbook of Human-Computer Interaction, pp. 402–441. Lawrence Erlbaum, Mahwah (2002)
14. Eagly, A.H.: Sex differences in influenceability. Psychol. Bull. **85**, 86–116 (1978)
15. Carli, L.L.: Gender, language, and influence. J. Pers. Soc. Psychol. **59**, 941–951 (1990)
16. Zanbaka, C., Goolkasian, P., Hodges, L.: Can a virtual cat persuade you? The role of gender and realism in speaker persuasiveness. In: Grinter, R., et al. (eds.) Proceedings of the SIGCHI, pp. 1153–1162. ACM, New York (2006)
17. Hall, J.A.: Nonverbal Sex Differences: Communication Accuracy and Expressive Style. Johns Hopkins University Press, Baltimore (1984)
18. Johnson, W., Marsella, S., Mote, N., Viljhalmsson, H., Narayanan, S., Choi, S.: Tactical language training system: supporting the rapid acquisition of foreign language and cultural skills. In: Proceedings of InSTIL/ICALLNLP and Speech Technologies in Advanced Language Learning Systems (2004)
19. Rehm, M., Andre, E., Bee, N., Endrass, B., Wissner, M., Nakano, Y., Nishida,T., Huang, H.: The CUBE-G approach-coaching culture-specific nonverbal behavior by virtual agents. In: Proceedings of Organizing and Learning Through Gaming and Simulation, ISAGA 2007, p. 313 (2007)
20. Rehm, M., Nakano, Y., André, E., Nishida, T.: Culture-specific first meeting encounters between virtual agents. In: Prendinger, H., Lester, J., Ishizuka, M. (eds.) IVA 2008. LNCS (LNAI), vol. 5208, pp. 223–236. Springer, Heidelberg (2008). doi:10.1007/978-3-540-85483-8_23
21. Aylett, R., Vannini, N., Andre, E., Paiva, A., Enz, S., Hall, L.: But that was in another country: agents and intercultural empathy. In: Proceedings of International Conference on Autonomous Agents and Multiagent Systems, vol. 1, pp. 329–336 (2009)
22. Koda, T., Ishida, T., Rehm, M., Andre, E.: Avatar culture: cross-cultural evaluations of avatar facial expressions. J. AI Soc. **24**(3), 237–250 (2009). Springer, London
23. Rehm, M., Nakano, Y., Koda, T., Winschiers-Theophilus, H.: Culturally aware agent communication. In: Zacarias, M., Oliveira, J.V. (eds.) Human-Computer Interaction: The Agency Perspective. SCI, vol. 396, pp. 411–436. Springer, Heidelberg (2012). doi:10.1007/978-3-642-25691-2_18

# Two Model Checking Approaches to Branch-and-Bound Optimization of a Flow Production System

Christoph Greulich$^{(\boxtimes)}$ and Stefan Edelkamp

Institute for Artificial Intelligence, University of Bremen, Bremen, Germany
{greulich,edelkamp}@cs.uni-bremen.de

**Abstract.** In this paper we introduce a novel application of model checking to find optimal planning solutions for a flow production system. Originally controlled by a multiagent system, the production system consists of autonomous products and asynchronous production stations with limited space for waiting products. In this work, we present two different approaches of application of the Spin model checker to optimize throughput in the given production system. Instead of mapping the multiagent system directly, we model the production line itself as a set of communicating processes. Each communication channel between two processes represents a one-way monorail connection from one station to another. Experiments show that both approaches derive valid and optimized plans with several thousands of steps using constrained branch-and-bound. However, experiments also indicate individual advantages of both approaches.

## 1 Introduction

The ongoing transformation of production industries causes a paradigm shift in manufacturing processes towards new technologies and innovative concepts, called *cyber, smart, digital* or *connected factory* [5]. The sector is entering its fourth revolution, characterized by a merging of computer networks and factory machines. At each link in production and supply chains, tools and workstations communicate constantly via Internet and local networks. Machines, systems, and products exchange information both among themselves and with the outside world.

*Flow production systems* are installed for products that are produced in high quantities. By optimizing the flow of production, manufacturers hope to speed up production at a lower cost, and in a more environmentally sound way. In manufacturing practice there are not only series flow lines (with stations arranged one behind the other), but also more complex networks of stations at which assembly operations are performed (assembly lines). The considerable difference from flow lines, which can be analyzed by known methods, is that a number of required components are brought together to form a single unit for further processing at the assembly stations. An assembly operation can begin only if all required parts are available.

© Springer International Publishing AG 2017
J. van den Herik and J. Filipe (Eds.): ICAART 2016, LNAI 10162, pp. 19–36, 2017.
DOI: 10.1007/978-3-319-53354-4_2

*Performance analysis* of flow production systems is generally needed during the planning phase regarding the system design, when the decision for a concrete configuration of such a system has to be made. The planning problem arises, e.g., with the introduction of a new model or the installation of a new manufacturing plant. Because of the investments involved, optimization of the system is crucial. The expenditure for new machines, for buffer or handling equipment, and the holding costs for the expected work-in-process face revenues from sold products. The performance of a concrete configuration is characterized by the throughput, i.e., the number of items that are produced per time unit. Other performance measures are the expected work in process or the idle times of machines or workers.

In this paper we consider *assembly-line networks with stations*, which are represented as a directed graph. Between any two successive nodes in the network, we assume a buffer of finite capacity. In the buffers between stations and other network elements, work pieces are stored, waiting for service. At assembly stations, service is given to work pieces. Travel time is measured and overall time is to be optimized.

Our running case study is the so called Z2, a physical monorail system for the assembling of tail-lights. Unlike most production systems, Z2 employs agent technology to represent autonomous products and assembly stations. The techniques developed, however, will be applicable to most flow production systems. We formalize the production floor as a system of communicating processes and apply the state-of-the-art model checker *Spin* [29] for analyzing its behavior. Using optimization mechanisms implemented on top of Spin, additional to the verification of the correctness of the model, we exploit its exploration process for optimization of production flow.

For the *optimization via model checking* we use many new language features from the latest version of the Spin model checker including loops and native c-code verification. The main contribution of this text, however, is *general cost-optimization via branch-and-bound*. The optimization approach originally invented for Spin was designed for state space trees [43, 44], while the proposed new approach also supports state space graphs, crucially reducing the running time and memory consumption of the algorithm, rendering otherwise intractable models to become analyzable.

The paper is structured as follows. First, we consider related work on agent-based industrial (flow) production, on model checking multiagent systems (MASs), and on planning via model checking. Next, we introduce the industrial case study, and its modeling as well as its simulation as an MAS. The simulator is used to measure the increments of the cost function to be optimized. Then, we turn to the intricacies of the Promela model specification and the parameterization of Spin, as well as to the novel branch-and-bound optimization scheme. Furthermore, we give a detailed overview over two different strategies to manage process synchronization and progression of time within the model. In the experiments we validate the conciseness and effectiveness of the model and the taken approaches.

# 2    Related Work

Especially in open, unpredictable, dynamic, and complex environments, MASs are applied to determine adequate solutions for transport problems. For example, agent-based commercial systems are used within the planning and control of industrial processes [12,27], as well as within other areas of logistics [7,17]. A comprehensive survey is provided by [40].

Flow line analysis is often done with queuing theory [8,36]. Pioneering work in analyzing assembly queuing systems with synchronization constraints analyzes assembly-like queues with unlimited buffer capacities [25]. It shows that the time an item has to wait for synchronization may grow without bound, while limitation of the number of items in the system works as a control mechanism and ensures stability. Work on assembly-like queues with finite buffers all assume exponential service times [2,30,34].

## 2.1    Model Checking Multiagent Systems

Model checking production flow is rare. Timed automata were used for simulating material flow in agricultural production [26]. There are, however, numerous attempts to apply model checking to validate the work of MASs.

The LORA framework [47,48] uses labeled transition and Kripke systems for characterizing the behavior of the agents (their belief, their desire and their intention), and temporal logics for expressing their interplay, as well as for the progression of knowledge. Alternatives consider an MAS as a game, in which agents – either in separation or cooperatively – optimize their individual outcome [45]. Communication between the agents is available via writing to and reading from channels, or via common access to shared variables. Other formalization approaches include work in the context of the MCMAS tool by Lomuscio[1]. Recently, there has been some approaches to formalize MASs as planning problems [39].

## 2.2    Planning and Model Checking

Since the origin of the term artificial intelligence, the automated generation of plans for a given task has been seen as an integral part of problem solving in a computer. In *action planning* [38], we are confronted with the descriptions of the initial state, the goal (states) and the available actions. Based on these we want to find a plan containing as few actions as possible (in case of unit-cost actions, or if no costs are specified at all) or with the lowest possible total cost (in case of general action costs).

The process of fully-automated property validation and correctness verification is referred to as *model checking* [11]. Given a formal model of a system $M$ and a property specification $\phi$ in some form of temporal logic like LTL [21], the task is to validate, whether or not the specification is satisfied in the model,

---

[1] http://vas.doc.ic.ac.uk/software/mcmas/.

$M \models \phi$. If not, a model checker usually returns a counterexample trace as a witness for the falsification of the property.

Planning and model checking have much in common [9, 22]. Both rely on the exploration of a potentially large state space of system states. Usually, model checkers only search for the existence of specification errors in the model, while planners search for a short path from the initial state to one of the goal states. Nonetheless, there is rising interest in planners that prove insolvability [28], and in model checkers to produce minimal counterexamples [15].

In terms of leveraging state space search, over the last decades there has been much cross-fertilization between the fields. For example, based on Satplan [32] *bounded model checkers* exploit SAT and SMT representations [1,3] of the system to be verified, while *directed model checkers* [13,33] exploit panning heuristics to improve the exploration for falsification; partial-order reduction [23,46] and symmetry detection [18,35] limit the number of successor states, while symbolic planners [10,14,31] apply functional data structures like BDDs to represent sets of states succinctly.

## 3    Case Study: Z2

One of the few successful real-world implementations of a multiagent flow production is the so called Z2 production floor unit [20,37]. The Z2 unit consists of six workstations where human workers assemble parts of automotive tail-lights. The system allows production of certain product variations and reacts dynamically to any change in the current order situation, e.g., a decrease or an increase in the number of orders of a certain variant. As individual production steps are performed at the different stations, all stations are interconnected by a monorail transport system. The structure of the transport system is shown in Fig. 1(a). On the rails, autonomously moving shuttles carry the products from one station to another, depending on the products' requirements. The monorail system has multiple switches which allow the shuttles to enter, leave or pass workstations and the central hubs. The goods transported by the shuttles are also autonomous,

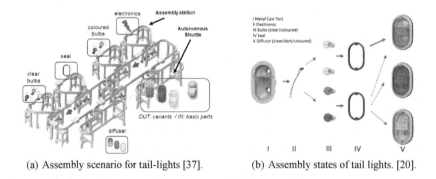

(a) Assembly scenario for tail-lights [37].          (b) Assembly states of tail lights. [20].

**Fig. 1.** Z2 Case study setup.

which means that each product decides on its own which variant to become and which station to visit. This way, a decentralized control of the production system is possible.

The modular system consists of six different workstations, each is operated manually by a human worker and dedicated to one specific production step. At production steps III and V, different parts can be used to assemble different variants of the tail-lights as illustrated in Fig. 1(b). At the first station, the basic metal-cast parts enter the monorail on a dedicated shuttle. The monorail connects all stations, each station is assigned to one specific task, such as adding bulbs or electronics. Each tail-light is transported from station to station until it is assembled completely.

### 3.1   Multiagent System Simulation

In the real-world implementation of the Z2 system, every assembly station, every mono-rail shuttle and every product is represented by a software agent. Even the RFID readers which keep track of product positions are represented by software agents which decide when a shuttle may pass or stop. The agent representation is based on the well-known Java Agent Development Kit (JADE) and relies heavily on its FIPA-compliant messaging components.

Most agents in this MAS resemble simple reflex agents as defined by Russell and Norvig [42]. These agents just react to requests or events which were caused by other agents or the human workers involved in the manufacturing process. In contrast, the agents which represent products are actively working towards their individual goal of becoming a complete tail-light and reaching the storage station. In order to complete its task, each product has to reach sub-goals which may change during production as the order situation may change. The number of possible actions is limited by sub-goals which already have been reached, since every possible production step has preconditions as illustrated in Fig. 2.

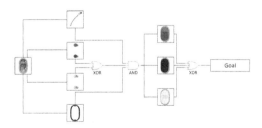

**Fig. 2.** Preconditions of the various manufacturing stages.

The product agents constantly request updates regarding queue lengths at the various stations and the overall order situation. The information is used to compute the utility of the expected outcome of every action which is currently available to the agent. High utility is given when an action leads to fulfillment of an outstanding order and takes as little time as possible. Time, in this case, is spent either on actions, such as moving along the railway or being processed, or on waiting in line at a station or a switch. By inferring a MATLAB server, each agent individually makes its decisions by applying a Fuzzy Logic model [41].

The Z2 MAS was developed strictly for the purpose of controlling the Z2 monorail hardware setup. Nonetheless, due to its hardware abstraction layer [37], the Z2 MAS can be adapted into other hardware or software environments. By replacing the hardware with other agents and adapting the monorail infrastructure into a directed graph, the Z2 MAS can be transferred to a virtual simulation environment [24]. Such an environment, which treats the original Z2 agents like black boxes, can easily be hosted by the JADE-based event-driven MAS simulation platform PlaSMA[2]. Experiments show how close the executions of the simulated and the real-world scenarios match.

For this study, we provided the PlaSMA model with timers to measure the time taken between two graph nodes. Since the hardware includes many RFID readers along the monorail, which all are represented by an agent and a node within the simulation, we simplified the graph and kept only three types of nodes: switches, production station entrances and production station exits. The resulting abstract model of the system is a weighted graph (see Fig. 3), where the weight of an edge denotes the traveling/processing time of the shuttle between two respective nodes.

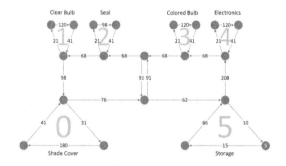

**Fig. 3.** Weighted graph model of the assembly scenario.

## 4    Formal Specification

Promela is the input language of the model checker Spin[3], the ACM-awarded popular open-source software verification tool, designed for the formal verification of multi-threaded software applications, and used by thousands of people worldwide. Promela defines asynchronously running communicating processes, which are compiled to finite state machines. It has a c-like syntax, and supports bounded channels for sending and receiving messages.

---

[2] http://plasma.informatik.uni-bremen.de/.
[3] http://spinroot.com/spin/whatispin.html.

Channels in Promela follow the FIFO principle. Therefore, they implicitly maintain order of incoming messages and can be limited to a certain buffer size. Consequently, we are able to map edges to communication channels. Unlike the original Z2 MAS, the products are not considered to be decision making entities within our Promela model. Instead, the products are represented by messages which are passed along the *node processes*, which resemble switches, station entrances and exits.

Unlike the original MAS and the resembling PlaSMA simulation, the Promela model is designed to apply a branch-and-bound optimization to evaluate the optimal throughput of the original system. Instead of local decision making, the various node agents have certain nondeterministic options of handling incoming messages, each leading to a different system state. The model checker systematically computes these states and memorizes paths to desirable outcomes when it ends up in a final state. As mentioned before, decreasing production time for a given number of products increases the utility of the final state.

We derive a formal model of the Z2 multiagent systems as follows. First, we define global setting on the number of stations and number of switches. We also define the data type storing the index of the shuttle/product to be `byte`.

In the Promela model, production nodes are realized as processes and edges between the nodes by the following channels.

```
chan entrance_to_exit[STATIONS]=[1] of {shuttle};
chan exit_to_switch[STATIONS]=[BUFFERSIZE] of {shuttle};
chan switch_to_switch[SWITCHES]=[BUFFERSIZE] of {shuttle};
chan switch_to_entrance[STATIONS]=[BUFFERSIZE] of {shuttle};
```

As global variables, we also have bit-vectors for the different assemblies being processed.

```
bit metalcast[SHUTTLES];
bit electronics[SHUTTLES];
bit bulb[SHUTTLES];
bit seal[SHUTTLES];
bit cover[SHUTTLES];
```

Additionally, we have a bit-vector that denotes when a shuttle with a fully assembled item has finally arrived at its goal location. A second bit-vector is used to set for each shuttle whether it has to acquire a colored or a clear bulb.

```
bit goals[SHUTTLES];
bit color[SHUTTLES];
```

A switch is a process that controls the flow of the shuttles. In the model, a non-deterministic choice is added to either enter the station or to continue traveling onwards on the cycle. Three of four switching options are made available, as immediate re-entering a station from its exit is prohibited.

```
proctype Switch(byte in; byte out; byte station)
{
  shuttle s;
  do
  :: exit_to_switch[station]?s; switch_to_switch[out]!s;
  :: switch_to_switch[in]?s; switch_to_switch[out]!s;
  :: switch_to_switch[in]?s; switch_to_entrance[station]!s;
  od
}
```

The entrance of a manufacturing station takes the item from the according switch and moves it to the exit. It also controls that the manufacturing complies with the capability of the station.

First, the assembling of product parts is different at each station, in the stations 1 and 3 we have the insertion of bulbs (station 1 provides colored bulbs, station 3 provides clear bulbs), station 2 assembles the seal, station 4 the electronics and station 0 the cover. Station 5 is the storage station where empty metal casts are placed on the monorail shuttles and finished products are removed to be taken into storage.

Secondly, there is a partial order of the respective product parts to allow flexible processing and a better optimization based on the current load of the ongoing production.

```
proctype Entrance(byte station)
{
  shuttle s;
  do
  ::  switch_to_entrance[station]?s;
      entrance_to_exit[station]!s
      if
      :: (station == 4) -> electronics[s] = 1;
      :: (station == 3 && !color[s]) -> bulb[s] = 1;
      :: (station == 2)-> seal[s] = 1;
      :: (station == 1 && color[s]) -> bulb[s] = 1;
      :: (station == 0 && seal[s]
          && bulb[s] && electronics[s])-> cover[s] = 1;
      :: (station == 5 && cover[s]) -> goals[s] = 1;
      :: else
      fi
  od
}
```

An exit is a node that is located at the end of a station, at which assembling took place. It is connected to the entrance of the station and the switch linked to it.

```
proctype Exit(byte station)
{
  shuttle s;
  do
  :: entrance_to_exit[station]?s;
     exit_to_switch[station]!s;
  od
}
```

A *hub* is a switch that is not connected to a station but provides a shortcut in the monorail network. Again, three of four possible shuttle movement options are provided

```
proctype Hub(byte in1; byte out1; byte in2; byte out2)
{
  shuttle s;
  do
  :: switch_to_switch[in1]?s; switch_to_switch[out1]!s;
  :: switch_to_switch[in1]?s; switch_to_switch[out2]!s;
  :: switch_to_switch[in2]?s; switch_to_switch[out1]!s;
  od
}
```

In the initial state, we start the individual processes, which represent nodes and hereby define the network of the monorail system. Moreover, initially we have that the metal cast of each product is already present on its carrier, the shuttle. The coloring of the tail-lights can be defined at the beginning or in the progress of the production. Last, but not least, we initialize the process by inserting shuttles on the starting rail (at station 5).

```
init {
  atomic {
    byte i;
    c_code { cost = 0; }
    c_code { best_cost = 100000; }
    for (i : 0 .. (SHUTTLES)/2)){ color[i] = 1; }
    for (i : 0 .. (SHUTTLES-1)) { metalcast[i] = 1; }
    for (i : 0 .. (STATIONS-1)) { run Entrance(i);
                                  run Exit(i); }
    run Switch(7,0,5); run Switch(0,1,4);
    run Switch(1,2,3); run Switch(3,4,2);
    run Switch(4,5,1); run Switch(5,6,0);
    run Hub(2,3,8,9); run Hub(6,7,9,8);
    for (i : 0 .. (SHUTTLES-1)) { exit_to_switch[5]!i; }
  }
}
```

We also heavily made use of the term `atomic`, which enhances the exploration for the model checker, allowing it to merge states within the search. In difference to the more aggressive `d_step` keyword, in an `atomic` block all communication queue action are still blocking, so that we chose to use an atomic block around each loop.

## 5   Constrained Branch-and-Bound Optimization

There are different options for finding optimized schedules with the help of a model checker that have been proposed in the literature. First, as in the *Soldier* model of [44], rendezvous communication to an additional synchronized process has been used to increase cost, dependent on the transition chosen, together with a specialized LTL property to limit the total cost for the model checking solver. This approach, however, turned out to be limited in its ability. An alternative proposal for branch-and-bound search is based on the support of native c-code in Spin (introduced in version 4.0) [43]. One running example is the traveling salesman problem (TSP), but the approach is generally applicable to many other optimization problems. However, as implemented, there are certain limitations to the scalability of state space problem graphs. Recall that the problem graph induced by the TSP is in fact a tree, generating all possible permutations for the cities.

Inspired by [6,13] and [43] we applied and improved branch-and-bound optimization within Spin. Essentially, the model checker can find traces of several hundreds of steps and provides trace optimization by finding the shortest path towards a counterexample if run with the parameter `./pan -i`. However, these traces are step-optimized, and not cost-optimized. Therefore, Ruys [43] proposed the introduction of a variable *cost*.

```
c_state "int best_cost" "Hidden"
c_code { int cost; }
c_track "cost" "sizeof(int)" "Matched"
```

While the cost variable increases the amount of memory required for each state, it also limits the power of Spins built-in duplicate detection, as two otherwise identical states are considered different if reached by different accumulated cost. If the search space is small, so that it can be explored even for the enlarged state vector, then this option is sound and complete, and finally returns the optimal solution to the optimization problem. However, as with our model, it might be that there are simply too many repetitions in the model so that introducing cost to the state vector leads to a drastic increase in state space size, so that otherwise checkable instances now become intractable. We noticed that even by concentrating on safety properties (such as the failed assertion mentioned), the insertion of costs causes troubles.

### 5.1   Optimization Goal

For our model, cost has to be tracked for every shuttle individually. The variable cost of the most expensive shuttle indicates the duration of the whole production process. Furthermore, the cost total provides insight regarding unnecessary detours or long waiting times. Hence, minimizing both criteria are the optimization goals of this model.

In Promela, every do-loop is allowed to contain an unlimited number of possible options for the model checker to choose from. The model checker randomly chooses between the options, however, it is possible to add an $if$-like condition to an option: If the first statement of a do option holds, Spin will start to execute the following statements, otherwise, it will pick a different option.

Since the model checker explores any possible state of the system, many of these states are technically reachable but completely useless from an optimization point of view. In order to reduce state space size to a manageable level, we add constraints to the relevant receiving options in the do-loops of every node process.

Peeking into the incoming queue to find out, which shuttle is waiting to be received is already considered a complete statement in Promela. Therefore, we exploit C-expressions (c_expr) to combine several operations into one atomic statement. For every station $t$ and every incoming channel $q$, a function $prerequisites(t, q)$ determines, if the first shuttle in $q$ meets the prerequisites for $t$, as given by Fig. 2.

```
shuttle s;
do
:: c_expr{prerequisites(Px->q,Px->t)} ->
    channel[q]?s;
    channel[out]!;
```

For branch-and-bound optimization, we now follow the guidelines of [43]. This enables the model checker to print values to the output, only if the values of the current max cost and sum cost have improved.

```
c_code {
 if (max < best_cost ||
     (max == best_cost && sum < best_sum_cost) {
    best_cost = max;
    best_sum_cost = sum;
    putrail();
    Nr_Trails--;
  };
}
```

# 6   Process Synchronization

Due to the nature of the state space search of the model checker, node agents in the Promela model do not make decisions. Nonetheless, the given Promela model is a distributed simulation consisting of a varying number of processes, which potentially influence each other if executed in parallel.

In parallel simulation, different notions of time have to be considered. Physical time is the time of occurrence of real world events, simulation time (or virtual time) is the adaptation of physical time into the simulation model. Furthermore, wall clock time refers to the real-world time which passes during computation of the simulation.

Parallel execution allows faster processes to overtake slower processes, even though the LVT of the slower process is lower. While Spin maintains the order of products and their respective costs implicitly by the FIFO queues as long as the products are passed along in a row, the so called causality problem [19] emerges, as soon as products part ways at any switch node.

We addressed this problem by examining two different approaches of process synchronization in order to maintain simulation consistency. Both approaches ensure that a product $p$ can only be removed from a queue $q$ if it is its turn to move. Therefore, we introduce an atomic boolean function $canreceive(q)$ which only holds if the first element $p$ in $q$ is allowed to move. The function $canreceive(q)$ is added to the prerequisite check at every node entrance.

```
  shuttle s;
  do
  ::  c_expr{canreceive(Px->q) &&
            prerequisites(Px->q, Px->t)} ->
        channel[q]?s;
        waittime[s]+=next_step_cost;
        channel[out]!s;
```

When no product $p$ is allowed to make a move, all current processes are unable to proceed. Within Spin, a global Boolean variable `timeout` is defined, which is automatically set to *true* whenever this situation occurs. Following a suggestion by Bošnački and Dams [4], we add a process that computes time progress whenever `timeout` occurs. Unlike Bošnački and Dams, however, we examine two event-driven discrete time models. To further constrain branching, the time-managing process also asserts that the time does not exceed the best_cost, since worse results do not need to be explored completely.

```
active proctype timemanager() {
    do
    :: timeout -> c_code{ increasetime(); };
                  assert(currenttime < best_cost);
    od
}
```

## 6.1  Discrete Event System

For the first approach, we created a discrete event system (DES) with event-based time progress [16]. Whenever a product $p$ travels along one of the edges, the corresponding message is put into a channel and the cost of the respective shuttle is increased by the cost of the given edge.

To maintain consistency in the DES, $canreceive(q)$ returns true for a product $p$ only if no $p_i \neq p$ exists with $cost(p_i) < cost(p)$. Consequently, the first item $p$ of $q$ can only be moved if it has minimal $cost(p)$.

Time progress is enforced as follows: if the minimum event is blocked (e.g., because it is not first in its queue), we compute the wake-up time of the second best event. If the two are of the same time, a time increment of 1 is enforced. In the other case, the second best event time is taken as the new one for the first. It is easy to see that this strategy eventually resolves all possible deadlocks. Algorithm 1.1 illustrates the procedure.

1: **procedure** INCREASETIME
2:     $first \leftarrow p_0 \in products$
3:     $min_a \leftarrow cost(p_0)$
4:     $min_b \leftarrow \infty$
5:     **for all** $p \neq p_0 \in products$ **do**
6:         **if** $cost(p) < min_a$ **then**
7:             $min_a \leftarrow cost(p)$
8:             $first \leftarrow p$
9:     **for all** $p \in products$ **do**
10:         **if** $cost(p) < min_b \wedge cost(p) > min_a$ **then**
11:             $min_b \leftarrow cost(p)$
12:     **if** $min_b = \infty$ **then**
13:         $cost(first) \leftarrow min_a + 1$
14:     **else**
15:         $cost(first) \leftarrow min_b$

**Algorithm 1.1.** DES time progress.

## 6.2  Local Virtual Time

While the DES approach already maintains consistency within the simulation model, it only considers actual traveling costs per edge for each shuttle while costs for waiting in queues are not taken into account. In order to be able to include them into the total production cost, we introduce an integer array waittime[SHUTTLES] to the Promela model. It enables each shuttle to keep track of its local virtual time (LVT), as the wait time will be increased by the cost of each action as soon as the action is executed.

Again, we introduce a function $canreceive(q)$, which returns true only if the first element $s$ of $q$ has $waittime(s) \leq 0$. Furthermore, we apply an event-driven discrete time model as described in Algorithm 1.2. In this model, whenever a `timeout` occurs, the waiting time until the earliest event is determined and subtracted from waiting times of every product simultaneously.

```
 1: procedure INCREASETIME
 2:     minimum ← ∞
 3:     delta ← 1
 4:     for all p ∈ products do
 5:         if 0 < waittime(p) < minimum then
 6:             minimum ← waittime(p)
 7:     if minimum < ∞ then
 8:         delta ← minimum
 9:     for all p ∈ products do
10:         if waittime(p) − delta ≥ 0 then
11:             waittime(p) ← waittime(p) − delta
12:         else
13:             waittime(p) ← 0
```

**Algorithm 1.2.** LVT time progress.

# 7  Evaluation

In this section, we present results of a series of experiments executing both synchronization models. For comparison, we also present results of simulation runs of the original MAS implementation [24].

Unlike the original system, the Promela models do not rely on local decision making but searches for an optimal solution systematically. Therefore, both Promela models resemble a centralized planning approach.

For executing the model checking, we chose version 6.4.3 of Spin. As a compiler we used *gcc* version 4.9.3, with the *posix* thread model. For the standard setting of trace optimization for safety checking (option -DSAFETY), we compiled the model as follows.

```
./spin -a z2.pr;
gcc -O2 -DREACH -DSAFETY -o pan pan.c;
./pan -i -m30000
```

Parameter -i stands for the incremental optimization of the counterexample length. We regularly increased the maximal tail length with option -m, as in some cases of our running example, the traces turned out to be longer than the standard setting of at most 10000 steps. Option -DREACH is needed to warrant minimal counterexamples at the end. To run experiments, we used a common notebook with an Intel(R) Core(TM) i7-4710HQ CPU at 2.50 GHz, 16 GB of RAM and Windows 10 (64 Bit).

## 7.1  Inflexible Product Variants

In each experiment run, a number of $n \in \{2 \ldots 20\}$ shuttles carry products through the facility. All shuttles with even IDs acquire clear bulbs, all shuttles with odd IDs acquire colored ones.

A close look at the experiment results of every simulation run reveals that, given the same number of products to produce, all three approaches result in different sequences of events. However, LVT and DES propose that the same sequence of production steps for each product. The example given in Table 1 shows that for all shuttles $0 \ldots 2$ the scheduling sequence is exactly the same in LVT and DES, while the original MAS often proposes a different schedule. In the given example, both LVT and DES propose a sequence of $4, 2, 1, 0, 5$ for shuttle 1. To the contrary, the MAS approach proposes $2, 1, 4, 0, 5$ for shuttle 1. The same phenomenon can be observed for every $n \in \{2 \ldots 20\}$ number of shuttles.

**Table 1.** Sequences of events for $n = 3$ products (*Product* $\Rightarrow$ *Station*, where $\Rightarrow$ indicates a finished production step).

| MAS | 0⇒4 | 1⇒2 | 0⇒3 | 2⇒1 | 0⇒2 | 1⇒4 | 0⇒0 | 2⇒4 | 0⇒5 | 1⇒1 | 2⇒2 | 1⇒0 | 2⇒0 | 1⇒5 | 2⇒5 |
|-----|-----|-----|-----|-----|-----|-----|-----|-----|-----|-----|-----|-----|-----|-----|-----|
| LVT | 0⇒4 | 1⇒4 | 2⇒4 | 0⇒3 | 2⇒3 | 1⇒2 | 1⇒1 | 2⇒2 | 1⇒0 | 0⇒2 | 2⇒0 | 0⇒0 | 1⇒5 | 2⇒5 | 0⇒5 |
| DES | 0⇒4 | 1⇒4 | 2⇒4 | 0⇒3 | 1⇒2 | 2⇒3 | 0⇒2 | 1⇒1 | 2⇒2 | 0⇒0 | 1⇒0 | 2⇒0 | 0⇒5 | 1⇒5 | 2⇒5 |

All three simulation models keep track of the local production time of each shuttle's product. However, in MAS and LVT simulation, minimizing maximum local production time is the optimization goal. Steady, synchronized progress of time is maintained centrally after every production step. Hence, whenever a shuttle has to wait in a queue, its total production time increases. For the DES model, progress of time is managed differently, as illustrated in Sect. 6.1. In the DES model, actual traveling costs per edge are summarized for each shuttle but costs for waiting in queues are not considered. Consequently, time in MAS and LVT includes idle time while time in DES does not. Therefore, results always show that max. production time in DES is lower than LVT and MAS production times in all cases.

For every experiment, the amount of RAM required by DES to determine an optimal solution is slightly lower than the amount required by LVT as shown in Table 2. While the LVT required several iterations to find an optimal solution, the first valid solution found by DES was already the optimal solution in every conducted experiment. However, the LVT model is able to search the whole state space within the 16 GB RAM limit (given by our machine) for $n \le 3$ shuttles, whereas the DES model is unable to search the whole state space for $n > 2$. For every experiment with $n > 3$ (LVT) or $n > 2$ (DES) shuttles respectively, searching the state space for better results was cancelled, when the 16 GB RAM limit was reached.

In general, experiments indicate that the DES model is faster and more memory efficient than the LVT model even though both approaches propose

**Table 2.** Simulated production times for $n$ products in the original MAS and Spin simulation, including the amount of RAM required to compute the given result. (* indicates that the whole state space was searched within the given RAM usage.)

| Products | MAS | LVT | | DES | |
|---|---|---|---|---|---|
| | Max. Prod. Time | Max. Prod. Time | RAM | Max. Prod. Time | RAM |
| 2 | 4:01 | 3:24 | 987 MB* | 2:53 | 731 MB* |
| 3 | 4:06 | 3:34 | 2154 MB* | 3:04 | 503 MB |
| 4 | 4:46 | 3:56 | 557 MB | 3:13 | 519 MB |
| 5 | 4:16 | 4:31 | 587 MB | 3:25 | 541 MB |
| 6 | 5:29 | 4:31 | 611 MB | 3:34 | 565 MB |
| 7 | 5:18 | 5:08 | 636 MB | 3:45 | 587 MB |
| 8 | 5:57 | 5:43 | 670 MB | 3:55 | 610 MB |
| 9 | 6:00 | 5:43 | 692 MB | 4:06 | 635 MB |
| 10 | 6:08 | 5:43 | 715 MB | 4:15 | 557 MB |
| 20 | 9:03 | 8:56 | 977 MB | 5:59 | 857 MB |

the same optimal production schedules for each shuttle. Both models follow a different notion of time and, therefore, a slightly different optimization goal. By excluding idle time, the DES model focuses strictly on minimizing the time spent moving along edges and being processed at stations. The LVT model includes idle time, hence, it minimizes the total time spent in the production system.

### 7.2   Flexible Product Variants

In a second series of experiments, we allowed the model checker to decide, which products to provide with a colored or clear bulb. In these experiments, a desirable final state is reached when all products have returned to the storage station (station 5) and the difference $d$ between the amount of both product variants is $0 \leq d \leq 1$.

In these experiments, the model checker has even more possibilities to branch its search space. Therefore, it is hardly surprising that problems with $n > 3$ shuttles could not be computed on our test machine. However, for $n = 2$ shuttles, the LVT model proposes a solution that takes 3:21 s and therefore is 3 s faster than the inflexible solution. For $n = 3$ shuttles, the difference is 10 s, as the production takes 3:24 s of simulation time.

## 8   Conclusions

In this paper, we introduced two different approaches to apply branch-and-bound optimization to a flow production system by employing model checking software. Our research is motivated by our interest in creating a benchmarking baseline for optimization of decentralized autonomous manufacturing.

Using model checking for optimizing DES is a relatively new playground for formal method tools in form of a new analysis paradigm. Our Promela model reflects the routing and scheduling of entities in a flow production system. We successfully adapted the monorail structure of our case study into a network of communicating channels which connect a number of concurrent processes. Additional constraints to the order of production steps enable to carry out a complex planning and scheduling task.

We introduced two different synchronization strategies. A close look at the limits and possibilities of LVT and DES revealed that both approaches have certain advantages and disadvantages.

In future work, we will consider applying an action planner or a general game player for comparison, even though we do not expect a drastic improvement in state space size. Also, we will use the baseline established in this paper as a reference to improve the decentralized planning for the original MAS implementation.

**Acknowledgements.** This research was partly funded by the International Graduate School for Dynamics in Logistics (IGS), University of Bremen, Germany.

# References

1. Armando, A., Mantovani, J., Platania, L.: Bounded model checking of software using SMT solvers instead of SAT solvers. In: Valmari, A. (ed.) SPIN 2006. LNCS, vol. 3925, pp. 146–162. Springer, Heidelberg (2006). doi:10.1007/11691617_9
2. Bhat, U.: Finite capacity assembly-like queues. Queueing Syst. **1**, 85–101 (1986)
3. Biere, A., Cimatti, A., Clarke, E., Zhu, Y.: Symbolic model checking without BDDs. In: Cleaveland, W.R. (ed.) TACAS 1999. LNCS, vol. 1579, pp. 193–207. Springer, Heidelberg (1999). doi:10.1007/3-540-49059-0_14
4. Bošnački, D., Dams, D.: Integrating real time into spin: a prototype implementation. In: Budkowski, S., Cavalli, A., Najm, E. (eds.) FORTE/PSTV, vol. 6, pp. 423–438. Springer, New York (1998)
5. Bracht, U., Geckler, D., Wenzel, S.: Digitale Fabrik: Methoden und Praxisbeispiele. Springer, Heidelberg (2011)
6. Brinksma, E., Mader, A.: Verification and optimization of a PLC control schedule. In: Havelund, K., Penix, J., Visser, W. (eds.) SPIN 2000. LNCS, vol. 1885, pp. 73–92. Springer, Heidelberg (2000). doi:10.1007/10722468_5
7. Bürckert, H.J., Fischer, K., Vierke, G.: Holonic transport scheduling with teletruck. Appl. Artif. Intell. **14**(7), 697–725 (2000)
8. Burman, M.: New results in flow line analysis. Ph.D. thesis, Massachusetts Institute of Technology (1995)
9. Cimatti, A., Giunchiglia, E., Giunchiglia, F., Traverso, P.: Planning via model checking: a decision procedure for AR. In: Steel, S., Alami, R. (eds.) ECP 1997. LNCS, vol. 1348, pp. 130–142. Springer, Heidelberg (1997). doi:10.1007/3-540-63912-8_81
10. Cimatti, A., Roveri, M., Traverso, P.: Automatic OBDD-based generation of universal plans in non-deterministic domains. In: AAAI, pp. 875–881 (1998)
11. Clarke, E., Grumberg, O., Peled, D.: Model Checking. MIT Press, Cambridge (2000)

12. Dorer, K., Calisti, M.: An adaptive solution to dynamic transport optimization. In: AAMAS, pp. 45–51. ACM (2005)
13. Edelkamp, S., Lafuente, A.L., Leue, S.: Directed explicit model checking with HSF-SPIN. In: Dwyer, M. (ed.) SPIN 2001. LNCS, vol. 2057, pp. 57–79. Springer, Heidelberg (2001). doi:10.1007/3-540-45139-0_5
14. Edelkamp, S., Reffel, F.: *OBDDs* in heuristic search. In: Herzog, O., Günter, A. (eds.) KI 1998. LNCS, vol. 1504, pp. 81–92. Springer, Heidelberg (1998). doi:10. 1007/BFb0095430
15. Edelkamp, S., Sulewski, D.: Flash-efficient LTL model checking with minimal counterexamples. In: SEFM, pp. 73–82 (2008)
16. Edelkamp, S., Greulich, C.: Using SPIN for the optimized scheduling of discrete event systems in manufacturing. In: Bošnački, D., Wijs, A. (eds.) SPIN 2016. LNCS, vol. 9641, pp. 57–77. Springer, Heidelberg (2016). doi:10.1007/ 978-3-319-32582-8_4
17. Fischer, K., Müller, J.R.P., Pischel, M.: Cooperative transportation scheduling: an application domain for DAI. Appl. Artif. Intell. **10**(1), 1–34 (1996)
18. Fox, M., Long, D.: The detection and exploration of symmetry in planning problems. In: IJCAI, pp. 956–961 (1999)
19. Fujimoto, R.: Parallel and Distributed Simulation Systems. Wiley, Hoboken (2000)
20. Ganji, F., Morales Kluge, E., Scholz-Reiter, B.: Bringing agents into application: intelligent products in autonomous logistics. In: Schill, K., Scholz-Reiter, B., Frommberger, L. (eds.) Artificial Intelligence and Logistics (AiLog) - Workshop at ECAI 2010, pp. 37–42 (2010)
21. Gerth, R., Peled, D., Vardi, M., Wolper, P.: Simple on-the-fly automatic verification of linear temporal logic. In: PSTV, pp. 3–18. Chapman & Hall (1995)
22. Giunchiglia, F., Traverso, P.: Planning as model checking. In: Biundo, S., Fox, M. (eds.) ECP 1999. LNCS (LNAI), vol. 1809, pp. 1–20. Springer, Heidelberg (2000). doi:10.1007/10720246_1
23. Godefroid, P.: Using partial orders to improve automatic verification methods. In: Clarke, E.M., Kurshan, R.P. (eds.) CAV 1990. LNCS, vol. 531, pp. 176–185. Springer, Heidelberg (1991). doi:10.1007/BFb0023731
24. Greulich, C., Edelkamp, S., Eicke, N.: Cyber-physical multiagent-simulation in production logistics. In: Müller, J.P., Ketter, W., Kaminka, G., Wagner, G., Bulling, N. (eds.) MATES 2015. LNCS (LNAI), vol. 9433, pp. 119–136. Springer, Heidelberg (2015). doi:10.1007/978-3-319-27343-3_7
25. Harrison, J.: Assembly-like queues. J. Appl. Probab. **10**, 354–367 (1973)
26. Helias, A., Guerrin, F., Steyer, J.P.: Using timed automata and model-checking to simulate material flow in agricultural production systems - application to animal waste management. Comput. Electron. Agric. **63**(2), 183–192 (2008)
27. Himoff, J., Rzevski, G., Skobelev, P.: Magenta technology multi-agent logistics i-scheduler for road transportation. In: AAMAS, pp. 1514–1521. ACM (2006)
28. Hoffmann, J., Kissmann, P., Torralba, Á.: "Distance"? Who cares? Tailoring merge-and-shrink heuristics to detect unsolvability. In: ECAI, pp. 441–446 (2014)
29. Holzmann, G.J.: The SPIN Model Checker - Primer and Reference Manual. Addison-Wesley, Boston (2004)
30. Hopp, W., Simon, J.: Bounds and heuristics for assembly-like queues. Queueing Syst. **4**, 137–156 (1989)
31. Jensen, R.M., Veloso, M.M., Bowling, M.H.: OBDD-based optimistic and strong cyclic adversarial planning. In: ECP (2001)
32. Kautz, H., Selman, B.: Pushing the envelope: planning propositional logic, and stochastic search. In: ECAI, pp. 1194–1201 (1996)

33. Kupferschmid, S., Hoffmann, J., Dierks, H., Behrmann, G.: Adapting an AI planning heuristic for directed model checking. In: Valmari, A. (ed.) SPIN 2006. LNCS, vol. 3925, pp. 35–52. Springer, Heidelberg (2006). doi:10.1007/11691617_3

34. Lipper, E., Sengupta, E.: Assembly-like queues with finite capacity: bounds, asymptotics and approximations. Queueing Syst. 1, 67–83 (1986)

35. Lluch-Lafuente, A.: Symmetry reduction and heuristic search for error detection in model checking. In: MOCHART, pp. 77–86 (2003)

36. Manitz, M.: Queueing-model based analysis of assembly lines with finite buffers and general service times. Comput. Oper. Res. 35(8), 2520–2536 (2008)

37. Morales Kluge, E., Ganji, F., Scholz-Reiter, B.: Intelligent products - towards autonomous logistic processes - a work in progress paper. In: PLM, Bremen, pp. 348–357 (2010)

38. Nau, D., Ghallab, M., Traverso, P.: Automated Planning: Theory & Practice. Morgan Kaufmann Publishers Inc., San Francisco (2004)

39. Nissim, R., Brafman, R.I.: Cost-optimal planning by self-interested agents. In: AAAI (2013)

40. Parragh, S.N., Doerner, K.F., Hartl, R.F.: A survey on pickup and delivery problems Part II: transportation between pickup and delivery locations. J. für Betriebswirtschaft 58(2), 81–117 (2008)

41. Rekersbrink, H., Ludwig, B., Scholz-Reiter, B.: Entscheidungen selbststeuernder logistischer Objekte. Ind. Manag. 23(4), 25–30 (2007)

42. Russell, S.J., Norvig, P.: Artificial Intelligence - A Modern Approach, 3rd edn. Pearson Education, Upper Saddle River (2010)

43. Ruys, T.C.: Optimal scheduling using branch and bound with SPIN 4.0. In: Ball, T., Rajamani, S.K. (eds.) SPIN 2003. LNCS, vol. 2648, pp. 1–17. Springer, Heidelberg (2003). doi:10.1007/3-540-44829-2_1

44. Ruys, T.C., Brinksma, E.: Experience with literate programming in the modelling and validation of systems. In: Steffen, B. (ed.) TACAS 1998. LNCS, vol. 1384, pp. 393–408. Springer, Heidelberg (1998). doi:10.1007/BFb0054185

45. Saffidine, A.: Solving games and all that. Ph.D. thesis, University Paris-Dauphine (2014)

46. Valmari, A.: A stubborn attack on state explosion. In: Clarke, E.M., Kurshan, R.P. (eds.) CAV 1990. LNCS, vol. 531, pp. 156–165. Springer, Heidelberg (1991). doi:10.1007/BFb0023729

47. Wooldridge, M.: Reasoning About Rational Agents. The MIT Press, Cambridge (2000)

48. Wooldridge, M.: An Introduction to Multi-agent Systems. Wiley, Chichester (2002)

# Adaptive Switching Behavioral Strategies for Effective Team Formation in Changing Environments

Masashi Hayano[✉], Yuki Miyashita, and Toshiharu Sugawara

Department of Computer Science and Communications Engineering,
Waseda University, Tokyo 1698555, Japan
{m.hayano,y.miyashita}@isl.cs.waseda.ac.jp, sugawara@waseda.jp

**Abstract.** This paper proposes a control method for in agents by switching their behavioral strategy between rationality and reciprocity depending on their internal states to achieve efficient team formation. Advances in computer science, telecommunications, and electronic devices have led to proposals of a variety of services on the Internet that are achieved by teams of different agents. To provide these services efficiently, the tasks to achieve them must be allocated to appropriate agents that have the required capabilities, and the agents must not be overloaded. Furthermore, agents have to adapt to dynamic environments, especially to frequent changes in workload. Conventional decentralized allocation methods often lead to conflicts in large and busy environments because high-capability agents are likely to be identified as the best team member by many agents, resulting in the entire system becoming inefficient due to the concentration of task allocation when the workload becomes high. Our proposed agents switch their strategies in accordance with their local evaluation to avoid conflicts occurring in busy environments. They also establish an organization in which a number of groups are autonomously generated in a bottom-up manner on the basis of dependability to avoid conflicts in advance while ignoring tasks allocated by undependable/unreliable agents. We experimentally evaluated our method in static and dynamic environments where the number of tasks varied.

**Keywords:** Allocation problem · Agent network · Bottom-up organization · Team formation · Reciprocity

## 1 Introduction

An increasing number of applications with services/goals that are achieved by teams of different agents have been proposed due to recent advances in information science, telecommunications, and electronics. For example, in the Internet of Things (IoT) [26], many types of intelligent nodes, such as sensors, actuators, robots, and processors are interconnected, and a variety of services are provided by intelligent programs using up-to-date information from these nodes.

© Springer International Publishing AG 2017
J. van den Herik and J. Filipe (Eds.): ICAART 2016, LNAI 10162, pp. 37–55, 2017.
DOI: 10.1007/978-3-319-53354-4_3

These services are achieved by executing the corresponding tasks within teams of cooperative agents, where agents are autonomous and intelligent programs for controlling nodes, network bandwidth, and computer resources or for providing specialized functionalities. Of course, the services are simultaneously requested by huge numbers of users. Thus, in these systems, the agents are massive and busy, they are located in a variety of positions and are deployed by different companies for their own purpose, and they operate in the Internet autonomously. However, they are still required to identify other agents' functions and performance appropriately, and they are allocated the suitable and executable components of the task (this component is called a *subtask* hereafter). Mismatching or excessive allocations of subtasks to agents results in delays or failures of services. Teams of agents for the required tasks need to be formed simultaneously on demand and in a realtime manner for timely and quick service provision.

Studies on the aforementioned decentralized task allocation problem have been conducted in the multi-agent system (MAS) context for a long time. For example, coalition structure formation is a theoretical approach in which (rational) agents find the optimal coalition structure (the set of agent groups) that provides the maximal utilities for a given set of tasks [5,21]. However, this approach assumes that the systems are static, relatively small, and unbusy because it assumes the (static) characteristic function to calculate the utility of an agent set. It also requires high computational costs to find (semi-)optimal solutions, making it impractical when the systems are large and busy. Another approach that is more closely related to our method is team formation (or task-oriented coalition formation) by rational agents. In this framework, a number of leaders that commit to forming teams for tasks first select the agent appropriate for executing each of the subtasks on the basis of the learning of past interactions, and they solicit the agents to form a team to execute the entire task. Agents that receive a number of solicitations accept one or a few of them depending on their local viewpoints. When a sufficient number of agents has accepted the solicitations, the team can successfully be formed for executing the target task. However, conflicts occur if many solicitations by leaders are concentrated to only a few capable agents, especially in large and busy MASs, so the success rate of team formation decreases considerably in busy environments.

In the real world, people often form teams to execute complicated tasks. Of course, we usually behave rationally, i.e., we decide who will provide the most utility. However, if conflicts in forming teams are expected to occur and if no prior negotiation is possible, we often try to find and ask reliable people with whom to work. Reliable people are usually identified through past success in cooperative work [6]. Furthermore, if the opportunities for group work are frequent, we try to form implicit or explicit collaborative structures based on (mutual) reliability. In an extreme case, we may ignore or understate offers from non-reliable people for the sake of possible future proposals with more reliable people. Such behavior based on reciprocity may be irrational because offers from non-reciprocal people are expected to be rewarding in at least some way. However, it can stabilize collaborative relationships and reduce the possibility of conflicts in team formations. Thus, we can expect steady benefits in the future through working based on reciprocity. To avoid conflicts and to improve efficiency in group work in computerized systems, we believe that agents should identify which agents are cooperative and build an agent network on the basis of mutual reliability that is appropriate for the request patterns and task structures of the service requirements.

To avoid conflicts in team formation in large and busy MASs, we propose a computational method of enabling efficient team formations that have fewer conflicts (thereby ensuring stability) by autonomously generating reliability from reciprocity. The proposed agents switch between two behavioral strategies, rationality and reciprocity: they initially form teams rationally and identify reliable so dependable agents through the success of past team work and then identify a number of dependable agents that behave reciprocally. Of course, they return to the rational strategy if the dependable relationships are dissolved. The concept behind this proposal is that many conflicts occur in the regime of only rational agents because such agents always pursue their own utilities. Conversely, the regime of only reciprocal agents experiences less conflict but seems to constrain the behavior of some agents in the cooperative structure without avail. We believe that the optimal ratio between rationality and reciprocity will result in better performance. However, the relationship between the ratios, performance, and the locations of agents in an agent network that behave rationally or reciprocally remains to be clarified. Thus, we propose agents that switch strategies in a bottom-up manner by directly observing the reciprocal behavior of others and the success rates of team formation.

We already discussed the method to switch behavioral strategies in a preliminary report [14] by building upon our previous work [13]. In this paper, we revised the experimental environments and conducted the experiments again to find more detailed insight. Particularly, we investigated the features of our method in dynamic environments where the system's workload, i.e., the number of tasks, gradually changed or explosively increased but only occasionally [2,29]. Our experimental results suggested that because our method enabled agents to establish stable cooperation relationships between them, it could instantly adapt to gradual and sudden changes in workload.

## 2   Related Work

Achieving allocations using an effective negotiation method or protocol in a decentralized environment is an attractive goal in MAS research. For example, the conventional *contract net protocol* (CNP) [25] approach and its extensions have been studied by many researchers. For example, Sandholm and Lesser [19] extended the CNP by introducing *levels of commitment* to make a commitment breakable with some penalty. One of the key problems in negotiation protocols is that the number of messages exchanged for agreement increases as the number of agents increases [18]. However, broadband networks have begun easing this problem at the link level, and agents (nodes) are now overloaded by excessive messages, instead. Furthermore, it has been pointed out that the eager-bidder problem, where a number of tasks are announced concurrently, occurs in large-scale MASs, in which the CNP with levels of commitment does not work well [20]. Gu and Ishida [12] also reported that busy environments decrease the performance of the CNP. Thus, these methods cannot be used in large-scale, busy environments.

Coalition structure formation is a theoretical approach based on an abstraction in which agents find the optimal coalition structure that provides the maximal utilities for a given set of tasks [5, 21–23]. Although this technique has many applications, it assumes static and relatively small environments because high computational costs to find (semi-)optimal solutions are required, and the static characteristic function for providing utilities of agent groups is assumed to be given. Market-based allocation is another theoretical approach based on game theory and auction protocol. In this approach, information concerning allocations is gathered during auction-like bidding. Although it can allocate tasks/resources optimally in the sense of maximizing social welfare, it cannot be applied to dynamic environments where optimal solutions vary. Team formation is another approach in which individual agents identify the most appropriate member agent for each subtask on the basis of the learning of functionality and the capabilities of other agents [1, 4, 10, 13, 15]. However, this may cause conflicts in large-scale and busy MASs, as mentioned in Sect. 1.

Many studies in computational biology, sociology, and economics have focused on the groups that have been organized in human societies [24]. For example, many studies have tried to explain irrational behaviors for collaboration in group work using reciprocity. The simplified findings of these studies are that people do not engage in selfish actions toward others and do not betray those who are reciprocal and cooperative, even if selfish/betraying actions could result in higher utilities [8, 11, 17]. For example, Panchanathan and Boyd [17] stated that cooperation could be established from indirect reciprocity [6], while the authors of [8, 11] insisted that fairness in cooperation may produce irrational behavior because rational agents prefer a higher payoff even though it may reduce the payoff to others. However, agents do not betray relevant reciprocal agents because such a betrayal would be unfair. Fehr and Fischbacher [6] demonstrated how payoffs shared among collaborators affected strategies and found that punishment towards those who distribute unfair payoffs is frequently observed, although administering the punishment can be costly [7]. In this paper, we attempt to introduce the aforementioned findings into the behaviors of computational agents.

## 3   Model

### 3.1   Agents and Tasks

Let $\mathcal{A} = \{1, \ldots, n\}$ be a set of agents. Agent $i \in \mathcal{A}$ has its associated resources (corresponding to functions or capabilities) $H_i = (h_i^1, \ldots, h_i^p)$, where $h_i^k$ is 1 or 0, and $p$ is the number of resource types. Parameter $h_i^k = 1$ means that $i$ has the capability for the $k$-th resources. Task $T$ consists of a number of subtasks $S_T = \{s_1, \ldots, s_l\}$, where $l = |S_T|$. Subtask $s_j$ requires some resources, which are denoted by $(r_{s_j}^1, \ldots, r_{s_j}^p)$, where $r_{s_j}^k = 0$ or $1$ and $r_{s_j}^k = 1$ means that the $k$-th resource is required to execute $s_j$. Agent $i$ can execute $s_j$ only when

$$h_i^k \geq r_j^k \text{ for } 1 \leq \forall k \leq p$$

is satisfied. We often identify subtask $s$ and its associated resource $s = (r_s^1, \ldots, r_s^p)$. We can say that task $T$ is executed when all the associated subtasks are executed.

## 3.2   Execution by a Team

Task $T$ is executed by a set of agents by appropriately allocating each subtask to an agent. A *team* for executing task $T$ is defined as $(G, \sigma, T)$, where $G$ is the set of agents. Surjective function

$$\sigma : S_T \longrightarrow G$$

describes the assignment of $S_T$, where subtask $s \in S_T$ is allocated to $\sigma(s) \in G$. We assume that $\sigma$ is a one-to-one function for simplicity, but we can omit this assumption in the following discussion. The team for executing $T$ has been successfully formed when the conditions

$$h_{\sigma(s)}^k \geq r_s^k \tag{1}$$

hold for $\forall s \in S_T$ and $1 \leq \forall k \leq p$.

After the success of team formation for task $T$, the team receives the associated utility $u_T \geq 0$. In general, the utility value may be correlated with, for example, the required resources and/or the priority. However, here we focus on improving the success rate of team formation by autonomously establishing groups based on dependability, so we simplify the utility calculation and distributions; hence, all agents involved in forming the team receive $u_T = 1$ equally when they have succeeded but receive $u_T = 0$ otherwise. Note that agents are confined to one team and cannot join another team simultaneously. This assumption is reasonable in some applications: for example, agents in a team are often required to be synchronized with other agents, and some sensors and actuators are exclusive resources. Another example is in robotics applications where the physical entities are not sharable due to spatial restrictions [30]. Even in a computer system that can schedule multiple subtasks, selecting one team corresponds to the decision on which subtasks should be done first.

## 3.3   Forming Teams

For a positive number $\lambda$, $\lambda$ tasks per tick are requested by the environment probabilistically and stored in the system's task queue $\mathcal{Q} = \langle T_1, T_2, \ldots \rangle$, where $\mathcal{Q}$ is an ordered set and *tick* is the unit of time used in our model. Parameter $\lambda$ is called the *workload* of the system. Agents in our model are in either an *inactive* or *active* state, where an agent in the active state is involved in forming a team and otherwise is inactive. Inactive agents first decide to play a role, *leader* or *member*; how they select the role is discussed later.

Inactive agent $i$ playing a leader role picks up task $T$ from the head of $\mathcal{Q}$ and becomes active. If $i$ cannot find any task, it stays inactive. Active agent $i$ then finds subtask $s \in S_T$ that $i$ can execute. Then, $i$ identifies $|S_T| - 1$ agents to allocate subtasks in $S_T \setminus \{s\}$. (If $i$ cannot find any executable subtask in $S_T$, it must identify $|S_T|$ agents. In our upcoming explanation, we assume that $i$ can execute one of the subtasks, but we can omit this assumption if needed.) How these agents are identified will be discussed in Sect. 4. The set of $i$ and the identified agents is called the *pre-team* and is denoted by $G_T^p$. Agent $i$ sends the agents in $G_T^p$ messages soliciting them to join the team, and it then waits for the response. If the agents that accept the solicitations satisfy condition (1), the team $(G, \sigma, T)$ is successfully formed, where $G$ is the set of agents to which the subtask in $S_T$ is allocated, and the assignment $\sigma$ is canonically defined on the basis of the acceptances. Then, $i$ notifies $G \setminus \{i\}$ of the successful team formation and all agents in $G$ continue to be active for $d_T$ ticks for task execution. At this point, $i$ (and agents in $G$) return to being inactive. However, if an insufficient number of agents for $T$ accept the solicitation, the team formation by $i$ fails, and $i$ discards $T$ and notifies the agents of the failure. The agents in $G$ then return to being inactive. Note that the failed tasks can be returned to $\mathcal{Q}$ without discarding them. However, because the propose of this paper is efficient team formation, we simply assume to discard them.

When agent $i$ decides to play a member, it looks at the solicitation messages from leaders and selects the message whose allocated subtask is executable in $i$. The strategy for selecting the solicitation message is described in Sect. 4. Note that $i$ selects only one message because $i$ can join only one team at a time. Agent $i$ enters the active state and sends an acceptance message to the leader $j$ of the selected solicitation and rejection messages to other leaders if they exist. Then, $i$ waits for the response to the acceptance. If it receives a failure message, it immediately returns to the inactive state. Otherwise, $i$ joins the team formed by $j$ and is confined for duration $d_T$ to its execution. After that, it receives $u_T = 1$ and returns to being inactive. If $i$ receives no solicitation messages, it continues in the inactive state.

Note that we set the time required for forming a team to $d_G$ ticks; thus, the total time for executing a task is $d_G + d_T$ ticks. We also note that leader agent $i$ can select pre-team members redundantly; for example, $i$ selects $R \geq 1$ agents for each subtask in $S_T$ (where $R$ is an integer). This can increase the success rate of team formation but may overly restrain other agents. We make our model simpler by setting $R = 2$, as our purpose is to improve efficiency by changing behavioral strategies.

## 4    Proposed Method

Our agents have three learning parameters. The first is called the *degree of expectation for cooperation* (DEC) and is used to decide which agents they should work with again. The other two are called the *degree of success as a leader* (DSL) and the *degree of success as a member* (DSM) and are used to identify which role is likely to be successful for forming teams. We define these parameters and explain how agents learn and use them in this section.

### 4.1    Learning for Cooperation

Agent $i$ has the DEC parameter $c_{ij}$ for $\forall j$ ($\in \mathcal{A} \setminus \{i\}$) with which $i$ has worked in the same team in the past. The DEC parameters are used differently depending on roles. When $i$ plays a leader, $i$ selects pre-team members in accordance with the DEC values, i.e., agents with higher DEC values are likely to be selected. How pre-team members are selected is discussed in Sect. 4.3. Then, the value of $c_{ij}$ is updated by

$$c_{ij} = (1 - \alpha_c) \cdot c_{ij} + \alpha_c \cdot \delta_c, \tag{2}$$

where $0 \leq \alpha_c \leq 1$ is the learning rate. When $j$ accepts $i$'s solicitation, $c_{ij}$ is updated with $\delta_c = 1$; otherwise, it is updated with $\delta_c = 0$. Therefore, $j$ with a high DEC value is expected to accept the solicitation by $i$.

After $i$ agrees to join the team that is initiated by leader $j$, $i$ also updates $c_{ij}$ using Eq. (2), where $\delta_c$ is the associated utility $u_T$, i.e., $\delta_c = 1$ when the team is successfully formed and $\delta_c = 0$ otherwise. Agent $i$ also selects the solicitation messages according to the DEC values with the $\varepsilon$-greedy strategy.

After the value of $c_{ij}$ in $i$ has increased, $j$ may become uncooperative for various reasons. To forget the outdated cooperative behavior, the DEC values are slightly decreased in every tick by

$$c_{ij} = max(c_{ij} - \nu_F, 0), \tag{3}$$

where $0 \leq \nu_F \ll 1$.

### 4.2    Role Selection and Learning

Agent $i$ learns the values of DSL and DSM to decide which role, leader or member, would result in a higher success rate of team formation. For this purpose, after the team formation trial for task $T$, parameters $e_i^{leader}$ and $e_i^{member}$ are updated by

$$e_i^{leader} = (1 - \alpha_r) \cdot e_i^{leader} + \alpha_r \cdot u_T \quad \text{and}$$
$$e_i^{member} = (1 - \alpha_r) \cdot e_i^{member} + \alpha_r \cdot u_T,$$

where $u_T$ is the received utility value that is 0 or 1, and $0 < \alpha_r < 1$ is the learning rate for the DSL and DSM.

When $i$ is inactive, it compares the values of DSL and DSM: specifically, if $e_i^{leader} > e_i^{member}$, $i$ decides to play a leader, and if $e_i^{leader} < e_i^{member}$, $i$ plays a member. If $e_i^{leader} = e_i^{member}$, its role is randomly selected. Note that when $i$ selects the leader as the role but can find no task in $\mathcal{Q}$, $i$ does nothing and will select its role again in the next tick.

### 4.3   Agent Switching Behavioral Strategies

Our main objective in this work was to design a new type of agent that switches its behavioral strategy, rational or reciprocal, depending on its internal state. In this section, we first discuss how worthy-to-cooperate agents (called *dependable* agents) are identified and then go over the behaviors of rational and reciprocal agents. Finally, we explain how agents select their behavioral strategies.

**Dependable Agents.** Agent $i$ has the set of dependable agents $D_i \subset \mathcal{A} \setminus \{i\}$ with the constraint $|D_i| \leq X_F$, where $X_F$ is a positive integer and is the upper limit of dependable agents. The elements of $D_i$ are decided as follows. For the given threshold value $T_D > 0$, after $c_{ij}$ is updated, if $c_{ij} \geq T_D$ and $|D_i| < X_F$ are satisfied, $i$ identifies $j$ as dependable by setting $D_i = D_i \cup \{j\}$. Conversely, if $\exists k \in D_i$ s.t. $c_{ik} < T_D$, $k$ is removed from $D_i$.

**Behaviors of Agents with Rational and Reciprocal Strategies.** Behavioral strategies mainly affect decisions regarding collaborators. Both leader agents with rational and reciprocal behavioral strategies select the members of the pre-team based on the DEC values with $\varepsilon$-greedy selection. Initially, agent $i$ sets $G_T^p = \{i\}$ and allocates itself to the subtask $s^0$ ($\in S_T$) executable in $i$.[1] Then, $\tilde{S}_T = S_T \setminus \{s^0\}$, and $i$ sorts the elements of $\mathcal{A}$ by descending order of the DEC values. For each subtask $s^k \in \tilde{S}_T$, $i$ seeks from the top of $\mathcal{A}$ an agent that can execute $s^k$ and that is not in $G_T^p$ and then adds it to $G_T^p$ with probability $1 - \varepsilon$. However, with probability $\varepsilon$, the agent for $s \in G_T^p$ is selected randomly. If $R = 1$, the current $G_T^p$ is the pre-team member for $T$. If $R > 1$, $i$ repeats $R - 1$ times the seek-and-add process for subtasks in $\tilde{S}_T$.

Behavioral differences appear when agents play members. An agent with a rational behavioral strategy selects the solicitation message sent by the leader whose DEC value is the highest among the received ones. An agent with a reciprocal behavioral strategy selects the solicitation message in the same way but ignores any solicitation messages sent by leaders not in $D_i$. Note that by ignoring non-dependable agents, no solicitation messages may remain in $i$ (i.e., all solicitations will be declined). We understand this situation in which $i$ does not accept the messages for the sake of possible future proposals from dependable agents. Thus, we can say that this ignorance may be irrational. All agents also adopt the $\varepsilon$-greedy selection of solicitation messages, whereby the selected solicitation message is replaced with another message randomly selected from the received messages with probability $\varepsilon$.

---

[1] $s^0$ may be *null*, as mentioned before.

### 4.4   Selection of Behavioral Strategies

When agent $i$ decides to play a member, it also decides its behavioral strategy on the basis of the DSM values $e_i^{member}$ and $D_i$. If the DSM $e_i^{member}$ is larger than the parameter $T_m$ ($> 0$) and if $D_i \neq \emptyset$, $i$ adopts the reciprocal strategy; otherwise, it adopts rationality. The parameter $T_m$ is a positive number used in the threshold for the criterion of whether or not $i$ has had a sufficient degree of success working as a member. Thus, $T_m$ is called the *member role threshold for reciprocity*. When $i$ plays a leader, its strategy is not affected by how members are selected.

We have to note that $i$ memorizes dependable agents on the basis of DEC values that reflect the success rates of team formation so that it can expect utility after that. In this sense, the DEC values are involved in rational selections. Therefore, dependable agents are identified on the basis of rational decision making. In our framework, after a number of dependable agents are identified, $i$ changes its behavior. Therefore, we can say that at first, $i$ pursues only the utilities. However, when it has identified a number of dependable agents that may bring utilities, $i$ tries not only to work with them preferentially but also to reduce the chances of unexpected uncooperative behaviors.

## 5   Experimental Evaluation

### 5.1   Experimental Setting

We conducted three experiments to evaluate our method. In the first experiment (Exp. 1), we investigated the performance (i.e., the number of successes) of team formation in the society of the proposed agents and the structure of behavioral strategies, and we then compared it with the performance of agents in the society of *rational agents* and that of the proposed agents of the static group regime whose structures are initially given and fixed. A rational agent always behaves on the basis of rationality, thereby corresponding to the case where $X_F = 0$. The agents with the static group regime are initially grouped into teams of six random agents, and any agent that initiates a task always allocates the associated subtasks to other agents in the same team. Thus, this type of agent corresponds to the case where $D_i$ is fixed to the members of the same group and $R = 1$. We call this type of agent the *static group-structured agents* or the SGS agents.[2]

In the second experiment (Exp. 2), we introduced dynamic environments where workload, $\lambda$, gradually increased or decreased over time, and investigated how agents with the proposed method, rational agents, and SGS agents could adapt to the gradual changes. Finally, we considered more bursty environments where workload varied in accordance with the Pareto (or power-law) distribution in the third experiment (Exp. 3). Our reason for conducting this experiment was the numbers of service requests over time on the Internet such as HTTP [29]

---

[2] We omit the networks of dependability and team formation achievement because they were reported by Hayano et al. [14].

and other service requests on the Internet [16] have the self-similarity that is characterized by this distribution.

Let the number of agents $|\mathcal{A}|$ be 500 (so 83 groups are initially established in the environment of SGS agents) and the number of resource types $p$ be six. The amount of the $k$-th resource of agent $i$, $h_i^k$, and the amount of the $k$-th resource required for task $s$, $r_s^k$, is 0 or 1. We assume that at least one resource in $H_i$ is set to 1 to avoid null-capability agents. However, only one resource is required in $s$, so $\exists k, r_s^k = 1$, and $r_s^{k'} = 0$ if $k' \neq k$. A task consists of three to six subtasks, so $|S_T|$ is an integer between three and six. The duration for forming a team, $d_G$, is set to two, and the duration for executing a task, $d_T$, is set to one. Other parameters used in Q-learning for agent behaviors are listed in Table 1. Note that while $\varepsilon$-greedy selection and Q-learning often used learning parameters, we used the shared learning rate $\alpha$ and random selection rate $\varepsilon$. The experimental data shown below are the mean values of ten independent trials.

Table 1. Parameter values in experiments.

| Parameter | Value |
|---|---|
| Initial value of DEC $c_i$ | 0.1 |
| Initial value of DSL $e_i^{leader}$ | 0.5 |
| Initial value of DSM $e_i^{member}$ | 0.5 |
| Learning rate $\alpha$ $(= \alpha_c, \alpha_r)$ | 0.05 |
| Epsilon in $\varepsilon$-greedy selection $\varepsilon$ | 0.01 |
| Decremented number $\gamma_F$ | 0.00005 |
| Threshold for dependability $T_D$ | 0.5 |
| Max. number of dependable agents $X_F$ | 5 |
| Member role threshold for reciprocity $T_m$ | 0.5 |

## 5.2 Performance Results

Figure 1 plots the number of successful teams every 50 ticks in societies consisting of the SGS, rational, and proposed agents when workload $\lambda$ is 10, 15, 25, and 35 in Exp. 1. Note that because all agents individually adopted $\varepsilon$-greedy selection with $\varepsilon = 0.01$ when selecting member roles and solicitation messages, approximately five to ten percent of tasks were used for challenges to find new solutions. However, in these situations, forming teams was likely to fail. We also note that $\lambda = 10, 15, 25$, and 35 correspond to the environment where work is low-loaded ($\lambda = 10, 15$), balanced (slightly lower than the system's limit of performance when $\lambda$ is around 25), and overloaded ($\lambda = 35$), respectively.

Figure 1 shows that the performance with the proposed agents outperformed those with other strategies except when $\lambda = 10$. When the system load was low, the performance with the SGS agents was stable, but when $\lambda = 25$ and 35, their performance gradually decreased. In the busy environment, an agent

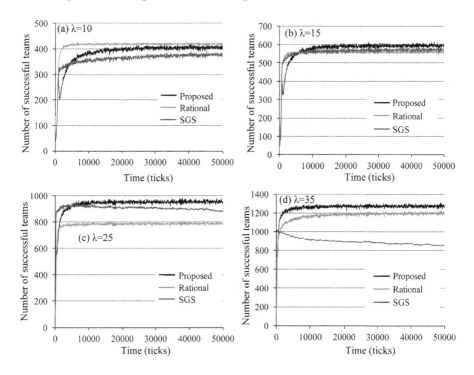

**Fig. 1.** Team formation performance.

that learned to play a leader in a group encountered many team formation failures, thereby starting to learn that it was ineffective as a leader. In such cases, other agents started to play the leader roles instead. However, among the SGS agents, groups are static and no leaders existed in a number of groups. Thus, the number of team formation failures increased. Because many conflicts occurred in the society of only the rational agents, their performance was lower than that with the proposed agents (except when $\lambda = 10$). However, in a busy environment ($\lambda = 35$), the performance by the proposed agents also reached a ceiling, and their difference decreased.

Because Fig. 1 suggests that the improvement ratios might vary depending on the work load, we plotted the ratios in Fig. 2, where the improvement ratio $I(str)$ was calculated as

$$I(str) = \frac{N(proposed) - N(str)}{N(proposed)} \times 100, \tag{4}$$

where $N(str)$ is the number of successful teams between 45,000 and 50,000 ticks with agents whose behavioral strategy is $str$, which is *"proposed," "SGS,"* or *"rational."*

Figure 2 indicates that the performance improvement ratio of the society of the SGS agents, $I(SGS)$, was small when the workload was low ($\lambda \leq 20$) but

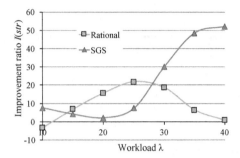

**Fig. 2.** Performance improvement ratios.

**Table 2.** Number of leaders at 50,000 ticks

| Workload ($\lambda$) | 10 | 15 | 20 | 25 | 30 | 35 | 40 |
|---|---|---|---|---|---|---|---|
| Proposed | 108.3 | 105.2 | 102.4 | 99.9 | 98.2 | 97.5 | 97.7 |
| Rational | 234.2 | 208.6 | 183.0 | 157.0 | 124.3 | 101.9 | 100.4 |
| SGS | 69.2 | 67.9 | 64.1 | 61.3 | 59.4 | 58.8 | 59.6 |

that it monotonically increased in accordance with the system's workload when $\lambda > 20$. The improvement ratios to the rational agents $I(rational)$ depict a characteristic curve, becoming maximal around $\lambda = 25$ and 30, which is near but below the system's limit, as aforementioned. We think this is the effect of autonomous organization in the society of the proposed method, as reported in [3]; we will discuss this topic in Sect. 5.5. Finally, when the workload was low ($\lambda \leq 10$), we could not observe any clear difference in the performances because conflict in team formation rarely occurred.

## 5.3   Behavioral Analysis

To understand why teams were effectively formed in the society of the proposed agents, we first analyzed the characteristics of the behavioral strategy and role selections. Table 2 lists the numbers of leader agents in which $e_i^{leader} > e_i^{member}$ were satisfied at the time of 50,000 ticks (so they played leaders) when $\lambda$ was varied. As shown, we found that the number of leader agents slightly decreased when the workload increased, but the number was almost invariant around 100 in the environments of the proposed agents. Thus, 400 agents were likely to play member roles. The number of subtasks required to complete a single task was fixed between three and six with uniform probability, and the structures of the task distribution did not change in our experiments. Hence, the number of leaders that initiated the team formation also seemed to be unchanged.

In contrast, the number of leaders changed considerably in the society of rational agents. When workload, $\lambda$, was small, fewer conflicts occurred, so many agents could continue to be leaders. However, as $\lambda$ increased, leader agents began to give up the leader role, and the number of leaders decreased to approximately one hundred. In the SGS regime, the number of leaders slightly changed around 60 to 69, which was smaller than the number of fixed groups, 83.

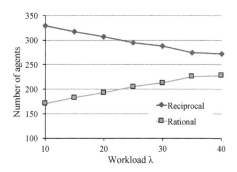

**Fig. 3.** Selected behavioral strategies at 50,000 ticks.

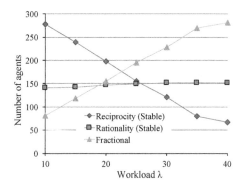

**Fig. 4.** Stability of behavioral strategies.

However, behavioral strategies were selected differently depending on the workload. The relationships between the workload and the structures of behavioral strategies at the end of the experiment are plotted in Fig. 3. The figure indicates that reciprocity was selected by over half of the agents, but this number gradually decreased as the workload increased. Furthermore, in Fig. 4, we plot the number of selected behavioral strategies during 49,000 to 50,000 ticks stably. For example, "reciprocity" in Fig. 4 means that they constantly selected reciprocity during 49,000 to 50,000 ticks, and "fractional (strategy)" means agents changed their strategy at least once during this period.

First, we can observe that the number of agents stably selecting reciprocity as their behavioral strategy decreased in accordance with the increase in workload. This is expected because they have a greater chance of forming teams as the workload increases, so they may have more chances to change their strategies. Nevertheless, the number of agents stably selecting rationality barely changed around 30 % of the agent population and if anything slightly increased in accordance with the workload. Hence, we can say that a number of the reciprocal agents occasionally became rational agents and worked like *freelancers*. We discuss this further in Sect. 5.5. Note that we found that all leader agents stably selected the reciprocal behavioral strategy.

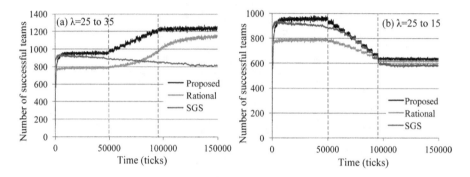

**Fig. 5.** Team formation performance in changing environments.

## 5.4 Performance in Changing Environments

In Exp. 2, we investigated the performance in dynamic environments, i.e., how the numbers of successful teams of agents with the proposed method, rational agents, and SGS agents, were affected by the gradual changes in workload. First, we fixed $\lambda = 25$ until 50,000 ticks. After that, (1) $\lambda$ increased by one every 5000 ticks until $\lambda = 35$ and was fixed until 150,000 ticks, and (2) $\lambda$ decreased by one every 5000 ticks until $\lambda = 15$ and was fixed until 150,000 ticks. The results are plotted in Fig. 5. The vertical dotted lines in the figure indicates when $\lambda$ started and stopped changing.

We can see from Fig. 5 that the number of successful teams of the proposed agents quickly and linearly increased or decreased in both cases. However, the number of successful teams with the rational agents increased behind the change in workload. This suggested that the proposed agents immediately adapted to the change in workload, but rational agents required additional time to adapt to the environmental changes. In the proposed method, agents already established the groups based on the dependability until 10,000 ticks, and this solid structures contributed to adapting to the changes in workload quickly. However, rational agents caused the structural change, especially the decrease in the number of leaders in accordance with the increase in workload as shown in Table 2. Therefore, they require additional time to adapt to the changes. In contrast, Fig. 5(a) indicates that the number of successful teams of the SGS agents constantly decreased, while the workload increased, like Fig. 1(c) and (d).

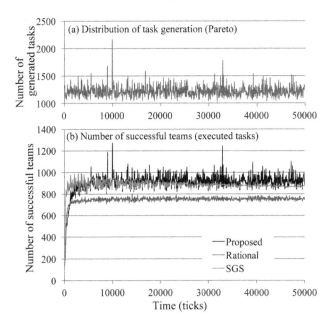

**Fig. 6.** Team formation performance in changing environments (Pareto distribution).

**Table 3.** Improvement ratio between 45,000 and 50,000 ticks (%)

| Value of $\alpha$ | 1.5 | 2.0 | 2.5 | 3.0 |
|---|---|---|---|---|
| Rational | 2.7 | 6.8 | 16.2 | 18.6 |
| SGS | 2.9 | 4.1 | 5.7 | 6.1 |

In Exp. 3, we introduced the Pareto distribution, whose cumulative distribution function, $F(x)$, is

$$F(x) = 1 - \left(\frac{x_0}{x}\right)^{\alpha},$$

and the mean was $\alpha x_0/(\alpha - 1)$ (for $\alpha > 1$). We fixed four instances of Pareto distribution whose $\alpha$ values were 1.5, 2.0, 2.5, and 3.0 (because a number of observations of service requests and network traffic reported that $\alpha$ was small) and whose mean values were 25. Then, we examined the number of successful teams when workload $\lambda$ varied every tick in accordance with each instance of distribution. Figure 6(a) indicates the example of the generated distribution of workload over time when $\alpha = 3$, and Fig. 6(b) indicates the numbers of successful teams over time under this workload distribution. We also list the improvement ratios, $I(str)$, defined by Formula (4) in Table 3.

Table 3 shows that the proposed agents exhibited better performance than those of rational and SGS agents, although their improvement ratios became slightly smaller than those in the constant workload (see also Fig. 2). When $\alpha = 3.0$ (the changes in workload were relatively moderate among the four

Pareto distributions), the number of successful teams of the proposed agents seems synchronized with the distribution of task generation (in particular, see a flood of task generations around 10,000 ticks in Fig. 6), but that of the rational agents did not correlate with the distribution. From these results, we can say that the proposed agents quickly adapted to the bursts of task requests. Of course, when tasks are generated in accordance with the Pareto distribution, if anytime a flood of service requests occur, many failures of forming teams are inevitable even with the proposed agents due to the bursty nature of the Pareto distribution. However, the failures are much smaller than those with rational and SGS agents.

## 5.5   Discussion

The results of Exp. 1 suggest that the mixture of reciprocity and rationality produces an efficient and effective society. The appropriate ratio between these behavioral strategies is still unknown and probably depends on a variety of factors such as task structure, workload, and topology of the agent network. Our study is the first attempt to pursue this ratio by introducing autonomous strategy decision making through social and local efficiency. We also believe that a bottom-up construction of organization, such as the group/association structures based on the dependability discussed in this paper, is another important issue to achieve a truly efficient society of computer agents like a human society. Thus, another aim of this study was to clarify the mechanism to establish such an organization in a bottom-up manner. Our experimental results also suggest that reciprocity is probably what generates the organization, but further experimentation is required to clarify this.

As shown in Fig. 2, if we look at the curve of $I(rational)$ from the society of the proposed agents, it peaked around $\lambda = 25$ to 30, which is near but below the system's limit of task execution. This peak, called the *sweet spot* by Corkill et al. [3], is caused by the appropriate organizational structure of the agent society. A similar phenomenon was also reported by Sugawara et al. [28]: a peak of performance appeared when the workload was right before the theoretical upper limit. In our case, the proposed agents established their groups on the basis of dependability through their experience of cooperation. We want to emphasize that this curve indicates an important feature of the organization: namely, that its benefit rises up to the surface when the efficiency is really required. When the system is not busy, any simple method works well, and when the system is beyond the limit of the theoretical performance, no method can help the situation. When the workload is near the system's limit, the potential capabilities of agents must be maximally elicited. The experimental results suggest that the organization generated by the proposed agents partly elicited their capabilities in situations where it was really required.

In Exp. 1, all leaders agents in our method stably selected rationality as their behavioral strategy. Thus, from Fig. 4, approximately fifty members were stable rational agents. Because the number of leaders was about a hundred, agents generated groups of mostly four or five members on the basis of their dependability [14]. Hence, they could form teams from only within their groups if the number of subtasks was less than or equal to four or five. When they were requested to form larger teams for larger tasks, only one or two agents were solicited from outside of the groups. Because these agents were not beneficial enough for them to stay in the groups of dependability, they dropped out and behaved rationally. If the solicited agents behaved reciprocally, the solicitation messages might be ignored, so rational agents are likely to be solicited. Therefore, rational agents work like freelancers, compensating for the lack of member agents in larger tasks. The role of rational agents from this viewpoint is essential, especially in busy environments: when the workload is high, the rational agents can earn more utilities, thereby increasing the ratio of rational agents as shown in Fig. 3.

The solid and stable group structure based on the aforementioned dependability also contributed to better performance when the workload quickly varied (Exp. 3), but this performance was not sufficient, although the Pareto distribution occasionally causes explosive peaks, and thus, many failures (or long delays) of forming teams are unavoidable. In the current experiments, we set the size of task queue $Q$ to infinity, but in reality it must be finite and often a small number, so many tasks will be dropped, resulting in task refusals. We believe that, for the actual systems, we have to consider intentional refusals of services, like a *random early detection* algorithm [9], which is a very effective method against congestion of network traffic and which also has a self-similarity nature; this is a future direction of our research.

## 6   Conclusion

We proposed agents that switch their behavioral strategy between rationality and reciprocity in accordance with internal states on the basis of past cooperative activities and success rates of task executions to achieve efficient team formation. Through their cooperative activities, agents with reciprocal behavior established groups of dependable agents, thereby improving the efficiency of team formation by avoiding conflicts, especially in large and busy environments. We experimentally investigated the performance of the society of the proposed agents, the structures of selected roles, and behavioral strategies. We also investigated the effect of changes in workload on the entire performance and experimentally showed that the proposed agents form a solid group structure based on dependability. Thus, they can adapt to changes without restructuring groups. This feature is quite useful in the actual systems where service requests may suddenly change.

Our future study is to investigate the mechanisms to identify rules or norms [27] to enable agents to behave efficiently to form more stable groups of dependability in the future. We also plan to introduce the concept of execution time and delay to evaluate our method in more realistic situations where tasks are requested by a phase-change distribution between Poisson and Pareto distributions.

**Acknowledgement.** This work was, in part, supported by KAKENHI (25280087).

## References


1. Abdallah, S., Lesser, V.R.: Organization-based cooperative coalition formation. In: 2004 IEEE/WIC/ACM International Conference on Intelligent Agent Technology (IAT 2004), pp. 162–168. IEEE Computer Society (2004)
2. Cameron, C.W., Low, S.H., Wei, D.X.: High-density model for server allocation and placement. In: Proceedings of the 2002 ACM SIGMETRICS International Conference on Measurement and Modeling of Computer Systems, SIGMETRICS 2002, pp. 152–159. ACM, New York (2002)
3. Corkill, D., Garant, D., Lesser, V.: Exploring the effectiveness of agent organizations. In: Proceedings of the 19th International Workshop on Coordination, Organizations, Institutions, and Norms in Multiagent Systems (COIN@AAMAS 2015), pp. 33–48 (2015)
4. Coviello, L., Franceschetti, M.: Distributed team formation in multi-agent systems: stability and approximation. In: Proceedings on 2012 IEEE 51st Annual Conference on Decision and Control (CDC), pp. 2755–2760, December 2012
5. Dunin-Keplicz, B.M., Verbrugge, R.: Teamwork in Multi-Agent Systems: A Formal Approach, 1st edn. Wiley, Hoboken (2010)
6. Fehr, E., Fischbacher, U.: Why social preferences matter - the impact of non-selfish motives on competition. Econ. J. **112**(478), C1–C33 (2002)
7. Fehr, E., Fischbacher, U.: Third-party punishment and social norms. Evol. Hum. Behav. **25**(2), 63–87 (2004)
8. Fehr, E., Fischbacher, U., Gächter, S.: Strong reciprocity, human cooperation, and the enforcement of social norms. Hum. Nat. **13**(1), 1–25 (2002)
9. Floyd, S., Jacobson, V.: Random early detection gateways for congestion avoidance. IEEE/ACM Trans. Netw. **1**(4), 397–413 (1993)
10. Genin, T., Aknine, S.: Coalition formation strategies for self-interested agents in task oriented domains. In: 2010 IEEE/WIC/ACM International Conference on Web Intelligence and Intelligent Agent Technology, vol. 2, pp. 205–212 (2010)
11. Gintis, H.: Strong reciprocity and human sociality. J. Theor. Biol. **206**(2), 169–179 (2000)
12. Gu, C., Ishida, T.: Analyzing the social behavior of contract net protocol. In: Velde, W., Perram, J.W. (eds.) MAAMAW 1996. LNCS, vol. 1038, pp. 116–127. Springer, Heidelberg (1996). doi:10.1007/BFb0031850
13. Hayano, M., Hamada, D., Sugawara, T.: Role and member selection in team formation using resource estimation for large-scale multi-agent systems. Neurocomputing **146**, 164–172 (2014)
14. Hayano, M., Miyashita, Y., Sugawara, T.: Switching behavioral strategies for effective team formation by autonomous agent organization. In: Proceedings of the 8th International Conference on Agents and Artificial Intelligence, pp. 56–65 (2016)
15. Katayanagi, R., Sugawara, T.: Efficient team formation based on learning and reorganization and influence of communication delay. In: International Conference on Computer and Information Technology, pp. 563–570 (2011)
16. Lu, X., Yin, J., Chen, H., Zhao, X.: An approach for bursty and self-similar workload generation. In: Lin, X., Manolopoulos, Y., Srivastava, D., Huang, G. (eds.) WISE 2013. LNCS, vol. 8181, pp. 347–360. Springer, Heidelberg (2013). doi:10.1007/978-3-642-41154-0_26

17. Panchanathan, K., Boyd, R.: Indirect reciprocity can stabilize cooperation without the second-order free rider problem. Nature **432**(7016), 499–502 (2004)
18. Parunak, H.V.D.: Manufacturing experience with the contract net. In: Huhns, M. (ed.) Distributed Artificial Intelligence, pp. 285–310. Pitman Publishing/Morgan Kaufmann, London/San Mateo (1987)
19. Sandholm, T., Lesser, V.: Issues in automated negotiation and electronic commerce: extending the contract net framework. In: Lesser, V. (ed.) Proceedings of the First International Conference on Multi-Agent Systems (ICMAS 1995), pp. 328–335. The MIT Press, Cambridge/San Francisco (1995)
20. Schillo, M., Kray, C., Fischer, K.: The eager bidder problem: a fundamental problem of DAI and selected solutions. In: Proceedings of First International Joint Conference on Autonomous Agents and Multiagent Systems (AAMAS 2002), pp. 599–606 (2002)
21. Sheholy, O., Kraus, S.: Methods for task allocation via agent coalition formation. J. Artif. Intell. **101**, 165–200 (1998)
22. Sims, M., Goldman, C.V., Lesser, V.: Self-organization through bottom-up coalition formation. In: Proceedings of the Second International Joint Conference on Autonomous Agents and Multiagent Systems, AAMAS 2003, pp. 867–874. ACM, New York (2003)
23. Sless, L., Hazon, N., Kraus, S., Wooldridge, M.: Forming coalitions and facilitating relationships for completing tasks in social networks. In: Proceedings of the 2014 International Conference on Autonomous Agents and Multi-agent Systems (AAMAS 2014), pp. 261–268 (2014)
24. Smith, J.M.: Group selection. Q. Rev. Biol. **51**(2), 277–283 (1976)
25. Smith, R.G.: The contract net protocol: high-level communication and control in a distributed problem solver. IEEE Trans. Comput. **C–29**(12), 1104–1113 (1980)
26. Stankovic, J.: Research directions for the internet of things. IEEE Internet Things J. **1**(1), 3–9 (2014)
27. Sugawara, T.: Emergence and stability of social conventions in conflict situations. In: International Joint Conference on Artificial Intelligence (IJCAI 2011), pp. 371–378 (2011)
28. Sugawara, T., Kurihara, S., Hirotsu, T., Fukuda, K., Sato, S., Akashi, O.: Total Performance by local agent selection strategies in multi-agent systems. In: Proceedings of 5th International Joint Conference on Autonomous Agents and Multiagent Systems (AAMAS 2006), pp. 601–608. ACM (2006)
29. Willinger, W., Paxson, V.: Where mathematics meets the Internet. Not. Am. Math. Soc. **45**(8), 961–970 (1998)
30. Zhang, Y., Parker, L.: Considering inter-task resource constraints in task allocation. Auton. Agent. Multi-Agent Syst. **26**(3), 389–419 (2013)

# From Reviews to Arguments and from Arguments Back to Reviewers' Behaviour

Simone Gabbriellini[1] and Francesco Santini[2(✉)]

[1] Dipartimento di Economia e Management, Università di Brescia, Brescia, Italy
simone.gabbriellini@unibs.it
[2] Dipartimento di Matematica e Informatica, Università di Perugia, Perugia, Italy
francesco.santini@dmi.unipg.it

**Abstract.** Our aim is to understand reviews from the point of view of the arguments they contain, and then do a first step from how arguments are distributed in such reviews towards the behaviour of the reviewers that posted them. We consider 253 reviews of a selected product (a ballet tutu for kids), extracted from the "Clothing, Shoes and Jeweller" section of Amazon.com. We explode these reviews into arguments, and we study how their characteristics, e.g., the distribution of positive (in favour of purchase) and negative ones (against purchase), change through a period of four years. Among other results, we discover that negative arguments tend to permeate also positive reviews. As a second step, by using such observations and distributions, we successfully replicate the reviewers' behaviour by simulating the review-posting process from their basic components, i.e., the arguments themselves.

## 1 Introduction

Online e-commerce stores like Amazon.com, or travel-related services like TripAdvisor.com are a common venue to let consumers voice their opinions. They represent a source of information for the companies, which can exploit such datasets to gain a better understanding of what consumers think about their products. Moreover, they also represent an important source of information about the quality of a product or the reliability of a service for other consumers who might be not aware of such quality/reliability before purchase.

Recent surveys have reported that 50% of on-line shoppers spend at least ten minutes reading reviews before making a decision about a purchase, and 26% of on-line shoppers read reviews on Amazon prior to making a purchase.[1] Such a flow of information among consumers has an impact on sales of products like books, CDs, and movies [5,31].

This paper reports an exploratory study of how customers use arguments in writing such reviews. We start from a well acknowledged result in the literature on on-line reviews: the more reviews a product gets, the more the rating tends

---

[1] http://www.forbes.com/sites/jeffbercovici/2013/01/25/how-amazon-should-fix-its-reviews-problem/.

© Springer International Publishing AG 2017
J. van den Herik and J. Filipe (Eds.): ICAART 2016, LNAI 10162, pp. 56–72, 2017.
DOI: 10.1007/978-3-319-53354-4_4

to decrease [25]. Such rating is, in many case, a simple scale from 1 to 5, where 1 is a low rating and 5 is the maximum possible rating.

This fact can be explained easily considering that first customers are more likely to be enthusiast of the product, then as the product gets momentum, more people have a chance to review it and inevitably the average rating tends to stabilise on some values lower than 5. Such a process, with a few enthusiast early adopters then followed by a majority of innovators, ultimately followed by late adopters that end the hype of an innovation, is a typical pattern in diffusion studies [25]. In on-line reviews however, when more people get involved in reviewing a product, we observe a lower level of satisfaction among them. More data is needed to assess the shape of diffusion of products through on-line reviews, but our initial investigation points in this direction. Some charts describing such phenomena are reported in Sect. 3.

However, the level of disagreement in product reviews remains a challenge: does it influence what other customers will do? In particular, what does it happen, on a micro level, that justifies such diminishing trend in ratings? Since reviewing a product is a communication process, and since we use arguments to communicate our opinions to others, and possibly convince them [21], it is evident that late reviews should contain enough negative arguments to explain such a negative trend in ratings - or that we are more susceptible to negative arguments.

The presence of extreme opinions on-line is a well-known issue grounded on the *reporting bias* and the *purchasing bias* of online customers - we will deepen this argument in the next section.

Our present study can be considered as "micro" because we focus on a single product only, even if with a quite large number of reviews (i.e., 253). Unfortunately, due to the lack of well-established tools for the automated extraction of arguments and attacks, we cannot extend our study "in the large" and draw more general considerations.

We extracted by hand, for each review about the selected product, both positive and negative arguments expressed, the associated rating (from one to five stars), and the time when the review has been posted. Afterwords, we analyse our data in terms of:

- how positive/negative arguments are posted through time;
- how many positive/negative arguments a review has (through time).

In particular, we argue that the reason why average ratings tend to decrease as a function of time depends not only on the fact that the number of negative reviews increases, but also on the fact that negative arguments tend to permeate positive reviews, decreasing de facto the average rating of these reviews.

As a second contribution of the paper, the goal is to replicate the behaviour of the reviewers of the investigated product as agents, by simulating how they assemble reviews in the form of arguments. The aim of this step is to translate our hypotheses on how customers write reviews into a computable form so to simulate them and attempt to reproduce the empirical patterns we have observed and described in the first part of the paper.

To accomplish this, we propose three different core mechanisms to understand the two main stylised facts observed in the data: *(i)* the tendency for average review rating to decrease with time, and *(ii)* the presence of negative arguments in reviews with positive ratings. The goal of this step is to evaluate the similarity between empirical and simulated data as per the correlations and distribution outlined in Sect. 4. To run our simulation on all such three mechanisms we use *NetLogo*, which is a programmable modelling environment for simulating natural and social phenomena.

The rest of the paper is structured as follows. Section 2 sets the scene where we settle our work: we introduce related proposals that aggregate Amazon.com reviews in order to produce an easy-to-understand summary of them. Afterwards, in Sect. 3 we describe the Amazon.com dataset from where we select our case-study. Section 4 plots how both positive and negative arguments dynamically change through time, zooming inside reviews with a more granular approach. Section 5 reproduce the observed phenomenon through a simulation of different mechanisms. Finally, Sect. 6 wraps up the paper and hints direction for future work.

## 2  Literature Review

Electronic Word-of-Mouth (e-WoM) is the passing of information from person to person, mediated through any electronic means. Over the years it has gained growing attention from scholars, as more and more customers started sharing their experience online [1,4,13,27,31]. Since e-WoM somewhat influences consumers' decision-making processes, many review systems have been implemented on a number of popular Web 2.0-based e-commerce websites (e.g., Amazon.com[2] and eBay.com[3]), product comparison websites (e.g., BizRate.com[4] and Epinions.com[5]), and news websites (e.g., MSNBC.com[6] and SlashDot.org[7]).

Unlike recommendation systems, which seek to personalise each user's Web experience by exploiting item-to-item and user-to-user correlations, review systems give access to others' opinions as well as an average rating for an item based on the reviews received so far. Two key facts have been assessed so far:

- *reporting bias*: customers with more extreme opinions have a higher than normal likelihood of reporting their opinion [1];
- *purchasing bias*: customers who like a product have a greater chance to buy it and leave a review on the positive side of the spectrum [5].

These conditions produce a J-shaped curve of ratings, with extreme ratings and positive ratings being more present. Thus a customer who wants to buy

---

[2] http://www.amazon.com.
[3] http://www.ebay.com.
[4] http://www.bizrate.com.
[5] http://www.epinions.com.
[6] http://www.msnbc.com.
[7] http://slashdot.org.

a product is not exposed to a fair and unbiased set of opinions. Scholars have started investigating the relation between reviews, ratings, and disagreement among customers [7,22]. In particular, one challenging question is: *does the disagreement about the quality of a product in previous reviews influence what new reviewers will post?*

A common approach to measure disagreement in reviews is to compute the standard deviation of ratings per product, but more refined indexes are possible [24]. The next step is to detect correlations among disagreement as a function of time [7,24]. We aim, however, at modelling a lower level, micro-founded mechanism that could account for how customers' reviewing behaviour evolves over time. We want to analyse reviews not only in terms of rating and length, but also in terms of what really constitutes the review itself, i.e., the arguments used by customers. We aim at explaining disagreement as a consequence of customers' behaviour, not only at describing it as a correlation among variables; an analytical and micro-founded modelling of social phenomena is well detailed in some works [14,19,26], and applied to on-line contexts as well [9].

However, before automatically reasoning on arguments, we have first to extract them from a text corpora of on-line reviews. On this side, research is still dawning, even if already promising [28,30]. In addition, we would like to mention other approaches that can be used to summarise the bulk of unstructured information (in natural language) provided by customer reviews. Some authors [15] summarise reviews by *(i)* mining product features that have been commented on by customers, *(ii)* identifying opinion sentences in each review and deciding whether each opinion sentence is positive or negative, and, finally, *(iii)* summarising the results. Several different techniques have been advanced to this, e.g., sentiment classification, frequent and infrequent features identification, or predicting the orientation of opinions (positive or negative).

## 3   Dataset

Amazon.com allows users to submit their reviews to the web page of each product, and the reviews can be accessed by all users. Each review consists of the reviewer's name (either the real name or a nickname), several lines of comments, a rating score (ranging from one to five stars), and the time-stamp of the review. All reviews are archived in the system, and the aggregated result, derived by averaging all the received ratings, is reported on the Web-page of each product. It has been shown that such reviews provide basic ideas about the popularity and dependability of corresponding items; hence, they have a substantial impact on cyber-shoppers' behaviour [5]. It is well known that the current Amazon.com reviewing system has some noticeable limits [29]. For instance, *(i)* the review results have the tendency to be skewed toward high scores, *(ii)* the ageing issue of reviews is not considered, and *(iii)* it has no means to assess reviews' helpfulness if the reviews are not evaluated by a sufficiently large number of users.

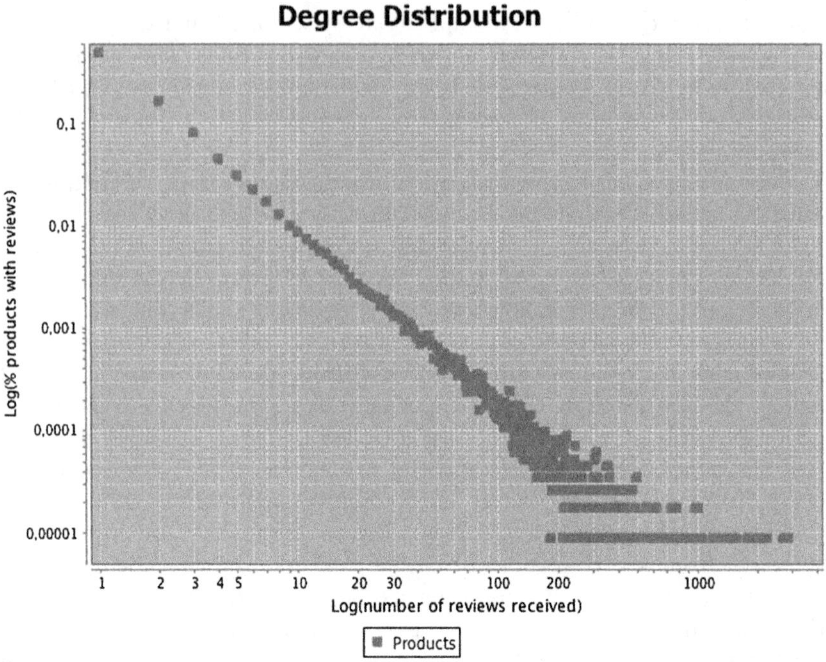

## Degree Distribution

**Fig. 1.** Degree distribution of reviews per product.

For our purposes, we retrieved the "Clothing, Shoes and Jeweller" products section of Amazon.com[8]. The dataset contains approximately 110k products and spans from 1999 to July 2014, for a total of more than one million reviews. The whole dataset contains 143.7 millions reviews.

We summarise here a quick description of such dataset. As can be seen in Fig. 1, the distribution of reviews per product is highly heterogeneous.

Figure 2 shows the disagreement in ratings tends to rise with the number of reviews until a point after which it starts to decay. Interestingly, for some highly reviewed products, the disagreement remains high: this means that only for specific products opinions polarise while, on average, reviewers tend to agree.[9]

Figure 3 shows that more recent reviews tend to get shorter, irrespectively of the number of reviews received, which is pretty much expectable: new reviewers might realise that some of what they wanted to say has already been stated in previous reviews.

Finally, Fig. 4 shows that more recent ratings tend to be lower, irrespectively of the number of reviews received.

---

[8] Courtesy of Julian McAuley and SNAP project (source: http://snap.stanford.edu/data/web-Amazon.html and https://snap.stanford.edu).

[9] Polarisation only on specific issues has already been observed in many off-line contexts, see [3].

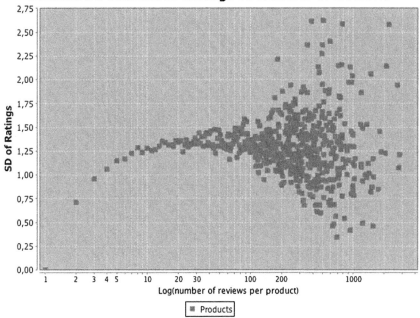

**Fig. 2.** The disagreement in ratings.

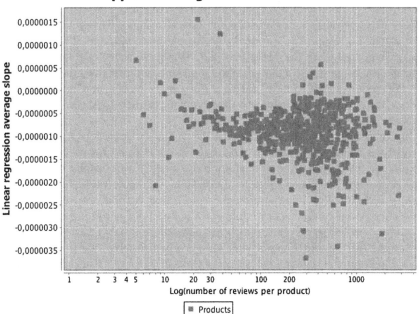

**Fig. 3.** Reviews tend to get shorter.

## What happens to ratings over time

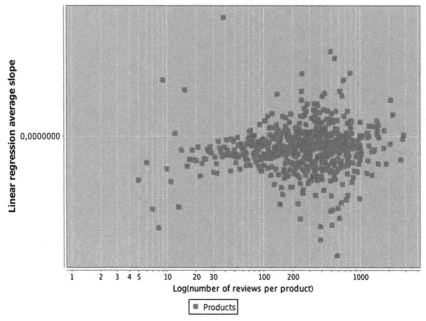

**Fig. 4.** The disagreement in ratings.

Coupling results from the second and fourth plots, it seems that disagreement in previous reviews does not affect much latest ratings - except for some cases which might correspond to products with polarised opinions. This result has already been found in the literature [22]. However, it has also already been challenged by Nagle and Riedl [24], who found that a higher disagreement among prior reviews does lead to lower ratings. They ascribe their new finding to their more accurate way of measuring the disagreement in such J-shaped distributions of ratings.

One of the main aims of this work is to understand how it is that new reviews tend to get lower ratings. Our hypothesis is that this phenomenon can be explained if we look at the level of arguments, i.e., if we consider the dynamics of the arguments used by customers, more than aggregate ratings.

Since techniques to mine arguments from a text corpora are yet in an early development stage, we focus on a single product and extract arguments by hand. We randomly select a product, which happens to be a ballet tutu for kids, and we examine all the 253 reviews that this product received between 2009 and July 2014. From the reviews, we collect a total of 24 positive arguments and 20 negative arguments, whose absolute frequencies are reported in Table 1.

There are of course many issues that arise when such a process is done by hand. First of all, an argument might seem positive to a reader and negative to another. For the purpose of this small example, we coded arguments together

**Table 1.** Positive and negative arguments, with their number of appearances in reviews between 2009 and July 2014.

| ID | Positive arguments | #App. | ID | Negative arguments | #App. |
|----|--------------------|-------|----|--------------------|-------|
| A | The kid loved it | 78 | a | It has a bad quality | 18 |
| B | It fits well | 65 | b | It is not sewed properly | 17 |
| C | It has a good quality/price ratio | 52 | c | It does not fit | 12 |
| D | It has a good quality | 44 | d | It is not full | 11 |
| E | It is durable | 31 | e | It is not as advertised | 8 |
| F | It is shipped fast | 25 | f | It is not durable | 7 |
| G | The kid looks adorable | 23 | g | It has a bad customer service | 4 |
| H | It has a good price | 21 | h | It is shipped slow | 3 |
| I | It has great colors | 21 | i | It smells chemically | 3 |
| J | It is full | 18 | j | You can see through it | 3 |
| K | It did its job | 11 | k | It cannot be used in real dance class | 2 |
| L | It is good for playing | 11 | l | It has a bad quality/price ratio | 2 |
| M | It is as advertised | 9 | m | It has a bad envelope | 1 |
| N | It can be used in real dance classes | 7 | n | It has a bad waistband | 1 |
| O | It is aesthetically appealing | 7 | o | It has bad colours | 1 |
| P | It has a good envelope | 2 | p | It has high shipping rates | 1 |
| Q | It is a great first tutu | 2 | q | It has no cleaning instructions | 1 |
| R | It is easier than build your own | 2 | r | It is not lined | 1 |
| S | It is sewed properly | 2 | s | It never arrived | 1 |
| T | It has a good customer service | 1 | t | It was damaged | 1 |
| U | It is secure | 1 | | | |
| V | It is simple but elegant | 1 | | | |
| W | You can customize it | 1 | | | |
| X | You cannot see through it | 1 | | | |

and, for each argument, tried to achieve the highest possible agreement on its polarity. A better routine, for larger studies, would be to have many coders operate autonomously and then check the consistency of their results. However, we didn't find case where an argument could be considered both positive and negative, maybe because the product itself didn't allow for complex reasoning. When we encountered a review with both positive and negative arguments, like "the kid loved it, but it is not sewed properly", we split the review counting one positive argument and one negative argument. The most interesting thing emerging from this study is the fact that, as reviews accumulate, they tend to contain more negative bits, even if the ratings remain high.

## 4    Analysis

In Fig. 6, the first plot on the left shows the monthly absolute frequencies of positive arguments in the specified time range. As it is easy to see, the number of positive arguments increases as time goes by, which can be a consequence of a success in sales: more happy consumers are reviewing the product. At the same time, the first plot on the right shows a similar trend for negative arguments, which is a signal that, as more customers purchase the product, some of them are not satisfied with it. According to what we expect from the literature (see Sect. 2), the higher volume of positive arguments is a consequence of the J-shaped curve in ratings, i.e., a consequence of reporting and selection biases. What is interesting to note though, is that the average review rating tends to decrease with time, as shown by the second row of plots in Fig. 6. This holds both for reviews containing positive arguments as well as for those containing negative arguments. In particular, the second plot on the right shows that, starting from 2012, negative arguments start to infiltrate "positive" reviews, that is reviews with a rating of 3 and above. Finally, the last row of plots in Fig. 6 shows that the average length of reviews decreases as time passes; this happens both for reviews with positive arguments and for reviews with negative arguments. However, such a decrease is much more steep for negative ones than for positive ones.

In Fig. 7 we can observe the distribution of positive and negative arguments.[10] Regarding positive arguments, we cannot exclude a power-law model for the distribution tail with x-min $= 18$ and $\alpha = 2.56$ ($pvalue = 0.54$)[11]. We also tested a log-normal model with x-min $= 9$, $\mu = 3.01$ and $\sigma = 0.81$ ($pvalue = 0.68$). We then searched a common x-min value to compare the two fitted distributions: for $x - min = 4$, both the log-normal ($\mu = 3.03$ and $\sigma = 0.78$) and the power-law ($\alpha = 1.55$) models still cannot be ruled out, with $p - value = 0.57$ and $pvalue = 0.54$ respectively. However, a comparison between the two leads to a two-sided $pvalue = 0.001$, which implies that one model is closer to the true distribution - in this case, the log-normal model performs better. For negative arguments, we replicated the distribution fitting: for xmin $= 2$, a power law model cannot be ruled out ($\alpha = 1.78$ and p-value $= 0.22$) as well as a log-normal model ($\mu = 1.48$ and $\sigma = 0.96$, $pvalue = 0.32$). Again, after comparing the fitted distributions, we cannot drop the hypotheses that both the distributions are equally far from the true distribution (two-sided $pvalue = 0.49$). In this case, too few data are present to make a wise choice.

Among the positive arguments (plot on the left), there are four arguments that represent, taken together, almost 44% of customers' opinions. These arguments are: *(i)* good because the kid loved it, *(ii)* good because it fits well, *(iii)* good because it has a good quality/price ratio, *(iv)* good because it has a good quality. Negative arguments represent, all together, less than 20% of opinions.

We have a clear view where the pros and cons of this product are stated as arguments: not surprisingly, the overall quality is the main reason why customers consider the product as a good or bad deal. Even among detractors, this product is not considered expensive, but quality still is an issue for most of them.

The plots in Fig. 5 show the cumulative frequencies and the rate at which new arguments are added as a function of time. In the left plot, it is interesting

---

[10] We used the R poweRlaw package for heavy tailed distributions (developed by Colin Gillespie [12]).

[11] We used the relatively conservative choice that the power law is ruled out if $pvalue = 0.1$ [6].

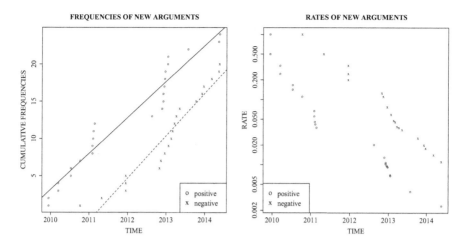

**Fig. 5.** Left plot: cumulative frequencies of new positive and negative arguments per month. Right plot: rate of new positive and negative arguments over total arguments per month.

to note that, despite the difference in volume (positive arguments are more cited than negative ones), the cumulative frequencies at which positive and negative arguments are added are almost identical. Positive arguments start being posted earlier than negative ones, consistently with the fact that enthusiast customers are the first that review the product. Moreover, it is interesting to note that no new positive argument is added in the 2011–2013 interval, while some negative ones arise in the reviews. Since 2013, positive and negative arguments follow a similar trajectory. However, as can be noted in the second plot on the right, new arguments are not added at the same pace. If we consider the total amount of added arguments, positive ones are repeated more often than negatives, and the rate at which a new positive argument is added is considerably lower than its counterpart. This information sheds a light on customers' behaviour: dissatisfied customers tend to post new reasons why they dislike the product, more than just repeating what other dissatisfied customers have already said.

## 5 Simulation with NetLogo

In this section we propose an agent-based model simulation to replicate empirical data about customers, reviews, and arguments, as described in Sect. 4. The aim of this step is to translate our hypotheses on how customers write reviews into a computable form so to simulate them and attempt to reproduce the empirical patterns we have observed and described in previous sections.

Following Moody [23], our aim is to specify a substance-specific model that can shed light on how customers behave when they have to review a product, thus to identify properties that make real-world and simulated data differ, without quantifying these differences with a statistical significance.

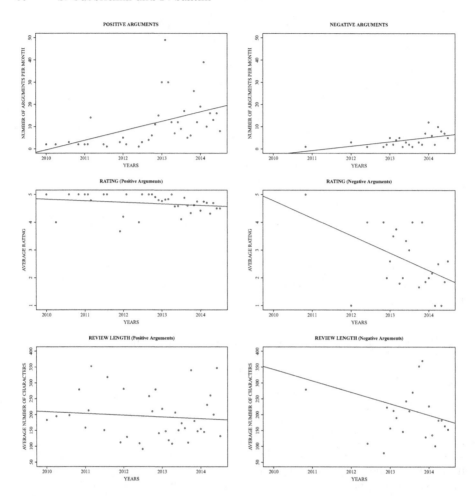

**Fig. 6.** Argument trends: (row1) absolute frequency of arguments per month, (row2) average rating of reviews per month, (row3) average review-length per month.

We opt for the *Agent-Based Modelling (ABM)* computational approach [18] to simulate arguments networks of online reviews from user behaviour. There is a growing literature that uses ABM in network studies [8,17]. ABM is a straightforward way to detail and implement substance-specific mechanisms in the form of computational models, i.e., software that generates entities with attributes and decision-making rules, and that is goal-oriented.

Despite the specific solution implemented, the main logic would be to test different specifications of a mechanism against empirical data and to refine such implementations until a satisfactory match is found or, alternatively, to get back to the blackboard and think again about the hypotheses.

An interesting analytical strategy to understand the robustness of an ABM is to compare its results against empirical data [20] in order to assess how realistic the model behaves - thus how plausible is the theory behind it. We will also

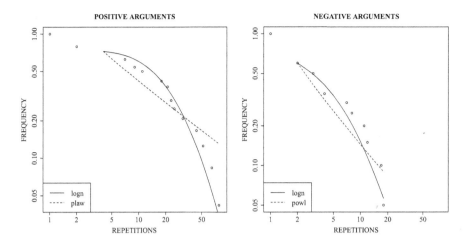

**Fig. 7.** Arguments distribution: probability of observing an argument repeated x times.

compare the results of our ABM against a random baseline in order to assess whether a simpler model can suffice to deal with the complexity of what we observed empirically. The idea is that our ABM should outperform the baseline model in approximating empirical data.

We adopt *NetLogo*[12], a programmable modelling environment in *Scala*[13] for simulating natural and social phenomena, to implement our model. NetLogo is particularly well suited for modelling complex systems developing over time. Modellers can give instructions to hundreds or thousands of agents all operating independently. This makes it possible to explore the connection between the micro-level behaviour of individuals and the macro-level patterns that emerge from their interaction. Figure 8 shows our simulation running in NetLogo.

Our simulation model assumes a few constraints from empirical data:

1. the size of simulated and empirical populations coincide and it is equal to 198;
2. reviewers decide to review with a probability proportional to observing a review in empirical data: the frequency of reviews is thus mimicked realistically, but each time reviewers are chosen randomly to avoid artefacts (i.e. reproducing the same order in which physical reviewers reviewed the product);
3. the percentages of happy and unhappy reviewers coincide in real and simulated scenarios (around 80% are happy about the product);
4. the average number of arguments per review is 2, with a minimum of 1 argument and a maximum of 4 arguments;
5. the number and distribution of both positive and negative arguments is held constant (24 positive arguments and 20 negative arguments) and possibly similar to the empirical one (we use a Poisson generator to assign to every reviewers positive and negative arguments among the 44 possible arguments).

---

[12] https://ccl.northwestern.edu/netlogo/.
[13] http://www.scala-lang.org.

We then propose three different core mechanisms to understand the two main stylized facts observed in the data: (a) the tendency for average review rating to decrease with time; (b) the presence of negative arguments in reviews with positive ratings.

The first mechanism, *Mechanism 1*, is used as a random baseline where arguments and ratings are not related: we start assigning to reviewers a rating for their reviews (a value between 1 and 5) and then we randomly assign positive or negative arguments, irrespective of the rating value.

With *Mechanism 2*, we assume that a strict correlation is in place between ratings and arguments, thus reviews with positive ratings contain only positive arguments and vice versa.

With *Mechanism 3* we relax Mechanism 2 a bit, assuming that positive reviews can contain also negative arguments. In this case, for a certain positive rating (3, 4 or 5) the probability to contain a positive arguments is given by:

$$1/1 + \exp(\alpha - \beta * x)$$

As in Mechanism 2, however, negative reviews contain only negative arguments.

We have a very simple scheduling: at each time step, reviewers examine their probability to review the product. If this is the case, then they "write" a review with their rating and all the arguments they know. Each reviewer can review just once. The result of this process is simply a list of lists, where every inner list represents an agent's review.

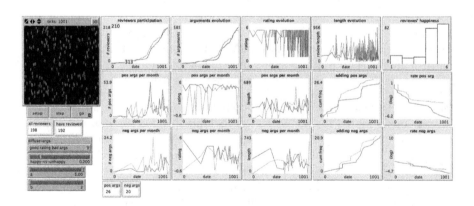

**Fig. 8.** Our simulation running in NetLogo.

We simulate each of the three mechanisms 100 times and we record, for each outcome, the distribution of positive and negative arguments, as well as the corresponding ratings. We then compare each simulated result against empirical data using the euclidean distance between the two curves, and report the distributions of distances as box-plots in Fig. 9.

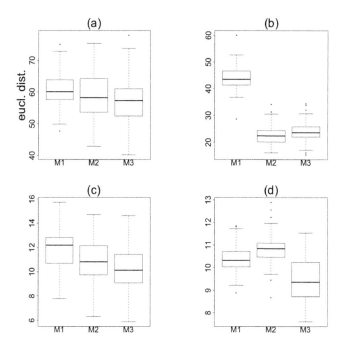

**Fig. 9.** Simulation results: each plot shows the distribution of euclidean distances between simulated curves and empirical ones over 100 replications. For Mechanism 3, $\alpha = 4.8$ and $\beta = 1.8$. From left to right in each figure, Mechanisms from 1 to 3.

Figure 9(a) shows, for each mechanism, the distribution of distances from the cumulative frequency curve of positive arguments. It is evident that all mechanisms can produce equally distant curves from the empirical one. When it comes to negative arguments, however, things are different. Figure 9(b) shows the distribution of distances from the cumulative frequency curve of negative arguments: it is evident that Mechanisms 2 and 3 do a better job. Figure 9(c) shows, for positive arguments, the distribution of distances from the curve of ratings over time. While it looks like Mechanism 3 is performing slightly better than the others, we can say that the three mechanisms are doing pretty much the same job. When it comes to the same measure, but for negative arguments, Fig. 9(d) shows clearly that Mechanism 3 performs better than the others, producing curves of ratings versus time that are statistically more close to the empirical one w.r.t. the other two mechanisms.

## 6   Conclusion

We have proposed an exploratory study on arguments in Amazon.com reviews. Firstly, we extract positive (in favour of purchase) and negative (against it) arguments from each review concerning a selected product. We have accomplished such information extraction manually, scanning all the related reviews. Secondly, we have linked the extracted arguments to the rating score, to the length, and to the date of reviews, in order to understand how they are connected. As a result, we have shown that negative arguments are quite sparse in the beginning of such social review-process, while positive arguments are more equally distributed along the timeline. As a second step, we have replicated the behaviour of reviewers as agents, by simulating (ABM) how they assemble reviews in the form of arguments. In such a way, we have shown we are able to mirror the measured experiment through a simulation that takes into account both positive and negative arguments.

With our model we are in the position to offer a possible explanation of reviewers' behaviour, but we still do not know much about why some opinions are in place among reviewers nor how they engage in discussions when they disagree. In other words, we still do not know anything about the arguments used by reviewers. Much research is at stake in computational argumentation and some frameworks for agent-based modelling with argumentative agents have been proposed. In the future, it would be interesting to mine the dataset for arguments and then model how argumentative frameworks evolve when disagreement is strong: a closer examinations of such exchanges should lead to more insightful conclusions.

In addition, reviews, reviewers, and products could be mapped as in [2]:

- reviewers and products are represented as two sets of nodes in a bipartite network;
- reviews are represented as links that connect consumers and products, where the weight of the link represents the rating of the review.

Different strategies are possible in order to check how much empirical and simulated networks share a common topology and to validate the realism of the mechanisms proposed in Sect. 5. An interesting approach is to use as more statistics as possible, coupling for example descriptive statistics and GOF statistics [9,19]. Following [11], we also plan to implement an Agent-Based Model with Argumentative Agents in order to explore the possible mechanisms, from a user's perspective.

We limited the horizon of our study to a "micro" dimension [10] due to the constraint imposed by the argument-mining field, which is still at its first steps: no well-established tool seems already exist to handle this task in our application, except for emerging approaches [16]. However, the ultimate aim is to widen our study to check the behaviour of consumers of products in different databases, not only the one dedicated to "Clothing, Shoes and Jeweller", as in this paper. Different classes of products may involve a different consumers' behaviour: the same consumers can interact on a different class of products (e.g., technology-related ones) with different attitudes.

# References

1. Anderson, E.W.: Customer satisfaction and word of mouth. J. Serv. Res. **1**(1), 5–17 (1998)
2. Balázs, K.: The duality of organizations and audiences, pp. 397–418. Wiley (2014). http://dx.doi.org/10.1002/9781118762707.ch16

3. Baldassarri, D., Bearman, P.: Dynamics of political polarization. Am. Sociol. Rev. **72**, 784–811 (2007)

4. Chatterjee, P.: Online reviews do consumers use them? In: Gilly, M.C., Myers-Levy, J. (eds.) ACR 2001 Proceedings, pp. 129–134. Association for Consumer Research (2001)

5. Chevalier, J., Mayzlin, D.: The effect of word of mouth on sales: online book reviews. J. Mark. **43**(3), 345–354 (2006)

6. Clauset, A., Shalizi, C., Newman, M.: Power-law distributions in empirical data. SIAM Rev. **51**(4), 661–703 (2009)

7. Dellarocas, C.: The digitization of word of mouth: promise and challenges of online feedback mechanisms. Manag. Sci. **49**(10), 1407–1424 (2003)

8. Flache, A., Macy, M.W.: Local convergence and global diversity: from interpersonal to social influence. J. Confl. Resolut. **55**(6), 970–995 (2011). http://jcr.sag epub.com/content/55/6/970.abstract

9. Gabbriellini, S.: The evolution of online forums as communication networks: an agent-based model. Rev. Francaise de Sociol. **4**(55), 805–826 (2014)

10. Gabbriellini, S., Santini, F.: A micro study on the evolution of arguments in Amazon.com's reviews. In: Chen, Q., Torroni, P., Villata, S., Hsu, J., Omicini, A. (eds.) PRIMA 2015. LNCS (LNAI), vol. 9387, pp. 284–300. Springer, Heidelberg (2015). doi:10.1007/978-3-319-25524-8_18

11. Gabbriellini, S., Torroni, P.: A new framework for abms based on argumentative reasoning. In: Kamiński, B., Koloch, G. (eds.) Advances in Social Simulation. AISC, vol. 229, pp. 25–36. Springer, Heidelberg (2014). doi:10.1007/978-3-642-39829-2_3

12. Gillespie, C.: Fitting heavy tailed distributions: the powerlaw package. J. Stat. Softw. **64**(2), 1–16 (2015)

13. Goldenberg, J., Libai, B., Muller, E.: Talk of the network: a complex systems look at the underlying process of word-of-mouth. Mark. Lett. **12**(3), 211–223 (2001)

14. Hedstrom, P.: Dissecting the Social: On the Principles of Analytical Sociology, 1st edn. Cambridge University Press, Cambridge (2005)

15. Hu, M., Liu, B.: Mining and summarizing customer reviews. In: Proceedings of the Tenth ACM SIGKDD International Conference on Knowledge Discovery and Data Mining, KDD 2004, pp. 168–177. ACM (2004)

16. Lippi, M., Torroni, P.: Context-independent claim detection for argument mining. In: Proceedings of the Twenty-Fourth International Joint Conference on Artificial Intelligence, IJCAI 2015, pp. 185–191. AAAI Press (2015)

17. Macy, M.W., Skvoretz, J.: The evolution of trust and cooperation between strangers: a computational model. Am. Sociol. Rev. **63**(5), 638–660 (1998). http://www.jstor.org/stable/2657332

18. Macy, M.W., Willer, R.: From factors to actors: computational sociology and agent-based modeling. Annu. Rev. Sociol. **28**, 143–166 (2002). http://www.jstor.org/stable/3069238

19. Manzo, G.: Educational choices and social interactions: a formal model and a computational test. Comp. Soc. Res. **30**, 47–100 (2013)

20. Manzo, G.: Variables, mechanisms, and simulations: can the three methods be synthesized? Rev. Francaise de Sociol. **48**, 156 (2007)

21. Mercier, H., Sperger, D.: Why do humans reason? Arguments for an argumentative theory. Behav. Brain Sci. **34**(2), 57–74 (2011)

22. Moe, W.W., Schweidel, D.A.: Online product opinions: incidence, evaluation, and evolution. Mark. Sci. **31**(3), 372–386 (2012)

23. Moody, J.: Network dynamics. In: Hedstrom, P., Bearman, P.S., pp. 447–474 (2008)
24. Nagle, F., Riedl, C.: Online word of mouth and product quality disagreement. In: ACAD MANAGE PROC. Meeting Abstract Supplement, Academy of Management (2014)
25. Rogers, E.: Diffusion of Innovations, 5th edn. Simone & Schuster, New York (2003)
26. Squazzoni, F.: Agent-Based Computational Sociology, 1st edn. Wiley, Hoboken (2012)
27. Stokes, D., Lomax, W.: Taking control of word of mouth marketing: the case of an entrepreneurial hotelier. J. Small Bus. Enterp. Dev. **9**(4), 349–357 (2002)
28. Villalba, M.P.G., Saint-Dizier, P.: A framework to extract arguments in opinion texts. IJCINI **6**(3), 62–87 (2012)
29. Wang, B.C., Zhu, W.Y., Chen, L.J.: Improving the Amazon review system by exploiting the credibility and time-decay of public reviews. In: Proceedings of the 2008 IEEE/WIC/ACM International Conference on Web Intelligence and Intelligent Agent Technology, WI-IAT 2008, vol. 3, pp. 123–126. IEEE Computer Society (2008)
30. Wyner, A., Schneider, J., Atkinson, K., Bench-Capon, T.J.M.: Semi-automated argumentative analysis of online product reviews. In: Computational Models of Argument - Proceedings of COMMA 2012, FAIA, vol. 245, pp. 43–50. IOS Press (2012)
31. Zhu, F., Zhang, X.: The influence of online consumer reviews on the demand for experience goods: the case of video games. In: Proceedings of the International Conference on Information Systems, ICIS, p. 25. Association for Information Systems (2006)

# Artificial Intelligence

# Integrating Graded Knowledge and Temporal Change in a Modal Fragment of OWL

Hans-Ulrich Krieger[✉]

German Research Center for Artificial Intelligence (DFKI),
Saarbrücken, Germany
krieger@dfki.de

**Abstract.** Natural language statements uttered in diagnosis, but more general in daily life are usually *graded*, i.e., are associated with a degree of *uncertainty* about the validity of an assessment and is often expressed through specific words in natural language. In this paper, we look into a *representation* of such graded statements by presenting a simple non-standard modal logic which comes with a set of modal operators, directly associated with the words indicating the uncertainty and interpreted through confidence intervals in the model theory. We complement the model theory by a set of RDFS-/OWL 2 RL-like entailment (*if-then*) rules, acting on the syntactic representation of modalized statements. After that, we extend the modal statements by *transaction time*, in order to implement a notion of temporal change. Our interest in such a formalization is related to the use of OWL as the *de facto* language in today's ontologies and its weakness to represent and reason about assertional knowledge that is *uncertain* and that changes over time.

## 1 Introduction

Medical natural language statements uttered by physicians or other health professionals and found in medical examination letters are usually *graded*, i.e., are associated with a degree of uncertainty about the validity of a medical assessment. This uncertainty is often expressed through specific *verbs, adverbs, adjectives*, or even *phrases* in natural language which we will call <u>gradation words</u> (related to *linguistic hedges*); e.g., *Dr. X <u>suspects</u> that Y suffers from Hepatitis* or *The patient <u>probably</u> has Hepatitis* or *(The <u>diagnosis of</u>) Hepatitis is <u>confirmed</u>.* Our approach is clearly not restricted to medical statements, but is applicable to graded statements in general, e.g., in technical diagnosis (*the engine is <u>probably</u> overheated*) or in everyday conversation (*I'm <u>pretty sure</u> that Joe has <u>signed a</u> contract with Foo Inc.*), involving *trust* (*I'm <u>not an expert</u>, but ...*) which can be seen as the common case (contrary to true *universal* statements).

In this paper, we look into a representation of such graded statements by presenting a simple *non-standard modal logic* which comes with a small set of *partially-ordered modal operators*, directly associated with the words indicating the uncertainty and interpreted through *confidence intervals* in the model theory. Our interest in such a formalization is related to the use of OWL in our projects

© Springer International Publishing AG 2017
J. van den Herik and J. Filipe (Eds.): ICAART 2016, LNAI 10162, pp. 75–95, 2017.
DOI: 10.1007/978-3-319-53354-4_5

as the *de facto standard* for ontologies today and its *weakness* to represent and reason about assertional knowledge that is uncertain [16] or that changes over time [10]. There are two principled ways to address such a restriction: *either* by sticking with the existing formalism (viz., OWL) and trying to find an encoding that still enables some useful forms of reasoning [16]; *or* by deviating from a defined standard in order to arrive, at best, at an easier, intuitive, and less error-prone representation [10].

Here, we follow the latter avenue, but employ and extend the standard entailment rules from [7,15,18] for positive binary relation instances in RDFS and OWL towards modalized *n*-ary relation instances, including transaction time and negation. These entailment rules talk about, e.g., subsumption, class membership, or transitivity, and have been found useful in many applications. The proposed solution has been implemented for the binary relation case (extended triples: quintuples) in *HFC* [11], a forward chaining engine that builds Herbrand models which are compatible with the open-world view underlying OWL.

This paper extends [12,14] by new material, addressing the *temporal change of graded statements*. We will introduce a special notion of *transaction time* [17] (the time period in which a database entry is valid), contrary to *valid time* which we have investigated in [10] for the non-modal case. Due to space restrictions, we let the interested reader refer to [12,14] for more material that we can not cover here, viz., (i) more on implementing modal entailments in *HFC*, (ii) specialized custom entailments, (iii) further kinds of modals (dual, in-the-middle), and (iv) related work, including the relation to the normal modal logic **K** and to *Subjective Logic* [8].

## 2   OWL Vs Modal Representation

We note here that the names of our *initial* modal operators were inspired by the *qualitative information parts* of diagnostic statements from [16] as shown in Fig. 1.

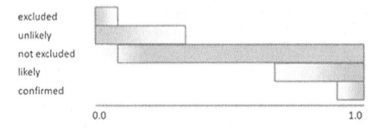

**Fig. 1.** Schematic mappings of the qualitative information parts *excluded* (*E*), *unlikely* (*U*), *not excluded* (*N*), *likely* (*L*), and *confirmed* (*C*) to *confidence intervals*. Picture taken from [16].

These qualitative parts were used in medical statements about, e.g., liver inflammation with varying levels of detail [16] in order to infer, e.g., if *Hepatitis is confirmed* **then** *Hepatitis is likely* but **not** *Hepatitis is unlikely*. And **if** *Viral*

*Hepatitis B is confirmed*, **then** both *Viral Hepatitis is confirmed* **and** *Hepatitis is confirmed* (generalization). Things "turn around" when we look at the adjectival modifiers *excluded* and *unlikely*: **if** *Hepatitis is excluded* **then** *Hepatitis is unlikely*, but **not** *Hepatitis is not excluded*. Furthermore, **if** *Hepatitis is excluded*, **then** both *Viral Hepatitis is excluded* **and** *Viral Hepatitis B is excluded* (specialization).

[16] consider five OWL encodings, from which only two were able to fully reproduce the *plausible* inferences for the above Hepatitis use case. The encodings in [16] were quite *cumbersome* as the primary interest was to stay within the limits of the underlying calculus. Besides coming up with complex encodings, only minor forms of reasoning were possible, viz., subsumption reasoning. Furthermore, each combination of disease and qualitative information part required a *new* OWL class definition/new class name, and there exist a lot of them! These disadvantages are a result of two conscious decisions: OWL only provides unary and binary relations (concepts and roles) and comes up with a (mostly) fixed set of entailment/tableaux rules.

In our approach, however, the *qualitative information parts* from Fig. 1 are first class citizens of the object language (the modal operators) and *diagnostic statements* from the Hepatitis use case are expressed through the binary property suffersForm between $p$ (patients, people) and $d$ (diseases, diagnoses). The plausible inferences are then simply a *byproduct* of the *instantiation* of the entailment rule schemas (G) from Sect. 5.1, and (S1) and (S0) from Sect. 5.2 for property suffersForm (the rule variables are universally quantified; $\top$ = *universal truth*; $C$ = *confirmed*; $L$ = *likely*), e.g.,

(S1) ViralHepatitisB $\sqsubseteq$ ViralHepatitis $\wedge$ ViralHepatitisB$(d)$
     $\rightarrow$ $\top$ViralHepatitis$(d)$
(G) $C$suffersFrom$(p, d) \rightarrow L$suffersFrom$(p, d)$

Two things are worth mentioning here. *Firstly*, not only OWL properties can be graded, such as $C$suffersFrom$(p, d)$ (= *it is confirmed that p suffers from d*), but also class membership, e.g., $C$ViralHepatitisB$(d)$ (= *it is confirmed that d is of type Viral Hepatitis B*). As the original OWL example from [16] can not make use of any modals, we employ the special modal $\top$ here: $\top$ViralHepatitisB$(d)$. *Secondly*, modal operators are only applied to assertional knowledge (the ABox in OWL)—neither TBox nor RBox axioms are being affected by modals in our approach, as they are supposed to express universal truth.

# 3   Confidence and Confidence Intervals

We address the *confidence* of an asserted (medical) statement [16] through *graded* modalities applied to propositional formulae: $E$ (*excluded*), $U$ (*unlikely*), $N$ (*not excluded*), $L$ (*likely*), and $C$ (*confirmed*). For various (technical) reasons, we add a *wildcard* modality ? (*unknown*), a complementary *failure* modality ! (*error*), plus two further modalities to syntactically state definite truth and falsity: $\top$

(*true,* or *top*) and $\perp$ (*false* or *bottom*).[1] Let $\triangle$ now denotes the set of all modalities: $\triangle := \{?, !, \top, \perp, E, U, N, L, C\}$.

A *measure function* $\mu : \triangle \mapsto [0,1] \times [0,1]$ is a mapping which returns the associated *confidence interval* $\mu(\delta) = [l, h]$ for a modality from $\delta \in \triangle$ $(l \leq h)$. We write $||\delta|| = h - l$ to denote the *length* of the confidence interval and presuppose that $\mu(?) = [0,1]$, $\mu(\top) = [1,1]$, $\mu(\perp) = [0,0]$, and $\mu(!) = \emptyset$.[2]

In addition, we define two disjoint subsets of $\triangle$, called $\underline{1} := \{\top, C, L, N\}$ and $\underline{0} := \{\perp, E, U\}$ and again make a presupposition: the confidence intervals for modals from $\underline{1}$ *end* in 1, whereas the confidence intervals for $\underline{0}$ modals always *start* with 0. It is worth noting that we do *not* make use of $\mu$ in the syntax of the modal language (for which we employ the modalities from $\triangle$), but in the semantics when dealing with the satisfaction relation of the model theory (see Sect. 4).

We have talked about *confidence intervals* now several times without saying what we actually mean by this. Suppose that a physician says that it is *confirmed* $(= C)$ that patient $p$ suffers from disease $d$, for a set of observed symptoms (or evidence) $S = \{S_1, \ldots, S_k\}$: $C\, suffersFrom(p, d)$.

Assuming that a different patient $p'$ shows the same symptoms $S$ (and only $S$, and perhaps further symptoms which are, however, *independent* from $S$), we would assume that the same doctor would diagnose $C\, suffersFrom(p', d)$.

Even an other, but similar trained physician is supposed to grade the two patients *similarly*. This similarity which originates from patients showing the same symptoms and from physicians being taught at the same medical school is addressed by confidence *intervals* and not through a *single* (posterior) probability, as there are still variations in diagnostic capacity and daily mental state of the physician. By using intervals (instead of single values), we can usually reach a consensus among people upon the *meaning* of gradation words, even though the low/high values of the confidence interval for, e.g., *confirmed* might depend on the context.

Being a bit more theoretic, we define a *confidence interval* as follows. Assume a *Bernoulli experiment* [9] that involves a large set of $n$ patients $P$, sharing the same symptoms $S$. W.r.t. our example, we would like to know whether $suffersFrom(p, d)$ or $\neg suffersFrom(p, d)$ is the case for every patient $p \in P$, sharing $S$. Given a Bernoulli trials sequence $\boldsymbol{X} = (X_1, \ldots, X_n)$ with indicator random variables $X_i \in \{0, 1\}$ for a patient sequence $(p_1, \ldots, p_n)$, we can approximate the *expected value* E for *suffersFrom* being *true*, given disease $d$ and background symptoms $S$ by the *arithmetic mean* A: $\mathrm{E}[\boldsymbol{X}] \approx \mathrm{A}[\boldsymbol{X}] = \frac{\sum_{i=1}^{n} X_i}{n}$.

---

[1] We also call $\top$ and $\perp$ *propositional* modals as they lift propositional statements to the modal domain. We refer to ? and ! as *completion* modals since they complete the modal hierarchy by adding unique most general and most specific elements (see Sect. 4.3).

[2] Recall that intervals are (usually infinite) sets of real numbers, together with an ordering relations (e.g., $<$ or $\leq$) over the elements, thus $\emptyset$ is a perfect, although degraded interval.

Due to the *law of large numbers*, we expect that if the number of elements in a trials sequence goes to infinity, the arithmetic mean will coincide with the expected value: $E[\boldsymbol{X}] = \lim_{n\to\infty} \frac{\sum_{i=1}^{n} X_i}{n}$.

Clearly, the arithmetic mean for each new *finite* trials sequence is different, but we can try to *locate* the expected value within an interval around the arithmetic mean: $E[\boldsymbol{X}] \in [A[\boldsymbol{X}] - \epsilon_1, A[\boldsymbol{X}] + \epsilon_2]$. For the moment, we assume $\epsilon_1 = \epsilon_2$, so that $A[\boldsymbol{X}]$ is in the center of this interval which we will call from now on *confidence interval*.

Coming back to our example and assuming $\mu(C) = [0.9, 1]$, $C$ *suffersFrom* $(p, d)$ can be read as being true in 95% of all cases *known* to the physician, involving patients $p$ potentially having disease $d$ and sharing the same prior symptoms (evidence) $S_1, \ldots, S_k$: $(\sum_{p \in P} \mathrm{Prob}(\mathit{suffersFrom}(p, d)|S))/n \approx 0.95$.

The variance of $\pm 5\%$ is related to varying diagnostic capabilities between (comparative) physicians, daily mental form, undiscovered important symptoms or examinations which have not been carried out (e.g., lab values), or perhaps even by the physical stature of the patient (crooked vs. upright) which unconsciously affects the final diagnosis, etc., as elaborated above. Thus the individual modals from $\triangle$ express (via $\mu$) different forms of the physician's *confidence*, depending on the set of already acquired symptoms as (potential) explanations for a specific disease.

## 4   Normal Form and Model Theory

Let $\mathcal{C}$ denote the set of constants that serve as the arguments of a relation instance. For instance, in an RDF/OWL setting, $\mathcal{C}$ would exclusively consist of XSD atoms, blank nodes, and URIs/IRIs. In order to define basic $n$-ary propositional formulae (ground atoms), let $p(\boldsymbol{c})$ abbreviates $p(c_1, \ldots, c_n)$, for $c_1, \ldots, c_n \in C$, given $length(\boldsymbol{c}) = n$. In case the number of arguments does not matter, we sometimes simply write $p$, instead of, e.g., $p(c, d)$ or $p(\boldsymbol{c})$. As before, we assume $\triangle = \{?, !, \top, \bot, E, U, N, L, C\}$. We inductively define the set of *well-formed formulae* $\phi$ of our modal language as follows:

$$\phi ::= p(\boldsymbol{c}) \mid \neg\phi \mid \phi \wedge \phi' \mid \phi \vee \phi' \mid \triangle\phi$$

### 4.1   Simplification and Normal Form

We now syntactically *simplify* the set $\Phi$ of well-formed formulae $\phi$ by restricting the uses of *negation* and *modalities* to the level of propositional letters $\pi$:

- $\pi ::= p(\boldsymbol{c}) \mid \neg p(\boldsymbol{c})$     - $\phi ::= \pi \mid \triangle\pi \mid \phi \wedge \phi' \mid \phi \vee \phi'$

The design of this language is driven by two main reasons: *firstly*, we want to effectively implement the logic (in our case, in *HFC*), and *secondly*, the application of the below semantic-preserving simplification rules in an offline preprocessing step makes the implementation easier and guarantees a more efficient runtime system. To address negation, we first need the notion of a *complement* modal $\delta^C$ for every $\delta \in \triangle$, where

$$\mu(\delta^C) := \mu(\delta)^C = \mu(?) \setminus \mu(\delta) = [0,1] \setminus \mu(\delta)$$

I.e., $\mu(\delta^C)$ is defined as the complementary interval of $\mu(\delta)$ (within the bounds of $[0,1]$, of course). For example, $E$ and $N$ (*excluded, not excluded*) or ? and ! (*unknown, error*) are already existing complementary modals.

We also require *mirror* modals $\delta^M$ for every $\delta \in \triangle$ whose confidence interval $\mu(\delta^M)$ is derived by "mirroring" $\mu(\delta)$ to the opposite side of the confidence interval, either to the left or to the right:[3]

$$\textbf{if } \mu(\delta) = [l,h] \textbf{ then } \mu(\delta^M) := [1-h, 1-l]$$

For example, $E$ and $C$ (*excluded, confirmed*) or $\top$ and $\bot$ (*top, bottom*) are mirror modals. In order to transform $\phi$ into its *negation normal form*, we need to apply simplification rules a finite number of times (until rules are no longer applicable). We depict those rules by using the $\vdash$ relation, read as *formula* $\vdash$ *simplified formula* ($\epsilon$ = empty word):

1. $?\phi \vdash \epsilon$                  ($?\phi$ is not informative at all)
2. $\neg\neg\phi \vdash \phi$
3. $\neg(\phi \wedge \phi') \vdash \neg\phi \vee \neg\phi'$
4. $\neg(\phi \vee \phi') \vdash \neg\phi \wedge \neg\phi'$
5. $\neg\triangle\phi \vdash \triangle^C\phi$         (example: $\neg E\phi = E^C\phi = N\phi$)
6. $\triangle\neg\phi \vdash \triangle^M\phi$         (example: $E\neg\phi = E^M\phi = C\phi$)

Clearly, the mirror modals $\delta^M$ ($\delta \in \triangle$) are not necessary as long as we explicitly allow for negated statements (which we do), and thus case 6 can, in principle, be dropped.

What is the result of simplifying $\triangle(\phi \wedge \phi')$ and $\triangle(\phi \vee \phi')$? Let us start with the former case and consider as an example the statement about an engine that *a mechanical failure m <u>and</u> an electrical failure e is <u>confirmed</u>*: $C(m \wedge e)$. It seems *plausible* to simplify this expression to $Cm \wedge Ce$. Commonsense tells us furthermore that neither $Em$ nor $Ee$ is compatible with this description (we should be alarmed if, e.g., both $Cm$ and $Em$ happen to be the case).

Now consider the "opposite" statement $E(m \wedge e)$ which must *not* be rewritten to $Em \wedge Ee$, as *either Cm or Ce* is well *compatible* with $E(m \wedge e)$. Instead, we rewrite this kind of "negated" statement as $Em \vee Ee$, and this works fine with either $Cm$ or $Ce$.

In order to address the other modal operators, we generalize these *plausible* inferences by making a distinction between $\underline{0}$ and $\underline{1}$ modals (cf. Sect. 3):

7a. $\underline{0}(\phi \wedge \phi') \vdash \underline{0}\phi \vee \underline{0}\phi'$
7b. $\underline{1}(\phi \wedge \phi') \vdash \underline{1}\phi \wedge \underline{1}\phi'$

---

[3] This construction procedure comes in handy when dealing with *in-the-middle* modals, such as *fifty-fifty* or *perhaps*, whose confidence intervals neither touch 0 nor 1. Such modals have a *real* background in (medical) diagnosis.

Let us now focus on disjunction inside the scope of a modal operator. As we do allow for the full set of Boolean operators, we are allowed to deduce

8. $\triangle(\phi \vee \phi') \vdash \triangle(\neg(\neg(\phi \vee \phi'))) \vdash \triangle(\neg(\neg\phi \wedge \neg\phi')) \vdash \triangle^M(\neg\phi \wedge \neg\phi')$

This is, again, a conjunction, so we apply schemas 7a and 7b, giving us

8a. $\underline{0}(\phi \vee \phi') \vdash \underline{0}^M(\neg\phi \wedge \neg\phi') \vdash \underline{1}(\neg\phi \wedge \neg\phi') \vdash \underline{1}\neg\phi \wedge \underline{1}\neg\phi' \vdash \underline{1}^M\phi \wedge \underline{1}^M\phi' \vdash \underline{0}\phi \wedge \underline{0}\phi'$
8b. $\underline{1}(\phi \vee \phi') \vdash \underline{1}^M(\neg\phi \wedge \neg\phi') \vdash \underline{0}(\neg\phi \wedge \neg\phi') \vdash \underline{0}\neg\phi \vee \underline{0}\neg\phi' \vdash \underline{0}^M\phi \vee \underline{0}^M\phi' \vdash \underline{1}\phi \vee \underline{1}\phi'$

Note how the modals from $\underline{0}$ in 7a and 8a act as a kind of *negation* operator to turn the logical operators into their counterparts, similar to de *Morgan's law*.

The final case considers two consecutive modals:

9. $\delta_1 \delta_2 \phi \vdash (\delta_1 \circ \delta_2)\phi$

We interpret the $\circ$ operator as a kind of *function composition*, leading to a new modal $\delta$ which is the result of $\delta_1 \circ \delta_2$. We take a liberal stance here of what the result is, but indicate that it depends on the domain and, again, plausible inferences we like to capture. The $\circ$ operator will probably be different from the related operation $\odot$ which is used in Sect. 5.3.

## 4.2   Model Theory

In the following, we extend the standard definition of modal (Kripke) frames and models [3] for *graded* modal operators from $\triangle$ by employing the confidence function $\mu$ and focussing on the minimal definition for $\phi$. A *frame* $\mathcal{F}$ for the probabilistic modal language is a pair $\mathcal{F} = \langle \mathcal{W}, \mathcal{R}_\triangle \rangle$ where $\mathcal{W}$ is a non-empty set of *worlds* (or *situations, states, points, vertices, etc.*) and $\mathcal{R}_\triangle$ a family of binary relations over $\mathcal{W} \times \mathcal{W}$, called *accessibility relations*. In the following, we write $R_\delta$ to depict the accessibility relation for modal $\delta \in \triangle$.

A *model* $\mathcal{M}$ for the probabilistic modal language is a triple $\mathcal{M} = \langle \mathcal{F}, \mathcal{V}, \mu \rangle$, such that $\mathcal{F}$ is a *frame*, $\mathcal{V} : \Phi \mapsto 2^{\mathcal{W}}$ is a *valuation*, assigning each proposition $\phi \in \Phi$ a subset of $\mathcal{W}$, viz., the set of worlds in which $\phi$ holds, and $\mu$ is a mapping, returning the confidence interval for a given modality from $\triangle$. Note that we only require a definition for $\mu$ in $\mathcal{M}$ (the model, but *not* in the frame), as $\mathcal{F}$ represents the relational structure without interpreting the edge labelling $R_\delta$ of the graph.

The *satisfaction relation* $\models$, given a model $\mathcal{M}$ and a specific world $w$ is inductively defined over the set of well-formed formulae in *negation normal form* (remember $\pi ::= p(c) \mid \neg p(c)$):

1. $\mathcal{M}, w \models p(c)$ **iff** $w \in \mathcal{V}(p(c))$ **and** $w \notin \mathcal{V}(\neg p(c))$
2. $\mathcal{M}, w \models \neg p(c)$ **iff** $w \in \mathcal{V}(\neg p(c))$ **and** $w \notin \mathcal{V}(p(c))$
3. $\mathcal{M}, w \models \phi \wedge \phi'$ **iff** $\mathcal{M}, w \models \phi$ **and** $\mathcal{M}, w \models \phi'$
4. $\mathcal{M}, w \models \phi \vee \phi'$ **iff** $\mathcal{M}, w \models \phi$ **or** $\mathcal{M}, w \models \phi'$
5. **for all** $\delta \in \underline{1}$: $\mathcal{M}, w \models \delta\pi$ **iff** $\frac{\#\{u|(w,u)\in R_\delta \text{ and } \mathcal{M},u\models\pi\}}{\#\cup_{\delta'\in\triangle}\{v|(w,v)\in R_{\delta'}\}} \in \mu(\delta)$
6. **for all** $\delta \in \underline{0}$: $\mathcal{M}, w \models \delta\pi$ **iff** $1 - \frac{\#\{u|(w,u)\in R_\delta \text{ and } \mathcal{M},u\models\pi\}}{\#\cup_{\delta'\in\triangle}\{v|(w,v)\in R_{\delta'}\}} \in \mu(\delta)$

The last two cases of the satisfaction relation addresses the modals: for a world $w$, we look for the successor states $u$ that are directly reachable via $R_\delta$ and in which $\pi$ holds, and divide the number of such states ($\# \cdot$) by the number of all worlds that are reachable from $w$ by an arbitrary $R_{\delta'}$ in the denominator. This number, lying between 0 and 1, is then required to be an element of the confidence interval $\mu(\delta)$ of $\delta$, in case $\delta \in \underline{1}$. For the modals whose confidence intervals start at 0, we clearly need to subtract this number from 1.

It is worth noting that the satisfaction relation above differs from the standard definition in its handling of $\mathcal{M}, w \models \neg p(\boldsymbol{c})$, as negation is *not* interpreted through the *absence* of $p(\boldsymbol{c})$ ($\mathcal{M}, w \not\models p(\boldsymbol{c})$), but through the *existence* of $\neg p(\boldsymbol{c})$. This treatment addresses the *open-world* nature in OWL and the evolvement of a (medical) domain over time.

We also note that the definition of the satisfaction relation for modalities (last clause) is related to the *possibility operators* $M_k \cdot$ ($= \Diamond^{\geq k} \cdot;\ k \in \mathbb{N}$) introduced by [5] and *counting modalities* $\cdot \geq n$ [1], used in modal logic characterizations of *description logics* with *cardinality* restrictions.

### 4.3    Two Constraints: Well-Behaved Frames

The definition of the satisfaction relation $\models$ above makes no assumptions about the underlying frame $\mathcal{F}$. For various reasons described below, we will now impose two constraints $(\mathcal{C}_1)$ and $(\mathcal{C}_2)$ on $\mathcal{F}$.

As we will see later, it is handy to assume that the graded modals are arranged in a kind of hierarchy—the more we move along the arrows in the hierarchy, the more a statement $\phi$ in the scope of a modal $\delta \in \triangle$ becomes *uncertain*. In order to address this, we slightly extend the notion of a *frame* by a third component $\preceq \subseteq \triangle \times \triangle$, a partial order (i.e., a reflexive, antisymmetric, and transitive binary relation) between modalities: $\mathcal{F} = \langle \mathcal{W}, \mathcal{R}_\triangle, \preceq \rangle$.

Let us consider the following modal hierarchy that we build from the set $\triangle$ of already introduced modals (cf. Fig. 1):

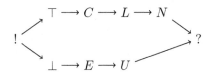

This graphical representation is just a compact way to specify a set of 33 binary relation instances over $\triangle \times \triangle$, such as $\top \preceq \top$, $\top \preceq N$, $C \preceq N$, $\bot \preceq ?$, or $! \preceq ?$. The above mentioned form of uncertainty is expressed by the measure function $\mu$ in that the associated confidence intervals become larger:

$$\text{if } \delta \preceq \delta' \text{ then } \mu(\delta) \subseteq \mu(\delta')$$

In order to arrive at a proper and intuitive model-theoretic semantics which mirrors intuitions such as **if** $\phi$ *is confirmed* ($C\phi$) **then** $\phi$ *is likely* ($L\phi$), we will focus here on *well-behaved* frames $\mathcal{F}$ which enforce the existence of edges in $\mathcal{W}$, given $\preceq$ and $\delta, \delta^\uparrow \in \triangle$:

$$(\mathcal{C}_1) \textbf{ if } (w, u) \in R_\delta \textbf{ and } \delta \preceq \delta^\uparrow$$
$$\textbf{then } (w, u) \in R_{\delta^\uparrow}$$

However, by imposing this constraint, we also need to adapt the last two cases of the satisfiability relation from Sect. 4.2:

5. **for all** $\delta \in \underline{1}$: $\mathcal{M}, w \models \delta\pi$ **iff** $\dfrac{\# \cup_{\delta^\uparrow \succeq \delta} \{u | (w,u) \in R_{\delta^\uparrow} \textbf{ and } \mathcal{M}, u \models \pi\}}{\# \cup_{\delta' \in \triangle} \{v | (w,v) \in R_{\delta'}\}} \in \mu(\delta)$

6. **for all** $\delta \in \underline{0}$: $\mathcal{M}, w \models \delta\pi$ **iff** $1 - \dfrac{\# \cup_{\delta^\uparrow \succeq \delta} \{u | (w,u) \in R_{\delta^\uparrow} \textbf{ and } \mathcal{M}, u \models \pi\}}{\# \cup_{\delta' \in \triangle} \{v | (w,v) \in R_{\delta'}\}} \in \mu(\delta)$

Not only are we scanning for edges $(w, u)$ labeled with $R_\delta$ and for successor states $u$ of $w$ in which $\pi$ holds in the numerator (original definition), but also take into account edges $R_{\delta^\uparrow}$ marked with more general modals $\delta^\uparrow$, given $\delta^\uparrow \succeq \delta$. This mechanism implements a kind of *built-in model completion* that is not necessary in ordinary modal logics as they deal with only a *single* relation (viz., unlabelled arcs).

We have also seen that negated propositions inside the scope of a modal can be formulated equivalently by using the mirror modal: $\delta\neg\phi \equiv \delta^M \phi$. Since $\mathcal{F}$ is only constrained by $(\mathcal{C}_1)$ so far, we impose a further restriction to guarantee that the satisfaction relation works properly for the interplay between negation and mirror modals as otherwise the fraction in case (5) will yield wrong numbers. In order to capture both the left-to-right and the right-to-left direction of the equivalence, we use $\pi$ here for abbreviating the propositional letters $\pi ::= p(\boldsymbol{c}) \mid \neg p(\boldsymbol{c})$ (see Sect. 4.1):

$$(\mathcal{C}_2) \textbf{ if } (w, u) \in R_\delta \textbf{ s.t. } u \in \mathcal{V}(\neg\pi)$$
$$\textbf{then } \exists u' \in \mathcal{W} \textbf{ s.t. } (w, u') \in R_{\delta^M} \textbf{ and } u' \in \mathcal{V}(\pi)$$

## 5   Entailment Rules

We now turn our attention, again, to the syntax of our language and to the syntactic consequence relation. This section addresses a restricted subset of entailment rules which will unveil new (or implicit) knowledge from already existing graded statements. Recall that these kind of statements (in negation normal form) are a consequence of the application of simplification rules as depicted in Sect. 4.1. Thus, we assume a *pre-processing step* here that "massages" more complex statements that arise from a representation of graded (medical) statements in *natural language*. The entailments which we will present in a moment can either be *directly* implemented in a *tuple*-based reasoner, such as *HFC* [11], or in *triple*-based engines (e.g., Jena [4] or *OWLIM* [2]) which need to *reify* the medical statements in order to be compliant with the RDF triple model.

## 5.1    Modal Entailments

The entailments presented in this section deal with *plausible* inference centered around modals $\delta, \delta' \in \triangle$ which are, in part, also addressed in [16] in a pure OWL setting. We use the implication sign $\rightarrow$ to depict the entailment rules *lhs* $\rightarrow$ *rhs* which act as *completion* (or *materialization*) rules the way as described in, e.g., [7] and [18], and used in today's *semantic repositories* (e.g., *OWLIM*). We sometimes even use the biconditional $\leftrightarrow$ to address that the LHS and the RHS are semantically equivalent, but will indicate the direction that should be used in a practical setting. As before, we define $\pi ::= p(c) \mid \neg p(c)$. We furthermore assume that for every modal $\delta \in \triangle$, a *complement* modal $\delta^C$ and a *mirror* modal $\delta^M$ exist (cf. Sect. 4.1).

**Lift    (L)** $\pi \leftrightarrow \top\pi$. This rule interprets propositional statements as special modal formulae. It might be dropped and can be seen as a pre-processing step. We have used it in the Hepatitis example above. Usage: left-to-right direction.

**Generalize (G)** $\delta\pi \wedge \delta \preceq \delta' \rightarrow \delta'\pi$. This rule schema can be instantiated in various ways, using the modal hierarchy from Sect. 4.3, e.g., $\top\pi \rightarrow C\pi$, $C\pi \rightarrow L\pi$, or $E\pi \rightarrow U\pi$. It has been used in the Hepatitis example.

**Complement (C)** $\neg\delta\pi \leftrightarrow \delta^C\pi$. In principle, (C) is not needed in case the statement is already in negation normal form. This schema might be useful for natural language paraphrasing (explanation). Given $\triangle$, there are four possible instantiations: $E\pi \leftrightarrow \neg N\pi$, $N\pi \leftrightarrow \neg E\pi$, $?\pi \leftrightarrow \neg!\pi$, and $!\pi \leftrightarrow \neg?\pi$.

**Mirror (M)** $\delta\neg\pi \leftrightarrow \delta^M\pi$. Again, (M) is in principle not needed as long as the modal proposition is in negation normal form, since we do allow for negated propositional statements $\neg p(c)$. This schema might be useful for natural language paraphrasing (explanation). For $\triangle$, there are six possible instantiations: $E\pi \leftrightarrow C\neg\pi$, $C\pi \leftrightarrow E\neg\pi$, $L\pi \leftrightarrow U\neg\pi$, $U\pi \leftrightarrow L\neg\pi$, $\top\pi \leftrightarrow \bot\neg\pi$, and $\bot\pi \leftrightarrow \top\neg\pi$.

**Uncertainty (U)** $\delta\pi \wedge \neg\delta\pi \leftrightarrow \delta\pi \wedge \delta^C\pi \leftrightarrow ?\pi$. The *co-occurrence* of $\delta\pi$ and $\neg\delta\pi$ does *not* imply logical *inconsistency* (propositional case: $\pi \wedge \neg\pi$), but leads to complete *uncertainty* about the validity of $\pi$. Usage: left-to-right direction. Remember that $\mu(?) = \mu(\delta) \uplus \mu(\delta^C) = [0, 1]$:

$$0 \hspace{5cm} 1$$
$$\mu : |\!-\!\delta^C\!-\!|\!-\!-\!\delta\!-\!-\!|$$
$$\pi \hspace{2cm} \pi$$

**Negation (N)** $\delta(\pi \wedge \neg\pi) \leftrightarrow \delta^M(\pi \wedge \neg\pi)$. (N) can be easily shown by applying the simplification rules from Sect. 4.1. $\delta(\pi \wedge \neg\pi)$ can be formulated equivalently by using the mirror modal $\delta^M$:

$$0 \hspace{5cm} 1$$
$$\mu : |\!-\!\delta^M\!-\!|\!-\!-\!-\!|\!-\!\delta\!-\!|$$
$$\pi \wedge \neg\pi \hspace{2cm} \pi \wedge \neg\pi$$

In general, (N) is *not* the modal counterpart of the *law of non-contradiction*, as $\pi \wedge \neg\pi$ is usually afflicted by uncertainty, meaning that from $\delta(\pi \wedge \neg\pi)$, we can *not* infer that $\pi \wedge \neg\pi$ is the case for the concrete example in question (recall the intention behind the confidence intervals; cf. Sect. 3). There is one notable exception, involving the $\top$ and $\bot$ modals. This is formulated by the next entailment rule.

**Error (E)** $\top(\pi \wedge \neg\pi) \leftrightarrow \bot(\pi \wedge \neg\pi) \rightarrow !(\pi \wedge \neg\pi) \leftrightarrow !\pi$. (E) *is* the modal counterpart of the *law of non-contradiction* (note: $\bot^{\mathsf{M}} = \top, \top^{\mathsf{M}} = \bot, !^{\mathsf{M}} = !$). For this reason and *by definition*, the *error* (or *failure*) modal ! from Sect. 3 comes into play here. The modal ! can serve as a hint to either stop a computation the first time it occurs, or to continue reasoning and to syntactically memorize the ground literal $\pi$. Usage: left-to-right direction.

## 5.2 Subsumption Entailments

As before, we define two subsets of $\triangle$, called $\underline{1} = \{\top, C, L, N\}$ and $\underline{0} = \{\bot, E, U\}$, thus effectively become $\underline{1} = \{\top, C, L, N, U^{\mathsf{C}}\}$ and $\underline{0} = \{\bot, U, E, C^{\mathsf{C}}, L^{\mathsf{C}}, N^{\mathsf{M}}\}$ due to the use of complement modals $\delta^{\mathsf{C}}$ and mirror modals $\delta^{\mathsf{M}}$ for every base modal $\delta \in \triangle$ and by assuming that $E = N^{\mathsf{C}}$, $E = C^{\mathsf{M}}$, $U = L^{\mathsf{M}}$, and $\bot = \top^{\mathsf{M}}$, together with the four "opposite" cases.

Now, let $\sqsubseteq$ abbreviate relation subsumption as known from description logics and realized through `subClassOf` and `subPropertyOf` in RDFS. Given this, we define two further very practical and plausible modal entailments which can be seen as the modal extension of the entailment rules (rdfs9) and (rdfs7) for classes and properties in RDFS [7]:

$$(\mathsf{S1})\ \underline{1}p(c) \wedge p \sqsubseteq q \rightarrow \underline{1}q(c) \qquad (\mathsf{S0})\ \underline{0}q(c) \wedge p \sqsubseteq q \rightarrow \underline{0}p(c)$$

Note how the use of $p$ and $q$ switches in the antecedent and the consequent, even though $p \sqsubseteq q$ holds in both cases. Note further that propositional statements $\pi$ are restricted to the positive case $p(c)$ and $q(c)$, as their negation in the antecedent will not lead to any valid entailments.

Here are two *instantiations* of (S0) and (S1) for the unary and binary case (remember, $E \in \underline{0}$ and $C \in \underline{1}$):

    ViralHepatitis $\sqsubseteq$ Hepatitis $\wedge$ $E$Hepatitis$(x) \rightarrow E$ViralHepatitis$(x)$
    deeplyEnclosedIn $\sqsubseteq$ containedIn $\wedge$ $C$deeplyEnclosedIn$(x, y) \rightarrow C$containedIn
$(x, y)$

## 5.3 Extended RDFS and OWL Entailments

In this section, we will consider further entailment rules for RDFS [7] and a restricted subset of OWL [15,18]. Remember that modals only head positive and negative propositional letters $\pi$, not TBox or RBox axioms. Concerning the original entailment rules, we will distinguish *four principal cases* to which the extended rules belong (we will only consider the unary and binary case here as used in description logics/OWL):

1. TBox and RBox axiom schemas will not undergo a modal extension;
2. rules get extended in the antecedent;
3. rules take over modals from the antecedent to the consequent;

4. rules aggregate several modals from the antecedent in the consequent.

We will illustrate the individual cases in the following with examples by using a kind of description logic rule syntax. Clearly, the set of extended entailments depicted here is *not complete*.

**Case-1: No Modals.** Entailment rule (rdfs11) from [7] deals with class subsumption: $C \sqsubseteq D \land D \sqsubseteq E \rightarrow C \sqsubseteq E$. As this is a terminological axiom schema, the rule stays *constant* in the modal domain. Example rule instantiation:

$\quad$ ViralHepatitisB $\sqsubseteq$ ViralHepatitis $\land$ ViralHepatitis $\sqsubseteq$ Hepatitis
$\quad \rightarrow$ ViralHepatitisB $\sqsubseteq$ Hepatitis

**Case-2: Modals on LHS, No Modals on RHS.** The following original rule (rdfs3) from [7] imposes a range restriction on objects of binary ABox relation instances: $\forall P.C \land P(x, y) \rightarrow C(y)$. The extended version needs to address the ABox proposition in the antecedent (*don't care* modal $\delta$), but must not change the consequent (even though we always use the $\top$ modality here—the range restriction $C(y)$ is always true, independent of the uncertainty of $P(x, y)$; cf. Sect. 2 example):

$$(\mathsf{Mrdfs3}) \quad \forall P.C \land \delta P(x, y) \rightarrow \top C(y)$$

Example rule instantiation:

$\quad \forall$ suffersFrom.Disease $\land$ $L$ suffersFrom$(x, y) \rightarrow \top$ Disease$(y)$

**Case-3: Keeping LHS Modals on RHS.** Inverse properties switch their arguments [18] as described by (rdfp8): $P \equiv Q^- \land P(x, y) \rightarrow Q(y, x)$. The extended version simply keeps the modal operator:

$$(\mathsf{Mrdfp8}) \quad P \equiv Q^- \land \delta P(x, y) \rightarrow \delta Q(y, x)$$

Example rule instantiation:
$\quad$ containedIn $\equiv$ contains$^-$ $\land$ $C$ containedIn$(x, y) \rightarrow C$ contains$(y, x)$

**Case-4: Aggregating LHS Modals on RHS.** Now comes the most interesting case of modalized RDFS & OWL entailment rules, that offers several possibilities on a varying scale between *skeptical* and *credulous* entailments, depending on the degree of uncertainty, as expressed by the measuring function $\mu$ of the modal operator. Consider the original rule (rdfp4) from [18] for transitive properties: $P^+ \sqsubseteq P \land P(x, y) \land P(y, z) \rightarrow P(x, z)$.

Now, how does the modal on the RHS of the extended rule look like, depending on the two LHS modals? There are several possibilities. By operating directly on the *modal hierarchy*, we are allowed to talk about, e.g., the *least upper bound* or the *greatest lower bound* of $\delta_1$ and $\delta_2$. When taking the associated *confidence intervals* into account, we might play with the low and high numbers of the intervals, say, by applying min/max, the *arithmetic mean* or even by *multiplying* the corresponding numbers. Let us first consider the general rule from which more specialized versions can be derived, simply by instantiating the combination operator $\odot$:

$$\text{(Mrdfp4)}\quad P^+ \sqsubseteq P \land \delta_1 P(x, y) \land \delta_2 P(y, z) \rightarrow (\delta_1 \odot \delta_2) P(x, z)$$

Here is an instantiation of (Mrdfp4) as used in *HFC*, dealing with the transitive relation contains from above, assuming that $\odot$ reduces to the *least upper bound* (i.e., $C \odot L = L$):

$$C\text{contains}(x, y) \land L\text{contains}(y, z) \rightarrow L\text{contains}(x, z)$$

What is the general result of $\delta_1 \odot \delta_2$? It depends, probably both on the application domain and the *epistemic commitment* one is willing to accept about the "meaning" of gradation words/modal operators. To enforce that $\odot$ is at least both *commutative* and *associative* (as is the least upper bound) is probably a good idea, making the sequence of modal clauses *order independent*. And to work on the modal hierarchy instead of combining low/high numbers of the corresponding intervals is probably a good decision for forward chaining engines, as the latter strategy might introduce *new* individuals through operations such as multiplication, thus posing a problem for the implementation of the generalization schema (G) (see Sect. 5.1).

# 6  Adding Time

*Temporal databases* [17] distinguish between (at least) two different notions of time and the representation of temporal change: *valid time*, the temporal interval in which a statement about the world is valid, and *transaction time*, the temporal duration during which a statement has been stored in a database (or ontology, in our case). Valid time is able to add information about the past, present, and future, given a moment in time, whereas transaction time add present time ($= now$) when a statement is entered to the database. At the end of this section, we will have established a transaction time extension for the modal fragment of OWL derived so far, including a set of entailment rules and a corresponding extended model theory.

## 6.1  Metric Linear Time

In the following, we assume that the temporal measuring system is based on a one-dimensional *metric linear time* $\langle \mathcal{T}, \leq \rangle$, so that we can compare starting/ending points, using operators, such as $\leq$, or pick out input arguments in aggregates, using *min* or *max*. We require, for reasons which will become clear, that time is *discrete* and represented by natural or rational numbers.

The implementation of *HFC* employs 8-byte long integers (XSD datatype long) to encode *milli* or even *nano* seconds w.r.t. a fixed starting point (Unix Epoch time, starting with 1 January 1970, 00:00:00). Alternatively, the XSD `dateTime` format can be used which provides an arbitrarily fine precision, if needed.

As a consequence, given a time point $t \in \mathcal{T}$, the next smallest or successor time point would then be $t + 1$ (after a potential normalization). We often use this kind of notation to derive the ending time of a valid proposition $\top \phi @ t$ from the time it gets invalidated: $\bot \phi @ t{+}1$; see Sect. 6.3.

## 6.2   Valid Time

Valid time is a useful concept when representing, e.g., biographical knowledge which has been obtained from the Web. Various forms of OWL representations involving time have been investigated [6,13,19]. However, reasoning and querying with such representations is extremely complex, expensive, and error-prone and standard OWL reasoning is no longer applicable. In [10], we have investigated *valid time* for a non-graded extension of RDFS and OWL (triples, binary relation instances), representing the time period of an atemporal statement by two further argument, giving us quintuples instead of triples in the end. This extension is a pure syntactic calculus, defined as a set of tableaux-like entailment rules à la [7,18], able to derive useful new information in a temporal environment. For instance, the standard entailment rule (rdfp4) in OWL for *transitive properties* (see Sect. 5.3)

$$\mathsf{P}^+ \sqsubseteq \mathsf{P} \wedge \mathsf{P}(\mathsf{x},\mathsf{y}) \wedge \mathsf{P}(\mathsf{y},\mathsf{z}) \to \mathsf{P}(\mathsf{x},\mathsf{z})$$

then becomes

$$\mathsf{P}^+ \sqsubseteq \mathsf{P} \wedge \mathsf{P}(\mathsf{x},\mathsf{y},b_1,e_1) \wedge \mathsf{P}(\mathsf{y},\mathsf{z},b_2,e_2) \wedge [b_1,e_1] \cap [b_2,e_2] \neq \emptyset \to \mathsf{P}(\mathsf{x},\mathsf{z},b,e)$$

where $[b_1,e_1]$ and $[b_2,e_2]$ are the temporal intervals during which $\mathsf{P}(\mathsf{x,y})$ and $\mathsf{P}(\mathsf{y,z})$ are valid, given $b = max(b_1,b_2)$ and $e = min(e_1,e_2)$. I.e., $\mathsf{P}(\mathsf{x,z})$ is only valid during the proper intersection of $[b_1,e_1]$ and $[b_2,e_2]$. This is depicted in the following figure:

Note that $\mathsf{P}(\mathsf{x,z})$ is definitely the case for $[b,e]$, but we do not know if it holds before $b$ or after $e$. This inference harmonizes well with the open-world assumption underlying OWL.

In *HFC*, the meaning of the *original* entailment rule (left) and the *extension* for valid time (right) can be straightforwardly derived from the abstract syntax above:

```
?p rdf:type owl:TransitiveProperty    ?p rdf:type owl:TransitiveProperty
?x ?p ?y                              ?x ?p ?y ?b1 ?e1
?y ?p ?z                              ?y ?p ?z ?b2 ?e2
->                                    ->
?x ?p ?z                              ?x ?p ?z ?b ?e
                                      @test
                                      IntersectionNotEmpty ?b1 ?e1 ?b2 ?e2
                                      @action
                                      ?b = Max ?b1 ?b2
                                      ?e = Min ?e1 ?e2
```

In *HFC*, `IntersectionNotEmpty` refers to the (Java) implementation of a specific method of the corresponding class which realizes the above intersection of the corresponding temporal intervals (pseudo code):

IntersectionNotEmpty start1 end1 start2 end2 $\equiv$
    start := $max$(start1, start2)
    end := $min$(end1, end2)
    **return** (start $\leq$ end)

This computationally cheap left-hand side test (cf. the `@test` section in the above *HFC* rule) is applied after LHS matching and before right-hand side instantiation. The RHS generation of the resulting interval $[b, e]$ is achieved by the two aggregates `Max` and `Min` whose return values are bound to the RHS-only rule variables ?b and ?e, resp. (cf. the `@action` section above). It is worth noting that these two aggregates do *not* generate brand-new individuals (contrary to addition, for example), thus a terminating rule set and so a finite model is guaranteed overall.

The interesting observation when adding *valid time* to the RDFS & ter Horst subset of OWL is that only an additional test (cf. `IntersectionNotEmpty`) and two aggregates (cf. `Max`, `Min`) are needed [10]. Almost the same is true when adding *transaction time* to the modal extension of RDFS & OWL that we have investigated so far in the first part of this article. The additional test in *HFC* is called `ValidInBetween` and the aggregates are `Min` and `Max`, as before.

## 6.3   Transaction Time

Like valid time, the original approach to transaction time makes use of temporal intervals in order to represent the time during which a fact is stored in the database, even though the ending time is not known in advance. This is indicated by the wildcard **?** which will later be *overwritten* by the concrete ending time.

We *deviate* here from the interval view by specifying both the starting time when an ABox statement is entered to an ontology, and, via a *separate* statement, the ending time when the statement is *invalidated*.[4] For this, we exploit the propositional modals $\top$ and $\bot$ from before. This idea is shown in the following figure for a binary relation P. We write P(c,d,b,e) to denote the row $< c, d, b, e >$ in the database table P for relation P.

| TIME | DATABASE VIEW | ONTOLOGY VIEW |
|---|---|---|
| $\vdots$ | $\vdots$ | $\vdots$ |
| $t_1$ | add: P(c,d,$t_1$,?) | add: $\top$P(c,d)@$t_1$ |
| $\vdots$ | $\vdots$ | $\vdots$ |
| $t_2$ | **overwrite**: P(c,d,$t_1$,$t_2$) | —— |
| $t_2 + 1$ | —— | **add**: $\bot$P(c,d)@$t_2$+1 |
| $\vdots$ | $\vdots$ | $\vdots$ |

As we see from this picture, the invalidation in the ontology happens at $t_2+1$, whereas $[t_1, t_2]$ specifies the transaction time in the database. Clearly, the same transaction time interval for P(c,d) in the ontology can be derived from the two statements $\top$P(c, d)@$t_1$ and $\bot$P(c, d)@$t_2 + 1$, assuming that there does *not* exist a $\bot$P(c, d)@$t$, such that $t_1 \leq t \leq t_2$ (we can effectively query for this by employing the `ValidInBetween` test).

Extending ontologies by transaction time the way we proceed here gives us a means to easily encode *time series data*, i.e., allows us to record the *history* of data that changes over time, and so simulating imperative *variables* in a declarative environment.

### 6.4   Entailment Rules for Graded Modals and Transaction Time

We have almost introduced the *abstract* syntax for graded propositions with transaction time ($\delta \in \triangle$)

$$\delta\phi@t$$

Here, we focus on the binary relation case in order to address the RDFS [7] and ter Horst extension of OWL [18] from above. For this, we will then write

$$\delta P(c, d)@t$$

The corresponding *quintuple* representation in *HFC* then becomes

$$\delta \ \ c \ \ P \ \ d \ \ t$$

We opt for a *uniform* representation, thus *axiomatic triples* need to be extended by two further arguments; for instance,

```
owl:sameAs rdf:type owl:TransitiveProperty
```

---

[4] When *we* say *transaction time* we usually mean the time a statement is *added* to the *ontology*, say $t_1$ or $t_2+1$ in the figure.

becomes

```
logic:true owl:sameAs rdf:type owl:TransitiveProperty"0"^^xsd:long
```

We read the above statement as *being true* ($\top = $ `logic:true`) *from the begin-ning of time* (long int 0 = `"0"^^xsd:long`). We are now ready to distinguish, again, between the *four principled cases* from Sect. 5.3, where we compared the original rules from [7,18] to the graded modal extension, but now extend them further by a transaction time argument.

**Case-1: Top Modals Only, Zero Time.** We have already seen that the entailment rule (rdfs11) from [7] deals with class subsumption: $C \sqsubseteq D \land D \sqsubseteq E \to C \sqsubseteq E$. As this rule concerns only terminological knowledge (TBox), we decided not to change it in the modal domain. Since we argued above for a uniform quaternary relation or quintuple representation, this rule leads us quite naturally to the extended version of (rdfs11):

$$\text{(TMrdfs11)} \quad \top C \sqsubseteq D@0 \land \top D \sqsubseteq E@0 \to \top C \sqsubseteq E@0$$

This notation simply highlights that the original class subsumption entail-ment *is true at every time*, i.e., expresses an universal truth (remember the meaning of $\top$ and transaction time 0, and compare this to the axiomatic triple from above).

**Case-2: Modals on LHS, Top Modals on RHS, Keeping Time.** The orig-inal rule (rdfs3) from [7] imposes a range restriction on P: $\forall P.C \land P(x,y) \to C(y)$. Adding modals gave us (Mrdfs3): $\forall P.C \land \delta P(x,y) \to \top C(y)$. Extending this rule with transaction time is easy:

$$\text{(TMrdfs3)} \quad \top \forall P.C@0 \land \delta P(x,y)@t \to \top C(y)@t$$

The range restriction is a universal RBox statement (thus $\top$ and 0). P(x,y) is graded ($\delta$) and happens at a specific time $t$. Thus, the class prediction C(y) of the range argument y at time $t$ is true ($\top$).

**Case-3: Keeping LHS Modals on RHS, Keeping Time.** Inverse proper-ties are described in [18] by (rdfp8): $P \equiv Q^- \land P(x,y) \to Q(y,x)$. The modalized version simply kept the modal operator (Mrdfp8): $P \equiv Q^- \land \delta P(x,y) \to \delta Q(y,x)$. The transaction time version furthermore takes over the temporal argument:

$$\text{(TMrdfp8)} \quad \top P \equiv Q^-@0 \land \delta P(x,y)@t \to \delta Q(y,x)@t$$

Again, $P \equiv Q^-$ is a universal RBox statement (use $\top$ and 0) and both the grading of P(x,y) and time $t$ is consequently transferred to Q(y,x).

**Case-4: Aggregating Modals, Aggregating Time.** This case is the most challenging and computationally expensive one. The concrete implementation in *HFC* employs the above-mentioned test `ValidInBetween` (two times use in lines 2 and 3 below in a different form) and the aggregates `Min` and `Max`. Again, we will focus on one specific rule here, viz., (rdfp4) from [18] for transitive properties: $P^+ \sqsubseteq P \wedge P(x,y) \wedge P(y,z) \rightarrow P(x,z)$. The modal extension led us to (Mrdfp4): $P^+ \sqsubseteq P \wedge \delta_1 P(x,y) \wedge \delta_2 P(y,z) \rightarrow (\delta_1 \odot \delta_2) P(x,z)$. This blueprint can be utilized to derive the final transaction time version:

$$\text{(TMrdfp4)} \quad \top P^+ \sqsubseteq P@0 \wedge \delta_1 P(x,y)@t_1 \wedge \delta_2 P(y,z)@t_2 \wedge$$

$$\texttt{ValidInBetween: } \nexists \delta_1^M P(x,y)@t \text{ s.t. } min(t_1,t_2) \leq t \leq max(t_1,t_2) \wedge$$

$$\texttt{ValidInBetween: } \nexists \delta_1^M P(y,z)@t' \text{ s.t. } min(t_1,t_2) \leq t' \leq max(t_1,t_2) \wedge$$

$$\rightarrow (\delta_1 \odot \delta_2) P(x,z)@max(t_1,t_2)$$

Lines 1 and 4 of (TMrdfp4) are easy to grasp when compared to the plain modal extension (Mrdfp4) and the fact that the transaction time for the consequent $(\delta_1 \odot \delta_2)P(x,z)$ is based on the time when *both* $\delta_1 P(x,y)$ and $\delta_2 P(y,z)$ are the case, i.e., $max(t_1,t_2)$:

Furthermore, lines 2 and 3 guarantee that graded *contradictory* information with an equal or *less* degree of uncertainty $||\delta_{1,2}^M||$ (i.e., equal or *more* trustworthiness) does *not* exist as it would argue too strongly against the graded entailment of $P(x,z)$. Here, it is important to understand the interplay between (TMrdfp4) and the extension of the binary generalization schema (G) from Sect. 5.1:

$$\text{(TG)} \quad \delta P(x,y)@t \wedge \top\delta \preceq \delta'@0 \rightarrow \delta'P(x,y)@t$$

Consider, for example, that $\delta_1 P(x,y)@t_1$ matches $CP(x,y)@30$ and $\delta_2 P(y,z)@t_2$ matches $LP(y,z)@42$ in (TMrdfp4). Given statement $EP(x,y)@40$ ($30 \leq 40 \leq 42$), we are thus *not* allowed to derive the instantiation of the antecedent of (TMrdfp4). The more *certain* statement $\perp P(x,y)@40$ does also *not* support the rule as (TG) would allow us to derive $EP(x,y)@40$ again. Only a *more uncertain* modal than $E$ will do the trick, e.g., $U$ (recall that $||\perp|| < ||E|| < ||U||$). Thus, $UP(x,y)@40$ is a necessary requirement for finally deriving $(C \odot L)P(x,z)@42$.

## 6.5 Model Theory for Graded Modals and Transaction Time

The model theory for graded modals including transaction time will not differ much from what we already introduced in Sects. 4.2 and 4.3. Time points $t \in \mathcal{T}$, indicated by the notation @$t$ relative to a proposition $\mathsf{P}(\mathsf{x},\mathsf{y})$, are related to what *hybrid logics* [3] call *nominals—handles to worlds* which are indexed by $t$ and which are made available in the syntax of the modal language via @$t$. In our setting and contrary to hybrid logics, $t$ does *not* refer to a single world, but to multiple ones.

For transaction time, we still keep the notion of a frame $\mathcal{F} = \langle \mathcal{W}, \mathcal{R}_{\triangle}, \preceq \rangle$ and, in principle, that of a model $\mathcal{M} = \langle \mathcal{F}, \mathcal{V}, \mu \rangle$ (see Sect. 4.2). However, we will *modify* the valuation function $\mathcal{V} : \Phi \mapsto 2^{\mathcal{W}}$ in that its domain now also takes time points from $\mathcal{T}$ into account; i.e., $\mathcal{V} : \Phi \times \mathcal{T} \mapsto 2^{\mathcal{W}}$ returns those worlds at which $\phi$@$t$ is valid, given $\phi \in \Phi$ and $t \in \mathcal{T}$. This directly leads us to the extension of the six cases for the satisfaction relation $\models$ from Sects. 4.2 and 4.3:

1. $\mathcal{M}, w \models p(c)$@$t$ **iff** $w \in \mathcal{V}(p(c), t)$ **and** $w \notin \mathcal{V}(\neg p(c), t)$
2. $\mathcal{M}, w \models \neg p(c)$@$t$ **iff** $w \in \mathcal{V}(\neg p(c), t)$ **and** $w \notin \mathcal{V}(p(c), t)$
3. $\mathcal{M}, w \models \phi$@$t \wedge \phi'$@$t'$ **iff** $\mathcal{M}, w \models \phi$@$t$ **and** $\mathcal{M}, w \models \phi'$@$t'$
4. $\mathcal{M}, w \models \phi$@$t \vee \phi'$@$t'$ **iff** $\mathcal{M}, w \models \phi$@$t$ **or** $\mathcal{M}, w \models \phi'$@$t'$
5. **for all** $\delta \in \underline{1}$: $\mathcal{M}, w \models \delta \pi$@$t$ **iff** $\dfrac{\# \cup_{\delta \uparrow \succ \delta} \{u | (w,u) \in R_{\delta \uparrow} \text{ and } \mathcal{M}, u \models \pi@t\}}{\# \cup_{\delta' \in \triangle} \{v | (w,v) \in R_{\delta'}\}} \in \mu(\delta)$
6. **for all** $\delta \in \underline{0}$: $\mathcal{M}, w \models \delta \pi$@$t$ **iff** $1 - \dfrac{\# \cup_{\delta \uparrow \succ \delta} \{u | (w,u) \in R_{\delta \uparrow} \text{ and } \mathcal{M}, u \models \pi@t\}}{\# \cup_{\delta' \in \triangle} \{v | (w,v) \in R_{\delta'}\}} \in \mu(\delta)$

We also keep constraint $(\mathcal{C}_1)$ for well-behaved frames, but need to modify constraint $(\mathcal{C}_2)$ to incorporate transaction time (cf. Sect. 4.3):

$(\mathcal{C}_2)$ **if** $(w, u) \in R_\delta$ **s.t.** $u \in \mathcal{V}(\neg \phi, t)$
　　　**then** $\exists u' \in \mathcal{W}$ **s.t.** $(w, u') \in R_{\delta^M}$ **and** $u' \in \mathcal{V}(\phi, t)$

Furthermore, we impose a third constraint on the relational structure $\mathcal{F}$ which models the intuition *if $\phi$ is valid at time $t$, so is $\phi$ at $t+1$*, in case nothing *argues heavily against* $\phi$ (compare this to a similar argumentation expressed by lines 2 and 3 in $(\mathsf{TMrdfp4})$ of case 4 in Sect. 6.4):

$(\mathcal{C}_3)$ **if** $(w, u) \in R_\delta$ **s.t.** $u \in \mathcal{V}(\phi, t)$ **and** $\nexists (w, v) \in R_{\delta^M}$ **s.t.** $v \in \mathcal{V}(\phi, t)$
　　　**then** $\exists (w, x) \in R_\delta$ **s.t.** $x \in \mathcal{V}(\phi, t+1)$

Here, however, we do not need to check for proposition $\delta^M \phi$ between $t$ and $t+1$, as time is discrete and normalized, so that $t+1$ is the *immediate* successor of $t$.

Constraint $(\mathcal{C}_3)$ can be seen as a kind of *forward monotonicity* in that valid propositions at time $t$ will always hold at time $t + 1$. As a consequence, this will give us an *infinite* frame (cf. the *existential* variable $x$ in the consequent), i.e., an infinite number of worlds. To implement such a kind of model behaviour in the syntax through a *finite* number of propositions, we make the following assumption. Propositions will *never* be brought to the *temporal forefront* (never being updated), i.e., there is *no* rule such as $\delta \phi$@$t \rightarrow \delta \phi$@$(t+1)$. Only if $\delta \phi$ needs to be *invalidated* at $t'$, we will add the further statement $\perp \phi$@$t'$. Thus, through the use of the test `ValidInBetween` from above, we are then able to query whether $\delta \phi$ is still valid at a different time $t'' > t$.

# 7   Summary

In this paper, we have explored a fragment of a non-standard modal logic, being able to represent graded statements about the world. The modal operators in the syntax of the modal language were derived from gradation words and were further extended through mirror and complement operations. The operators were interpreted through confidence intervals in the model theory for expressing the uncertainty about the validity of a proposition. The model theory was complemented by a set of RDFS-/OWL-like entailment rules, acting on the syntactic representation of modalized statements. Finally, we extended the framework by transaction time in order to implement a notion of temporal change. The framework has been implemented in *HFC* for the case of binary propositions.

**Acknowledgements.** The research described in this paper has been co-funded by the Horizon 2020 Framework Programme of the European Union within the project **PAL** (Personal Assistant for healthy Lifestyle) under Grant agreement no. 643783 *and* by the German Federal Ministry of Education and Research (BMBF) through the project **HySociaTea** (Hybrid Social Teams for Long-Term Collaboration in Cyber-Physical Environments, grant no. 01IW14001). My colleagues Miroslav Janíček, Bernd Kiefer, and Stefan Schulz have lend me their ears and I have profited from discussions with them. I would also like to thank the ICAART reviewers for their detailed and useful suggestions—thank you all guys!

# References

1. Areces, C., Hoffmann, G., Denis, A.: Modal logics with counting. In: Dawar, A., Queiroz, R. (eds.) WoLLIC 2010. LNCS (LNAI), vol. 6188, pp. 98–109. Springer, Heidelberg (2010). doi:10.1007/978-3-642-13824-9_9
2. Bishop, B., Kiryakov, A., Ognyanoff, D., Peikov, I., Tashev, Z., Velkov, R.: OWLIM: a family of scalable semantic repositories. Semant. Web **2**(1), 33–42 (2011)
3. Blackburn, P., de Rijke, M., Venema, Y.: Modal Logic. Cambridge Tracts in Theoretical Computer Science. Cambridge University Press, Cambridge (2001)
4. Carroll, J.J., Dickinson, I., Dollin, C., Reynolds, D., Seaborne, A., Wilkinson, K.: Jena: implementing the semantic web recommendations. In: Proceedings of the 13th international World Wide Web conference (WWW), pp. 74–83 (2004)
5. Fine, K.: In so many possible worlds. Notre Dame J. Formal Log. **13**(4), 516–520 (1972)
6. Gangemi, A., Presutti, V.: A multi-dimensional comparison of ontology design patterns for representing $n$-ary relations. In: 39th International Conference on Current Trends in Theory and Practice of Computer Science, pp. 86–105 (2013)
7. Hayes, P.: RDF semantics. Technical report, W3C (2004)
8. Jøsang, A.: A logic for uncertain probabilities. Int. J. Uncertain. Fuzzyness Knowl. Based Syst. **9**(3), 279–311 (2001)
9. Krengel, U.: Einführung in die Wahrscheinlichkeitstheorie und Statistik. Vieweg, 7th edn. (2003). (in German)
10. Krieger, H.U.: A temporal extension of the Hayes/ter Horst entailment rules and an alternative to W3C's N-ary relations. In: Proceedings of the 7th International Conference on Formal Ontology in Information Systems (FOIS), pp. 323–336 (2012)

11. Krieger, H.U.: An efficient implementation of equivalence relations in OWL via rule and query rewriting. In: Proceedings of the 7th IEEE International Conference on Semantic Computing (ICSC), pp. 260–263 (2013)
12. Krieger, H.U.: Capturing graded knowledge and uncertainty in a modalized fragment of OWL. In: Proceedings of the 8th International Conference on Agents and Artificial Intelligence (ICAART), pp. 19–30 (2016)
13. Krieger, H.U., Declerck, T.: An OWL ontology for biographical knowledge. Representing time-dependent factual knowledge. In: Proceedings of the Workshop on Biographical Data in a Digital World, pp. 101–110 (2015)
14. Krieger, H.U., Schulz, S.: A modal representation of graded medical statements. In: Proceedings of the 20th Conference on Formal Grammar (2015)
15. Motik, B., Cuenca Grau, B., Horrocks, I., Wu, Z., Fokoue, A., Lutz, C.: OWL 2 web ontology language profiles. Technical report, W3C (2012), W3C Recommendation 11 December 2012
16. Schulz, S., Martínez-Costa, C., Karlsson, D., Cornet, R., Brochhausen, M., Rector, A.: An ontological analysis of reference in health record statements. In: Proceedings of the 8th International Conference on Formal Ontology in Information Systems (FOIS 2014), pp. 289–302 (2014)
17. Snodgrass, R.T.: Developing Time-Oriented Database Applications in SQL. Morgan Kaufmann, San Francisco (2000)
18. ter Horst, H.J.: Completeness, decidability and complexity of entailment for RDF schema and a semantic extension involving the OWL vocabulary. J. Web Semant. **3**, 79–115 (2005)
19. Welty, C., Fikes, R.: A reusable ontology for fluents in OWL. In: Proceedings of 4th FOIS, pp. 226–236 (2006)

# An Agent-Based Architecture for Personalized Recommendations

Amel Ben Othmane[1]([✉]), Andrea Tettamanzi[3], Serena Villata[2],
Nhan LE Thanh[3], and Michel Buffa[3]

[1] WIMMICS Research Team, Inria, I3S, UMR 7271 Sophia Antipolis, France
`amel.ben-othmane@inria.fr`
[2] CNRS, I3S, UMR 7271 Sophia Antipolis, France
`villata@i3s.unice.fr`
[3] Univ. Nice Sophia Antipolis, I3S, UMR 7271 Sophia Antipolis, France
`{andrea.tettamanzi,nhan.le-thanh,michel.buffa}@unice.fr`

**Abstract.** This paper proposes a design framework for a personalized multi-agent recommender system. More precisely, the proposed framework is a multi-context based recommender system that takes into account user preferences to generate a plan satisfying those preferences. Agents in this framework have a Belief-Desire-Intention (BDI) component based on the well-known BDI architecture. These BDI agents are empowered with cognitive capabilities in order to interact with others agents. They are also able to adapt to the environment changes and to the information coming from other agents. The architecture includes also a planning module based on ontologies in order to represent and reason about plans and intentions. The applicability of the proposed model is shown through a simulation in the NetLogo environment.

## 1 Introduction and Motivation

Human activities take place in particular locations at specific times. The increasing use of wearable devices enables the collection of information about these activities from an heterogeneous set of actors varying in physical, cultural, and socioeconomic characteristics. Generally, the places you have spent regularly or occasionally time in, reflect your lifestyle, which is strongly associated to your socioeconomic features. This amount of information about people, their relations, and their activities are valuable elements to personalize healthcare being sensitive to medical, social, and personal characteristics of individuals. Besides this, the decision-making process in human beings is based not only on logical objective elements, but also emotional ones that are typically extra-logical. As a result, the behavior can also be explained by other approaches, which additionally consider emotions, intentions, beliefs, motives, cultural and social constraints, impulsive actions, and even the simple willingness to try. Hence, building recommender systems that take user behavior into account requires a step toward personalization.

© Springer International Publishing AG 2017
J. van den Herik and J. Filipe (Eds.): ICAART 2016, LNAI 10162, pp. 96–113, 2017.
DOI: 10.1007/978-3-319-53354-4_6

To the best of our knowledge, there are no recommender systems that combine all these features at the same time. Consider the following motivating example that had driven this research: Bob, a 40 year-old adult, wants to get back to a regular physical activity (*pa*). Bob believes that a regular physical activity reduces the risk of developing a non-insulin dependant diabetes mellitus (*rd*). Mechanisms that are responsible for this are weight reduction (*wr*), increased insulin sensitivity, and improved glucose metabolism. Due to his busy schedule (*bs*), Bob is available on weekends (*av*) only. Hence, he would be happy if he can do his exercises only on weekends (*w*). Bob prefers also not to change his eating habits (*eh*). Besides all the aforementioned preferences, Bob should take into account his medical concerns and refer to a healthcare provider for monitoring. This scenario exposes the following problem: how can we help Bob to select the best plan to achieve his goal based on his current preferences and restrictions? This problem raises different challenges. First, the proposed solution should take into account Bob's preferences and restrictions (e.g., medical and physical concerns) in the recommendation process. Second, information about the environment in which Bob acts and people that might be in relationship with him may have impact in his decision-making process. Third, the system should be able to keep a trace of Bob's activities in order to adapt the recommendation according to his progress. Finally, the information or data about Bob's activities is distributed geographically and temporarily.

In order to address these challenges, multi-agent systems stand as a promising way to understand, manage and use distributed, large-scale, dynamic, and heterogeneous information. The idea is to develop recommender systems able to help users confronted with situations in which they have too many options to choose from, with the aim of assisting them to explore and filter out their preferences from a number of different possibilities. Based on this real-world application scenario, we propose in this paper a multi-agent-based recommender system where agents are described using the BDI model as a multi-context system. The system's goal is to recommend a list of activities according to the user preferences. We propose also an extension of the BDI model to deal with the social dimension and the uncertainty in dynamic environments.

The originality of what we propose with respect to existing works is the combination of an extended possibilistic BDI approach with multi-context systems. The resulting framework is then used as a healthcare recommender system. There are several advantages deriving from such combination. First, the use of a multi-context architecture allows us to have different syntaxes, e.g., the ontology to represent and reason about plans and intentions. Besides this, we believe that extending the classical BDI model with goals and social contexts better reflects human behavior. Moreover, the proposed approach deals with goal-belief consistency, and defines a belief revision process. However, the idea of extending the BDI model with social contexts is not novel: different works explored trust or reputation [1,2]. In our approach, we consider trust measures between two agents only if they are similar.

The reminder of this paper is organized as follows: Sect. 2 includes a literature overview about the related work. In Sect. 3, we summarize the main concepts on which this work is based. We introduce after, in Sect. 4, the multi-context BDI agent framework. In order to show how the model works, we describe in Sect. 5 a real-world scenario in healthcare domain, and we describe its simulation in Sect. 6. Conclusions end the paper.

## 2  Related Work

Research in agent-based recommender systems is increasing in order to address the challenges raised by a growing number of real-world applications. For a taxonomy of recommender agents on the Internet, we refer the reader to [3]. Several works propose to use a cognitive architecture as a base for a recommender system. Next, we will focus on works using the well known BDI architecture.

Casali *et al.* proposed in [4] a Travel Assistant agent that helps a tourist to choose holiday packages. They used a graded BDI agent model based on multi-context systems to deal with information uncertainty and graded notions of beliefs, desires and intentions, and a modal many-valued logic approach for modeling agents. An implementation of the proposed model is later presented in [5,6]. Results concluded that BDI agents are useful to build recommender systems. Nevertheless, as pointed in [7], this approach needs further research to adapt the agent behavior in a dynamic environment.

In [8], the authors propose a framework for personalized recommendations in e-commerce. They use the cognitive architecture as a middle layer between the user, and a set of recommenders instead of using it as a recommender. However, the proposed framework still in a preliminary stage and needs further improvements, e.g., to enable the communication with the user.

Another example of a multi-agent recommender system using a BDI architecture is studied in [9]. The proposed system, SHOpping Multi-Agent System (SHOMAS), aims at helping users to identify a shopping or leisure plan. The architecture of the user agent is based on both Case-Based Reasoning and the Beliefs Desires Intentions architectures (CBR-BDI). The combination of the two architectures allows dynamic re-planning in a dynamic environment.

In [10], an Interest Based Recommender System (IBRS) is proposed for the personalization of recommendations. The IBRS is an agent-based recommender system that takes into account users' preferences to generate personalized recommendations. Agents are based on the BDI architecture empowered with cognitive capabilities and interact with other users using argumentation. A travel case study is used to experiment the model.

Our work takes a different approach compared to the aforementioned approaches. It is based on a full-fledged possibilistic approach and includes a revision process for beliefs and intentions.

## 3  Background

In this section, we summarize the main insights on which the present contribution is based.

An agent in a BDI architecture is defined by its beliefs, desires and intentions. Beliefs encode the agent's understanding of the environment, desires are those states of affairs that an agent would like to accomplish and intentions those desires that the agent has chosen to act upon. Many approaches tried to formalize such mental attitudes (e.g., [11–14]). However, all these works concentrated on the human decision-making process as a single approach without considering social influences. They did not take the gradual nature of beliefs, desires, and intentions into account. Incorporating uncertainty and different degrees of attitudes will help the agent in the decision-making process. In order to represent and reason about uncertainty and graded notions of beliefs, desires, and intentions, we follow the approach proposed in [15], where uncertainty reasoning is dealt with by possibility theory. Possibility theory is an uncertainty theory dedicated to handle incomplete information. It was introduced by [16] as an extension to fuzzy sets which are sets that have degrees of membership in $[0, 1]$. Possibility theory differs from probability theory by the use of dual set functions (possibility and necessity measures) instead of only one. A possibility distribution assigns to each element $\omega$ in a set $\Omega$ of interpretations a degree of possibility $\pi(\omega) \in [0, 1]$ of being the right description of a state of affairs. It represents a flexible restriction on what is the actual state with the following conventions:

- $\pi(\omega) = 0$ means that state $\omega$ is rejected as impossible;
- $\pi(\omega) = 1$ means that state $\omega$ is totally possible (plausible).

While we chose to adopt a possibilistic BDI model to include gradual mental attitudes, unlike [15], we use multi-context systems (MCS) [17] to represent our BDI agents. According to this approach, a BDI model is defined as a group of interconnected units $\{C_i\}, i \in I, \Delta_{br}$, where:

- For each $i \in I$, $C_i = \langle L_i, A_i, \Delta_i \rangle$ is an axiomatic formal system where $L_i, A_i$ and $\Delta_i$ are the language, axioms, and inference rules respectively. They define the logic for context $C_i$ whose basic behavior is constrained by the axioms.
- $\Delta_{br}$ is a set of bridge rules, i.e., rules of inference which relate formulas in different units.

The way we use these components to model BDI agents is to have separate units for belief $B$, desires $D$ and intentions $I$, each with their own logic. The theories in each unit encode the beliefs, desires, and intentions of specific agents and the bridge rules ($\Delta_{br}$) encode the relationships between beliefs, desires and intentions. We also have two functional units $C$ and $P$, which handle communication among agents and allow to choose plans that satisfy users desires. To summarize, using the multi-context approach, a BDI model is defined as follows:

$$Ag = (\{BC, DC, IC, PC, CC\}, \Delta_{br})$$

where $BC$, $DC$, $IC$ represent respectively the Belief Context, the Desire Context and the Intention Context. $PC$ and $CC$ are two functional contexts corresponding to Planning and Communication Contexts.

The use of MCS offers several advantages when modeling agent architectures: it gives a neat modular way of defining agents, which allows from a software perspective to support modular architectures and encapsulation.

## 4    The Multi-context BDI Framework

The BDI agent architecture we are proposing in this paper extends Rao and Georgeffs well-known BDI architecture [12]. We define a BDI agent as a multi-context system being inspired by the work of [17]. Following this approach, our BDI agent model, visualized in Fig. 1, is defined as follows:

$$Ag = (\{BC, DC, GC, SC, PC, IC, CC\}, \Delta_{br})$$

where $GC$ and $SC$ represent the Goal and the Social Contexts, respectively.

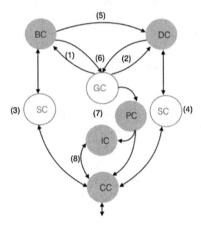

**Fig. 1.** The extended multi-context BDI agent model.

In order to reason about beliefs, desires, goals and social contexts we follow the approach developed by da Costa Pereira and Tettamanzi [15,18] where they adopt a classical propositional language for representation and possibility theory to deal with uncertainty.

Let $\mathcal{A}$ be a finite set of atomic propositions, and $\mathcal{L}$ be the propositional language such that $\mathcal{A} \cup \{\top, \bot\} \subseteq \mathcal{L}$ and $\forall \phi, \psi \in \mathcal{L}, \neg \phi \in \mathcal{L}, \phi \vee \psi \in \mathcal{L}, \phi \wedge \psi \in \mathcal{L}$. These propositions can contain temporal elements that are left as future work. As in [15], $\mathcal{L}$ is extended, and we will denote with $\Omega = \{0,1\}^{\mathcal{A}}$ the set of all interpretations on $\mathcal{A}$. An interpretation $\omega \in \Omega$ is a function $\omega : \mathcal{A} \rightarrow \{0,1\}$ assigning a truth value $p^{\omega}$ to every atomic proposition $p \in \mathcal{A}$ and, by extension, a truth value $\phi^{\omega}$ to all formula $\phi \in \mathcal{L}$. $[\phi]$ denotes the set of all interpretations satisfying $\phi$. (i.e., $[\phi] = \{\omega \in \Omega : \omega \models \phi\}$).

In the planning and intentions contexts, we propose an ontological representation for plans and intentions to provide the agents with a computer-interpretable description of the services they offer, and the information they have access to (workout plans in our case). In the following subsections, we will outline the different theories defined for each context in order to complete the specification of our multi-context agent model.

## 4.1   Belief Context

**The BC Language and Semantics.** In order to represent beliefs, we use the classical propositional language with additional connectives, following [15]. We introduce also a fuzzy operator $B$ over this logic to represent agents beliefs. The belief of an agent is then represented as a possibility distribution $\pi$. A possibility distribution $\pi$ can represent a complete preorder on the set of possible interpretations $\omega \in \Omega$. This is the reason why, intuitively, at a semantic level, a possibility distribution can represent the available knowledge (or beliefs) of an agent. When representing knowledge, $\pi(\omega)$ acts as a restriction on possible interpretations and represents the degree of compatibility of the interpretation $\omega$ with the available knowledge about the real world. $\pi(\omega) = 1$ means that is totally possible for $\omega$ to be the real world. As in [15], a graded belief is regarded as a necessity degree induced by a normalized possibility distribution $\pi$ on the possible worlds $\omega$. The degree to which an agent believes that a formula $\Phi$ is true is given by:

$$B(\phi) = N([\phi]) = 1 - \max_{\omega \nvDash \phi}\{\pi(\omega)\} \tag{1}$$

An agent's belief can change over time because new information arrives from the environment or from other agents. A belief change operator is proposed in [15], which allows to update the possibility distribution $\pi$ according to new trusted information. This possibility distribution $\pi'$, which induces the new belief set $B'$ after receiving information $\phi$, is computed from the possibility distribution $\pi$ with respect to the previous belief set $B$ ($B' = B * \frac{\tau}{\Phi}, \pi' = \pi * \frac{\tau}{\Phi}$) as follows: for all interpretations $\omega$,

$$\pi'(\omega) = \begin{cases} \frac{\pi(\omega)}{\Pi(\{\phi\})} & \text{if } \omega \vDash \phi \text{ and } B(\neg\phi) < 1; \\ 1 & \text{if } \omega \vDash \phi \text{ and } B(\neg\phi) = 1; \\ \min\{\pi(\omega), (1-\tau)\} & \text{if } \omega \nvDash \phi. \end{cases} \tag{2}$$

where $\tau$ is the trust degree towards a source about an incoming information $\phi$.

**BC Axioms and Rules.** Belief context axioms include all axioms from classical propositional logic with weight 1 as in [19]. Since a belief is defined as a necessity measure, all the properties of necessity measures are applicable in this context. Hence, the belief modality in our approach is taken to satisfy these properties that can be regarded as axioms. The following axiom is then added to the belief unit:

$$BC : B(\phi) > 0 \rightarrow B(\neg\phi) = 0$$

It is a straightforward consequence of the properties of possibility and necessity measures, meaning that if an agent believes $\phi$ to a certain degree then it cannot believe $\neg\phi$ at all. Other consequences are:

$$B(\phi \wedge \psi) \equiv \min\{B(\phi), B(\psi)\}$$
$$B(\phi \vee \psi) \geq \max\{B(\phi), B(\psi)\}$$

The inference rules are:

- $B(\neg p \vee q) \geq \alpha, B(p) \geq \beta \vdash B(q) \geq \min(\alpha, \beta)$ (modus ponens)
- $\beta \leq \alpha, B(p) \geq \alpha \vdash B(p) \geq \beta$ (weight weakening)

where $\vdash$ denotes the syntactic inference of possibilistic logic.

## 4.2   Desire Context

Desires represent a BDI agent's motivational state regardless its perception of the environment. Desires may not always be consistent. For example, an agent may desire to be healthy, but also to smoke; the two desires may lead to a contradiction. Furthermore, an agent may have unrealizable desires; that is, desires that conflict with what it believes possible.

**The DC Language and Semantics.** In this context, we make a difference between desires and goals. Desires are used to generate a list of coherent goals regardless to the agent's perception of the environment and its beliefs. Inspired from [18], the language of $DC$ ($L_{DC}$) is defined as an extension of a classical propositional language. We define a fuzzy operator $D^+$, which is associated with a satisfaction degree ($D^+(\phi)$ means that the agent positively desires $\phi$) in contrast with a negative desire, which reflects what is rejected as unsatisfactory. For sake of simplicity, we will only consider the positive side of desires in this work, and the introduction of negative desires is left as future work.

In this theory, da Costa Pereira and Tettamanzi [15] use possibility measures to express the degree of positive desires. Let $u(\omega)$ be a possibility distribution called also qualitative utility (e.g., $u(\omega) = 1$ means that $\omega$ is fully satisfactory). Given a qualitative utility assignment $u$ (formally, a possibility distribution), the degree to which the agent desires $\phi \in L_{DC}$ is given by:

$$D(\phi) = \Delta([\phi]) = \min_{\omega \models \phi}\{u(\omega)\} \tag{3}$$

where $\Delta$ is a guaranteed possibility measure that, given a possibility distribution $\pi$, is defined as follows:

$$\Delta(\Omega) = \min_{\omega \in \Omega}\{\pi(\Omega)\} \tag{4}$$

**DC Axioms and Rules.** The axioms consist of all properties of possibility measures such as $D(\phi \vee \psi) \equiv \min\{D(\phi), D(\psi)\}$. The basic inference rules, in the propositional case, associated with $\Delta$ are:

- $[D(\neg p \wedge q) \geq \alpha], [D(p \wedge r) \geq \beta] \vdash [D(q \wedge r) \geq min(\alpha, \beta)]$ (resolution rule)
- if $p$ entails $q$ classically, $[D(p) \geq \alpha] \vdash [D(q) \geq \alpha]$ (formula weakening)
- for $\beta \leq \alpha$, $[D(p) \geq \alpha] \vdash [D(p) \geq \beta]$ (weight weakening)
- $[D(p) \geq \alpha]; [D(p) \geq \beta] \vdash [D(p) \geq max(\alpha, \beta)]$ (weight fusion).

### 4.3    Goal Context

Goals are sets of desires that, besides being logically "consistent", are also maximally desirable, i.e., maximally justified. Even though an agent may choose some of its goals among its desires, nonetheless there may be desires that are not necessarily goals. The desires that are also goals represent those states of the world that the agent might be expected to bring about precisely because they reflect what the agent wishes to achieve. In this case, the agent's selection of goals among its desires is constrained by three conditions. First, since goals must be consistent and desires may be inconsistent, only the subsets of consistent desires can be the potential candidates for being promoted to goal-status, and also the selected subsets of consistent desires must be consistent with each other. Second, since desires may be unrealizable whereas goals must be consistent with beliefs (justified desires), only a set of feasible (and consistent) desires can be potentially transformed into goals. Third, desires that might be potential candidates to be goals should be desired at least to a degree $\alpha$. Then, only the most desirable, consistent, and possible desires can be elected as goals.

**The $GC$ Language and Semantics.** The language $L_{GC}$ to represent the Goal Context is defined over the propositional language $L$ extended by a fuzzy operator $G$ having the same syntactic restrictions as $D^+$. $G(\phi)$ means that the agent has goal $\phi$. As explained above, goals are a subset of consistent and possible desires. Desires are adopted as goals because they are justified and achievable. A desire is justified because the world is in a particular state that warrants its adoption. For example, one might desire to go for a walk because he believes it is a sunny day and may drop that desire if it starts raining. A desire is achievable, on the other hand, if the agent has a plan that allows it to achieve that desire.

*$GC$ Axioms and Rules.* Unlike desires, goals should be consistent, meaning that they can be expressed by the $D_G$ axiom ($D$ from the KD45 axioms [12]) as follows:

$$D_G \quad GC : G(\phi) > 0 \rightarrow G(\neg\phi) = 0$$

Furthermore, since goals are a set of desires, we use the same axioms and deduction rules as in $DC$. Goals-beliefs and goals-desires consistency will be expressed with bridge rules as we will discuss later on in the paper.

### 4.4    Social Context

One of the benefits of the BDI model is to consider the mental attitude in the decision-making process, which makes it more realistic than a purely logical model. However, this architecture overlooks an important factor that influences this attitude, namely the *sociality* of an agent. There are a number of ways in which agents can influence each other mental states, e.g., authority where an agent may be influenced by another to adopt a mental attitude whenever the latter has the power to guide the behavior of the former, trust where an agent may be influenced by another to adopt a mental attitude merely on the strength of its confidence in the latter, or persuasion where an agent may be influenced to adopt another agent mental state via a process of argumentation or negotiation. In this work, we will only consider trust as a way by which agents can influence each others.

**The $SC$ Language and Semantics.** In our model, we consider a multi-agent system MAS consisting of a set of $N$ agents $\{a_1, .., a_i, ..a_N\}$. The idea is that these agents are connected in a social network such as agents with the same goal. Each agent has links to a number of other agents (neighbors) that change over time. In this paper, we do not consider dynamic changes in the social network, but we assume to deal with the network in a specific time instant. Between neighbors, we assume a trust relationship holds. The trustworthiness of an agent $a_i$ towards an agent $a_j$ about an information $\phi$ is interpreted as a necessity measure $\tau \in [0, 1]$, as in [20], and is expressed by the following equation:

$$T_{a_i, a_j}(\phi) = \tau \qquad (5)$$

where $a_i, a_j \in MAS = \{a_1, .., a_i, .., a_N\}$. Trust is transitive in our model, which means that, trust does not hold only between agents having a direct link to each other, but indirect links are also considered. Namely if agent $a_i$ trusts agent $a_k$ to a degree $\tau_1$, and $a_k$ trusts agent $a_j$ with a trust degree $\tau_2$ then $a_i$ can infer its trust for agent $a_j$, and $T_{a_i, a_j}(\psi) = min\{\tau_1, \tau_2\}$.

**$SC$ Axioms and Rules.** As sociality is expressed as a trust measure, which is interpreted as a necessity measure, $SC$ axioms include properties of necessity measures as in $BC$ (e.g., $N(\phi \wedge \psi) \equiv \min\{N(\phi), N(\psi)\}$).
When an agent is socially influenced to change its mental attitude, by adopting a set of beliefs and/or desires, the latter should maintain a degree of consistency. Those rules will be expressed with bridge rules that link the social context to the belief and the desire contexts.

## 4.5   Planning and Intention Contexts

The aim of this functional context is to extend the BDI architecture in order to represent plans available to agents and provide a way to reason over them. In this context, we are inspired by [21] to represent and reason about plans and intentions. Plans are described using ontologies. [22] defines an ontology as 'the specification of conceptualizations used to help programs and humans to share knowledge'. According to the World Wide Web Consortium[1] (W3C), ontologies or vocabularies define the concepts and relationships used to describe and represent an area of concern. We use the 5W[2] (Who, What, Where, When, Why) vocabulary which is relevant for describing different concepts and constraints in our scenario. The main concepts and relationships of this ontology are illustrated in Fig. 2.

---

[1] http://www.w3.org/standards/semanticweb/ontology.
[2] http://ns.inria.fr/huto/5w/.

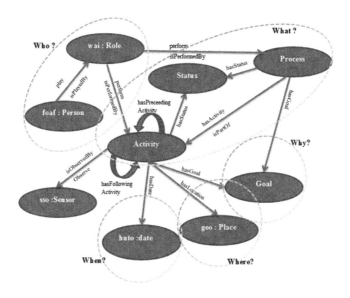

**Fig. 2.** The main concepts and relationships of the 5W ontology.

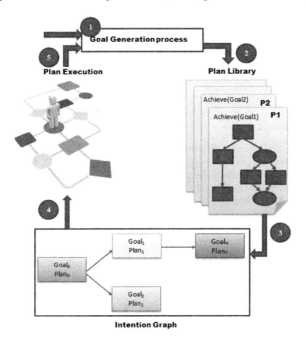

**Fig. 3.** Planning and intention contexts.

The main task of this context is to select plans that satisfy maximally the agents goals. To go from the abstract notions of desires and beliefs to the more concrete concepts of goals and plans, as illustrated in Fig. 3, the following steps are considered: (1) new information arrives and updates beliefs or/and desires which trigger goals update; (2) these goal changes invoke the Plan Library. The selection process is expressed by Algorithm 1 which looks in a knowledge base (KB) for all plans that satisfy maximally these goals; $CB$ and/or $CF$ techniques can be used in the selection process but will be investigated more thoroughly in further work. The algorithm complexity is significantly reduced since we discard from the beginning goals without plans; (3) one or more of these plans is then chosen and moved to the intention structure; and (4) a task (intention) is selected for execution and once executed or failed this leads to the update of the agents beliefs (5).

---

**Data:** G
**Result:** S //S is a list of plans
$G^* = \{\phi_1, \phi_2, .., \phi_n\}$
$m \leftarrow 0; S' \leftarrow \emptyset; G' \leftarrow \emptyset;$
**for** *each* $\phi_i$ *in* $G^*$ **do**
  //*Search in the KB for a plan satisfying* $\phi_i$
  $S_{\phi_i} \leftarrow SearchInKB(\phi_i);$
  **if** $S_{\phi_i} \neq \emptyset$ **then**
    //*Discard goals without plans*
    $Append(G', S_{\phi_i});$
  **end**
**end**
**for** $i$ *in* $1..Lenght(G')$ **do**
  //*Combination of i elements in* $G'$
  $S' \leftarrow Combination(G', i);$
  **for** $j$ *in* $1..Length(S')$ **do**
    **if** $S'[j] \neq \emptyset$ **then**
      //*Compute the satisfaction degree of* $S'$
      $\alpha_i = G(S'[j]);$
      //*Select the maximum* $\alpha_i$
      **if** $\alpha_i > m$ **then**
        $m \leftarrow \alpha_i;$
        Initialize(S);
        Append(S, S');
      **else**
        **if** $\alpha_i = m$ **then**
          | Append(S,S');
        **end**
      **end**
    **end**
  **end**
**end**
Return S;

**Algorithm 1.** *RequestForPlan* Function.

## 4.6   Bridge Rules

There are a number of relationships between contexts that are captured by so-called bridge rules. A bridge rule is of the form:

$$u1 : \phi, u2 : \psi \rightarrow u3 : \theta$$

and it can be read as: if the formula $\phi$ can be deduced in context $u1$, and $\psi$ in $u2$, then the formula $\theta$ has to be added to the theory of context $u3$. A bridge rule allows to relate formulae in one context to those in another one. In this section, we present the most relevant rules, illustrated by numbers in Fig. 1. For all the agents in the MAS, the first rule relating goals to beliefs can be expressed as follows:

$$(1) \vDash GC : G(a_i, \phi) > 0 \rightarrow BC : B(a_i, \neg\phi) = 0$$

which means that if agent $a_i$ adopts a goal $\phi$ with a satisfaction degree equal to $\beta_\phi$ then $\phi$ is believed possible to a degree $\beta_\phi$ by $a_i$. Concerning rule (2) relating the goal context to the desire context, if $\phi$ is adopted as goal then it is positively desired with the same satisfaction degree.

$$(2) \vDash GC : G(a_i, \phi) = \delta_\phi \rightarrow DC : D^+(a_i, \phi) = \delta_\phi$$

An agent may be influenced to adopt new beliefs or desires. Beliefs coming from other agents are not necessarily consistent with the agent's individual beliefs. This can be expressed by the following rule:

$$(3) \vDash BC : B(a_j, \phi) = \beta_\phi, SC : T_{a_i, a_j}(\phi) = t \rightarrow BC : B(a_i, \phi) = \beta'_\phi$$

where $\beta'_\phi$ is calculated using Eq. 1 with $\tau = min\{\beta_\phi, t\}$ to compute the possibility distribution, and Eq. 1 to deduce the Belief degree.

**Data:** B,D
**Result:** $G^*$, $\gamma^*$
$\bar{\gamma} \leftarrow 0$;
**repeat**
  Compute $G_{\bar{\gamma}}$ by Algorithm 3;
  **if** $G_{\bar{\gamma}} = \emptyset$ **then**
    //Move to the next more believed value in B
    $\bar{\gamma} \leftarrow \begin{cases} min\{\alpha \in Img(B) \mid \alpha > \bar{\gamma}\} \\ 1 \qquad\qquad\qquad\quad if \nexists \alpha > \bar{\gamma} \end{cases}$
  **end**
**until** $\bar{\gamma} < 1$ *and* $G_{\bar{\gamma}} = \emptyset$;
$\gamma^* = 1 - \bar{\gamma}, G^* = G_{\bar{\gamma}}$;

**Algorithm 2.** The goal election function.

Similarly to beliefs, desires coming from other agents need not to be consistent with the agent's individual desires. For example, an agent may be influenced by another agent to adopt the desire to smoke, and at the same time having the desire to be healthy, as shown by the following rule:

$$(4) \vDash DC : D^+(a_j, \psi) = \delta_\psi, SC : T_{a_i, a_j}(\psi) = \tau \rightarrow DC : D^+(a_i, \psi) = \delta'_\psi$$

where $\delta'_\psi = min\{\delta_\psi, \tau\}$. Desire-generation rules can be expressed by the following rule:

$$(5) \vDash BC : min\{B(\phi_1) \wedge \ldots \wedge B(\phi_n)\} = \beta, DC :$$
$$min\{D^+(\psi_1) \wedge \ldots \wedge D^+(\psi_n))\} = \delta \rightarrow DC : D^+(\Psi) \geq min\{\beta, \delta\}$$

Namely, if an agent has the beliefs $B(\phi_1) \wedge \ldots \wedge B(\phi_n)$ with a degree $\beta$ and it positively desires $D^+(\psi_1) \wedge \ldots \wedge D^+(\psi_n)$ to a degree $\delta$, then it positively desires $\Psi$ to a degree greater or equal to $min\{\beta, \delta\}$. According to [18], goals are a set of desires that, besides being logically 'consistent', are also maximally desirable, i.e., maximally justified and possible. This is expressed by the following bridge rule:

$$(6) \vDash BC : B(a_i, \phi) = \beta_\phi, DC : D^+(a_i, \psi) = \delta_\psi \rightarrow GC : G(\chi(\phi, \psi)) = \delta$$

where $\chi(\phi, \psi) = ElectGoal(\phi, \psi)$, as specified in Algorithm 2, is a function that allows to elect the most desirable and possible desires as goals. If *ElectGoal* returns $\emptyset$, then $G(\emptyset) = 0$, i.e., no goal is elected.

As expressed by the bridge rule above, once goals are generated, our agent will look for plans satisfying goal $\phi$ by applying the *RequestForPlan* function and do the first action of the recommended plan.

$$(7) \vDash GC : G(a_i, \phi) = \delta, PC : RequestForPlan(\phi) \rightarrow IC :$$
$$I(act_i, PostConditon(act_i))$$

where *RequestForPlan* is a function that looks for plans satisfying goal $\phi$ in the plan library, as specified in Algorithm 1. Rule (8) means that if an agent has the intention of doing an action $act_i$ with $PostCondition(act_i)$ then it passes this information to the communication unit and via it to other agents and to the user.

---

**Data:** $B, D, \bar{\gamma}$
**Result:** $G_{\bar{\gamma}}$
$//Img(D)$ *is the level set of D, i.e., the set of membership degrees of D*
$\delta \leftarrow max \, Img(D)$;
$//Find$ *the most desired $\delta$-cut $D_\delta$ of D which is believed possible*
**while** $min_{\psi \in D_\delta} B(\neg\psi) \leq \bar{\gamma}$ and $\delta > 0$ **do**
   | $//while$ *not found, move to the next lower level of desire*
   | $\delta \leftarrow \begin{cases} max\{\alpha \in Img(D) \mid \alpha < \delta\} \\ 0 \qquad\qquad\qquad\quad if \nexists \, \alpha < \delta \end{cases}$
**end**
**if** $\delta > 0$ **then** $G_{\bar{\gamma}} = D_\delta$;
**else** $G_{\bar{\gamma}} = \emptyset$;

**Algorithm 3.** Computation of $G_{\bar{\gamma}}$.

---

$$(8) \vDash IC : I(act_i, PostConditon(act_i)) \rightarrow CC : C(does(act_i, PostConditon(act_i)))$$

If the communication unit obtains some information that some action has been completed then the agent adds it to its beliefs set using rule (3) with $B(PostConditon(act_i)) = 1$.

# 5   Illustrative Example

To illustrate the reasoning process of our BDI architecture, we use our Bob's running example. To implement such a scenario using the BDI formalism, a recommender agent has a knowledge base (KB) like the one shown in Table 1, initially specified by Bob.

**Table 1.** Initial knowledge base of Bob's recommender agent.

| Beliefs | Desires |
|---------|---------|
| $B(pa \rightarrow rd) = 0.75$ | $D^+(pa) = 0.8$ |
| $B(wr \rightarrow rd) = 0.8$ | $D^+(wr) = 0.8$ |
| $B(\neg eh) = 0.4$ | $D^+(eh) = 0.9$ |
| $B(bs) = 0.9$ | $D^+(w) = 0.75$ |

The belief set is represented by formulae describing the world (e.g., $B(\psi_1) = 1$ means that $\psi_1$ is necessary and totally possible). Desires are all possible states that the agent wishes to achieve. Notice that they can be conflicting like $D^+(wr)$ and $D^+(\neg eh)$. $D^+(wr) = 0.8$ means that $wr$ is desired to a degree equal to 0.8. Desire-generation rules from bridge rule (5) can be described as follows:

$$R_{5_1} : \quad BC : B(pa \rightarrow rd), DC : D^+(rd) \rightarrow DC : D^+(pa),$$
$$R_{5_2} : \quad BC : B(wr \rightarrow rd), DC : D^+(rd) \rightarrow DC : D^+(wr),$$
$$R_{5_3} : \qquad\quad BC : B(bs), DC : D^+(pa) \rightarrow DC : D^+(w),$$
$$R_{5_4} : BC : B(pa \rightarrow wr), DC : D^+(wr) \rightarrow DC : D^+(\neg eh).$$

Then, the desire base of Bob, derived from desire-generation rules, will be as follows:

$$D = \{(pa, 0.8), (wr, 0.8), (w, 0.75), (\neg eh, 0.9)\}$$

We may now apply rule (6) to elect Bob's goals, given his belief base and his desire base. This rule will apply the function *electGoal()* which will choose from the desire base the most desirable and possible desires. Then, $Img(B) = \{0.75, 0.8, 0.9, 0.4\}$ and $Img(D) = \{0.75, 0.8, 0.9\}$. We begin by calling Algorithm 2 with $\gamma = 0$; $\delta$ is set to $maxImg(D) = 0.9$ and the corresponding desire in $D$ is $D_\delta = \{\neg eh\}$. Now if we verify $B(\neg(\neg eh)) = 0.4 > \gamma$ we move to the next less desired value which sets $\delta$ to $Img(D) = 0.8 < \delta = 0.9$. $\delta = 0.8 > 0$, then we go back to Step 2. In this case, $D_\delta = \{(pa, wr\}$. Now $B(\neg pa) = B(pa) = 0$ because we ignore yet whether $pa$ is possible or nor. Similarly, $B(\neg wr) = 0$ and Algorithm 2 will terminate with $G^* = G_\gamma = \{pa, wr\}$, i.e., Bob's recommender agent will elect as goal 'get back to a regular physical activity and reduce weight'.

Given these goals, Bob's agent ($a_1$) will look in the plan library for a plan satisfying them. As explained in rule (7), the agent will invoke function *Request-ForPlan*, which will look for a plan satisfying $pa$ and $wr$. Applying Algorithm 1, we have $G' = \{pa, wr\}$ and $S' = [pa, wr, \{pa, wr\}]$ with the same satisfaction degree $\alpha_1 = \alpha_2 = \alpha_3 = 0.8$. Suppose that it returns three plans $p_1$, $p_2$ and $p_3$ satisfying respectively goals $pa$, $wr$ and $\{pa, wr\}$. Bob's recommender agent will propose plan $p_3$ to the user because it meets more Bob's requirements with the same satisfaction degree. We suppose that Bob chooses plan $p_3$. Therefore, the first action (activity) in plan $p_3$ will become the agent's intention. The intended action will be proposed to the user via the communication unit by applying rule (8). Finally, if Bob starts executing the activity, information such as speed, distance or heart rate are collected via sensors (i.e., a smart watch) and transmitted to the communication unit in order to update the agent's beliefs. The revision mechanism of beliefs is the same as in [15], defined by Eq. 2. Once the activity is completed, rule (3) is triggered in order to update the belief set of Bob's agent with $B(postCondition(action1) = 1)$ which will permit to move to the next action in plan $\alpha$.

In order to illustrate the social influence between agents, we suppose that Bob's doctor uses our application with the same goal as Bob, i.e., to reduce his diabetes risk. Then, there is a direct link between agents $a_1, a_2$ representing Bob and Bob's doctor, respectively, with $T_{a_1,a_2}(\phi) = 0.9$ where $\phi$ represents any message coming from Bob's doctor (see [20] for more details). Now that Bob is executing his plan in order to get back to a physical activity, his recommender agent receives the following information from $a_2$ : $B(\neg pa) = 1$ which means that Bob's doctor believes that physical activity is not possible (not recommended). This information will trigger bridge rule (3). Knowing the belief degree of $a_2$ about $pa$ and given the trust degree of $a_1$ toward $a_2$ about information $pa$ ($T_{a_1,a_2}(pa)$), $a_1$ decides to update its mental state according to Eq. 2, and sets the new belief to $B'(pa) = 0$ according to Eq. 1. This will trigger the goal generation process, which updates the elected goals. $pa$ will be removed because $B(\neg pa) = 1$. Hence, a new plan is proposed to Bob.

## 6   Simulation

Aiming to illustrate the applicability of our model, the case study used in the previous section has been implemented and simulated in the NetLogo[3] environment. Netlogo [23] is a multi-agent programming language and modelling environment for simulating complex phenomena. It stands out from other agent-based simulation platforms for its ease of use and excellent documentation. We decided to use Netlogo for this work for those reasons, but also because it has a support for the BDI architecture and the Agent Communication Language (ACL).

The agent-based model is composed of 2 types of agents: a user agent which represents Bob, and a doctor agent representing Bob's doctor. The behavior of Bob's agent reproduces the behavior described in Sect. 4 with some simplifications, e.g., in the planning context, plans are a list of activities (moving from one destination to another) defined using Netlogo procedures. The behavior of the doctor agent is similar to Bob's agent one, but in this scenario its role is

---

[3] https://ccl.northwestern.edu/netlogo/.

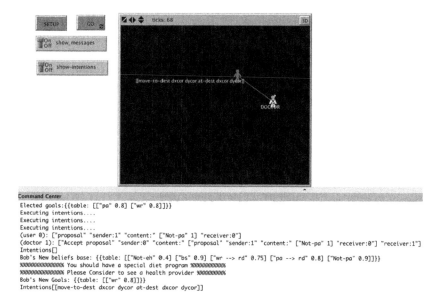

**Fig. 4.** A view of the simulation of our running scenario in Netlogo.

limited in communicating its recommendation about physical activity to Bob's agent. Beliefs and desires are initialized according to Table 1 for Bob's agent. For the doctor agent, we initialize only its beliefs to $B(\neg pa) = 1$. Figure 4 shows a general view of the implemented agent-based scenario.

As expected, in this simulation agents behave as described in the previous Section. Once the recommendation is calculated, Bob's agent starts to execute its intentions. It changes its plan when it receives information from its doctor's agent, who is considered as trustworthy. The analysis of the behavior of agents in this scenario allowed to support the design of the agent-based framework, tuning and refining its specification. The simulation is available online at the following link: http://modelingcommons.org/browse/one_model/4602.

## 7   Conclusions

Using cognitive agents architectures in the recommendation process is relevant especially in real-world applications [6]. To this end, we have presented a recommender system based on the BDI architecture. We used multi-context systems to define the BDI agent architecture with additional reasoning capabilities. First, we extended the traditional BDI architecture with a social context in which similar agents can communicate and influence each other to adopt mental attitudes. Second, we used ontologies to represent and reason about plans and intentions which offer the possibility of sharable and reusable data. The use of ontologies allow also to query streaming data. Unlike current approaches to agents recommendations, the agents (i.e., users) in our approach are active participants in the recommendation process, as they involve their personal social network based on their own perception of similarity. When applying the proposed framework to a running example, we showed it to be applicable and appropriate. As for future work, a more sophisticated evaluation of the framework with different metrics and agent strategies will be provided. As long term goals, a proof-of-concept implementation of the proposed framework is conceivable following approaches like [24].

Finally, our BDI agents operate in a dynamic environment which is dynamic both on the temporal and on the space side. Consequently, they are sensitive to the context and its changes especially spatio-temporal ones. Extending the proposed framework in order to handle spatio-temporal reasoning is then necessary. For that aim, approaches such as [25] will be explored.

# References

1. Koster, A., Schorlemmer, M., Sabater-Mir, J.: Opening the black box of trust: reasoning about trust models in a BDI agent. J. Log. Comput. **23**(1), exs003–58 (2012)
2. Pinyol, I., Sabater-Mir, J., Dellunde, P., Paolucci, M.: Reputation-based decisions for logic-based cognitive agents. Auton. Agent. Multi-Agent Syst. **24**, 175–216 (2012)
3. Montaner, M., López, B., De La Rosa, J.L.: A taxonomy of recommender agents on the internet. Artif. Intell. Rev. **19**, 285–330 (2003)
4. Casali, A., Godo, L., Sierra, C.: Modeling travel assistant agents: a graded BDI approach. In: Bramer, M. (ed.) IFIP AI 2006. IIFIP, vol. 217, pp. 415–424. Springer, Heidelberg (2006). doi:10.1007/978-0-387-34747-9_43
5. Casali, A., Godo, L., Sierra, C.: A tourism recommender agent: from theory to practice. Inteligencia artificial: Revista Iberoamericana de Inteligencia Artificial **12**, 23–38 (2008)
6. Casali, A., Godo, L., Sierra, C.: Validation and experimentation of a tourism recommender agent based on a graded BDI model. In: CCIA, pp. 41–50 (2008)
7. Casali, A., Godo, L., Sierra, C.: A graded BDI agent model to represent and reason about preferences. Artif. Intell. **175**, 1468–1478 (2011)
8. Sabater-Mir, J., Cuadros, J., Garcia, P.: Towards a framework that allows using a cognitive architecture to personalize recommendations in e-commerce. In: EUMAS, pp. 3–17 (2013)
9. Bajo, J., De Luis, A., Gonzalez, A., Saavedra, A., Corchado, J.M.: A shopping mall multiagent system: ambient intelligence in practice. In: 2nd International Workshop on Ubiquitous Computing & Ambient Intelligence, pp. 115–125 (2006)
10. Vashisth, P., Bedi, P.: Interest-based personalized recommender system. In: 2011 World Congress on Information and Communication Technologies (WICT), pp. 245–250. IEEE (2011)
11. Cohen, P.R., Levesque, H.J.: Intention is choice with commitment. Artif. Intell. **42**, 213–261 (1990)
12. Rao, A.S., Georgeff, M.P., et al.: BDI agents: from theory to practice. In: ICMAS, vol. 95, pp. 312–319 (1995)
13. Wooldridge, M., Jennings, N.R., Kinny, D.: The Gaia methodology for agent-oriented analysis and design. Auton. Agents Multi-agent Syst. **3**, 285–312 (2000)

14. Singh, M.P.: Semantical considerations on intention dynamics for BDI agents. J. Exp. Theoret. Artif. Intell. **10**, 551–564 (1998)
15. da Costa Pereira, C., Tettamanzi, A.G.: An integrated possibilistic framework for goal generation in cognitive agents. In: Proceedings of 9th International Conference on Autonomous Agents and Multiagent Systems, vol. 1, pp. 1239–1246 (2010)
16. Negoita, C., Zadeh, L., Zimmermann, H.: Fuzzy sets as a basis for a theory of possibility. Fuzzy Sets Syst. **1**, 3–28 (1978)
17. Parsons, S., Jennings, N.R., Sabater, J., Sierra, C.: Agent specification using multi-context systems. In: d'Inverno, M., Luck, M., Fisher, M., Preist, C. (eds.) Foundations and Applications of Multi-Agent Systems. LNCS (LNAI), vol. 2403, pp. 205–226. Springer, Heidelberg (2002). doi:10.1007/3-540-45634-1_13
18. da Costa Pereira, C., Tettamanzi, A.G.: Syntactic possibilistic goal generation. In: ECAI 2014–21st European Conference on Artificial Intelligence, vol. 263, pp. 711–716. IOS Press (2014)
19. Dubois, D., Prade, H.: Possibility theory and its applications: a retrospective and prospective view. In: Riccia, G.D., Dubois, D., Kruse, R., Lenz, H.-J. (eds.) Decision Theory and Multi-Agent Planning, vol. 482, pp. 89–109. Springer, Heidlelberg (2006). doi:10.1007/3-211-38167-8_6
20. Paglieri, F., Castelfranchi, C., da Costa Pereira, C., Costa Pereira, C., Falcone, R., Tettamanzi, A., Villata, S.: Trusting the messenger because of the message: feedback dynamics from information quality to source evaluation. Comput. Math. Organ. Theory **20**, 176–194 (2014)
21. Batet, M., Moreno, A., Sánchez, D., Isern, D., Valls, A.: Turist@: agent-based personalised recommendation of tourist activities. Expert Syst. Appl. **39**, 7319–7329 (2012)
22. Gruber, T.: Ontology. Encyclopedia of Database Systems, pp. 1963–1965 (2009)
23. Tisue, S., Wilensky, U.: Netlogo: A simple environment for modeling complexity. In: International Conference on Complex Systems, Boston, MA, vol. 21 (2004)
24. Bergenti, F., Caire, G., Gotta, D.: Agents on the move: JADE for android devices. In: Proceedings of Workshop From Objects to Agents (2014)
25. Jonker, C.M., Terziyan, V., Treur, J.: Temporal and spatial analysis to personalise an agent's dynamic belief, desire, and intention profiles. In: Klusch, M., Omicini, A., Ossowski, S., Laamanen, H. (eds.) CIA 2003. LNCS (LNAI), vol. 2782, pp. 298–315. Springer, Heidelberg (2003). doi:10.1007/978-3-540-45217-1_22

# Enhancing Support Vector Decoders by Integrating an Uncertainty Model

Jörg Bremer[✉] and Sebastian Lehnhoff

University of Oldenburg, 26129 Oldenburg, Germany
{joerg.bremer,sebastian.lehnhoff}@uni-oldenburg.de

**Abstract.** Predictive scheduling is a frequently executed task within the control process of energy grids. Relying on different predictions, planning results are naturally subject to uncertainties. Robust proactive planning of day-ahead real power provision must incorporate uncertainty in feasibility when trading off different schedules against each other during the predictive planning phase. Deviations from the expected initial operational state of an energy unit may easily foil a planned schedule commitment and provoke the need for costly ancillary services. The integration of confidence information into the optimization model allows for a consideration of uncertainty at planning time; resulting in more robust plans. Hence, control power and costs arising from deviations from agreed energy product delivery can be minimized. Integrating uncertainty information can be easily done when using a surrogate model. We extend an existing surrogate model that has been successfully used in energy management for checking feasibility during constraint-based optimization. The surrogate is extended to incorporate confidence scores based on expected feasibility under changed operational conditions. We compare the new surrogate model with the old one and demonstrate the superiority of the new model by results from several simulation studies.

**Keywords:** Uncertainty · SVDD · Smart grid · Distributed generation

## 1  Introduction

The ongoing transition in the changing electricity grid regarding control schemes leads to growing complexity and a need for new control schemes [25]. A steadily growing number of renewable energy resources like photovoltaics (PV), wind energy conversion (WEC) or co-generation of heat and power (CHP) has to be integrated into the electricity grid. This fact leads to a growing share of hardly predictable feed-in. The behavior of such renewable energy units often depends on uncertain prediction of projected weather conditions, user interaction (e.g. hot water usage), or similar. An algorithm for robust control would coordinate distributed energy resources (DER) with a proactive planning that already takes into account such uncertainty issues for scheduling in order to minimize the need for ancillary services in case of deviation from planned electricity delivery. Without loss of generality, we will focus on algorithms for virtual power plants (VPP)

© Springer International Publishing AG 2017
J. van den Herik and J. Filipe (Eds.): ICAART 2016, LNAI 10162, pp. 114–132, 2017.
DOI: 10.1007/978-3-319-53354-4_7

as an established control concept for renewables' integration [27] for the rest of the paper. All concepts are nevertheless applicable for different coordination schemes and smart grid Architectures, too.

Many balancing algorithms for a bunch of different control schemes have already been proposed as a solution to the problem of assigning a suitable, feasible schedule to each energy unit such that the sum of all schedules resembles a desired load profile while concurrently other objectives like minimal cost are met, too. Among such solutions are centralized algorithms as well as decentralized approaches for VPP as organizational entity. A VPP can be seen as a cluster of distributed energy resources (generators as well as controllable consumers) that are connected by communication means for control. Seen from the outside, the VPP cluster behaves like a large, single power plant. A VPP may offer services for real power provision as well as for ancillary services [4, 21, 25].

Traditionally, energy management is implemented as centralized control. However, given the increasing share of DER as well as more and more flexible loads in the distribution grid today, it is unlikely for such centralized control schemes to be able to cope with the rapidly growing problem size. The evolution of the classical, rather static (from an architectural point of view) power system to a dynamic, continuously reconfiguring system of individual decision makers (e.g. as described in [18, 24]) also leads to distributed problems. Thus, the seminal work of [43] identified the need for decentralized control. Examples for VPP are given in [14, 27]. An overview on existing control schemes and a research agenda can e.g. be found in [22, 31].

In order to additionally address the integration of the current market situation as well as volatile grid states, [24] introduces the concept of a dynamic virtual power plant (DVPP) for an on demand formation and situational composition of energy resources to a jointly operating VPP. In that approach VPPs gather dynamically together with respect to concrete electricity products at an energy market and will diverge right after delivery. Such dynamic organization even more relies on assumptions and predictions about individual flexibilities of each (possibly so far unknown) energy unit when going into load planning.

Anyway, a general problem for all algorithms is the presence of individual local constraints that restrict possible operations of all distributed energy resource within a virtual power plant. Each DER first and foremost has to serve the purpose it has been built for. But, usually this purpose may be achieved in different alternative ways. It is for instance the intended purpose of a CHP to deliver enough heat for the varying heat demand in a building at every moment in time. Nevertheless, if heat usage can be decoupled from heat production by using a thermal buffer store, different production profiles may be used for generating the same heat production profile. This leads, in turn, to different respective electric load profiles that may be offered as alternatives to a VPP controller. The set of all schedules that a DER may operate without violating any technical constraint (or soft constraint like comfort) is the sub-search-space with respect to this specific DER from which a scheduling algorithm may choose solution candidates. Geometrically seen, this set forms a sub-space $\mathcal{F} \subseteq \mathbb{R}^d$ in the space of all possible schedules.

In [7] a model has been proposed to derive a description for this sub-space of feasible solutions that abstracts from any DER model and its specific constraint formulations. These surrogate models for the search spaces of different DER may be automatically combined to a dynamic optimization model by serving as a means that guides an arbitrary algorithm where to look for feasible solutions. Due to the abstract formulations all DER may be treated the same by the algorithm and thus the control mechanism can be developed independently of any knowledge on the energy units that are controlled afterwards.

Up to now, this approach takes into account merely a hard margin that isolates feasible and infeasible schedules. A schedule is either feasible or not. But, for problems in real life this feasibility depends on predictions about the initial operational state of the unit from which the schedule is operated. If this initial state deviates from the predicted one, the schedule might or might not still be operable. The uncertainty in predicting the initial state of the unit is reflected by an uncertainty about the feasibility of any schedule. This fact results in a need for a fuzzy definition of the feasible region that contains all feasible schedules of a unit. In [6], the model given in [7] has been extended to unsupervised fuzzy decision boundaries after [20].

In this contribution we will further elaborate on this extension. We demonstrate the superior quality when deciding on feasibility of schedules under uncertain conditions and give some additional insights into the reasons. We start with a discussion on related work and briefly recap the used model technique before we define the extension and propose a measure for the confidence of arbitrary schedules. We conclude with several simulation results that support the extended approach.

## 2    Related Work

### 2.1    Uncertainty in the Smart Grid

Several works scrutinize the problem of uncertainty within the smart grid in general; mainly by using predefined stochastic models [1]. Uncertainty in long term development examinations like [46] are not in the scope of this work. Lots of work has been done in the field of wind (or photovoltaics) forecasting, e.g. [37,44], or on integration into stochastic unit commitment approaches [40], respectively. But, so far surprisingly low effort has been spent on integration into energy resource modeling for the case of operability. In [41] uncertainty about demand response is integrated directly into a multi agent decision making process, but in an unit specific and not in an abstract way. Integrating models of correlation in unit behaviour may be handled by using factory approaches for the scenario as has been demonstrated for the energy sector e.g. in [5]. An example for modeling reliability and assessment differentiated for different unit types is given in [3]. In [36] statistical models are used for observing the devices to predict possible operations over a day. By statistically averaging over large numbers of devices, the substantial unreliability can be reduced.

On the other hand, a need for an abstract and unit-independent surrogate model of individual feasible regions in distributed generation scenarios can for example be derived from [16,25] and more recently from [35]. An example for implementing such model is recapped in the next section.

## 2.2   Surrogate Models for der

Abstract surrogate models in the energy management sector are usually built with the help of a set of feasible schedules that serve as a training set for deriving the surrogate model. In this sense, we regard a schedule of an energy unit as a vector $s = (s_0, \ldots, s_d) \in \mathcal{F}^{(U_i)} \subset \mathbb{R}^d$ with each element $s_i$ denoting mean active power generated (or consumed) during the $i$th time interval. $\mathcal{F}^{U_i}$ defines the feasible region specifically associated with unit $U_i \in \mathcal{U}$ in the group of all unites $\mathcal{U}$. Figure 1 shows a simple 2-dimensional example for a single unit. With a maximum of 100 % rated power (and a minimum of zero) as the only constraint, the space of feasible schedules would be the whole unit square (or hyper-cube in the general case) $\mathcal{F} = [0,1]^d$. That would be the whole area depicted in Fig. 1. Different constraints prohibit the use of different regions. Figure 1 shows the following examples for constraints on the operation of a single modulating CHP:

$C_1$ **Energy Level Restrictions:** Modulating CHP are usually able to vary their electricity generation between a minimum $(p_{min})$ and a maximum $(p_{max})$ load. Shutting down the device $(p = 0)$ is sometimes an additional valid option. Therefore, such constraint prohibits the region $p_1 \in ]0, p_{min}[$ $(C_{1a})$ and $p_2 \in ]0, p_{min}[$ $(C_{1b})$.

$C_2$ **Limited Acceleration:** Due to inertia effects, physical devices cannot instantaneously change behavior. Sometimes, additional reasons prohibit a too quick change of the energy generation level. Constraint $C_2$ prohibits all schedules with a difference $\|p_1 - p_2\| > d_{max}$ above a given threshold $d_{max}$. This constraint also gives an example for a not continuous region. It decomposes into $C_{2a}$ and $C_{2b}$.

$C_3$ **Nearly Charged Storage:** Every co-generation plant needs to have the concurrently generated thermal energy used or buffered. If the buffer is nearly charged and no heat is used, the sum $p_1 + p_2$ might be limited by an upper bound as shown with constraint $C_3$.

Only the remaining region (white color) represents the scope of action of the energy resource from which schedules are to be taken for consideration during optimization. The feasible part at the axes (zero power) has been artificially enlarged for visualization purposes. In general it can be stated that the remaining part usually consist of a set of (separated) regions [23]. In addition, it has been shown in [10] that the feasible region is not always a convex polytope.

The procedure for generating the training set starts with initializing a unit behavior model with a parametrization from the physical unit or – in case of simulation – from its simulation model. These parameters may be directly read from the unit controller reflecting its current operation state or may be further

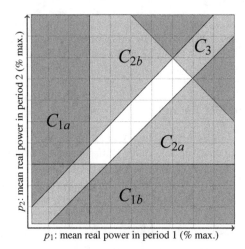

**Fig. 1.** Geometrical interpretation of operable schedules and exemplary restricting technical constraints of a modulating co-generation unit after [10].

projected onto a future state using the current operation schedule and predictions on future operation conditions.

Whereas in the first case exact parameters are derived, the latter case usually suffers from uncertainty from different forecast sources. The initialization defines the initial state of the unit at the starting point from whence alternative schedules are to be determined by sampling a behavior model which simulates the future flexibilities of the energy unit. If the initial operational state of the unit at the start of the time frame over which the energy load is balanced or optimized is fixed, a surrogate model can be derived that abstracts from the specific unit at hand and allows for an ad hoc integration at runtime into the scheduling algorithm.

Appropriate black-box models based on support vector approaches have been presented e.g. in [7]. We will briefly recap this technique before extending the ideas to uncertainty integration. The model is based on support vector data description (SVDD) as introduced by [39]. The goal of building such a model is to learn the feasible region of the schedules of a DER by harnessing SVDD to learn the enclosing boundary around the whole set of operable schedules.

We will briefly introduce the SVDD approach as for instance described in [2,7]. The modeling task is achieved by determining a mapping function $\Phi :$ $\mathcal{X} \subset \mathbb{R}^d \to \mathcal{H}$, with $\boldsymbol{x} \mapsto \Phi(\boldsymbol{x})$ such that all data points from a given region $\mathcal{X}$ is mapped to a minimal hypersphere in some high- or indefinite-dimensional space $\mathcal{H}$. Actually, the images go onto a manifold whose dimension is at maximum the cardinality of the training set [33]. The minimal sphere with radius $R$ and center $a$ in $\mathcal{H}$ that encloses $\{\Phi(\boldsymbol{x}_i)\}_N$ can be derived from minimizing $\|\Phi(\boldsymbol{x}_i) - a\|^2 \leq R^2 + \xi_i$ with $\|\cdot\|$ denoting the Euclidean norm and with slack variables $\xi_i \geq 0$ that introduce soft constraints for sphere determination. Introducing $\boldsymbol{\beta}$ and $\boldsymbol{\mu}$ as the

Lagrangian multipliers, the minimization problem for finding the smallest sphere becomes

$$L(\boldsymbol{\xi}, \boldsymbol{\mu}, \boldsymbol{\beta}) = R^2 - \sum_i (R^2 + \xi_i - \|\Phi(\boldsymbol{x}_i) - a^2)\|\beta_i$$
$$- \sum_i \xi_i \mu_i + C \sum_i \xi_i. \tag{1}$$

$C \sum_i \xi_i$ is a penalty term and determines size and accuracy of the resulting sphere by determining the number of rejected outliers. Usually, $C$ reflects an a priori fixed rejection rate.

After introducing Lagrangian multipliers and further relaxing to the Wolfe dual form, the well known Mercer's theorem may be harnessed for calculating dot products in $\mathcal{H}$ by means of a Mercer kernel in data space: $\Phi(\boldsymbol{x}_i) \cdot \Phi(\boldsymbol{x}_j) = k(\boldsymbol{x}_i, \boldsymbol{x}_j)$; cf. [33]. In order to gain a more smooth adaption, it is known [2] to be advantageous to use a Gaussian kernel:

$$k_G(\boldsymbol{x}_i, \boldsymbol{x}_j) = e^{-\frac{1}{2\sigma^2}\|\boldsymbol{x}_i - \boldsymbol{x}_j\|^2}. \tag{2}$$

Putting it all together, the equation that has to be maximized in order to determine the desired sphere is:

$$W(\boldsymbol{\beta}) = \sum_i k(\boldsymbol{x}_i, \boldsymbol{x}_i)\beta_i - \sum_{i,j} \beta_i \beta_j k(\boldsymbol{x}_i, \boldsymbol{x}_j). \tag{3}$$

With $k = k_G$ we get two main results: the center $a = \sum_i \beta_i \Phi(\boldsymbol{x}_i)$ of the sphere in terms of an expansion into $\mathcal{H}$ and a function $R : \mathbb{R}^d \to \mathbb{R}$ that allows to determine the distance of the image of an arbitrary point from $a \in \mathcal{H}$, calculated in $\mathbb{R}^d$ by:

$$R^2(\boldsymbol{x}) = 1 - 2\sum_i \beta_i k_G(\boldsymbol{x}_i, \boldsymbol{x}) + \sum_{i,j} \beta_i \beta_j k_G(\boldsymbol{x}_i, \boldsymbol{x}_j). \tag{4}$$

Because all support vectors are mapped right onto the surface of the sphere, the radius $R_{\mathbb{S}}$ of the sphere $\mathbb{S}$ can be easily determined by the distance of an arbitrary support vector. Thus the feasible region can now be modeled as

$$\mathcal{F} = \{\boldsymbol{x} \in \mathbb{R}^d | R(\boldsymbol{x}) \leq R_{\mathbb{S}}\} \approx \mathcal{X}. \tag{5}$$

Initially, such models have for example been used for handwritten digit or face recognition, pattern denoising, or anomaly detection [12,28,32]. A relatively new application is that of modeling feasible regions and constraint abstraction for distributed optimization problems especially in the field of energy management, e.g. as used in [16].

Using SVDD as surrogate model within a VPP control algorithm starts with generating a training set of feasible schedules for a specific energy unit with the help of a simulation model of this unit [9]. Thus, a schedule is a vector $\boldsymbol{x} \in \mathbb{R}^d$ consisting of $d$ values for mean active power to be operated during the respective time inerval. In a first step, the simulation model is parametrized with the estimated initial operation state of the unit (e.g. the temperature of

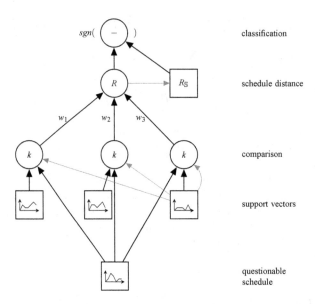

**Fig. 2.** Scheme for using SVDD as surrogate model for checking feasibility of operation schedules in distributed energy management after [34].

a thermal buffer store attached to a co-generation plant) at the future point in time that marks the start of the time frame for which a cluster schedule for the VPP is to be found. A cluster schedule as result of an (distributed) optimization process assigns a schedule to each energy unit within the VPP such that the sum of all individual schedules resembles a given target schedule (often an energy product to be sold at market) as close as possible. This simple case is an instance of the multiple choice constraint optimization problem [17]; for each unit a schedule has to be chosen from the feasible region of that unit. Often, further objectives like cost are concurrently optimized. Because the units are not necessarily known at compile-time and in order to be able to implement the control strategy independently, surrogates with a well-defined interface are used for checking feasibility during optimization. In this way, a simulation model for each unit is parametrized with a predicted initial operation state and generates a training set of feasible schedules for training the SVDD classifier that in turn is used by the problem solver for checking feasibility [7]. The process of checking feasibility for the VPP case is depicted in Fig. 2.

A so far sparcely addressed problem is that of integrating uncertainty issues in such models. A first attempt was made in [6]. Integrating uncertainty into support vector data description has so far led to only a few approaches. For instance, [45] introduced a fuzzy approach for the data clustering use case. With the help of a fuzzy definition of membership that determines for each point whether it belongs to the training set or not, they control the rate of hyper volume and outlier acceptance. Another approach with fuzzy constraint treatment is given by [15]. A different approach is taken in [20]. An individual weighting is introduced allowing for a differentiated consideration of accepted errors. Thus, data points with a higher confidence have a larger impact on the decision boundary. Equation (6) shows the respective extension to (1) in the last term.

$$L(\xi, \mu, \beta) = R^2 - \sum_i (R^2 + \xi_i - \|\Phi(x_i) - a\|^2)\beta_i$$
$$- \sum_i \xi_i \mu_i + C \sum_i (\kappa[x_i]\xi_i).$$

(6)

A definition of a problem specific differentiated confidence value for weighting has so far not been introduced. Liu et al. used the SVDD distance of a first training run as weighting for a second run. For our use case, we may later harness some a priori information for a more specific weighting.

In Eq. (6) the last term determines the trade-off between accepted error and hypersphere volume like the last term in Eq. (1). In contrast to the standard version Eq. (1), each point $x_i$ is individually weighted according to its individual confidence of membership to the positive class by $\kappa[x_i]$. $\kappa$ gives a measure for the reasonability of $x_i$.

We will later use this approach for modelling uncertainty in the use case of energy management. Beforehand we briefly discuss a specialized application for the SVDD model of feasible region: the ability to be used as decoder.

## 2.3 Decoders for Scheduling

In order to be able to systematically generate feasible solutions directly from the search space model, a decoder approach had been developed on top of the support vector model to go beyond just telling feasible and infeasible schedules apart. In [8] the support vector decoder has been introduced. In general, a decoder is a constraint handling technique that gives an algorithm hints on where in the free search space to look for feasible solutions. It imposes a relationship between a decoder solution (genotype representation) and a feasible solution (phenotype) and gives instructions on how to construct a feasible solution [13]. For example, [19] proposed a homomorphous mapping between an $n$-dimensional hyper cube and the feasible region in order to transform the problem into a topological equivalent one that is easier to handle. In order to be able to derive such a decoder mapping automatically from any given energy unit model, [8] developed an approach based on the mentioned support vector model [7].

Provided the feasible region of an energy unit has been encoded by SVDD, a decoder can be derived as follows. The set of alternatively feasible schedules after encoding by SVDD is represented as pre-image of a high-dimensional sphere $\mathbb{S}$. Figure 3 shows the situation. This representation has some advantageous properties. Although the pre-image might be some arbitrary shaped non-continuous blob in $\mathbb{R}^d$, the high-dimensional representation is a ball and geometrically easier to handle with the following relations: If a schedule is feasible, i.e. can be operated by the unit without violating any technical constraint, it lies inside the feasible region (grey area on the left hand side in Fig. 3). Thus, the schedule is

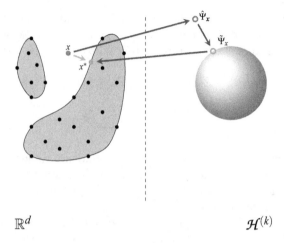

$$\mathbb{R}^d \qquad\qquad\qquad\qquad \mathcal{H}^{(k)}$$

**Fig. 3.** Basic idea of a decoder for constraint-handling based on SVDD [11].

inside the pre-image (that represents the feasible region) of the ball and thus its image in the high-dimensional representation lies inside the sphere. An infeasible schedule (e.g. $x$ in Fig. 3) lies outside the feasible region and thus its image $\hat{\Psi}_x$ lies outside the ball. But, some important relations are known: the center of the ball, the distance of the image from the center and the radius of the ball. One can now move the image of an infeasible schedule along the difference vector towards the center until it touches the ball. Finally, the pre-image of the moved image $\tilde{\Psi}_x$ is calculated to get a schedule at the boundary of the feasible region: a repaired schedule $x^*$ that is now feasible. No mathematical description of the original feasible region or of the constraints are needed to do this. More sophisticated variants of transformation are e.g. given in [8].

**Table 1.** Improved classification for a boiler with different water drawing profiles and different variations in usage prediction.

| $\sigma/kJ$ | draught $w_1$ | | draught $w_2$ | | draught $w_3$ | | $\overline{\Delta}/\%$ |
|---|---|---|---|---|---|---|---|
| | SVDD | csw-SVDD | SVDD | csw-SVDD | SVDD | csw-SVDD | |
| 135 | $0.313 \pm 0.341$ | $0.513 \pm 0.381$ | $0.281 \pm 0.324$ | $0.501 \pm 0.372$ | $0.308 \pm 0.339$ | $0.505 \pm 0.384$ | 74.37 |
| 90 | $0.527 \pm 0.341$ | $0.674 \pm 0.319$ | $0.532 \pm 0.340$ | $0.699 \pm 0.298$ | $0.527 \pm 0.341$ | $0.674 \pm 0.319$ | 30.24 |
| 45 | $0.841 \pm 0.190$ | $0.904 \pm 0.149$ | $0.860 \pm 0.187$ | $0.918 \pm 0.120$ | $0.841 \pm 0.190$ | $0.904 \pm 0.149$ | 6.99 |
| 27 | $0.943 \pm 0.085$ | $0.965 \pm 0.072$ | $0.949 \pm 0.081$ | $0.969 \pm 0.066$ | $0.943 \pm 0.085$ | $0.965 \pm 0.072$ | 2.15 |
| 18 | $0.969 \pm 0.053$ | $0.981 \pm 0.048$ | $0.973 \pm 0.047$ | $0.984 \pm 0.038$ | $0.970 \pm 0.053$ | $0.981 \pm 0.048$ | 0.91 |

## 3    Modeling Confidence

In order to model the uncertainty in a schedule's operability we define the confidence of a schedule as the share of variations of the initial state that still allows

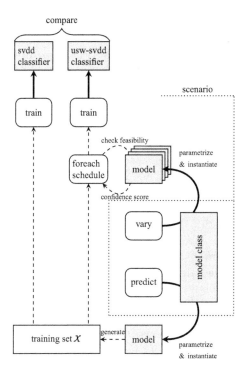

**Fig. 4.** Integration of confidence scores and evaluation scheme for comparing both classifiers.

operating the schedule without any modification. Let $\mathcal{X}$ be a set of $d$-dimensional schedules $\boldsymbol{x}_i$ that is going to serve as training set for building the SVDD model of unit $U$. $\mathcal{X}$ has been generated by assuming operation of a unit $U$ starting from an initial operation state $z_0 \in \boldsymbol{Z}_U$ at a certain future point in time with the set $\boldsymbol{Z}_U$ of all possible operation states. This set is unit specific. To give an example, $\boldsymbol{Z}_U$ in the case of a co-generation plant might be in the simplest version the set of assignments for the state of charge (SOC) of an associated thermal buffer store. Let $\Omega(z_0)$ bet a set of variations of $z_0$ and $\mathcal{F}[\Omega(z_0)]$ the set of schedules $\boldsymbol{x}_i \in \mathcal{X}$ that are operable from any state in $\Omega(z_0)$ without modification. We now define the confidence of a schedule $\boldsymbol{p} \in \mathcal{X}$ as the ratio

$$\kappa[\boldsymbol{p}] = P(\boldsymbol{p} \in \mathcal{F}[\Omega(z_0)] | \boldsymbol{p} \in \mathcal{F}[z_0]) = \frac{|\{\boldsymbol{p}|\boldsymbol{p} \in \mathcal{F}[z] \forall z \in \Omega(z_0)\}|}{|\Omega(z_0)|}. \qquad (7)$$

In this way, the confidence is the probability of still being operable if a given variation is applied to the initial operation state that had been taken as assumption for generating the training set of feasible schedules.

The question that remains open is the definition of actual variation in initial states in the real world. The actual design of such variation highly depends on the unit type at hand and on its embedding into the actual operation site. For this reason, this question cannot be answered in general here. In this paper we define variations for our simulations in a scenario specific way.

By using Eq. (6) instead of Eq. (1) in the SVDD part of the surrogate model for the feasible regions of energy units (and for the derived decoder) and by using the expectation value of the feasibility of a schedule under changed conditions for the units operations as defined in (7) as a score for the confidence of the schedule, we define the confidence score weighted extension to the surrogate model (csw-SVDD) used in [7].

## 4    Results

We tested the approach with a simulation study. For this purpose we used appliances with a characteristics that allows for a well defined simulated variation in initial operation state. We have chosen an under-counter water boiler, a co-generation plant and a fridge as example units for electricity generation as well as demand. All models had already been used in several studies and projects for evaluation [8, 10, 16, 23, 26].

**Fridge:** A fridge allows for modelling different variations. For this first approach, we tested two variants: variations in changing the thermal mass (different amount of reefer cargo at start of time horizon) and variation of the expected start temperature.

**Co-generation:** For co-generation plants (CHP) we modeled errors in expected weather conditions resulting in differences for the usage of the concurrently produced heat. Hence, we co-simulated CHP together with the heat losses of a house based on weather forecasts.

**Water Boiler:** By keeping a water reservoir within a certain temperature range by an electrical heating device, electricity consumption can be scheduled with rather few constraints. Assuming the technical insulation setting as fixed, losses are merely dependent on the ambient temperature difference. On the other hand, possible variations in scheduling load depend on the predicted usage profile for water drawing. Setting the ambient temperature fixed, the initial state for scheduling is determined by the temperature of the water in the tank and the profile for predicted water drawing during the scheduling horizon. For variations, we modeled different prediction errors for the usage profile.

In order to evaluate the improvement of the modified model we trained two models with basically the same training set of feasible schedules generated from the simulation model of the unit which is also used for evaluation of both surrogates. Figure 4 shows the setting of the basic evaluation procedure.

Each scenario comprises a specific model class for an energy unit and a prediction for an initial state which serves as parametrization for instantiating a model of the energy unit. From this model a training set $\mathcal{X}$ of feasible schedules is generated. Each schedule consists of a fixed number $d$ of values for consecutive

**Table 2.** Comparison of decoding errors as portion of correctly constructed schedules for different forecast deviations using the example of a boiler with predicted hot water demand.

| σ/kJ | SVDD | csw-SVDD |
|------|------|----------|
| 9 | $0.074 \pm 0.243$ | $0.003 \pm 0.056$ |
| 18 | $0.350 \pm 0.445$ | $0.025 \pm 0.152$ |
| 27 | $0.524 \pm 0.469$ | $0.098 \pm 0.293$ |
| 45 | $0.738 \pm 0.411$ | $0.594 \pm 0.468$ |
| 67.5 | $0.842 \pm 0.355$ | $0.804 \pm 0.387$ |

mean real power at which the unit can be operated without violating any constraint. This training set serves for training a classic SVDD classifier surrogate model for testing feasibility of a given schedule without needing to use the actual energy unit model. At the same time, each scenario contains a unit specific definition of variation σ for the initial state. This variation is used to generate a set of models, each with a random variation. Each schedule in the training set is then checked for feasibility with each of these varied models. The expectation value of feasibility under a certain variety of initial operation states (given the schedule $x$ was feasible under the fixed, predicted initial operation state) serves as confidence score $\kappa[x]$ for training a csw-SVDD. Finally, both classifiers can be compared by using classical classifier evaluation methods [30, 42]. To evaluate the classifier performance, we calculated the confusion matrix by comparing classifier and the original model that had been used for generating the training set and derived standard indicators for comparison [29]. Feasibility of a randomly (equally distributed) generated schedule is tested for feasibility once with the help of the classifier and once with the help of the unit model. In each scenario, 10000 variations have been used to find the expectation value κ.

Table 1 shows some first results for a water boiler. In this scenario we estimated a given water profile for hot water drawing as predicted usage. Hot water usage strongly determines feasibility of a given electrical profile. As variations we generated random deviations from the given water profile of a given size by adding normally distributed values with given standard deviation σ (negative drawings were corrected to zero for plausibility) ranging from 18 to 135 kJ per 15 min time interval. We tested scenarios with a duration of one hour with a 15 min resolution and the following artificial drawing profiles: $w_1 = (180 \, \text{kJ}, 0 \, \text{kJ}, 0 \, \text{kJ}, 720 \, \text{kJ})$, $w_2 = (0 \, \text{kJ}, 1440 \, \text{kJ}, 180 \, \text{kJ}, 540 \, \text{kJ})$ and $w_3 = (180 \, \text{kJ}, 90 \, \text{kJ}, 90 \, \text{kJ}, 180 \, \text{kJ})$.

The absolute performance (depicted is the recall value) degrades fast with growing uncertainty in both classifiers. This is as expected because of the growing deviation from the expected initial state. Nevertheless, the csw-SVDD performs better in all cases and the mean relative improvement and thus the advantage grows with growing error in prediction. Table 2 shows the results (error rate of not correctly generated schedules) for a decoder built from the respective

**Table 3.** Comparison of classifier recall indicators (higher values are better) for further scenarios.

| Scenario | SVDD | csw-SVDD |
|---|---|---|
| Fridge 1 | $0.927 \pm 0.045$ | $0.994 \pm 0.025$ |
| Fridge 2 | $0.747 \pm 0.028$ | $0.829 \pm 0.085$ |
| CHP | $0.838 \pm 0.260$ | $0.884 \pm 0.226$ |

classifier for profile 3 only. The results for the decoder part are not as good as for the classifier model part but nevertheless significant.

For evaluating the classifiers we primarily use the recall indicator. The precision degrades in both cases significantly. This is immediately apparent. The precision reflects the likelihood of a found schedule being feasible [29]. Because feasibility here is checked under changed preconditions and feasibility is a property of the schedules, precision degrades in both classifiers at approximately the same level. The new csw-SVDD classifier for energy resources surrogate modeling shows but a higher recall behavior, because the recall reflects the likelihood of a found schedule being feasible even under changed conditions. But this is exactly what is needed for the use case of checking feasibility of a schedule during energy management operations.

Table 3 shows some further results for a 2 h time frame. For fridge 1 an unpredictable user interaction was simulated by adding a random thermal mass ($30 \pm 5$ kJ, equating to about 500 g of food with room temperature) to the reefer cargo in the fridge. For the second fridge a variation of the predicted starting temperature was introduced. In the CHP scenario the thermal demand was varied to simulate a deviation from the weather forecast.

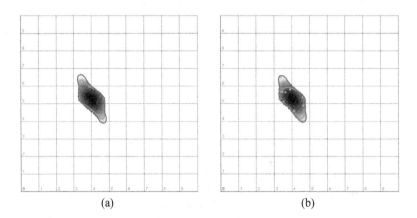

(a)                                                        (b)

**Fig. 5.** Comparison of different resulting decision boundaries. The right side also shows resulting (bounded) support vectors. (Color figure online)

Figure 5 gives a visual impression of the impact of confidence weights on the SVDD training process. The decision boundary is adapted to omitting regions with low confidence without forcing a threshold that decided explicitly whether a given point belongs to the positive class or not. In case of an approach that a priori excludes ill evaluated point from the training set, a from case to case decision had to be taken from every new optimization process. The confidence weighted approach on the other hand is unsupervised and allows the integration into a fully automated overall process flow. The figure shows in both cases the search space (again 2-dimensional for demonstration purposes) of a hot water boiler. The color denotes the confidence of each schedule; the darker the higher the probability of staying operable when things go astray. The confidence has been determined as in the experiment from Table 3. The decision boundary of the modified SVDD variant (brighter in color) is shifted towards schedules with higher confidence. Figure 5(b) also shows the resulting support vectors. A subset of the support vectors (pale color) results in so called bounded support vectors in data space but outside of the enclosing envelope defined by the decision boundary. Bounded support vectors are in general false classified schedules from the training set. There images lie outside the sphere although they contribute to the definition of the decision boundary. They lead to a better separation of different clusters in the data set or in the case of confidence integration to an unsupervised detection of undesired schedules with densities overlapping with the density of the desired schedules [2]. This effect is due to a mean decrease of parameter $C$ that controls the trade-off between accepted outliers and size of the envelope. As these bounded support vectors also have an effect on the quality of the derived decoder, it becomes clear that the decoder does not benefit to the same degree from the modified SVDD.

Table 4. Comparison of classifier accuracy for a simulated boiler with 24-dimensional schedules and deviations ($\sigma$) in predicted water usage of different size in a different number of time intervals.

| $\sigma$, $n$ | SVDD | csw-SVDD |
|---|---|---|
| 60, 3 | $0.8431 \pm 0.0939$ | $0.9371 \pm 0.0966$ |
| 120, 1 | $0.8644 \pm 0.1323$ | $0.9507 \pm 0.1051$ |
| 120, 2 | $0.6802 \pm 0.2196$ | $0.9372 \pm 0.1062$ |
| 120, 3 | $0.5175 \pm 0.2658$ | $0.9027 \pm 0.1291$ |

Finally, Table 4 shows some results for longer time periods with 24-dimensional schedules. Again, these are boilers; this time with variations in a limited number of $n$ time periods.

Due to a lack of real world data, a normal distribution of the variations has been assumed in all simulations according to [38]. This assumption is likely to become invalid in practice. Nevertheless, an advantage of the chosen approach for the csw-SVDD surrogate is the ability to derive the decision boundary unsupervised from the confidence scores of the individual schedules in the training set regardless of the underlying distributions. In this way, the approach can be used unchanged for individual variations of newly implemented and integrated energy resource models; even if they are introduced later at run time.

## 5    Conclusion

Feasibility of solutions is a crucial key factor for the success and wide acceptance of any kind of algorithm within the future smart grid. Automation will be the key factor to distribute electricity generation as well as responsibility for grid control. If the future smart grid is going to shift to a system with independent and self-dependently operated small and distributed entities, automated abstraction from specific units and individual flexibility modeling widely becomes an essential requirement especially for decentralized coordination algorithms.

Predictive energy management for balancing or planning electricity demand and production according to operation schedules needs predictions of future operation alternatives and thus information about flexibilities of all devices for the scheduler to choose from. Meta-models as representations of individually restricted search spaces lean on such predictions on flexibility. By using these predictions on possible alternatives as training set, individual representations of search spaces and their traits are learned. Whether a predicted operation schedule in the training set is actually still operable when it comes to finally operating the assigned (optimal) ones depends on several certain predictions that where made while constructing the training set of probably feasible schedules.

A robust planning algorithm should take into account this uncertainty of operability already during the planning phase. Determining an exact global optimum is, in any case, not possible in practice until ex post due to uncertainties and forecast errors. Nevertheless, the likelihood of gaining a plan that cannot be operated due to changes in external precondition may be minimized by selecting preferably schedules with a higher probability of being still operable even under changed conditions.

For the use case scrutinized in this contribution, robustness of a schedule is defined by the operability even under changed circumstances and preconditions. This ability of a schedule is condensed into a confidence value that allows individual weighting during the training phase of the search space meta-model. Nevertheless, future work still has to derive appropriate data on real world variations.

To already achieve the mathematical goal of integration information on uncertainty, we adapted an approach for confidence integration in classification, added a confidence model specific for electric flexibilities for operation schedules, and demonstrated its applicability with several use cases. The results are already promising for the model part and call for further extension especially regarding concrete definitions of variety and confidence for specific unit types.

Future work will have to target a better integration of uncertainty into decoders as well. If this is achieved, a more robust scheduling within virtual power plants will lead to a better support for the integration of fluctuating renewable resources. For the case of surrogate modelling this was already improved with the approach proposed here.

# References

1. Alharbi, W., Raahemifar, K.: Probabilistic coordination of microgrid energy resources operation considering uncertainties. Electr. Power Syst. Res. **128**, 1–10 (2015). http://www.sciencedirect.com/science/article/pii/S0378779615001856
2. Ben-Hur, A., Siegelmann, H.T., Horn, D., Vapnik, V.: Support vector clustering. J. Mach. Learn. Res. **2**, 125–137 (2001)
3. Blank, M., Lehnhoff, S.: Correlations in reliability assessment of agent-based ancillary-service coalitions. In: Power Systems Computation Conference (PSCC), pp. 1–7, August 2014
4. Tröschel, M., Appelrath, H.-J.: Towards reactive scheduling for large-scale virtual power plants. In: Braubach, L., van der Hoek, W., Petta, P., Pokahr, A. (eds.) MATES 2009. LNCS (LNAI), vol. 5774, pp. 141–152. Springer, Heidelberg (2009). doi:10.1007/978-3-642-04143-3_13
5. Bremer, J., Andreßen, S., Rapp, B., Sonnenschein, M., Stadler, M.: A modelling tool for interaction and correlation in demand-side market behaviour. In: New Methods for Energy Market Modelling, pp. 77–92 (2008)
6. Bremer, J., Lehnhoff, S.: Modeling uncertainty in support vector surrogates of distributed energy resources: enabling robust smart grid scheduling. In: van den Herik, J., Filipe, J. (eds.) ICAART 2016 - Proceedings of the 8th International Conference on Agents and Artificial Intelligence, vol. 2, pp. 42–50. SciTePress, Science and Technology Publications, Lda., Rome (2016, in press)
7. Bremer, J., Rapp, B., Sonnenschein, M.: Encoding distributed search spaces for virtual power plants. In: IEEE Symposium Series on Computational Intelligence 2011 (SSCI 2011), Paris, France, April 2011
8. Bremer, J., Sonnenschein, M.: Constraint-handling for optimization with support vector surrogate models - a novel decoder approach. In: Filipe, J., Fred, A. (eds.) ICAART 2013 - Proceedings of the 5th International Conference on Agents and Artificial Intelligence, vol. 2, pp. 91–105. SciTePress, Barcelona (2013)
9. Bremer, J., Sonnenschein, M.: Sampling the search space of energy resources for self-organized, agent-based planning of active power provision. In: Page, B., Fleischer, A.G., Göbel, J., Wohlgemuth, V. (eds.) 27th International Conference on Environmental Informatics for Environmental Protection, Sustainable Development and Risk Management, EnviroInfo 2013, Hamburg, Germany, 2–4 September 2013, Proceedings, pp. 214–222. Berichte aus der Umweltinformatik, Shaker (2013)
10. Bremer, J., Rapp, B., Sonnenschein, M.: Support vector based encoding of distributed energy resources' feasible load spaces. In: IEEE PES Conference on Innovative Smart Grid Technologies Europe. Chalmers Lindholmen, Gothenburg (2010)
11. Bremer, J., Sonnenschein, M.: Constraint-handling with support vector decoders. In: Filipe, J., Fred, A. (eds.) ICAART 2013. CCIS, vol. 449, pp. 228–244. Springer, Heidelberg (2014). doi:10.1007/978-3-662-44440-5_14
12. Chang, W.C., Lee, C.P., Lin, C.J.: A revisit to support vector data description (SVDD). Technical report, Department of Computer Science, National Taiwan University, Taipei 10617, Taiwan (2013)

13. Coello Coello, C.A.: Theoretical and numerical constraint-handling techniques used with evolutionary algorithms: a survey of the state of the art. Comput. Methods Appl. Mech. Eng. **191**(11–12), 1245–1287 (2002)
14. Coll-Mayor, D., Picos, R., Garciá-Moreno, E.: State of the art of the virtual utility: the smart distributed generation network. Int. J. Energy Res. **28**(1), 65–80 (2004)
15. GhasemiGol, M., Sabzekar, M., Monsefi, R., Naghibzadeh, M., Yazdi, H.S.: A new support vector data description with fuzzy constraints. In: Proceedings of the 2010 International Conference on Intelligent Systems, Modelling and Simulation ISMS 2010, pp. 10–14. IEEE Computer Society, Washington (2010)
16. Hinrichs, C., Bremer, J., Sonnenschein, M.: Distributed hybrid constraint handling in large scale virtual power plants. In: IEEE PES Conference on Innovative Smart Grid Technologies Europe (ISGT Europe 2013). IEEE Power and Energy Society (2013). http://www-ui.informatik.uni-oldenburg.de/download/Publikationen/HBS13.pdf
17. Hinrichs, C., Sonnenschein, M., Lehnhoff, S.: Evaluation of a self-organizing heuristic for interdependent distributed search spaces. In: Filipe, J., Fred, A.L.N. (eds.) International Conference on Agents and Artificial Intelligence (ICAART 2013), vol. 1 - Agents, pp. 25–34. SciTePress (2013)
18. Ilić, M.D.: From hierarchical to open access electric power systems. Proc. IEEE **95**(5), 1060–1084 (2007)
19. Koziel, S., Michalewicz, Z.: Evolutionary algorithms, homomorphous mappings, and constrained parameter optimization. Evol. Comput. **7**, 19–44 (1999)
20. Liu, B., Xiao, Y., Cao, L., Hao, Z., Deng, F.: SVDD-based outlier detection on uncertain data. Knowl. Inf. Syst. **34**(3), 597–618 (2013). http://dx.doi.org/10.1007/s10115-012-0484-y
21. Lukovic, S., Kaitovic, I., Mura, M., Bondi, U.: Virtual power plant as a bridge between distributed energy resources and smart grid. In: Hawaii International Conference on System Sciences, pp. 1–8 (2010)
22. McArthur, S., Davidson, E., Catterson, V., Dimeas, A., Hatziargyriou, N., Ponci, F., Funabashi, T.: Multi-agent systems for power engineering applications - part I: concepts, approaches, and technical challenges. IEEE Trans. Power Syst. **22**(4), 1743–1752 (2007)
23. Neugebauer, J., Kramer, O., Sonnenschein, M.: Classification cascades of overlapping feature ensembles for energy time series data. In: Woon, W.L., Aung, Z., Madnick, S. (eds.) DARE 2015. LNCS (LNAI), vol. 9518, pp. 76–93. Springer, Heidelberg (2015). doi:10.1007/978-3-319-27430-0_6
24. Nieße, A., Beer, S., Bremer, J., Hinrichs, C., Lünsdorf, O., Sonnenschein, M.: Conjoint dynamic aggregation and scheduling for dynamic virtual power plants. In: Ganzha, M., Maciaszek, L.A., Paprzycki, M. (eds.) Federated Conference on Computer Science and Information Systems - FedCSIS 2014, Warsaw, Poland, September 2014
25. Nieße, A., Lehnhoff, S., Tröschel, M., Uslar, M., Wissing, C., Appelrath, H.J., Sonnenschein, M.: Market-based self-organized provision of active power and ancillary services: an agent-based approach for smart distribution grids. In: COMPENG, pp. 1–5. IEEE (2012)
26. Nieße, A., Sonnenschein, M.: Using grid related cluster schedule resemblance for energy rescheduling - goals and concepts for rescheduling of clusters in decentralized energy systems. In: Donnellan, B., Martins, J.F., Helfert, M., Krempels, K.H. (eds.) SMARTGREENS, pp. 22–31. SciTePress, Setúbal (2013)

27. Nikonowicz, L.B., Milewski, J.: Virtual power plants - general review: structure, application and optimization. J. Power Technol. **92**(3), 135–149 (2012). http://papers.itc.pw.edu.pl/index.php/JPT/article/view/284/492
28. Park, J., Kang, D., Kim, J., Kwok, J.T., Tsang, I.W.: SVDD-based pattern denoising. Neural Comput. **19**(7), 1919–1938 (2007)
29. Powers, D.M.W.: Evaluation: from precision, recall and f-measure to roc., informedness, markedness & correlation. J. Mach. Learn. Technol. **2**(1), 37–63 (2011)
30. Powers, D.M.W.: Evaluation evaluation. In: Proceedings of the 2008 Conference on ECAI 2008: 18th European Conference on Artificial Intelligence, pp. 843–844. IOS Press, Amsterdam (2008). http://dl.acm.org/citation.cfm?id=1567281.1567498
31. Ramchurn, S.D., Vytelingum, P., Rogers, A., Jennings, N.R.: Putting the 'smarts' into the smart grid: a grand challenge for artificial intelligence. Commun. ACM **55**(4), 86–97 (2012)
32. Rapp, B., Bremer, J.: Design of an event engine for next generation cemis: a use case. In: Arndt, H.-K., Gerlinde Knetsch, W.P.E. (eds.) EnviroInfo 2012 - 26th International Conference on Informatics for Environmental Protection, pp. 753–760. Shaker Verlag (2012). ISBN 978-3-8440-1248-4
33. Schölkopf, B., Mika, S., Burges, C., Knirsch, P., Müller, K.R., Rätsch, G., Smola, A.: Input space vs. feature space in kernel-based methods. IEEE Trans. Neural Netw. **10**(5), 1000–1017 (1999)
34. Schölkopf, B.: Support Vector Learning. Dissertation, Fachbereich 13 Informatik der Technischen Universität Berlin, Oldenbourg Verlag, München (1997)
35. Sonnenschein, M., Appelrath, H.J., Canders, W.R., Henke, M., Uslar, M., Beer, S., Bremer, J., Lünsdorf, O., Nieße, A., Psola, J.H., et al.: Decentralized provision of active power. In: Smart Nord - Final Report. Hartmann GmbH, Hannover (2015)
36. Sonnenschein, M., Lünsdorf, O., Bremer, J., Tröschel, M.: Decentralized control of units in smart grids for the support of renewable energy supply. Environ. Impact Assess. Rev. **52**, 40–52 (2015)
37. Súri, M., Huld, T., Dunlop, E.D., Albuisson, M., Lefevre, M., Wald, L.: Uncertainties in photovoltaic electricity yield prediction from fluctuation of solar radiation. In: 22nd European Photovoltaic Solar Energy Conference (2007)
38. Stadler, I.: Demand Response: Nichtelektrische Speicher für Elektrizitätsversorgungssysteme mit hohem Anteil erneuerbarer Energien. Habilitation Fachbereich Elektrotechnik Universität Kassel, October 2005
39. Tax, D.M.J., Duin, R.P.W.: Support vector data description. Mach. Learn. **54**(1), 45–66 (2004)
40. Wang, J., Botterud, A., Bessa, R., Keko, H., Carvalho, L., Issicaba, D., Sumaili, J., Miranda, V.: Wind power forecasting uncertainty and unit commitment. Appl. Energy **88**(11), 4014–4023 (2011). http://www.sciencedirect.com/science/article/pii/S0306261911002339
41. Wildt, T.: Modelling uncertainty of household decision - making process in smart grid appliances adoption. In: Behave Energy Conference, Oxford, UK (2014)
42. Witten, I.H., Frank, E., Hall, M.A.: Data Mining: Practical Machine Learning Tools and Techniques, 3rd edn. Morgan Kaufmann, Amsterdam (2011). http://www.sciencedirect.com/science/book/9780123748560
43. Wu, F., Moslehi, K., Bose, A.: Power system control centers: past, present, and future. Proc. IEEE **93**(11), 1890–1908 (2005)
44. Zhang, J., Hodge, B.M., Gomez-Lazaro, E., Lovholm, A., Berge, E., Miettinen, J., Holttinen, H., Cutululis, N.: Analysis of Variability and Uncertainty in Wind Power Forecasting: An International Comparison. Energynautics GmbH (2013)

45. Zheng, E.-H., Yang, M., Li, P., Song, Z.-H.: Fuzzy support vector clustering. In: Wang, J., Yi, Z., Zurada, J.M., Lu, B.-L., Yin, H. (eds.) ISNN 2006. LNCS, vol. 3971, pp. 1050–1056. Springer, Heidelberg (2006). doi:10.1007/11759966_154. http://dblp.uni-trier.de/db/conf/isnn/isnn2006-1.html#ZhengYLS06

46. Zio, E., Aven, T.: Uncertainties in smart grids behavior and modeling: what are the risks and vulnerabilities? How to analyze them? Energy Policy **39**(10), 6308–6320 (2011). Sustainability of biofuels. http://www.sciencedirect.com/science/article/pii/S0301421511005544

# Natural Language Argumentation for Text Exploration

Elena Cabrio[1] and Serena Villata[2(✉)]

[1] University of Nice Sophia Antipolis, Sophia Antipolis, France
elena.cabrio@unice.fr
[2] CNRS - I3S Laboratory, Sophia Antipolis, France
villata@i3s.unice.fr

**Abstract.** Argumentation mining aims at automatically extracting natural language arguments from textual documents. In the last years, it has become a hot topic due to its potential in processing information originating from the Web in innovative ways. In this paper, we propose to apply the argument mining pipeline to the text exploration task. First, starting from the arguments put forward in online debates, we introduce *bipolar entailment graphs* to predict the relation among the textual arguments, i.e., entailment or non entailment relation. Second, we exploit the well know formalism called *abstract dialectical frameworks* to define acceptance conditions answering the needs of the text exploration task. The evaluation of the proposed approach shows its feasibility.

## 1 Introduction

In the last ten years, the Textual Entailment (TE) framework [13] has gained popularity in Natural Language Processing (NLP) applications like information extraction and question answering, providing a suitable model for capturing major semantic inference needs at textual level, taking into account the language variability. Given a pair of textual fragments, a TE system assigns an *entailment* or a *non entailment* relation to the pair. However, in real world scenarios as analyzing costumers' interactions about a service or a product, or online debates, these pairs extracted from the interactions cannot be considered as independent. This means that they need to be collected together into a single graph, e.g., all the reviews about a certain service are collected together to understand which are the overall problems/merits of the service.[1] This combination of TE pairs into a unique graph aims at supporting text exploration, whose goal is the extraction of specific information from users interactions evaluated as relevant in a particular domain or task. The challenge is thus to propose an automated framework able to compute such relevant information starting from the TE pairs returned by the system and collected into a graph.

---

[1] As discussed also in the keynote talk of the Joint Symposium on Semantic Processing (http://jssp2013.fbk.eu/).

© Springer International Publishing AG 2017
J. van den Herik and J. Filipe (Eds.): ICAART 2016, LNAI 10162, pp. 133–150, 2017.
DOI: 10.1007/978-3-319-53354-4_8

In this paper, we answer the research question:

– How to guide text exploration by highlighting relevant information?

Differently from standard entailment graphs [4,27] where the nodes are connected by entailment relations only, in this paper we consider *bipolar entailment graphs* (BEG), where the nodes are the text fragments of TE pairs, and both relations returned by TE systems (i.e., *entailment* and *non entailment*) are considered as the graph links. A recent proposal by Cabrio and Villata [8] suggests that TE pairs can be collected together to construct an abstract argumentation framework [11,14] where the *entailment* relation is mapped with the *support* relation in argumentation, and the *non entailment* relation is mapped with the *attack* relation. Argumentation theory [14] is used to compute the set of accepted arguments in the online debates they analyze. While we believe that strong connections hold between TE and argumentation theory, we detect the following drawbacks in their combined approach: *(i)* the *non entailment* relation is considered as equivalent to a contradiction and directly translated into an attack relation. This is not always the case: *non entailment* means that the two text spans are either *unrelated* or contradicting each other; *(ii)* the support relation affects arguments' acceptability only if supported arguments are also attacked (new attacks are introduced when a support holds [11]), making the resulting framework more complex; and *(iii)* applying standard acceptability semantics [14] to TE graphs does not give the possibility to express detailed task-dependent conditions to be satisfied, in order to have the arguments accepted.

Our research question breaks down into the following sub-questions:

– How to cast bipolar entailment graphs in the argumentation setting such that the semantics of the relations is maintained?
– How to define specific arguments' acceptance conditions such that information we consider as relevant in our task is extracted?

First, we answer the research questions by adopting *abstract dialectical frameworks* (ADF) [5,6], a generalization of Dung's abstract argumentation frameworks where different kinds of links among statements are represented. We cast bipolar entailment graphs in abstract dialectical frameworks where the links represent entailment and non entailment.

Second, considering positive (entailing) and negative (non entailing) links, and the weights assigned to such links by the TE system, we define and evaluate two acceptance conditions which allow us to extract in an automated way the set of arguments, i.e., text fragments, relevant for our text exploration task.

The goal of the proposed framework is to highlight the information that is relevant to explore (i.e. to understand, and in a certain sense, to summarize) humans interactions in natural language (e.g. in a debate, or in a reviewing service). Our proposal is a natural language based knowledge representation framework grounded on natural language constructs rather than on a formal pre-defined terminology. On the one side we provide an automated way to compute relevant information, and on the other side we apply abstract dialectical frameworks to a real application where texts are the primary source of knowledge.

In the remainder of the paper, Sect. 2 compares the proposed approach to the related work. Section 3 presents the TE framework. Section 4 introduces ADFs and the two acceptance conditions we define. Experimental setting is described in Sect. 5. Section 6 shows the whole pipeline over a real debate example. Conclusions end the paper.

# 2   Related Work

The term *entailment graph* is not new in the literature, and it has been firstly introduced by Berant et al. [4] as a structure to model entailment relations between propositional templates. The nodes of an entailment graph are propositional templates, i.e., a path in a dependency tree between two arguments of a common predicate [25]. In a dependency parse, such a path passes through the predicate; a variable must appear in at least one of the argument positions, and each sense of a polysemous predicate corresponds to a separate template (and a separate graph node): $X \xleftarrow{subj} treat\#1 \xrightarrow{obj} Y$ and $X \, subj \xleftarrow{subj} treat\#1 \xrightarrow{obj} nausea$ are propositional templates for the first sense of the predicate *treat*. An edge $(u, v)$ represents the fact that template $u$ entails template $v$. Berant and colleagues [4] assume a user interested in retrieving information about a target concept (e.g., *nausea*). The proposed approach automatically extracts from a corpus the set of propositions where *nausea* is an argument, and learns an entailment graph over propositional templates derived from the extracted propositions.

While Berant and colleagues [3,4] model the problem of learning entailment relations between predicates represented as propositional templates as a graph learning problem (to search for the best graph under a global transitivity constraint), we collect both entailment and non entailment relations returned by the system to use both of them during the computation of relevant information. In the context of the topic labeling task, Mehdad et al. [27] propose to build a multidirectional entailment graph over the phrases extracted for a given set of sentences (covering the same topic). Since many of such phrases include redundant information which are semantically equivalent but vary in lexical choices, they exploit the entailment graphs to discover if the information in one phrase is semantically equivalent, novel, or more/less informative with respect to the content of the other phrase.

Also the combination of argumentation theory and NLP is not new, and some existing works combine NLP and argumentation theory [1,10,12,16,28,36] with different purposes, ranging from policy making support up to recommendations on language patterns using indices, to automated arguments generation. However, only few of them [10,16,28] actually process the textual content of the arguments, but their goals, i.e., arguments generation [10], and arguments classification in texts [16,28] differ from ours.

Moreover, systems like Avicenna [29], Carneades [21], Araucaria [30] (based on argumentation schemes [35]), and ArguMed [34] use natural language arguments, but the text remains unanalyzed as users are requested to indicate the kind of relationship holding between two arguments. Finally, approaches like [17,22,24] show the added value of applying argumentation theory to understand on-line discussions and user opinions in decision support and business oriented websites. Again texts here are not the source of knowledge, and the linguistic content is not analyzed. All these approaches show the need to make the two communities communicate and jointly address such kind of open issues.

Up to our knowledge, the only work which tries to combine TE with argumentation theory is in [8]. The drawbacks of this work have been previously detailed. For sake of completeness, we have to mention that they [8] are aware about the first drawback we identified in their approach, i.e., the fact that the non entailment relation is mapped to the attack relation even if the meaning of the two is different, and they present a data-driven comparison of the meanings of entailment/support and non entailment/attack in [9]. However, the drawback still holds, and a more general framework is required to obtain a proper combination of TE and argumentation.

The added value of using argumentation theory in on-line discussions and user reviews to support decision making on business oriented websites has been shown by Gabriellini and Santini [18], while an interesting approach to support argumentative discussions on social networks, and more precisely on Twitter, has been explored by Gabriellini and Torroni [19,20]. We share with these approaches the adoption of argumentation theory to support intelligent interactions with other users or big amount of data.

Finally, in the last years, the argument mining research topic has become more and more relevant in the Artificial Intelligence and Natural Language Processing communities, as witnessed by the success of the 'Argument Mining' workshop[2]. An interesting approach that is worth mentioning in particular has been recently presented by Lippi and Torroni [26]. The authors propose a method that exploits structured parsing information to detect claims without resorting to contextual information. Even if the goal of the two approaches is different, they go in the same direction of developing supporting systems for users who interact with big amount of data and need to be guided to achieve an intelligent exploration experience.

# 3    Bipolar Entailment Graphs

This section introduces the Textual Entailment framework (Sect. 3.1), and its extension into bipolar entailment graphs (Sect. 3.2).

## 3.1    Textual Entailment

In the NLP field, the notion of Textual Entailment [13] refers to a directional relation between two textual fragments, termed *Text (T)* and *Hypothesis (H)*, respectively. The relation holds (i.e. $T \Rightarrow H$) whenever the truth of one text fragment follows from another text, as interpreted by a typical language user.

---

[2] https://www.cs.cornell.edu/home/cardie/naacl-2nd-arg-mining/.

The TE relation is directional, since the meaning of one expression may usually entail the other, while entailment in the other direction is much less certain. Consider the pairs in Examples 1, 2, and 3:

*Example 1.*
**T (id=3)**: People should be at liberty to treat their bodies how they want to. Indeed, people are allowed to eat and drink to their detriment and even death, so why shouldn't they be able to harm themselves with marijuana use? This is, of course, assuming that their use does not harm anyone else.
**H (id=1)**: Individuals should be free to use marijuana. If individuals want to harm themselves, they should be free to do so.

*Example 2 (Continued).*
**T (id=2)**: Even if marijuana's effects were isolated to the individual, there is room for the state to protect individuals from harming themselves.
**H (id=1)**: Individuals should be free to use marijuana. If individuals want to harm themselves, they should be free to do so.

*Example 3 (Continued).*
**T (id=4)**: Individuals should be at liberty to experience the punishment of a poor choice.
**H (id=2)**: Even if marijuana's effects were isolated to the individual, there is room for the state to protect individuals from harming themselves.

In Example 1, we can identify an *entailment* relation between T and H (i.e. the meaning of H can be derived from the meaning of T), in Example 2, T *contradicts* H, while in Example 3, even if the topic is the same, the truth of H cannot be verified on the bases of the information present in T (i.e. the relation is said to be *unknown*).[3] The notion of TE has been proposed as an applied framework to capture major semantic inference needs across applications in NLP (e.g. information extraction, text summarization, and reading comprehension systems) [13]. The task of recognizing TE is therefore carried out by automatic systems, mainly implemented using Machine Learning techniques (typically SVM), logical inference, cross-pair similarity measures between T and H, and word alignment.[4] While entailment in its logical definition pertains to the meaning of language expressions, the TE model does not represent meanings explicitly, avoiding any semantic interpretation into a meaning representation level. Instead, in this applied model inferences are performed directly over lexical-syntactic representations of the texts. TE allows to overcome the main limitations showed by formal approaches (where the inference task is carried out by logical theorem provers), i.e. *(i)* the computational costs of dealing with huge amounts of available but noisy data present in the Web; *(ii)* the fact that formal approaches address forms of deductive reasoning, exhibiting a too

---

[3] In the two-way classification task, contradiction and unknown relations are collapsed into a unique relation, i.e. *non entailment.*
[4] [13] provides an overview of the recent advances in TE.

high level of precision and strictness as compared to human judgments, that allow for uncertainties typical of inductive reasoning. But while methods for automated deduction assume that the arguments in input are already expressed in some formal representation (e.g. first order logic), addressing the inference task at a textual level opens different and new challenges from those encountered in formal deduction. Indeed, more emphasis is put on informal reasoning, lexical semantic knowledge, and variability of linguistic expressions.

### 3.2  From Pairs to Graphs

As defined in the previous section, TE is a directional relation between two textual fragments. However, in various real world scenarios, these pairs cannot be considered as independent. This means that they need to be collected together into a single graph. A new framework involving *entailment graphs* is therefore needed, where the semantic relations are not only identified between pairs of textual fragments, but such pairs are also part of a graph that provides an overall view of the statements' interactions, such that the influences of some statements on the others emerge. Therefore, we introduce the notion of *bipolar entailment graphs (BEG)*, where two kinds of edges are considered, i.e., entailment and non entailment, and nodes are the text fragments of TE pairs.

**Definition 1 (Bipolar Entailment Graph).** *A bipolar entailment graph is a tuple $BEG = \langle T, E, NE \rangle$ where*

- *$T$ is a set of text fragments;*
- *$E \subseteq T \times T$ is an entailment relation between text fragments;*
- *$NE \subseteq T \times T$ is a non entailment relation between text fragments.*

This opens new challenges for TE, that in the original definition considers the T-H pairs as "self-contained" (i.e., the meaning of H has to be derived from the meaning of T). On the contrary, in arguments extracted from human linguistic interactions a lot is left implicit (following Grice's conversational Maxim of Quantity), and anaphoric expressions should be solved to correctly assign semantic relations among arguments.

## 4  Text Exploration Through Argumentation

In this section, we first introduce abstract dialectical frameworks (Sect. 4.1), and then we describe which acceptability measures we choose for our text exploration task (Sect. 4.2).

### 4.1  Abstract Dialectical Frameworks

Abstract dialectical frameworks [6] have been introduced as a generalization of Dung-style abstract argumentation frameworks [14] where each node is associated with an acceptance condition. The slogan of abstract dialectical frameworks is: $ADF = dependency\ graphs + acceptance\ conditions$, meaning that, in contrast with Dung frameworks where links between nodes represent the type of relationship called *attack*, in this framework different dependencies can be represented in a flexible way.

An ADF is a directed graph whose nodes represent statements which can be accepted or not. The links between the nodes represent dependencies: the status (i.e., accepted, not accepted) of a node $s$ depends only on the status of its parents $par(s)$, i.e., those nodes connected to $s$ by a direct link. Each node $s$ is then associated to an *acceptance condition* $C_s$ which specifies the exact conditions under which argument $s$ is accepted. $C_s$ is a function assigning to each subset of $par(s)$ one of the values *in* or *out*, where *in* means that these arguments are accepted and *out* means that they are rejected. Roughly, if for $R \subseteq par(s)$ we have $C_s(R) = in$, this means that $s$ will be accepted if the nodes in $R$ are accepted and those in $par(s) \setminus R$ are rejected.

**Definition 2 (Abstract Dialectical Framework [6]).** *An abstract dialectical framework is a tuple $D = \langle S, L, C \rangle$ where*

- $S$ *is a set of statements (i.e., nodes);*
- $L \subseteq S \times S$ *is a set of links;*
- $C = \{C_s\}_{s \in S}$ *is a set of total functions $C_s : 2^{par(s)} \to \{in, out\}$, one for each statement $s$. $C_s$ is called the acceptance condition of $s$.*

For instance, Dung-style argumentation frameworks are associated to the ADF $D_{Dung} = \langle Args, att, C \rangle$ where the acceptance conditions for all nodes $s \in S$ is $C_s(R) = in$ if and only if $R = \emptyset$, and $C_s(R) = out$ otherwise. An example of an abstract dialectical framework from [6] is visualized in Fig. 1, where grey nodes are the accepted arguments, and acceptance conditions are expressed as propositional formulas over the nodes. For more details see [6].

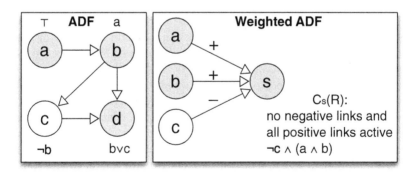

**Fig. 1.** Examples of ADF and weighted ADF together with the acceptance conditions defined for nodes.

[6] underline that ADF acceptance conditions can be defined also through *positive* and *negative* weights associated to links. In particular, they introduce weighted ADFs presenting their usefulness in the specific context of legal

argumentation, i.e., modeling five standards of proof. In this paper, we start from weighted ADFs presented in [6], and we adapt them to represent our bipolar entailment graphs. Note that weighted argumentation frameworks have been studied also by [15], where weights are used for handling inconsistencies, but there weights are not exploited to compute the acceptance or rejection of the arguments. The advantage of using ADFs to model bipolar entailment graphs, in contrast with the approach proposed in [8], is that the resulting "bipolar" argumentation graphs are not forced to interpret the negative weighted links as being attacks and therefore leading to a misconception about the meaning of the non entailment relation in TE.

### 4.2   Extracting Meaningful Information Using ADF

To explore texts searching for information which satisfies specific constraints and shows certain features, we adopt weighted abstract dialectical frameworks [6], and we define two acceptance conditions such that they allow us to select, starting from a bipolar entailment graph, only the information we are looking for. First, we define a general weighted ADF (to which we map $BEG$s) where an additional function is introduced to associate each link to a weight, similarly to what was proposed in [6].

**Definition 3 (Weighted Abstract Dialectical Frameworks).** *A weighted abstract dialectical framework is a tuple $D = \langle S, L, C, v \rangle$ where*

- *$S$ is a set of nodes;*
- *$L \subseteq S \times S$ is a set of links;*
- *$C = \{C_s\}_{s \in S}$ is a set of total functions $C_s : 2^{par(s)} \to \{in, out\}$, one for each statement $s$. $C_s$ is called the acceptance condition of $s$;*
- *$v : L \to W$ is a function associating weights to the links, where $W$ is a set of weights.*

Mapping a BEG into a weighted ADF, we can highlight two kinds of possible weights in bipolar entailment graphs: *(i)* qualitative weights, where we distinguish between *positive* vs. *negative* weights $W = \{+, -\}$, i.e., we consider the entailment links as associated to a positive weight and non entailment links as associated to a negative weight, and *(ii)* numerical weights, where we exploit the weights the TE system assigns to each link as its confidence, i.e., we consider a range $W \in [-1, 1]$ such that the more the link weight approaches $-1$, the more the system is confident it is a non entailment relation and the more the link weight approaches 1, the more the system is confident it is an entailment relation. Figure 1 shows an example of a weighted ADF, where $C_s$ is described.

Starting from the defined weighted ADFs, we have now to define the acceptance conditions we want to adopt to guide the selection of the nodes in the graph that we consider as relevant in our task. We consider two use cases for text exploration: *(a)* a huge online debate composed by several arguments, and we want to retrieve the arguments that are entailed by at least one accepted statement and no negative link is directed against them from accepted statements; and *(b)* a set of users' interactions about a service have to be explored in order to retrieve those statements which are highly entailed by other statements in the *BEG*, and not much non entailed by other statements (i.e., if the difference of their weights is above a certain threshold). These two domain independent acceptance conditions represent our *heuristics* to retrieve inside huge bipolar entailment graphs, the set of information satisfying the goal of our text exploration task.

The two acceptance conditions are formalized as follows:

1. $C_s(R) = in$ if and only if

$$\exists r \in R : v((r, s)) \in \{+\} \wedge \forall t \in R : v((t, s)) \notin \{-\} \tag{1}$$

2. $C_s(R) = in$ if and only if, given $r, t \in R$,

$$\max v_+((r, s)) - |\max v_-((t, s))| > k \tag{2}$$

where $k$ is a certain threshold.

The first acceptance condition models use case *(a)*: statement $s$ is accepted if and only if $R$ contains no node with a negative link towards $s$ and at least one node with a positive link towards $s$, i.e., no node not entailing $s$ and at least one node entailing $s$. The second acceptance condition models use case *(b)*: statement $s$ is accepted if and only if the difference between the maximal positive weight and the absolute value of the maximal negative weight is above a given threshold $k$. Concerning those nodes which have no incident links (i.e., $par(s) = \emptyset$), we apply the following acceptance condition: $C_s$ is $in$ (constant function). Note that we do not claim that these are the only possible acceptance conditions for identifying relevant information during text exploration in *BEGs*. We define such acceptance conditions because they provide us with the information satisfying our text exploration features. However, weighted ADFs applied to text exploration based on bipolar entailment graphs provide a flexible framework such that more complex acceptance conditions can be defined depending on the kind of information to be retrieved.

Brewka and Woltran [7] recently proposed GRAPPA, a semantical framework that allows to define Dung-style semantics for arbitrary labelled graphs, proposing acceptance functions based on multisets of labels. In this paper, we have not explored its adoption but this is left as future work. This framework could allow to simplify the definition of the acceptance functions thanks to the introduced pattern language, enhancing the automated evaluation of our framework. Defining new acceptance functions using such pattern language would ease the process, allowing to better fit the users' information need in the text exploration task.

## 5    Experimental Setting

This section evaluates the automated framework we propose to support text exploration. As a first step, we run a TE system to assign the entailment and the non entailment relations to the pairs of arguments. Then, a bipolar entailment graph is built, where the arguments are the nodes of the graph, and the automatically assigned relations correspond to the links of the graphs. Finally, we adopt the abstract dialectical frameworks to define acceptance conditions for the nodes of the bipolar entailment graph. The dataset of argument pairs on which we run the experiments is described in Sect. 5.1, while the framework evaluation is reported in Sect. 5.2.

## 5.1    Dataset

We experiment our framework on the Debatepedia dataset[5] (described in [8]). It is composed of 200 pairs, balanced between entailment and non entailment pairs, and split into a training set (100 pairs), and a test set (100 pairs). The pairs are extracted from a sample of Debatepedia[6] debates, an encyclopedia of pro and con arguments on critical issues (e.g. China one-child policy, vegetarianism, gay marriages). To the best of our knowledge, it is the only available dataset of T-H pairs that can be represented as bipolar entailment graphs.

Since [8] show on a learning curve that augmenting the number of training pairs actually improves the TE system performances on the test set, we decided to contribute to the extension of the Debatepedia data set manually annotating 60 more pairs (30 entailment and 30 non entailment pairs). We followed the methodology described in [8] for the annotation phase, and we added the newly created pairs to the original training set. We consider this enriched dataset of 260 pairs as the goldstandard in our experiments (where entailment/non entailment relations are correctly assigned), against which we will compare the TE system performances.

Starting from the pairs in the Debatepedia dataset, we then build a bipolar entailment graph for each of the topic in the dataset (12 topics in the training set and 10 topics in the test set, listed in [8]). The arguments are the nodes of the graph, and the relations among the arguments correspond to the links of the graphs.

To create the goldstandards to check the validity of the two proposed acceptance conditions, we separately applied both conditions on the bipolar entailment graphs built using manually annotated relations. In particular, for the second acceptance condition that consider the weights assigned on the links (see Sect. 4), we consider the max weight of 1 to be attributed to the entailment link (maximal confidence on the entailment relation assignment), and the max weight of −1 to be attributed to the non entailment link (maximal confidence on the non entailment relation assignment).

---

[5] The Recognizing Textual Entailment (RTE) data are not suitable for our goal, since the pairs are not interconnected (i.e. they cannot be transformed into argumentation graphs).

[6] http://idebate.org/.

We are aware that the dataset we used is smaller than the datasets provided in RTE challenges[7], but we consider it as a representative test set to prove the validity of our approach.

## 5.2   Evaluation

We carry out a two-step evaluation of our framework: first, we assess the TE system accuracy in correctly assigning the entailment and the non entailment relations to the pairs of arguments in the dataset. Then, we evaluate how much such accuracy impacts on ADF graphs, i.e. how much a wrong assignment of a relation to a pair of arguments is propagated in the ADF by the acceptance conditions.

**Table 1.** First step evaluation (results on Debatepedia test set, i.e. 100 pairs). Systems are trained on Debatepedia training set (160 pairs).

| EOP configuration | Accuracy | Recall | Precision | F-measure |
|---|---|---|---|---|
| BIUTEE | 0.71 | 0.94 | 0.66 | 0.78 |
| EditDistanceEDA | 0.58 | 0.61 | 0.59 | 0.59 |

To detect which kind of relation underlies each couple of arguments, we experiment the EXCITEMENT Open Platform (EOP)[8], that provides a generic architecture for a multilingual textual inference platform. We tested the three state-of-the-art entailment algorithms in the EOP (i.e., BIUTEE [32], TIE and EDITS [23]) on Debatepedia dataset, experimenting several different configurations, and adding knowledge resources.

The best results for the first evaluation step on Debatepedia are obtained with BIUTEE, adopting the configuration that exploits all available knowledge resources (e.g. WordNet, Wikipedia, FrameNet) (see Table 1). BIUTEE follows the transformation-based paradigm, which recognizes TE by converting the text into the hypothesis via a sequence of transformations. Such sequence is referred to as a *proof*, and is performed over the syntactic representation of the text (i.e. the text parse tree). A transformation modifies a given parse tree, resulting in a generation of a new parse tree, which can be further modified by subsequent transformations. The main type of transformations is the application of entailment-rules [2] (e.g. lexical rules, active/passive rules, coreference).

As baseline in this first experiment we use a token-based version of the Levenshtein distance algorithm, i.e. EditDistanceEDA in the EOP, as shown in Table 1. In this table, we do not report the results of the TIE system as it is not relevant with respect to the present evaluation, as we fixed EditDistanceEDA as our baseline and the best performing system for our task in the EOP is BIUTEE.

---

[7] http://bit.ly/RTE-challenge.
[8] http://hltfbk.github.io/Excitement-Open-Platform/.

The obtained results are in line with the average systems performances at RTE ($\sim$0.65 F-measure[9]).

As a second step of our evaluation, we consider the impact of the best TE configuration on the acceptability of the arguments, i.e. how much a wrong assignment of a relation to a pair of arguments affects the acceptability of the arguments in the ADF. We use the acceptance conditions we defined in Sect. 4 to identify the accepted arguments both on *(i)* the goldstandard entailment graphs of Debatepedia topics (see Sect. 5.1), and *(ii)* on the graphs generated using the relations and the weights assigned by BIUTEE on Debatepedia (since it is the system that obtained the best performances, see Table 1).

BIUTEE allows many types of transformations, by which an hypothesis can be proven from any text. Given a T-H pair, the system finds a proof which generates H from T, and estimates the proof validity [32]. Finding such a proof is a sequential process, conducted by a search algorithm. In each step of the proof construction the system examines all the possible transformations that can be applied, generates new trees by applying the selected transformations, and calculates their costs by constructing appropriate feature-vectors for them. Eventually, the search algorithm finds the (approximately) lowest cost proof. If the proof cost is below a threshold (automatically learned on the training set, for details see [31]), then the system concludes that T entails H. The inverse of this cost is normalized as a score between 0 (where T and H are completely different) and 1 (where T and H are identical), and returned as output. In other words, the score returned by the system indicates how likely it is that the obtained proof is valid, i.e., the transformations along the proof preserve entailment from the meaning of T.

In order to apply the second acceptance condition described in Sect. 4 using the scores returned by BIUTEE as the weights on the links between nodes, we need to have positive values (from 0 to 1) corresponding to the confidence of BIUTEE in assigning the entailment relation to the pair, and negative values (from 0 to –1) corresponding to the confidence of BIUTEE in assigning a non entailment relation to the pair. Since the scores that BIUTEE returns are normalized between 0 and 1, where the threshold learned on the Debatepedia training set is set to 0.5, we need to shift such scores on the scale demanded by such acceptance condition, setting the threshold to 0 and normalizing the scores produced by BIUTEE accordingly. In this new scale, *(i)* the more the system is confident that there is a non entailment relation between two arguments, the more its score (i.e. the link weight) approaches –1; *(ii)* the more the system is confident that there is an entailment relation, the more its score (i.e. the link weight) approaches 1; *(iii)* the more the system is uncertain about the assigned relation, the more the system score (i.e. the link weight) approaches 0 (both on the negative and on the positive scale).

Table 2 reports on the results of this second evaluation phase, where we evaluate the impact of BIUTEE on the arguments acceptability, adopting admissible

---

[9] The F-measure is a measure of accuracy. It considers both the precision and the recall of the test to compute the score.

**Table 2.** Results of the second evaluation (Debatepedia test set). Precision (avg): arguments accepted by the automatic system and by the goldstandard with respect to an entailment graph; recall (avg): arguments accepted in the goldstandard and retrieved as accepted by the automatic system.

| Acc. condition | # graphs | avg # links per graph | Precision | Recall | F-measure |
| --- | --- | --- | --- | --- | --- |
| First | 10 | 9.1 | 0.89 | 0.98 | 0.93 |
| Second | 10 | 9.1 | 0.894 | 0.98 | 0.95 |

based semantics, with respect to a goldstandard where the relations on the links have been assigned by human annotators (Sect. 5.1). In general, the TE system mistakes in relation assignment propagate in the argumentation framework, but results are still satisfying.

We are aware that in Debatepedia entailment graphs the error propagation is also limited by *(i)* their size (see Table 2, column *avg # links per graph*); and *(ii)* the heuristic we applied in computing the arguments acceptability, according to which the arguments that have no negative incident links are accepted, augmenting the number of the accepted nodes in the graphs. Concerning time complexity, the weighted ADF module takes ∼1 s to analyze a weighted ADF of 100 pairs, returning the relevant arguments with respect to the selected acceptance condition.[10] The results reported in Table 2 cannot be strictly compared with the results shown in [8], since the underlying role of the entailment relation in the selection of the accepted argument is different. In this paper, we do not address a comparison with the existing ADF software, such as DIAMOND and QADF[11], as the purpose of the present paper is not to evaluate the performances in computing ADFs, but the goodness of our system in retrieving natural language arguments for topics exploration. However, we plan as future research to adopt such systems for computing the acceptability of the arguments, and to evaluate their performances with respect to our specific task. Note that this evaluation is not intended to evaluate the performances of argumentation systems to compute the acceptability of the arguments[12], but it is meant to show the accuracy of the combined system (i.e., TE plus ADFs) in detecting the arguments satisfying the specified features, so that it can be exploited for a text exploration task.

Note that the acceptance conditions could be modified to consider the fact that the relations assigned to a pair by the system with a low confidence (around 0) are more uncertain than those assigned with a higher confidence. More specifically, for future work, we will consider to associate to the confidence values (from −1 to 1) a probability distribution, to improve the system ability in assigning the semantic relation to the pair, depending on the presence of the entailment relation.

---

[10] Complexity results for ADFs have been studied by [6].

[11] http://www.dbai.tuwien.ac.at/research/project/adf/.

[12] We refer the interested reader to the results of the First International Competition on Computational Models of Argumentation [33].

In general, we consider the results we obtained experimenting our framework on the Debatepedia dataset as promising, fostering further research in this direction. An analysis of arguments returned by the acceptability conditions has been addressed, and results show that the selected arguments contain relevant information for the topics exploration.

## 6    Examples

In this section, we show discuss on two real examples how the pipeline we described actually works. First, let us consider the $BEG$ whose text fragments are presented in Sect. 3. In Fig. 2, the resulting $ADF_1$ shows the weighted ADF, together with the nodes selected through the first acceptance condition. Note that statement "Individuals should be free to use marijuana. If individuals want to harm themselves, they should be free to do so" is selected as it has an incident negative link but coming from a rejected argument, and it is entailed by "People should be at liberty to treat their bodies how they want to. Indeed, people are allowed to eat and drink to their detriment and even death, so why shouldn't they be able to harm themselves with marijuana use? [...]".

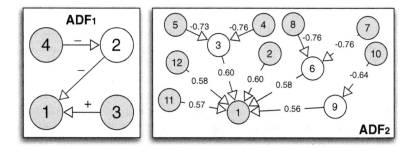

**Fig. 2.** Two examples from our dataset ($ADF_1$ - positive/negative weights, $ADF_2$ - numerical weights).

Let us consider now the debate about "Gas Vehicles" from our dataset. The arguments and their relations are as follows:

Pair id="152" topic="Gasvehicles" entailment="YES"

**2 (T):** *As the nation looks for ways to reduce air pollution from vehicles, natural gas is the ideal environmental alternative to gasoline. For starters, natural gas is clean. (It's the same clean-burning natural gas that you use to cook or heat your home). Vehicles fueled with natural gas can dramatically reduce emissions of carbon monoxide and reactive hydrocarbons-which interact with sunlight to produce ozone, the principal com- ponent of smog. Natural Gas Vehicles also reduce emissions of carbon dioxide, the principal "greenhouse" gas.*
**1 (H):** *Natural gas vehicles help cut emissions and fight global warming.*

Pair id="153" topic="Gasvehicles" entailment="YES"

**3 (T):** *Compared with their petroleum-powered counterparts, natural gas vehicles greatly reduce greenhouse gas emissions. The exhaust created from natural gas contains 70 percent less carbon monoxide, nearly 90 percent less nitrogen oxide and non-methane organic gas, and virtually no particulate matter.*

**1 (H)**: *Natural gas vehicles help cut emissions and fight global warming.*

Pair id="154" topic="Gasvehicles" entailment="NO"

**4 (T)**: *Natural gas hardly reduces emissions compared to petroleum. When natural gas replaces gasoline, greenhouse gases are reduced by just 20 to 30%. When natural gas is used instead of diesel in trucks, greenhouse gases are reduced just 10 to 20%. If diesel is almost comparable, then it makes more sense to fund that as a stop gap as that infrastructure is already in place.*

**3 (H)**: *Compared with their petroleum-powered counterparts, natural gas vehicles greatly reduce greenhouse gas emissions. The exhaust created from natural gas contains 70 percent less carbon monoxide, nearly 90 percent less nitrogen oxide and non-methane organic gas, and virtually no particulate matter.*

Pair id="155" topic="Gasvehicles" entailment="YES"

**5 (T)**: *Natural gas is much cleaner-burning than gasoline. According to the Environmental Protection Agency, natural gas can reduce carbon-monoxide emissions by 90 to 97 percent and nitrogen-oxide emissions by 35 to 60 percent when compared with gasoline. Natural gas can also potentially reduce non-methane hydrocarbon emissions by 50 to 75 percent, while producing fewer carcinogenic pollutants and little or no particulate matter.*

**3 (H)**: *Compared with their petroleum-powered counterparts, natural gas vehicles greatly reduce greenhouse gas emissions. The exhaust created from natural gas contains 70 percent less carbon monoxide, nearly 90 percent less nitrogen oxide and non-methane organic gas, and virtually no particulate matter.*

Pair id="156" topic="Gasvehicles" entailment="NO"

**6 (T)**: *On the surface, natural gas cars seem alright, but the topic becomes a bit different when these cars are competing against "zero emission" alternatives such as electric cars that are powered utilizing a solar grid.*

**1 (H)**: *Natural gas vehicles help cut emissions and fight global warming.*

Pair id="157" topic="Gasvehicles" entailment="YES"

**7 (T)**: *Natural gas vehicles run on natural gas, a fossil fuel, so emit significant amounts of greenhouse gases into the atmosphere, albeit smaller amounts than gasoline-fueled cars (roughly 30% less). If our goal is to aggressively fight global warming, does it make sense to invest in slightly cleaner technologies, or fully 0-emission ones? If we are serious about combating global warming, we should be focusing our energies and investments solely on 0-emission electric vehicles.*

**6 (H)**: *On the surface, natural gas cars seem alright, but the topic becomes a bit different when these cars are competing against "zero emission" alternatives such as electric cars that are powered utilizing a solar grid.*

Pair id="158" topic="Gasvehicles" entailment="NO"

**8 (T)**: *Natural gas is the cleanest transportation fuel available today. The important conclusion is that, if we want to immediately begin the process of significantly reducing greenhouse gas emissions, natural gas can help now. Other alternatives cannot be pursued as quickly.*

**6 (H)**: *On the surface, natural gas cars seem alright, but the topic becomes a bit different when these cars are competing against "zero emission" alternatives such as electric cars that are powered utilizing a solar grid.*

Pair id="159" topic="Gasvehicles" entailment="YES"

**9 (T)**: *Gasoline vehicles can be converted to run on natural gas. This means that heavy-polluting vehicles can be transformed into much lower-emission vehicles. This is key, as the millions of gasoline vehicles on the road currently cannot be immediately removed from the road.*

**1 (H)**: *Natural gas vehicles help cut emissions and fight global warming.*

Pair id="160" topic="Gasvehicles" entailment="NO"

**10 (T)**: *Gasoline/petrol vehicles converted to run on natural gas suffer because of the low compression ratio of their engines, resulting in a cropping of delivered power while running on natural gas (10%-15%). This inefficiency is costly economically and in terms of global warming.*

**9 (H)**: *Gasoline vehicles can be converted to run on natural gas. This means that heavy-polluting vehicles can be transformed into much lower-emission vehicles. This is key, as the millions of gasoline vehicles on the road currently cannot be immediately removed from the road.*

Pair id="161" topic="Gasvehicles" entailment="NO"

**11 (T)**: *Natural gas will simply relieve demand pressures on coal and petroleum and, subsequently, decrease prices. This will only make it easier for people to buy and consume oil and coal. Natural gas will not, therefore, replace coal and petroleum. It will only add to the absolute amount of fossil fuels we are burning, and greenhouse gases we are emitting.*

**1 (H):** *Natural gas vehicles help cut emissions and fight global warming.*

Pair id="162" topic="Gasvehicles" entailment="NO"

**12 (T):** *Methane is a much worse greenhouse gas than C02. Methane is very prominent within "natural gas". This is of concern because the drilling and transportation of natural gas will inevitably lead to leaks and large-scale "spills" that will release this highly harmful gas into the atmosphere and contribute substantially to global warming. These risks should not be taken.*
**1 (H):** *Natural gas vehicles help cut emissions and fight global warming.*

In Fig. 2, $ADF_2$ shows the weighted ADF we obtain for this debate, where the links are weighted with the confidence the TE system associates to the assigned relations. In this case, we first assign to the arguments the acceptability degree computed following the formula of the second acceptance condition, and if the computed value is above the threshold the argument is selected, i.e., it is evaluated as *in*, otherwise it is discarded. Note that the resulting selected arguments (in grey) satisfy the second heuristics we proposed, and returns a coherent set of arguments with respect to the text exploration task.

## 7   Conclusions

The text exploration task aims at retrieving from natural language texts meaningful information with respect to the user needs. In this paper, we propose to combine natural language processing techniques, namely the *textual entailment* framework, with argumentation-based reasoning ones, namely *abstract dialectical frameworks*, to address this challenging task. We introduce the notion of *bipolar entailment graph* in order to cast the information returned by the TE framework into a bipolar graph, where both entailment and non entailment edges are represented. Then, we exploit ADFs to represent in a formal way the goal of the text exploration task, i.e., to retrieve all those arguments that are more supported than attacked. We propose two heuristics for text exploration, and we show the feasibility of the proposed approach on a dataset of online debate interactions. Concrete examples from the dataset are presented and discussed. The evaluation shows the feasibility of the proposed approach and encourage further research in this direction. Both the enriched Debatepedia dataset (260 pairs), and the generated ADF are available for research purposes.[13]

As for future work, we will test further acceptance conditions to suit different information needs from the users. Moreover, we are currently studying how to integrate sentiment analysis techniques in our combined framework: the idea is that the polarity associated to the arguments can be used to define more insightful acceptance conditions. In this way, the text exploration task will take into account the polarity of the arguments and the relations among them.

## References

1. Amgoud, L., Prade, H.: Can AI models capture natural language argumentation? IJCINI **6**(3), 19–32 (2012)

---

[13] http://bit.ly/DebatepediaExtended.

2. Bar-Haim, R., Dagan, I., Greental, I., Shnarch, E.: Semantic inference at the lexical-syntactic level. In: AAAI, pp. 871–876 (2007)
3. Berant, J., Dagan, I., Adler, M., Goldberger, J.: Efficient tree-based approximation for entailment graph learning. In: ACL, vol. 1, pp. 117–125 (2012)
4. Berant, J., Dagan, I., Goldberger, J.: Global learning of focused entailment graphs. In: ACL, pp. 1220–1229 (2010)
5. Brewka, G., Strass, H., Ellmauthaler, S., Wallner, J.P., Woltran, S.: Abstract dialectical frameworks revisited. In: IJCAI (2013)
6. Brewka, G., Woltran, S.: Abstract dialectical frameworks. In: KR (2010)
7. Brewka, G., Woltran, S.: GRAPPA: a semantical framework for graph-based argument processing. In: Schaub, T., Friedrich, G., O'Sullivan, B. (eds.) ECAI 2014-21st European Conference on Artificial Intelligence, 18–22 August 2014, Prague, Czech Republic - Including Prestigious Applications of Intelligent Systems (PAIS 2014). Frontiers in Artificial Intelligence and Applications, vol. 263, pp. 153–158. IOS Press, August 2014. http://dx.doi.org/10.3233/978-1-61499-419-0-153
8. Cabrio, E., Villata, S.: Natural language arguments: a combined approach. In: ECAI, pp. 205–210 (2012)
9. Cabrio, E., Villata, S.: A natural language bipolar argumentation approach to support users in online debate interactions. Argument Comput. **4**(3), 209–230 (2013)
10. Carenini, G., Moore, J.D.: Generating and evaluating evaluative arguments. Artif. Intell. **170**(11), 925–952 (2006)
11. Cayrol, C., Lagasquie-Schiex, M.C.: Bipolarity in argumentation graphs: towards a better understanding. Int. J. Approx. Reason. **54**(7), 876–899 (2013)
12. Chesñevar, C.I., Maguitman, A.: An argumentative approach to assessing natural language usage based on the web corpus. In: ECAI, pp. 581–585 (2004)
13. Dagan, I., Dolan, B., Magnini, B., Roth, D.: Recognizing textual entailment: rational, evaluation and approaches. Nat. Lang. Eng. (JNLE) **15**(4), 1–17 (2009)
14. Dung, P.: On the acceptability of arguments and its fundamental role in non-monotonic reasoning, logic programming and n-person games. Artif. Intell. **77**(2), 321–358 (1995)
15. Dunne, P.E., Hunter, A., McBurney, P., Parsons, S., Wooldridge, M.: Weighted argument systems: basic definitions, algorithms, and complexity results. Artif. Intell. **175**(2), 457–486 (2011)
16. Feng, V.W., Hirst, G.: Classifying arguments by scheme. In: ACL, pp. 987–996 (2011)
17. Gabbriellini, S., Torroni, P.: NetArg: an agent-based social simulator with argumentative agents. In: AAMAS, pp. 1365–1366 (2013)
18. Gabbriellini, S., Santini, F.: A micro study on the evolution of arguments in amazon.com's reviews. In: Chen, Q., Torroni, P., Villata, S., Hsu, J., Omicini, A. (eds.) PRIMA 2015. LNCS (LNAI), vol. 9387, pp. 284–300. Springer, Heidelberg (2015). doi:10.1007/978-3-319-25524-8_18
19. Gabbriellini, S., Torroni, P.: Large scale agreements via microdebates. In: Ossowski, S., Toni, F., Vouros, G.A. (eds.) Proceedings of the First International Conference on Agreement Technologies, AT 2012, Dubrovnik, Croatia, 15–16 October 2012. CEUR Workshop Proceedings, vol. 918, pp. 366–377. CEUR-WS.org (2012). http://ceur-ws.org/Vol-918/111110366.pdf
20. Gabbriellini, S., Torroni, P.: Arguments in social networks. In: Gini, M.L., Shehory, O., Ito, T., Jonker, C.M. (eds.) International conference on Autonomous Agents and Multi-agent Systems, AAMAS 2013, Saint Paul, MN, USA, 6–10 May 2013, pp. 1119–1120. IFAAMAS (2013). http://dl.acm.org/citation.cfm?id=2485100

21. Gordon, T., Prakken, H., Walton, D.: The carneades model of argument and burden of proof. Artif. Intell. **171**(10–15), 875–896 (2007)
22. Heras, S., Atkinson, K., Botti, V.J., Grasso, F., Julián, V., McBurney, P.: Research opportunities for argumentation in social networks. Artif. Intell. Rev. **39**(1), 39–62 (2013)
23. Kouylekov, M., Negri, M.: An open-source package for recognizing textual entailment. In: ACL (System Demonstrations), pp. 42–47 (2010)
24. Leite, J., Martins, J.: Social abstract argumentation. In: IJCAI, pp. 2287–2292 (2011)
25. Lin, D., Pantel, P.: Discovery of inference rules for question answering. Nat. Lang. Eng. **7**, 343–360 (2001)
26. Lippi, M., Torroni, P.: Context-independent claim detection for argument mining. In: Yang, Q., Wooldridge, M. (eds.) Proceedings of the Twenty-Fourth International Joint Conference on Artificial Intelligence, IJCAI 2015, Buenos Aires, Argentina, 25–31 July, pp. 185–191. AAAI Press (2015). http://ijcai.org/papers15/Abstracts/IJCAI15-033.html
27. Mehdad, Y., Carenini, G., Ng, R.T., Joty, S.R.: Towards topic labeling with phrase entailment and aggregation. In: HLT-NAACL, pp. 179–189 (2013)
28. Moens, M.F., Boiy, E., Palau, R.M., Reed, C.: Automatic detection of arguments in legal texts. In: ICAIL, pp. 225–230 (2007)
29. Rahwan, I., Banihashemi, B., Reed, C., Walton, D., Abdallah, S.: Representing and classifying arguments on the semantic web. Knowl. Eng. Rev. **26**(4), 487–511 (2011)
30. Reed, C., Rowe, G.: Araucaria: software for argument analysis, diagramming and representation. Int. J. Artif. Intell. Tools **13**(4), 961–980 (2004)
31. Stern, A., Dagan, I.: A confidence model for syntactically-motivated entailment proofs. In: RANLP, pp. 455–462 (2011)
32. Stern, A., Dagan, I.: Biutee: a modular open-source system for recognizing textual entailment. In: ACL (Demo), pp. 73–78 (2012)
33. Thimm, M., Villata, S.: System descriptions of the first international competition on computational models of argumentation (ICCMA 2015). CoRR abs/1510.05373 (2015). http://arxiv.org/abs/1510.05373
34. Verheij, B.: Argumed - a template-based argument mediation system for lawyers and legal knowledge based systems. In: JURIX, pp. 113–130 (1998)
35. Walton, D., Reed, C., Macagno, F.: Argumentation Schemes. Cambridge University Press, Cambridge (2008)
36. Wyner, A., van Engers, T.: A framework for enriched, controlled on-line discussion forums for e-government policy-making. In: eGov (2010)

# Instance Selection and Outlier Generation
# to Improve the Cascade Classifier Precision

Judith Neugebauer[(✉)], Oliver Kramer, and Michael Sonnenschein

Department of Computing Science, Carl von Ossietzky University Oldenburg,
Oldenburg, Germany
{judith.neugebauer,oliver.kramer,michael.sonnenschein}@uni-oldenburg.de

**Abstract.** Classification of high-dimensional time series with imbalanced classes is a challenging task. For such classification tasks, the cascade classifier has been proposed. The cascade classifier tackles high-dimensionality and imbalance by splitting the classification task into several low-dimensional classification tasks and aggregating the intermediate results. Therefore the high-dimensional data set is projected onto low-dimensional subsets. But these subsets can employ unfavorable and not representative data distributions, that hamper classifiction again. Data preprocessing can overcome these problems. Small improvements in the low-dimensional data subsets of the cascade classifier lead to an improvement of the aggregated overall results. We present two data preprocessing methods, instance selection and outlier generation. Both methods are based on point distances in low-dimensional space. The instance selection method selects representative feasible examples and the outlier generation method generates artificial infeasible examples near the class boundary. In an experimental study, we analyse the precision improvement of the cascade classifier due to the presented data preprocessing methods for power production time series of a micro Combined Heat and Power plant and an artificial and complex data set. The precision increase is due to an increased selectivity of the learned decision boundaries. This paper is an extended version of [19], where we have proposed the two data preprocessing methods. In this paper we extend the analysis of both algorithms by a parameter sensitivity analysis of the distance parameters from the preprocessing methods. Both distance parameters depend on each other and have to be chosen carefully. We study the influence of these distance parameters on the classification precision of the cascade model and derive parameter fitting rules for the $\mu$CHP data set. The experiments yield a region of optimal parameter value combinations leading to a high classification precision.

**Keywords:** Time series classification · High-dimensional classification · Imbalanced learning · Data preprocessing

# 1  Introduction

Classification of high-dimensional data sets with imbalanced or even severely imbalanced classes is influenced by the curse of dimensionality. This is also true

© Springer International Publishing AG 2017
J. van den Herik and J. Filipe (Eds.): ICAART 2016, LNAI 10162, pp. 151–170, 2017.
DOI: 10.1007/978-3-319-53354-4_9

for time series classification tasks, where the ordering of the features (time steps) is important, [1]. Such tasks can be e.g., energy time series, where neighboring time steps are correlated. For these high dimensional time series classification tasks with imbalanced classes we have proposed the cascade classification model [18]. This model employs a cascade of classifiers based on features of overlapping time series steps. Therefore the high-dimensional feasible time series are projected on all neighboring pairs of time steps. In the low-dimensional space of the data subsets, the curse of dimensionality is no longer a problem.

Classification precision depends strongly on the distribution of the underlying data set, [16]. Therefore, an improvement of the data distribution could improve classification precision. Time series classification tasks with a cascade classifier have mainly two reason for unfavorable data distributions. Beside the original often not homogeneous distribution of the time series in feature space, the projection of feasible time series leads to an inhomogeneous distribution in low-dimensional space. A selection of more homogeneously distributed feasible examples (instances) would lead to an improvement in classification precision for a constant number of training examples or decrease the number of training examples, that are necessary to achieve a certain classification precision. In [19] we have proposed a resampling algorithm for feasible low-dimensional examples. The algorithm is based on distances between nearest neighbors. If the distance is greater than a certain threshold, the respective example is part of the new more homogeneous data set.

Additionally, infeasible examples can further improve the classification precision by increasing the selectivity of the decision boundaries, [27]. If there are enough infeasible examples, binary classification can be applied and yield better results than one-class classification, see [3]. But even if there are infeasible examples available in high-dimensional space, they can not be used for training of the low-dimensional classifiers. Energy time series e.g., are only feasible, if all time steps are feasible. Due to this property infeasible power production time series projected to low-dimensional space can be located in the region of feasible ones. Since projection of high-dimensional infeasible examples does not work, we have proposed a sampling procedure for artificial infeasible examples for the low-dimensional data subsets in [19]. Sampling of artificial infeasible examples is based on minimal distances to the nearest feasible neighbor. The infeasible examples are generated near the class boundary to improve the selectivity of the classifiers.

This paper is an extended version of [19]. The experiments in the original paper revealed that both distance parameters in the preprocessing methods have to be chosen carefully. Therefore we analyze additionally the combined effect of the distance parameters on the cascade classifier precision in this paper. We conduct the sensitivity analysis exemplarily for the combined heat and power plant power output data set and derive parameter fitting rules for the preprocessing methods.

This paper is structured as follows. In Sect. 2, we provide an overview on related work, instance selection, generation of artificial infeasible examples (outliers) and sensitivity analysis. In Sect. 3 we describe the cascade classification approach and in Sect. 4 we introduce our data preprocessing methods to improve the cascade classifier. In Sect. 5, we compare the classification precision of the cascade approach with and without data preprocessing in an experimental study. This study is conducted on simulated micro combined heat and power plant ($\mu$CHP) data and an artificial complex data set. A sensitivity analysis of the distance parameters from the data preprocessing methods is presented in Sect. 6. In Sect. 7, we summarize and draw conclusions.

## 2    Related Work

In classification tasks, a lot of problems can arise due to not optimally distributed data, like not representative data samples or inhomogeneously distributed samples.

For the cascade classifier, [18], the projection of the feasible examples from high to low-dimensional space leads to additional inhomogeneity in the distribution of feasible examples. Unfavorable data distributions hamper classification, [16]. But data preprocessing methods that select representative examples from the data set and maintain the integrity of the original data set while reducing the data set can help to overcome the classification problems. Depending on the data distribution and the application several instance selection (also called record reduction/numerosity reduction/prototype selection) approaches have been developed. Beside data compression and classification precision improvement instance selection also works as noise filter and prototype selector, [4,24,25]. In the last years, several instance selection approaches have been proposed and an overview can be found e.g., in [9,13,17]. Based on these algorithms advanced instance selection algorithms e.g. based on ensembles, [4], genetic algorithms, [24] or instance selection for time series classification with hubs, [23] were developed. But all these instance selection approaches have more or less high computational complexity, because they are developed for d-dimensional data sets, while the cascade classifier has several similar structured data subsets in low-dimensional space. Therefore, we propose a simple and fast instance selection method for low-dimensional space.

As far as infeasible examples (outliers, counter examples) can improve (one-class) classification, [27], algorithms to sample infeasible examples have been proposed. One such algorithm generates counter examples around the feasible class based on points near the class boundary, [2]. Another algorithm presented in [22] can sample outliers from a hyperbox or a hypersphere, that cover the target object (feasible class). The artificial infeasible examples of these algorithms comprise either high computational complexity or contain some feasible examples. But the cascade classifier requires a fast and simple sampling approach for all low-dimensional data subsets, where the generated infeasible examples are located in the region of the infeasible class. Thus we propose an artificial outlier generation method for the data subsets of the cascade classifier.

Instance selection and outlier generation are applied to increase classification precision of the cascade classification model. The magnitude of precision increase depends on the one hand on the application and on the other hand on the parametrization of the data preprocessing methods.

This influence of the preprocessing method parametrization on the classification precision can be analyzed with a sensitivity analysis. Sensitivity analysis (SA), also known as elastic theory, response surface methodology or design of experiment, examines the response of model output parameters to input parameter variations. For the sensitivity analysis of mathematical and statistical models several methodes have been proposed see e.g., [5, 8, 10, 15, 26]. Sensitivity analysis is e.g., applied to data mining models in [7, 8] to analyze the black box behaviour of data mining models and to increase their interpretability. Several sensitivity analysis methods have been proposed in literature for local, global and screen methods, see [12]. Local methods are used to study the influence of one parameter on the output, while all other parameters are kept constant. Global methods are used to evaluate the influence of one parameter by varying all other parameters as well. Screen methods are used for complex tasks, where global methods are computationally too expensive.

Concerning the influence of data preprocessing parameters on the cascade model precision, only some parameters are of interest and therefore local methods are appropriate. The simplest approach is the one-at-a-time method (OAT), [10] where one parameter is varied within a given parameter range, while all other parameters are kept constant. The influence of the input parameters on the model output can be determined qualitatively e.g., with scatter plots or quantitatively e.g., with correlation coefficients or regression analysis, see [8, 10].

## 3   Cascade of Overlapping Feature Classifiers

In this section, we introduce the cascade approach for time series classification [18]. As the classification of the high-dimensional time series is difficult, a step-wise classifier has been proposed. The cascade classification model is developed for high-dimensional binary time series classification tasks with (severely) imbalanced classes. The small interesting class is surrounded by the other class. Both classes fill together a hypervolume, e.g. a hypercube. Furthermore the cascade classifier requires data sets with clearly separable classes, where the small interesting class has a strong correlation between neighboring features (time steps). The low-dimensional data subsets of the small class should preferably employ only one concept (cluster) and a shape, that can be easily learned.

The model consists of a cascade of classifiers, each based on two neighboring time series steps (features) with a feature overlap between the classifiers. The cascade approach works as follows. Let $(\mathbf{x}_1, y_1), (\mathbf{x}_2, y_2), \ldots, (\mathbf{x}_N, y_N)$ be a training set of $N$ time series $\mathbf{x}_i = (x_i^1, x_i^2, \ldots, x_i^d)^T \in \mathbb{R}^d$ of $d$ time steps and $y_i \in \{+1, -1\}$ the information about their feasibility. For each 2-dimensional training set

$$((x_1^j, x_1^{j+1}), y_1), \ldots, ((x_N^j, x_N^{j+1}), y_N) \tag{1}$$

a classifier is trained. All $d - 1$ classification tasks can be solved with arbitrary baseline classifiers, depending on the given data. Single classifiers employ similarly structured data spaces and thus less effort is needed for parameter tuning. Most of the times only feasible low-dimensional examples are available and in this case baseline classifiers from one-class classification are suitable. The predictions $f_1, \ldots, f_{d-1}$ of all $d-1$ classifiers are aggregated to a final result

$$F(\mathbf{x}) = \begin{cases} +1 & \text{if } f_i \neq -1 \ \forall i = 1, \ldots, d-1 \\ -1 & \text{else} \end{cases} \qquad (2)$$

for a time series $\mathbf{x}$. A new time series $\mathbf{x}$ is feasible, only if all classifiers in the cascade predict each time step as feasible The cascade classification approach can be modified and extended, e.g., concerning the length of the time series intervals, respectively the dimensionality of the low-dimensional data subsets.

## 4    Data Preprocessing Methods

In this section the two data preprocessing methods for the cascade classification model are presented. Both methods operate on the low dimensional training subsets. The low-dimensional subsets fulfill the cascade model requirements. Both classes are clearly separable. The low-dimensional subsets incorporate similar structures in feature space and employ values in the same ranges for all time steps (features). For convenience all features are scaled, preferably to values between 0 and 1. Scaling of the features allows the use of the same parametrization for the data preprocessing methods for all low-dimensional subsets of the cascade classifier.

In the following we present two data preprocessing methods, an instance selection algorithm and an outlier generation algorithm for 2-dimensional training subsets. But just like the dimensionality of the low-dimensional subsets of the cascade approach could be changed, the proposed data preprocessing methods could be also applied to data subsets of other dimensionality.

### 4.1    Selection of Feasible Examples

Selection of feasible examples is an instance selection method for the low-dimensional feasible training subsets of the cascade classifier. The goal is to achieve more representative training examples by homogenizing the point density of the training subsets, see Fig. 1.

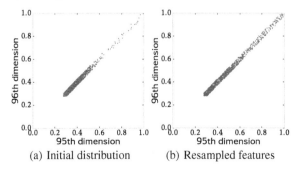

(a) Initial distribution     (b) Resampled features

**Fig. 1.** 1000 examples of the $95th$ and $96th$ dimensions of the feasible class of the $\mu$CHP data set (initial and resampled).

The example figures for selection of feasible examples show an increase in the point density in the upper right corner and a decrease in the point density in the lower left corner, see Fig. 1(b) in comparison to the original distribution shown in Fig. 1(a). Homogenization is achieved by selecting feasible examples for the training subsets based on the distance to the nearest feasible neighbors. Therefore a large set of feasible examples is needed, from which representative examples can be chosen. We assume that the inhomogeneous distribution of the training examples and their rarity in some regions is due to relative rarity. Relative rarity means examples are observed (sampled) less frequently than others, see e.g., [11]. But the rare examples constitute a certain percentage of a data set and an increase of the number of examples in the data set increases the absolute number of rare examples. If the rarity would be an absolute rarity, the absolute number of rare examples could not be increased with an increase of examples in the data set, see e.g., [11]. For this reason selection of feasible examples can only increase homogeneity of training examples, if rarity is relative. Based on the data properties resulting from the cascade classifier and the above described requirements, selection of $sn$ feasible examples works as follows for each low-dimensional training subset, see Algorithm 1.

---

**Algorithm 1.** Selection of feasible examples.

---
**Require:** 2-dimensional data set $\mathbf{X}$ with $n$ feasible examples
1: choose $t$ start examples $S$ from $\mathbf{X}$
2: **repeat**
3:     choose $t$ new examples $E$ from $\mathbf{X}$
4:     calculate euclidean distance $\delta$ of the examples in $E$ to their nearest neighbors in $S$
5:     **if** $\delta \geq \epsilon$ **then**
6:         append respective examples to $S$
7:     **end if**
8: **until** all $n$ examples are processed
9: shuffle $S$

---

$t$ feasible examples are chosen from the given data set $X$. These $t$ examples are the first examples of the homogenized training set $S$. Then $t$ new examples (set $E$) are taken and the distance between them and their nearest neighbors in $S$ is computed. An example from $E$ is added to the set $S$ if the distance $\delta$ to its nearest neighbor in $S$ is larger than or equals a certain distance $\epsilon$. This procedure is repeated until all examples in $X$ are processed. The algorithm parameters $t$ and $\epsilon$ depend on each other and the data set. The number of examples used for each comparison iteration is $t \geq 1$. The upper bound for the value of $t$ depends on the number of selected feasible examples $sn$ in $S$ and should be about $(t < sn/3)$. The smaller $\epsilon$ the larger can be $t$. An appropriate value for $\epsilon$ has to be chosen in pre-tests in such a way, that the examples in set $S$ are more or less homogeneously distributed for all low-dimensional training sets of the cascade classifier. Furthermore the number of selected feasible examples $sn$ in $S$ should be not much larger than the desired number of training and probably also validation examples. These conditions guarantee a good data representation of the feasible class, because nearly all $sn$ examples are used to train (and validate) the classifier. If the data sets are scaled to values between 0 and 1, $\epsilon$ values from the interval $[0.0005, 0.005]$ can be tried as initial values.

Training examples for the cascade classifier are taken from the respective set $S$ for each training subset and validation examples can be also taken from the homogenized set $S$ or from the remaining feasible examples, that do not belong to $S$.

## 4.2    Sampling of Infeasible Examples Near the Class Boundaries

Sampling of infeasible examples near the class boundary is an outlier generation algorithm for low-dimensional space. The aim of this algorithm is the generation of low-dimensional infeasible examples near the true class boundary as additional training and or validation examples, see Fig. 2.

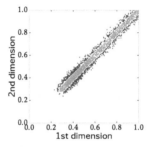

**Fig. 2.** Resampled examples of the $1st$ and $2nd$ dimension of the feasible class of the $\mu$CHP data set with artificial infeasible examples. The feasible class shown as gray points is surrounded by artificial infeasible examples (blue points). (Color figure online)

Low-dimensional infeasible examples are generated at a certain distance to their nearest feasible neighbor. Due to this distance dependence to the feasible class, examples of the feasible class are required. These examples have to represent the feasible class as good as possible and furthermore they have to be distributed more or less homogeneously. Sampling of infeasible examples strongly relies on the cascade classification model requirement of clearly separable classes. Additionally the class boundaries should be clear lines in low-dimensional space. With consideration of these requirements, generation of artificial infeasible examples near the class boundaries can be applied as a second data preprocessing method after selection of feasible examples. The algorithm works as described in Algorithm 2 for all low-dimensional training subsets of the cascade classifier.

---

**Algorithm 2.** Sampling of infeasible examples.

---

**Require:** 2-dimensional data set $\mathbf{X}$ with $n$ feasible examples, where the distance
between infeasibles and their feasible nearest neighbors $\delta_b \gg \epsilon_b$ in about 95%
of all cases
1: $Y = \mathbf{X} + \mathcal{N}(\mu, \sigma) \cdot \alpha$
2: calculate euclidean distance $\delta_b$ of all examples in $Y$ to their nearest feasible
    neighbors in $X$
3: **if** $\delta_b \geq \epsilon_b$ **then**
4:     examples are infeasible examples ($\Gamma$)
5: **end if**
6: **repeat**
7:     $Y = \Gamma + \mathcal{N}(\mu, \sigma) \cdot \alpha$
8:     calculate euclidean distance $\delta_b$ of all examples in $Y$ to their nearest neigh-
    bors in $X$
9:     **if** $\delta_b \geq \epsilon_b$ **then**
10:         append example to $\Gamma$
11:     **end if**
12: **until** number of examples in $\Gamma$ is sufficient
13: shuffle $\Gamma$

---

The low-dimensional feasible examples $X$ are perturbed with gaussian noise $\mathcal{N}(\mu, \sigma) \cdot \alpha$ and yield a new data set $Y$. Then the distance between the examples in $Y$ and their nearest feasible neighbors in $X$ is computed. A value in $Y$ belongs to the set of artificial infeasible examples $\Gamma$ if the distance to the nearest feasible neighbor $\delta_b$ is larger than or equals a certain value $\epsilon_b$. To receive enough infeasible examples around the feasible class, the above described procedure is repeated with a perturbation of all examples in $\Gamma$ instead of the examples in $X$ until the set $\Gamma$ contains a sufficient number of examples. The algorithm employs the parameter for the minimal distance between infeasible examples and their nearest feasible neighbors $\epsilon_b$ and the gaussian distribution $\mathcal{N}(\mu, \sigma) \cdot \alpha$. The parameters depend on the distribution of feasible examples, mainly the distance between feasible nearest neighbors $\epsilon$. Therefore $\epsilon_b$ has to be chosen in such a way, that $\epsilon_b \gg \epsilon$ form the instance selection algorithm. The parameter $\epsilon_b$ has to be chosen carefully, see Sect. 6.2. The $\epsilon_b$ value should be at least so high, that at least 95% off all generated artificial infeasible examples lie outside the region of the feasible class. As far as the true class boundary is not known, the percentage of real feasible examples among the artificial infeasible ones has to be approximated. If the distance $\delta_b$ between generated infeasible examples and their nearest feasible neighbors is $\delta_b \gg \epsilon_b$ for at least 95% of all generated infeasible examples, then most of the generated infeasible examples are actually infeasible ones. The approximation relies on the requirement, that the examples of the feasible class are representatively and homogeneously distributed.

The closer the infeasible examples are located to the class boundary, the greater is the improvement of classification specificity. But the closer the infeasible examples are located to the class boundary, the higher is the probability, that these artificial infeasible examples could be located in the region of the feasible class. False artificial infeasible examples can hamper classification improvement. Therefore a careful parametrization of the algorithm is necessary. All in all the minimum distance $\epsilon_b$ between infeasible examples and their nearest feasible neighbors should be as small as possible and as large as necessary.

Noise for the generation of potentially infeasible examples should scatter in all directions without a drift. Therefore the gaussian distribution is chosen with a mean value of $\mu = 0$. The larger $\epsilon_b$ the larger may be the standard deviation $\sigma$. A good initial choice is $\sigma = 0.01$. The range in which perturbed values can be found can be stretched with the factor $\alpha$. The default value is $\alpha = 1$.

# 5 Experimental Study

In this section, the effect of the proposed data preprocessing methods on the precision of the cascade classification approach is evaluated on two data sets. The first data set is an energy time series data set of micro combined heat and power plant ($\mu$CHP) power production time series. The second data set is an artificial complex data set where the small interesting class has a *Hyperbanana* shape. *Banana* and *Hyperbanana* data sets are often used to test new classifiers, because they are considered as difficult classification tasks. Therefore we take the test with the *Hyperbanana* data set as a representative result.

The experimental study is done with cascade classifiers on each data set. Altogether three classification experiments are conducted on both data sets. The first experiment is done without preprocessing (no prepro.), the second with selected feasible examples (fs) and the third with selected feasibles and artificial infeasible examples (fs + infs). For all experiments a one-class baseline classifier is used. The third experiment is also done with binary baseline classifiers.

The experimental study is divided into a description of the data sets, the experimental setup and the results.

## 5.1 Data Sets

The experiments are conducted with simulated $\mu$CHP power output time series and an artificial *Hyperbanana* data set. Both data sets have 96 dimensions (time steps, resp. features).

$\mu$**CHP.** A $\mu$CHP is a small decentralized power and heat generation unit. The $\mu$CHP power production time series are simulated with a $\mu$CHP simulation model[1]. The $\mu$CHP simulation model includes a $\mu$CHP model, a thermal buffer and the thermal demand of a detached house. A $\mu$CHP can be operated in different modes, where its technical constraints, the constraints of the thermal buffer and the conditions of the thermal demand of the building are complied. Power output time series can be either feasible or infeasible depending on these constraints. The $\mu$CHP simulation model calculates the power production time

---

[1] Data are available for download on our department website http://www.uni-oldenburg.de/informatik/ui/forschung/themen/cascade/.

series for feasible operation modes, but also infeasible power output time series can be generated, where at least one constraint is violated. Due to the different constraints the class of feasible power production time series consists of several clusters. For convenience only such feasible power output time series are chosen, where the power production is greater than 0 at each time step. Infeasible power output time series are sampled from the whole volume of the infeasible class. In data space the class of infeasible power output time series occupies a much larger volume than the class of feasible ones, [6]. The classes are severely imbalanced, but the experiments are conducted with equal numbers of examples from both classes.

The feasible and infeasible $\mu$CHP power output time series are scaled according to the maximal power production to values between 0 and 1.

**Hyperbanana.** As far as there is no 96-dimensional *Hyperbanana* data set, we have generated a data set from the extended d-dimensional Rosenbrock function, [21].

$$f(x) = \sum_{i=1}^{d-1}[100(x_i^2 - x_{i+1})^2 + (x_i - 1)^2] \tag{3}$$

The small and interesting class, or here also called feasible class is sampled from the Rosenbrock valley with $f(x) < 100$ and the infeasible class with $f(x) >= 100$ is sampled only near the class boundary to test the sensitivity of the decision boundaries of the classifiers.

Sampling of the banana shaped valley is done by disturbing the minimum of the extended 96-dimensional Rosenbrock function with gaussian distributed values ($\mathcal{N}(0,1) \cdot \beta$ with $\beta \in \{40, 50, 60, 70\}$). The minima of the Rosenbrock function are presented in [21] for different dimensionalities, but the minimum for 96 dimensions is missing. Therefore we approximated the minimum with regard to the other minima with $-0.99$ for the first dimension and 0.99 for all other dimensions. The procedure of disturbing and selecting values from the Rosenbrock valley is repeated with the sampled values until enough data points are found. As far as it is difficult to sample the banana "arms" all at the same time, we sampled them separately by generating points that are <or> than a certain value and continued sampling by repeating disturbance and selection with these values. Values from all these repetitions were aggregated to one data set and shuffled. Finally all dimensions (features) $x_i$ of the data set are scaled to values between 0 and 1 by $x_i = [x_i + (\min(x_i) + \text{offset})]/[\max(x_i) + \text{offset} - \min(x_i) + \text{offset}]$ with offset = 0.2.

The samples generated by this procedure are not homogeneously distributed in the Rosenbrock valley and they do not represent all *Hyperbanana* "arms" equally.

The 96-dimensional infeasible examples near the class boundary are sampled in the same way as the feasible ones but starting with the feasible *Hyperbanana* samples and selecting samples in the range $100 \le f(x) \le 500$.

## 5.2 Experimental Setting

The experimental setting is divided into two parts: data preprocessing and classification. All calculations are done in Python. The first part, data preprocessing (selection of feasible examples and generation of infeasible examples) is done according to Sects. 4.1 and 4.2.

Selection of feasible examples is parametrized differently for both data sets as a result of pre-studies. The pre-studies were conducted with different minimal distances $\epsilon$ and $\epsilon_b$ and evaluated according to the number of resulting feasible examples $sn$ and their distribution in the 2-dimensional data subset. For the $\mu$CHP data set instance selection is parametrized as follows, the minimal distance between feasible examples is set to $\epsilon = 0.001$ and the number of new examples used for each iteration $t$ is set to $t = 1000$. Generation of artificial infeasible examples is parameterized with $n = 15000$ initially feasible examples disturbance $= \mathcal{N}(0, 0.01) \cdot \alpha$ with $\alpha = 1$ and minimal distance between infeasible examples and their nearest feasible neighbors $\epsilon_b = 0.025$. For the *Hyperbanana* data set the instance selection parameters are set to $\epsilon = 0.002$ and $t = 1000$ and parameters for generating artificial infeasible examples are set to $n = 20000$, disturbance $= \mathcal{N}(0, 0.02) \cdot \alpha$ with $\alpha = 1$ and $\epsilon_b = 0.025$.

The second part of the experimental study, the three classification experiments, are done with the cascade classifier, see Sect. 3, with different baseline classifiers from SCIKIT-LEARN, [20], a One-Class SVM (OCSVM) and two binary classifiers, k-nearest neighbors (kNN) and Support Vector Machines (SVMs). The OCSVM baseline classifier is used for all three experiments. The two binary classifiers kNN and binary SVM are used for the third experiment with both preprocessing methods (fs + infs).

All experiments are conducted identically on both data sets except for the parametrization. For all experiments the number of feasible training examples $N$ is varied in the range of $N = \{1000, 2000, \ldots, 5000\}$ for the $\mu$CHP data set and $N = \{1000, 2000, \ldots, 10000\}$ for the *Hyperbanana* data set. For binary classification $N$ infeasible examples are added to the $N$ feasible training examples.

Parameter optimization is done with grid-search on separate validation sets with the same number of feasible examples $N$ as the training sets and also $N$ artificial infeasible examples for the third experiment. For the first experiment (no prepro.) and the second experiment (fs) the parameters are optimized according to true positive rates (TP rate or only TP), (TP rate = (true positives)/(number of feasible examples)).

For the third experiment, where the validation is done with $N$ additional infeasible examples, parameters are optimized according to accuracy (acc = (true positives + true negatives)/(number of positive examples + number of negative examples)). The OCSVM parameters are optimized in the ranges $\nu \in \{0.0001, 0.0005, 0.001, 0.002, \ldots, 0.009, 0.01\}$, $\gamma \in \{50, 60, \ldots, 200\}$, the SVM parameters in $C \in \{1, 10, 50, 100, 500, 1000, 2000\}$, $\gamma \in \{1, 5, 10, 15, 20\}$ and the kNN parameter in $k \in \{1, 2, \ldots, 26\}$.

Evaluation of the trained classifiers is done on a separate independent data set with 10000 feasible and 10000 real infeasible 96-dimensional examples according to TP and TN values for varying numbers of training examples $N$. The classification results could be evaluated with more advanced measures, see e.g. [11,14]. For better comparability of the results on both data sets and the option to distinguish effects on the classification of feasible and infeasible examples we use the simple TP and TN values. TN values on both data sets are difficult to compare, because the infeasible $\mu$CHP power output time series are distributed in the whole region of infeasible examples, while the infeasible *Hyperbanana* examples are distributed only near the class boundary. As far as most classification errors occur near the class boundary, the TN values of the *Hyperbanana* set are expected to be lower than the TN values on the $\mu$CHP data set.

## 5.3   Results

The proposed data preprocessing methods, selection of feasible examples and generation of artificial infeasible examples show an increase in classification precision of the cascade classifier in the experiments.

On both data sets ($\mu$CHP and *Hyperbanana*) data preprocessing leads to more precise decision boundaries than without data preprocessing, see Figs. 3(a) and 4. This can be also seen in the TP and TN values of the classification results, see Figs. 3(b) and 5.

For the $\mu$CHP data set, all three experiments lead to TN values of 1, therefore only the TP values are plotted in Fig. 3(b). But high TN valuess for the $\mu$CHP data set do not necessarily mean, that further infeasible time series are classified correctly. The applied infeasible test examples are taken from the whole volume of the large infeasible class and therefore most of the examples are not located

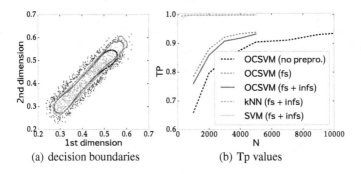

(a) decision boundaries            (b) Tp values

**Fig. 3.** Decision boundaries and TP values. The left figure showes the decision boundaries on the 1st and 2nd dimension of the $\mu$CHP data set trained with $N = 1000$ feasible (+1000 infeasible) training examples, no prepro. (dashed black), fs (dashed green), OCSVM (fs + infs) (red), kNN (fs + infs) (olive) and SVM (fs + infs) (yellow). The gray points indicate 500 of the selected feasible training examples and the blue points 500 of the artificial infeasible examples. The right figure shows the corresponding TP values on the high-dimensional data set. (Color figure online)

near the class boundary. The first experiment without data preprocessing (no prepro.) yields the lowest TP values of all experiments for all numbers of training values $N$ and the second experiment with selection of feasible examples (fs) leads already to higher TP values. The third experiment with selection of feasible examples and artificial infeasible examples (fs + infs) leads to different results with the OCSVM baseline classifier and the binary SVM and kNN baseline classifiers. While the OCSVM (fs + infs) achieves slightly lower TP values than OCSVM (fs) in the second experiment, the binary baseline classifiers SVM (fs + infs) and kNN (fs + infs) achieve TP values near 1.

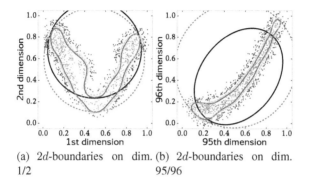

(a) 2*d*-boundaries on dim. (b) 2*d*-boundaries on dim.
1/2                              95/96

**Fig. 4.** Decision boundaries on the *Hyperbanana* data set trained with $N = 1000$ feasible (+1000 infeasible) training examples, no prepro. (dashed black), fs (dashed green), OCSVM (fs + infs) (red), kNN (fs + infs) (olive) and SVM (fs + infs) (yellow). The gray points indicate 500 of the selected feasible training examples and the blue points 500 of the artificial infeasible examples. (Color figure online)

For the *Hyperbanana* data set with a more complex data structure, data preprocessing influences the TP values, see Fig. 5(a) and the TN values, Fig. 5(b) of the classification results. In the first experiment (no prepro.) and second experiment (fs) the classification achieves relatively high TP values and at the same time the lowest TN values of all experiments due to an overestimation of the feasible class, see Fig. 4. The third experiment (fs + infs) revealed an opposed behavior of the OCSVM baseline classifier and the SVM and kNN baseline classifiers. The OCSVM (fs + infs) achieves lower TP values than the OCSVM in the previous experiments but also the highest TN values of all experiments. SVM and kNN baseline classifiers with (fs + infs) achieve the highest TP values of all experiments and at the same time lower TN values than the OCSVM (fs + infs).

In summary, data preprocessing increases the classification precision of the cascade classifier on both data sets. While the selection of feasible examples increases the classification precision, artificial infeasible examples can lead to an even greater increase depending on the data set and the baseline classifier.

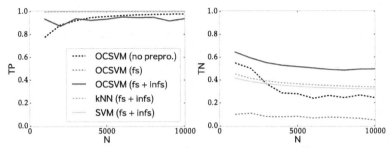

(a) TP values on a differently prepro-  (b) TN values on a differently preprocessed *Hyperbanana* set                cessed *Hyperbanana* set

**Fig. 5.** TP and TN values on the *Hyperbanana* data set for different preprocessing steps and different baseline classifiers. The legend in Fig. 5(a) is also valid for Fig. 5(b). The green line of OCSVM (fs) in Fig. 5(a) is covered by the olive and the yellow lines. (Color figure online)

# 6    Parameter Sensitivity Study and Parameter Fitting Rules

In this section the influence of the data preprocessing distance parameters on the cascade classifier precision is analyzed and parameter fitting rules are derived. Therefore selection of feasible instances is applied first with different values of the minimal distance $\epsilon$ between feasible nearest neighbors. Then outlier generation is applied to the different data sets of selected feasible examples. Outlier generation is conducted with different minimal distances $\epsilon_b$ between infeasibles and their nearest feasible neighbors. Next a cascade classifier is built on each preprocessed data set and the classification precision is tested on a test set. The cascade classifier precision is measured as true positive rates (TP) and true negative rates (TN). Based on high TP and TN values a region with optimal distance parameter value combinations is identified.

## 6.1    Experimental Setup

The classification precision experiments are conducted with various combinations of both data preprocessing distance parameter values. The experiments are performed on the $\mu$CHP data set from Sect. 5.1, consisting of $239, 131$ feasible and $1, 000, 000$ infeasible examples.

First of all both data preprocessing methods are applied and after that the preprocessed data sets are classified with the cascade classification model. Data preprocessing starts with the selection of feasible examples on all 2-dimensional data subsets of the $\mu$CHP data set. The parameter $t = 100$ remains constant and the value of the distance parameter $\epsilon$ is increased. The $\epsilon$ values are chosen with respect to the range of the power production values $[0, 1]$ at each time step and the number of required training and validation examples. The number of selected feasible examples $sn$ decreases for increasing values of $\epsilon$, see Fig. 6.

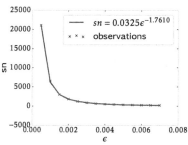
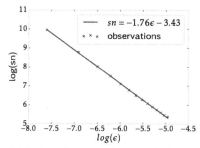

(a) functional relation between $\epsilon$ and $sn$

(b) loglog plot of the functional relation between $\epsilon$ and $sn$

**Fig. 6.** Functional relationship between the minimal distance between nearest feasible neighbors $\epsilon$ and the number of selected examples $sn$ of the subset with the fewest selected examples. The selected feasible examples have to be divided into training and validation sets or can be used only as training data while validation examples are taken from the remaining feasible examples, that were not selected.

But the number of selected feasible examples $sn$, resulting from one *epsilon* value, differ among the low-dimensional data subsets of the high-dimensional data set. Therefore the smallest number $sn$ of all low-dimensional data sets is used for all low-dimensional data subsets resulting from the same $\epsilon$ value. Overall the adapted number of selected examples $sn$ decreases for increasing values of $\epsilon$ with a power function $sn = 0.0325\epsilon^{-1.7610}$, see Fig. 6. In the previous experiments with data preprocessing for the $\mu$CHP data set in Sect. 5, training sets with more than $N = 250$ feasible training examples turned out to be reasonable for the kNN baseline classifier, see Fig. 3(b). With respect to the minimum number of feasible training examples $N$ and the constant parametrization of $t = 100$, we have chosen the number of feasible training examples as $N \in [100, 10000]$ examples. In the experiments we employ $N = sn/2$ as training examples and the remaining $sn/2$ examples as validation values, therefore $sn$ has to be twice as large as the number of training examples $sn = 2N$. These numbers of feasible training examples and the respective $sn$ values correspond to $\epsilon \in \{0.001, 0.0015, 0.002, \ldots, 0.0055\}$.

Then artificial infeasible outliers are generated for each of the new data sets $S$ consisting of $sn$ selected feasible examples. Outlier generation is parametrized as follows. Noise is taken from $\mathcal{N}(\mu, \sigma) \cdot \alpha$ with $\mu = 0$, $\sigma = 0.01$ and $\alpha = 1$ and $\epsilon_b$ is increased for all data sets generated with the different $\epsilon$ values. The $\epsilon_b$ values are chosen from $\{0.001, 0.002, \ldots, 0.05\}$ with $\epsilon_b \geq \epsilon$. Depending on $\epsilon_b$ the number of algorithm iterations is adapted until at least the same number of outlier examples are generated as the respective number of selected feasible examples $sn$.

Next the cascade classifiers are built on all preprocessed data sets with the k nearest neighbor baseline classifier from *scikit learn*, [20]. The training sets contain $(N = n/2)$ half of the number of selected feasible examples. Additionally

the training sets contain the same number of artificial infeasible examples as
feasible training examples. The number of nearest neighbors $k$ for each classifier is taken from $k \in \{1, 2, \ldots, 26\}$ and optimized with a validation set. The
validation set contains the same number of feasible and infeasible examples as
the training set. Feasible and infeasible examples are taken from the remaining
selected feasible ones and the remaining artificial infeasibles.

The classifiers are tested on a set of $10,000$ feasible and $10,000$ infeasible
high-dimensional examples without data preprocessing. TP and TN values of the
cascade classifier are stored for all preprocessed data sets. The cascade classifier
precision is evaluated graphically on the achieved TP and TN values according
to the underlying data preprocessing distance parameter value combinations.

## 6.2   Results

The cascade classifier precision yielded different TP values for the differently
preprocessed data sets shown in Fig. 7(a) and $TN = 1$. The high TN values are
due to the location of the infeasible high-dimensional test examples far away
from the class boundary, see Sect. 5.1.

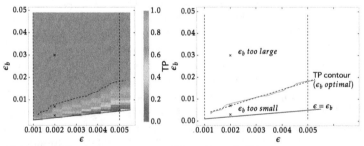

(a) TP for different parameter combinations of $\epsilon$ and $\epsilon_b$

(b) regions of different parameter combinations with different effects

**Fig. 7.** The left figure shows the TP values for the differently preprocessed $\mu$CHP data
set with the corresponding distance parameter values. The two vertical dashed black
lines mark the range of reasonable $\epsilon$ values and the solid black line at the bottom
indicates the lowest bound for $\epsilon_b$: $\epsilon = \epsilon_b$. The black line above is the contour with
TP $= 0.99$. The figure on the left shows the same boundary lines. Furthermore the
resulting regions are indicated. The three points in both figures mark the parameter
combinations used for Fig. 8.

Based on the TP values different regions of classification precision are identified and separated by the restrictions resulting from the distance parameters, see
Fig. 7(b). The regions of different distance parameter combinations are bounded
for this $\mu$CHP data set in the $\epsilon$ range and the $\epsilon_b$ range. The $\epsilon$ range is bounded
by the number of selected feasible examples, see Sect. 6.1. After excluding insen-
sible $\epsilon$ values ($\epsilon < 0.001$ and $\epsilon > 0.0055$), the $\epsilon_b$ values can be divided into three

groups, too small $\epsilon_b$ values, optimal values and too large values. For each of these groups the distribution of the preprocessed data sets and the learned decision boundaries are shown exemplarily in Fig. 8.

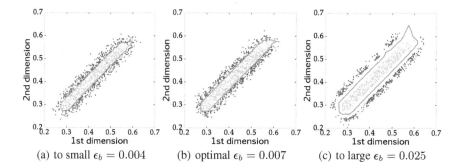

(a) to small $\epsilon_b = 0.004$     (b) optimal $\epsilon_b = 0.007$     (c) to large $\epsilon_b = 0.025$

**Fig. 8.** Decision boundaries learned for the first and second dimension on the $\mu$CHP data set for $\epsilon_b$ values from the different regions and a fixed value of $\epsilon = 0.002$. These parameter value combinations are marked in Fig. 7. (Color figure online)

The region of too small $\epsilon_b$ values is bounded by $\epsilon_b = \epsilon$ at the lower bound and the TP $= 0.99$ contour at the upper bound. The TP contour can be approximated by a linear function with linear regression: $\epsilon_b = 3.7251\epsilon - 0.0005$. In the region of too small $\epsilon_b$ values more or less artificial infeasible examples are generated in the region of the feasible class. This can be seen in Fig. 8(a) showing some artificial infeasible examples (blue points) between the gray points in the region of feasibles. This mixture of feasible and artificial infeasible examples leads to non smooth class boundaries and relatively low TP values.

The region of optimal $epsilon_b$ values is only described by the TP $= 0.99$ contour for the $\mu$CHP data set, because TN $= 1$ for all parameter value combinations. If there would be infeasible test examples near the true class boundary, the TN values should decrease for increasing $\epsilon_b$ values. From these decreasing TN values a respective TN contour could be computed. This TN contour could be used in combination with the TP contour to determine the optimal value region. The corresponding artificial infeasible examples are distributed around the feasible ones with a small gap in between the classes and hardly any overlap, see Fig. 8(b). Due to the gap feasible and infeasible examples are clearly separable and TP and TN values are high in this region.

The region of too large $\epsilon_b$ values has a lower bound resulting from the TP contour for the $\mu$CHP data set. But the lower bound could be also determined by a TN contour, if there would be infeasible test examples near the true class boundary. As far as the $\mu$CHP data set contains hardly any infeasible examples near the class boundary, the lower bound cannot be determined by a TN contour. But wrong classification results are due to incorrect decision boundaries. If the $\epsilon_b$ value is too large, feasible and infeasible examples are clearly separable and there is a large gap between the examples of both classes, see Fig. 8(c). The learned decision boundary is located in the middle of this gap. The larger the gap, the further is the decision boundary away from the feasible examples. This phenomenon is an overestimation of the feasible class and infeasible test examples near the true class boundary would be classified as feasible.

Even though the parameter $\epsilon_b$ has to be chosen carefully, the parameter sensitivity analysis yielded a region of optimal data preprocessing distance parameter value combinations, where the cascade classifier performs best. Deviations from the optimal parameter value combinations lead either to an over- or underestimation of the feasible class with decreasing (TN) or TP values.

# 7    Conclusions

In this paper, we presented two data preprocessing methods to improve the precision of the cascade classification model (selection of feasible examples and generation of artificial infeasible examples). Both methods operate on the low-dimensional data sets. Selection of feasible examples leads to more representative training data and artificial infeasible examples lead to more precise decision boundaries, due to the availability of infeasible examples near the class boundary. Depending on the baseline classifier, the application of both data preprocessing methods yields for the $\mu$CHP power output time series data set and an artificial and complex *Hyperbanana* data set the best classification precision. The application of only selection of feasible examples and no data preprocessing yielded always worse results, that can be observed as lower TP values on the $\mu$CHP data set and especially very low TN values on the *Hyperbanana* data set. Additionally the parameter sensitivity of the distance parameters of both data preprocessing methods was analyzed with respect to the cascade classifier precision on the $\mu$CHP data set. The analysis yielded a region of optimal parameter value combinations and their boundaries. Parameter value combinations from outside the optimal region lead to a lower classification precision with either lower TP or lower TN values. In the first case with lower TP values the precision decreases due to an overlap of feasible and infeasible training examples. This overlap causes an under estimation of the feasible class. In the second case low TN values near the class boundary are due to a large gap between feasible and infeasible examples. This gap leads to an over estimation of the feasible class.

Overall we recommend a careful parametrization of the data preprocessing methods with some pre-test to increase the cascade classifier precision.

We intend to repeat the sensitivity analysis on the *Hyperbanana* data set to study the behavior of infeasible examples near the class boundary, because the analyzed $\mu$CHP data set does not have infeasible examples near the class boundary. Furthermore we plan a comparison of traditional one class classifiers with the cascade classification model with preprocessing.

**Acknowledgement.** This work was funded by the Ministry for Science and Culture of Lower Saxony with the PhD program System Integration of Renewable Energy (SEE).

# References

1. Bagnall, A., Davis, L.M., Hills, J., Lines, J.: Transformation based ensembles for time series classification. In: Proceedings of the 12th SIAM International Conference on Data Mining, pp. 307–318 (2012)
2. Bánhalmi, A., Kocsor, A., Busa-Fekete, R.: Counter-example generation-based one-class classification. In: Kok, J.N., Koronacki, J., Mantaras, R.L., Matwin, S., Mladenič, D., Skowron, A. (eds.) ECML 2007. LNCS (LNAI), vol. 4701, pp. 543–550. Springer, Heidelberg (2007). doi:10.1007/978-3-540-74958-5_51
3. Bellinger, C., Sharma, S., Japkowicz, N.: One-class versus binary classification: which and when? In: 11th International Conference on Machine Learning and Applications, ICMLA 2012, vol. 2, pp. 102–106, December 2012
4. Blachnik, M.: Ensembles of instance selection methods based on feature subset. Procedia Comput. Sci. **35**, 388–396 (2014). Knowledge-Based and Intelligent Information and Engineering Systems 18th Annual Conference, KES-2014 Gdynia, Poland, September 2014 Proceedings
5. Borgonovo, E., Plischke, E.: Sensitivity analysis: a review of recent advances. Eur. J. Oper. Res. **248**(3), 869–887 (2016)
6. Bremer, J., Rapp, B., Sonnenschein, M.: Support vector based encoding of distributed energy resources' feasible load spaces. In: Innovative Smart Grid Technologies Conference Europe IEEE PES (2010)
7. Cortez, P., Embrechts, M.: Opening black box data mining models using sensitivity analysis. In: 2011 IEEE Symposium on Computational Intelligence and Data Mining (CIDM), pp. 341–348, April 2011
8. Cortez, P., Embrechts, M.J.: Using sensitivity analysis and visualization techniques to open black box data mining models. Inf. Sci. **225**, 1–17 (2013)
9. Garcia, S., Derrac, J., Cano, J., Herrera, F.: Prototype selection for nearest neighbor classification: taxonomy and empirical study. IEEE Trans. Pattern Anal. Mach. Intell. **34**(3), 417–435 (2012)
10. Hamby, D.M.: A review of techniques for parameter sensitivity analysis of environmental models. Environ. Monit. Assess. **32**, 135–154 (1994)
11. He, H., Garcia, E.: Learning from imbalanced data. IEEE Trans. Knowl. Data Eng. **21**(9), 1263–1284 (2009)
12. Heiselberg, P., Brohus, H., Hesselholt, A., Rasmussen, H., Seinre, E., Thomas, S.: Application of sensitivity analysis in design of sustainable buildings. Renew. Energy **34**(9), 2030–2036 (2009). Special Issue: Building and Urban Sustainability
13. Jankowski, N., Grochowski, M.: Comparison of instances seletion algorithms I. Algorithms survey. In: Rutkowski, L., Siekmann, J.H., Tadeusiewicz, R., Zadeh, L.A. (eds.) ICAISC 2004. LNCS (LNAI), vol. 3070, pp. 598–603. Springer, Heidelberg (2004). doi:10.1007/978-3-540-24844-6_90
14. Japkowicz, N.: Assessment Metrics for Imbalanced Learning, pp. 187–206. Wiley, Hoboken (2013)
15. Kleijnen, J.P.C.: Design and Analysis of Simulation Experiments. International Series in Operations Research and Management Science. Springer, Heidelberg (2015)
16. Lin, W.J., Chen, J.J.: Class-imbalanced classifiers for high-dimensional data. Brief. Bioinform. **14**(1), 13–26 (2013)
17. Liu, H., Motoda, H., Gu, B., Hu, F., Reeves, C.R., Bush, D.R.: Instance Selection and Construction for Data Mining. The Springer International Series in Engineering and Computer Science, vol. 608, 1st edn. Springer US, New York (2001)

18. Neugebauer, J., Kramer, O., Sonnenschein, M.: Classification cascades of overlapping feature ensembles for energy time series data. In: Woon, W.L., Aung, Z., Madnick, S. (eds.) DARE 2015. LNCS (LNAI), vol. 9518, pp. 76–93. Springer, Heidelberg (2015). doi:10.1007/978-3-319-27430-0_6

19. Neugebauer, J., Kramer, O., Sonnenschein, M.: Improving cascade classifier precision by instance selection and outlier generation. In: ICAART, vol. 8 (2016, in print)

20. Pedregosa, F., Varoquaux, G., Gramfort, A., Michel, V., Thirion, B., Grisel, O., Blondel, M., Prettenhofer, P., Weiss, R., Dubourg, V., Vanderplas, J., Passos, A., Cournapeau, D., Brucher, M., Perrot, M., Duchesnay, E.: Scikit-learn: machine learning in Python. J. Mach. Learn. Res. **12**, 2825–2830 (2011)

21. Shang, Y.W., Qiu, Y.H.: A note on the extended Rosenbrock function. Evol. Comput. **14**(1), 119–126 (2006)

22. Tax, D.M.J., Duin, R.P.W.: Uniform object generation for optimizing one-class classifiers. J. Mach. Learn. Res. **2**, 155–173 (2002)

23. Tomašev, N., Buza, K., Marussy, K., Kis, P.B.: Hubness-aware classification, instance selection and feature construction: survey and extensions to time-series. In: Stańczyk, U., Jain, L.C. (eds.) Feature Selection for Data and Pattern Recognition. SCI, vol. 584, pp. 231–262. Springer, Heidelberg (2015). doi:10.1007/978-3-662-45620-0_11

24. Tsai, C.F., Eberle, W., Chu, C.Y.: Genetic algorithms in feature and instance selection. Knowl.-Based Syst. **39**, 240–247 (2013)

25. Wilson, D., Martinez, T.: Reduction techniques for instance-based learning algorithms. Mach. Learn. **38**(3), 257–286 (2000)

26. Wu, J., Dhingra, R., Gambhir, M., Remais, J.V.: Sensitivity analysis of infectious disease models: methods, advances and their application. J. R. Soc. Interface **10**(86), 1–14 (2013)

27. Zhuang, L., Dai, H.: Parameter optimization of kernel-based one-class classifier on imbalance text learning. In: Yang, Q., Webb, G. (eds.) PRICAI 2006. LNCS (LNAI), vol. 4099, pp. 434–443. Springer, Heidelberg (2006). doi:10.1007/978-3-540-36668-3_47

# Qualitative Possibilistic Decisions: Decomposition and Sequential Decisions Making

Salem Benferhat[1], Khaoula Boutouhami[1,2], Hadja Faiza Khellaf-Haned[2($\boxtimes$)], and Ismahane Zeddigha[1,2]

[1] CRIL, University of Artois, CNRS UMR 8188, 62307 Lens, France
benferhat@cril.fr
[2] RIIMA, University of Sciences and Technology Houari Boumediene, Algiers, Algeria
{kboutouhami,fkhellaf,izeddigha}@usthb.dz

**Abstract.** Min-based possibilistic influence diagrams offer a compact modeling of decision problems under uncertainty. Uncertainty and preferential relations are expressed on the same structure by using ordinal data. In many applications, it may be natural to represent expert knowledge and preferences separately and treat all nodes similarly. This work shows how an influence diagram can be equivalently represented by two possibilistic networks: the first one represents knowledge of an agent and the second one represents agent's preferences. Thus, the decision evaluation process is based on more compact possibilistic network. Then, we show that the computation of sequential optimal decisions (strategy) comes down to compute a normalization degree of the junction tree associated with the graph representing the fusion of agents beliefs and its preferences resulting from the proposed decomposition process.

## 1 Introduction

Graphical decision models provide efficient decision tools. In fact, they allow a compact and a simple representation of decision problems under uncertainty. Most of decision graphical models are based on Influence Diagrams (ID) [17] for representing decision maker's beliefs and preferences on sequences of decisions to be made under uncertainty. The evaluation of Influence Diagrams ensures optimal decisions while maximizing the decision maker's expected utilities [6,16,17]. Min-based possibilistic Influence Diagrams (PID) [10] allow a gradual expression of both agent's preferences and knowledge. The graphical part of possibilistic Influence Diagrams is exactly the same as the one of standard Influence Diagrams. Uncertainty is expressed by possibility degrees and preferences are considered as satisfaction degrees.

Unlike probabilistic decision theory, which is based on one expected utility criteria to evaluate optimal decisions, a qualitative possibilistic decision theory

---

This is an extended and revised version of the conference paper: S. Benferhat, H.F. Khellaf-Haned, I. Zeddigha, "On the Decomposition of Min-Based PIDs". The 8th conference of Agent and Artificial Intelligence ICAART-2016. Roma, February 2016.

© Springer International Publishing AG 2017
J. van den Herik and J. Filipe (Eds.): ICAART 2016, LNAI 10162, pp. 171–188, 2017.
DOI: 10.1007/978-3-319-53354-4_10

[5,8] provides several qualitative utility criteria for decision approaches under uncertainty. Among these criteria, one can mention the pessimistic and optimistic utilities proposed in [7], the binary utility proposed in [12], etc. As standard Influence Diagrams, direct [10] and an indirect methods [10,13] have been proposed to evaluate a min-based PID. Besides, Influence Diagrams represent agent's beliefs and preferences on the same structure and they operate on three types of nodes: chance, decision and utility nodes. In practice, it will be easier for an agent to express its knowledge and preferences separately. Furthermore, it is more simple to treat all nodes in the same way. In [3], authors have proposed a new compact graphical model for representing decision making under uncertainty based on the use of possibilistic networks. Agent's knowledge and preferences are expressed in qualitative way by two distinct qualitative possibilistic networks. This new representation, for decision making under uncertainty based on min-based possibilistic networks, benefits from the simplicity of possibilistic networks.

In this chapter, we show first how to decompose an initial min-based Influence Diagram into two min-based possibilistic networks: the first one represents agent's beliefs and the second one encodes its preferences. Then, we define the required steps for splitting a qualitative Influence Diagram into two min-based possibilistic networks preserving the same possibility distribution and the same qualitative utility. Then, this decomposition process provides also the opportunity to exploit the inference algorithms [1,2] developed for min-based possibilistic networks to solve qualitative Influence Diagrams. This procedure allows us to obtain a more compact qualitative possibilistic network for computing optimal strategy based on the fusion of possibilistic networks. In this context, we present an efficient and unified way of computing optimal optimistic strategy using inference process based on the junction tree associated with the fusion of agents beliefs and preferences networks.

This chapter is organized as follows. Next section briefly recalls basic concepts of graphical frameworks for possibilistic qualitative decision: min-Based Possibilistic Influence Diagrams and min-based possibilistic networks. Section 3 describes how the decomposition process can be efficiently used for encoding an Influence Diagram into two possibilistic networks. Section 4 describes how propagation process can be efficiently used for computing optimal optimistic strategy. Section 5 present an experimental studies. Section 6 concludes the chapter.

## 2     Graphical Frameworks for Possibilistic Qualitative Decision

### 2.1     Min-Based Possibilistic Influence Diagrams

A min-based possibilistic Influence Diagram, denoted by $\Pi ID_{min}(G_{ID}, \pi_{min}^{ID}, \mu_{min}^{ID})$, have two components: the graphical part which is the same as the one of standard Influence Diagrams and the numerical part which consists in evaluating different links in the graph. The uncertainty is expressed by possibility degrees and preferences are considered as satisfaction degrees.

1. **A Graphical Component:** which is represented by a DAG, denoted by $G_{ID} = (\mathcal{X}, \mathcal{A})$ where $\mathcal{X} = \mathcal{C} \cup \mathcal{D} \cup \mathcal{U}$ represents a set of variables containing three different kinds of nodes. $\mathcal{A}$ is a set of arcs representing either causal influences or information influences between variables.
   - **Chance Nodes:** are represented by circles. They represent state variables $X_i \in \mathcal{C} = \{X_1, ..., X_n\}$. Chance nodes reflect uncertain factors of a decision problem. A combination $x = \{x_{1i}, ..., x_{nj}\}$ of state variable values represents a state.
   - **Decision Nodes:** are represented by rectangles. They represent decision variables $D_j \in \mathcal{D} = \{D_1, ..., D_p\}$ which depict decision options. A combination $d = \{d_{1i}, ..., d_{pj}\}$ of values represents a decision.
   - **Utility Nodes:** $V_k \in \mathcal{V} = \{V_1, ..., V_q\}$ are represented by diamonds. They represent local utility functions (local satisfaction degrees) $\mu_k \in \{\mu_1, ..., \mu_q\}$.
   A conventional assumption that an Influence Diagram must respect is that utility nodes have no children.
2. **Numerical Components:** Uncertainty is described by means of a priori and conditional possibility distributions relative to chance nodes. More precisely:
   - For every chance node $X \in \mathcal{C}$, uncertainty is represented by:
     - If $X$ is a root node, a priori possibility degree $\pi_{ID}(x)$ will be associated for each instance $x \in \mathbb{D}_X$, such that $\max\limits_{x \in \mathbb{D}_X} \pi_{ID}(x) = 1$.
     - If $X$ has parents, the conditional possibility degree $\pi_{ID}(x \mid u_X)$ will be associated for each instance $x \in \mathbb{D}_X$ and $u_X \in \mathbb{D}_{Par(X)} = \times_{X_j \in Par(X)} \mathbb{D}_{X_j}$, such that $\max\limits_{x \in \mathbb{D}_X} \pi_{ID}(x \mid u_x) = 1$, for any $u_X$.
   - Decision nodes are not quantified. Indeed, a value of decision node $D_j$ is deterministic, it will be fixed by the decision maker.
   Once a decision $d = \{d_{1i}, ..., d_{pj}\} \in \mathcal{D}$ is fixed, chance nodes of the min-based ID form a qualitative possibilistic network induces a unique joint conditional possibility distribution relative to chance node interpretations $x = \{x_{1i}, ..., x_{nj}\}$, in the context of $d$.

$$\pi^{ID}_{min}(x \mid d) = \min_{i=1..n} \pi_{ID}(x_{il} \mid u_{X_i}). \tag{1}$$

where $x_{il} \in \mathbb{D}_{X_i}$ and $u_{X_i} \in \mathbb{D}_{Par(X_i)} = \times_{X_m \in Par(X_i), D_j \in Par(X_i)} \mathbb{D}_{X_m} \cup \mathbb{D}_{D_j}$.
   - For each utility node $V_{k=1..q} \in \mathcal{V}$, ordinal values $\mu_k(u_{V_k})$ are assigned to every possible instantiations $u_{V_k}$ of the parent variables $Par(V_k)$. Ordinal values $\mu_k$ represent satisfaction degrees associated with local instantiations of parents variables.
The global satisfaction degree $\mu^{ID}_{min}(x, d)$ relative to the global instantiation $(x, d)$ of all variables can be computed as the minimum of the local satisfaction degrees:

$$\mu^{ID}_{min}(x, d) = \min_{k=1..q} \mu_k(u_{V_k}). \tag{2}$$

where $u_{V_k} \in \mathbb{D}_{Par(V_k)} = \times_{X_i \in Par(V_k), D_j \in Par(V_k)} \mathbb{D}_{X_i} \cup \mathbb{D}_{D_j}$.

## 2.2   Min-Based Possibilistic Networks

A min-based possibilistic network [12,13] over a set of variables V denoted by $\Pi_{min} = (G; \pi)$ is characterized by:

- **A Graphical Component:** is represented by a DAG, the nodes correspond to variables and arcs represent dependence relations between variables.
- **Numerical Components:** these components quantify different links in the DAG by using local possibility distributions for each node $A$ in the context of its parents denoted by $U_A$. More precisely:
  - For every root node $A$, a priori possibility degree $\pi(a)$ will be associated for each $a \in D_A$, such that $max\pi(a) = 1$.
  - For the rest of the nodes $U_A \neq \varnothing$, the conditional possibility degree $\pi(a|U_A)$ will be associated for each $a \in D_A$ and $U_A \in D_A$, such that $\max \pi(a|U_A) = 1$, for any $U_A$.

The a priori and the conditional possibility degrees induce a unique joint possibility distribution defined by:

$$\pi_G(A_1, .., A_n) = \pi_{min}(A_i|U_{A_i}) \tag{3}$$

Given two min-based possibilistic networks $\Pi G = (G; \pi_G)$ and $\Pi G' = (G'; \pi_{G'})$, the result of merging $\Pi G$ and $\Pi G'$ is the possibilistic network $\Pi G_\oplus = (G_\oplus; \pi_\oplus)$ [9], such that:

$$\forall \omega, \pi_{G_\oplus}(\omega) = min(\pi_G(\omega), \pi_{G'}(\omega)) \tag{4}$$

The syntactic counterpart of the fusion of two possibility distributions, associated to two possibilistic networks, using the min operator is a new min-based possibilistic network. In [9], the authors propose two principal classes for merging min-based possibilistic networks:

- Fusion of two possibilistic networks $\Pi G$ and $\Pi G'$ having the same network structure.
- Fusion of two possibilistic networks $\Pi G$ and $\Pi G'$ with different structures.

For more details on the fusion of possibilistic networks see [9].

## 3   Decomposition of Min-Based Possibilistic Influence Diagram

This section discuss how a qualitative PID can be modeled by two possibility distributions, one representing agent's beliefs and the other representing the qualitative utility. So, we propose a decomposition process of min-based PID $\Pi ID_{min}(G_{ID}, \pi_{min}^{ID}, \mu_{min}^{ID})$ into two min-based possibilistic networks:

1. Agent's knowledge $\Pi K_{min} = (G_K, \pi)$. This qualitative possibilistic network should codify the same joint conditional possibility distribution $\pi_{min}^{ID}$ induced by the PID.
2. Agent's preferences $\Pi P_{min} = (G_P, \mu)$. Again, this preference-based possibilistic network must codify the same qualitative utility $\mu_{min}^{ID}$ induced by the PID.

## 3.1   The Construction of a Knowledge-Based Qualitative Possibilistic Network

The knowledge-based qualitative possibilistic network $\Pi K_{min} = (G_K, \pi)$ encodes agent's beliefs. It induces a unique possibility distribution $\pi_K$ using Eq. 3. The graphical component $G_K$ of the new qualitative possibilistic network $\Pi K_{min}$ is defined on the set of variables $\mathcal{Y} = \mathcal{X} \cup \mathcal{D} = \{Y_1, ..., Y_{n+p}\}$ of chance and decision nodes (where $n = |\mathcal{X}|$ and $p = |\mathcal{D}|$). The building of the knowledge-based possibilistic network $\Pi K_{min}$ can be summarized by Algorithm 1.

---

**Algorithm 1.** Building knowledge-based network.

---

**Require:** $\Pi I D_{min}(G_{ID}, \pi_{min}^{ID}, \mu_{min}^{ID})$, a min-based PID.
**Ensure:** $\Pi K_{min} = (G_K, \pi)$ {knowledge-based network}
   **for** $D_j \in \mathcal{D}$ **do**
      Transform each decision node $D_j$ into chance node $\{\forall D_j \in \mathcal{D}, \ \pi(d_{jl} \mid u_{D_j}) = 1.\}$
      **for** $X_i \in \mathcal{C}$ **do**
         Quantify each chance node $X_i$ $\{\forall X_i \in \mathcal{C}, \ \pi(x_{il} \mid u_{X_i}) = \pi_{ID}(x_{il} \mid u_{X_i})\}$
         Remove utility nodes $\{V_1, ..., V_q\}$
      **end for**
   **end for**

---

The new min-based possibilistic network $\Pi K_{min} = (G_K, \pi)$ induces a unique joint possibility distribution $\pi_K$ defined by the min-based chain rule.

The following proposition ensures that the joint possibility distribution induced by the new possibilistic network $\Pi K_{min}$ encodes the same states represented by the Influence Diagram $\Pi I D_{min}$.

**Proposition 1.** *Let* $\Pi K_{min} = (G_K, \pi)$ *be a min-based possibilistic network obtained using Algorithm 1. The joint possibility distribution* $\pi_K$ *induced by* $\Pi K_{min}$ *is equal to the one induced by the Influence Diagram* $\Pi I D_{min}$. *Namely,*

$$\pi_K(Y_1, ..., Y_{n+p}) = \pi_{min}^{ID}(X_1, ..., X_n \mid D_1, ..., D_p) = \min_{X_i \in \mathcal{C}} \pi_{ID}(X_i \mid U_i) \qquad (5)$$

## 3.2   Building Preference-Based Qualitative Possibilistic Network

The second qualitative possibilistic network $\Pi P_{min} = (G_P, \mu)$ represents agent's preferences associated with the qualitative utility. $\Pi P_{min}$ induces a unique qualitative utility $\mu_P$ using Eq. 3. This section shows that this qualitative utility is equal to the qualitative utility $\mu_{min}^{ID}$ (Eq. 2) encoded by the Influence Diagram $\Pi I D_{min}$. The graphical component $G_P$ of the new qualitative possibilistic network $\Pi P_{min}$ is defined on the set of variables $\mathcal{Z} = \{Z_1, ..., Z_m\} \subset \mathcal{X} \cup \mathcal{D}$ of chance and decision nodes. The set of nodes $\mathcal{Z}$ represents the union of the parent variables of all utility nodes $\{V_1, ..., V_q\}$ in the Influence Diagram. Namely, $\mathcal{Z} = \{Z_1, ..., Z_m\} = Par(V_1) \cup ... \cup Par(V_q)$, where $m = |Par(V_1) \cup ... \cup Par(V_q)|$ represents the total of parent variables of all utility nodes in $\Pi I D_{min}$. During the construction phase of the graph $G_P$, we need to make sure that the generated graph is a DAG structure. We should also avoid the creation of loops at the merging step of the evaluation process [3]. So, before enumerating the decomposition process of an Influence Diagram $\Pi ID_{min}$, the notion of topological order generated by a DAG is recalled:

**Definition 1.** *A Directed Acyclic Graph is a linear ordering of its nodes such that for every arc from node $X_i$ to node $X_j$, $X_i$ comes before $X_j$ in the ordering. Any DAG has at least one topological ordering.*

The construction of a topological ordering associated to any DAG is known to be achieved in a linear time. The usual algorithm for topological ordering consists in finding a "start node" having no incoming edges. Then, edges outgoing this node must be removed. This process will be repeated until all nodes will be visited.

We first propose a naive solution that requires a preliminary step which consists to reduce all utility nodes into a single one. This node will inherit the parents of all value nodes. A more advanced solution preserving the initial structure is then proposed. Hence, operating on the initial structure of the Influence Diagram induces a more compact representation.

**Decomposition Process with a Single Utility Node:**
The first solution consists in reducing all utility nodes into a single one. Hence, it amounts to perform preliminary on the initial Influence Diagram before its decomposition. Formally, the preliminary step consists to reduce the number of value nodes to one, noted $V_r$, that will inherit the parents of all value nodes $(Par(V_1), ..., Par(V_q))$ i.e. $Par(V_r) = Par(V_1) \cup ... \cup Par(V_q)$. The utility value associated to the new utility node $V_r$ corresponds to the minimum of utilities, which is equivalent to the global satisfaction degree. Namely:

$$\mu_r(u_{V_r}) = \mu_{min}^{ID}(x, d) = \min_{k=1..q} \mu_k(u_{V_k}). \tag{6}$$

where $u_{V_r} \in \mathbb{D}_{Par(V_r)}$ and $u_{V_k} \in \mathbb{D}_{Par(V_k)}$. The construction of preference-based possibilistic network $\Pi P_{min}$ can be summarized by Algorithm 2.

---

**Algorithm 2.** Construction of preference-based possibilistic network.

---

**Require:** $\{V_1, Par(V_1)\}, ..., \{V_q, Par(V_q)\}$, utility nodes and their parents in the qualitative Influence Diagram..
**Ensure:** $\Pi P_{min} = (G_P, \mu)$ {preference-based possibilistic network}
$\quad \mathcal{Z} \leftarrow \{Par(V_1) \cup ... \cup Par(V_q)\}$
$\quad$ Reduce all utility nodes to a single node $V_r$
$\quad$ Select a node $Z_k \in Par(V_r)$ to be child of the remaining parent variables according to the topological ordering induced by the reduced ID
$\quad$ Quantifying chance node $Z_k$ $\{ \mu(z_{kl} \mid u_{Z_k}) = \mu_{min}^{ID}(u_{V_r})\}$
$\quad$ **for** $Z_j \neq Z_k$ **do**
$\quad\quad$ Quantifying $Z_j$ $\{\forall z_{jl} \in \mathbb{D}_{Z_j}, \mu(z_{jl}) = 1.\}$
$\quad$ **end for**

---

The following proposition indicates that the min-based possibilistic network $\Pi P_{min} = (G_P, \mu)$ constructed from the previous steps, codifies the same qualitative utility encoded by the qualitative Influence Diagram $\Pi ID_{min}(G_{ID}, \pi_{min}^{ID}, \mu_{min}^{ID})$.

**Proposition 2.** *Let $\Pi ID_{min}(G_{ID}, \pi_{min}^{ID}, \mu_{min}^{ID})$ be a min-based PID. Let $\Pi P_{min}$ $= (G_P, \mu)$ be a min-based possibilistic network obtained using Algorithm 2. The joint qualitative utility $\mu_P$ induced by $\Pi P_{min}$ is equivalent to the one induced by the Influence Diagram $\Pi ID_{min}$. Namely,*

$$\mu_P(Z_1, ..., Z_m) = \mu_{min}^{ID}(X_1, ..., X_n, D_1, ..., D_p). \tag{7}$$

**Decomposition Process Based on the Initial Influence Diagram:**
The solution proposed in this section is to try to have the structure of a preference-based network as close as possible to the initial structure of the Influence Diagram. Hence, as we will see, operating on the initial structure of the ID allows a more compact representation than if we have used the reduced ID. The construction of preference-based possibilistic network $\Pi P_{min}$ can be summarized by Algorithm 3.

---

**Algorithm 3.** Preference-based possibilistic network.

---

**Require:** $\{V_1, Par(V_1)\}, ..., \{V_q, Par(V_q)\}$, utility nodes and their parents in the PID.
**Ensure:** $\Pi P_{min} = (G_P, \mu)$ {preference-based possibilistic network}
  $\mathcal{Z} \leftarrow \emptyset$.
  $Child \leftarrow \emptyset$.
  **for** $V_k \in \{V_1, ..., V_q\}$ **do**
    $List - order(V_k) \leftarrow \{Par(V_k)\}$ ordered in the same way that the order induced by $\Pi ID_{min}$.
    $Candidate(V_k) \leftarrow \{$ the variables with the last rank in the $List - order(V_k)\}$.
    Select a variable $Z_k \in Candidate(V_k)$ and $Z_k \notin Child$.
    **if** $Z_k$ exists **then**
      $Child \leftarrow Child \cup \{Z_k\}$./*$Z_k$ presents child in $G_P$*/
      Create nodes $Par(V_k) \notin \mathcal{Z}$./*creating nodes that not appear in $G_P$*/
      Create arcs from $\{Par(V_k) - Z_k\}$ to $Z_k$./*creating arcs from the remaining parent variables to the selected node $Z_k$*/
      Quantifying chance node $Z_k$ {}$\mu(z_{kl} \mid u_{Z_k}) = \mu_k(u_{V_k})$
    **else**
      Select a variable $Z_k \in Candidate(V_k)$ and $|Par(Z_k)|$ in $G_P$ is the smallest.
      Create nodes $Par(V_k) \notin \mathcal{Z}$.
      Create arcs from $\{Par(V_k) - Z_k\}$ to $Z_k$.
      Quantifying chance node $Z_k$ $\{\mu(z_{kl} \mid u_{Z_k}) = \min[\mu(z_{kl} \mid u_{Z_k}), \mu_k(u_{V_k})]\}$
    **end if**
    **for** $Z_j \in Par(V_k)$ and $Z_j \neq Z_k$ **do**
      **if** $Z_j \notin Child$ **then**
        Quantifying chance node $Z_j$ $\{\forall z_{jl} \in \mathbb{D}_{Z_j}, \mu(z_{jl}) = 1.\}$
      **end if**
    **end for**
  **end for**

---

The proposed algorithm generates the qualitative min-based possibilistic network $\Pi P_{min} = (G_P, \mu)$ step by step. Indeed, for each utility node, the algorithm selects the candidate parents that can be a child of the remaining parents in the DAG $G_P$ under construction. These candidate nodes appear in the last rank of the topological ordering generated by the ID. Among the candidates, if there exists a node that has not yet been introduced in $G_P$ or it presents a root node, so it will be selected as the child of the remaining parent variables in the DAG $G_P$ under construction. Otherwise, if such node does not exist then it means that all candidate nodes are already integrated in the DAG $G_P$ and they have parents. According to the selected node status an utility will be associated to this node. A total ignorance possibility distribution will be associated with the remaining parent variables.

It is evident that the last solution which operates on the initial ID structure allows a compact representation of the qualitative utility.

It should be noted that in the case of an ID with multiple utility nodes having no common parents, the preference-based qualitative possibilistic network will in fact be disconnected. Indeed, each component of the graph encodes local satisfaction degrees associated to one utility node.

The following proposition shows that the qualitative possibilistic network $\Pi P_{min} = (G_P, \mu)$, built following the previous steps, encodes the same qualitative utility encoded by the qualitative Influence Diagram $\Pi ID_{min}$ $(G_{ID}, \pi_{min}^{ID}, \mu_{min}^{ID})$.

**Proposition 3.** Let $\Pi ID_{min}(G_{ID}, \pi_{min}^{ID}, \mu_{min}^{ID})$ be a min-based PID. Let $\Pi P_{min} = (G_P, \mu)$ be a preferences-based possibilistic network obtained using Algorithm 3. The joint qualitative utility $\mu_P$ induced by $\Pi P_{min}$ is equal to the one induced by $\Pi ID_{min}$. Namely,

$$\mu_P(Z_1, ..., Z_m) = \mu_{min}^{ID}(X_1, ..., X_n, D_1, ..., D_p). \tag{8}$$

## 4    On the Computation of Optimal Optimistic Strategy

### 4.1    Qualitative Possibilistic Decision

The sequential decisions problem under uncertainty [15] is modeled by a finite set of possible states of the world $S = \{s_1, s_2, ..., s_n\}$, a set of decisions $D = \{D_1, D_2, ..., D_m\}$ and a set of preferences among the consequences. In the same way, a decision $D$ is represented by a combination of values of decision variables $D_i = \{d_1, d_2, ..., d_p\}$ chosen by a decision maker.

The problem of finding a strategy $\delta$ in sequential decisions problem under uncertainty turns out to be intractable in systems with a large state space on a long planning horizon. The high dimensionality of the state space is partly due to the fact that the states are generally defined as a simple conjunction of all the variables describing the different aspects of the state. Formally, this amounts to define a strategy $\delta : S \rightarrow D$ which assigns a decision instantiation $d$ to any global instantiation $s$ of the state variables: $d = \delta(s)$. A strategy expresses the way in which the values of decision variables are chosen, depending on the values of the state variables observed at the time of the choice.

In qualitative possibilistic framework, the uncertainty of the decision-maker about the effect of strategy $\delta$ is represented by a normalized possibility distribution $\pi_\delta$ which is a function from states to a simply ordered scale $L$ of plausibility: for a world $\omega$, $\pi_\delta(\omega) \in L$ represents the degree of likelihood that $\omega$ is the real state of the world and the preferences of the agent are expressed by means of a possibility distribution representing a qualitative utility function $\mu$ taking its values in the interval $[0, 1]$. The qualitative utility function $\mu : S \times D \longrightarrow U$ represents the agent's preferences. $\mu$ takes its values in a simply orderly scale in $[0, 1]$. As in Savage theory, an action is represented by a function $d$ that associates to a world an element of $s$ [14]. The utility of an action (decision) $d$ in a state $\omega$ and whose consequence is $d(\omega) \in S$ can be evaluated by combining the possibility degrees $\pi_\delta(\omega)$ and the utilities $\mu(d(\omega))$ in an appropriate manner for all the possible states of the world.

In order to evaluate a strategy $\delta$, two qualitative decision criteria have been proposed in [11]. In this chapter, we only deal with optimistic decision making where the qualitative utility function, denoted by $U^*$, and associated to a strategy $\delta$ is defined by:

$$U^*(\delta) = \max_{\omega \in \Omega} \min(\pi_\delta(\omega), \mu(\omega)) \tag{9}$$

A strategy $\delta$ specifies a value $d$ of all the decision variables $D$ according to the value $s$ of all state variables. The possibility distribution $\pi_\delta(\omega)$ is computed as follows:

$$\pi_\delta(\omega) = \min_{\omega \in \Omega}(\pi_K(\omega), \pi_{d \wedge \varepsilon}(\omega)) \tag{10}$$

Such that $\varepsilon$ is the set of evidence updated at every step $i - 1$ of the computation process of the optimal optimistic utility of decision $d_i$.

$$\pi_{d \wedge \varepsilon}(\omega) = \begin{cases} 1 \text{ if } \omega \models d \wedge \varepsilon \\ \\ 0 \text{ otherwise} \end{cases} \tag{11}$$

Using Eq. 11, the optimistic utility decision $U^*(\delta)$ becomes:

$$U^*(\delta) = \max_{\omega \in \Omega} \min(\min(\pi_K(\omega), \mu(\omega)), \pi_{d \wedge \varepsilon}(\omega))). \tag{12}$$

Using technical merging of two min-based possibilistic networks (Eq. 12) becomes:

$$U^*(\delta) = \max_{\omega \in \Omega} \min(\pi_\oplus(\omega), \pi_{d \wedge \varepsilon}(\omega))). \tag{13}$$

Where $\pi_\oplus(\omega) = \min(\pi_K(\omega), \mu(\omega))$.

*Example 1.* Let us consider a simple decision problem represented by a min-based Influence Diagram $\Pi ID_{min}(G_{ID}, \pi_{min}^{ID}, \mu_{min}^{ID})$. The graphical component $G_{ID}$ is given by Fig. 1. We suppose that all variables are binary. The numerical components are represented in Tables 1 and 2.

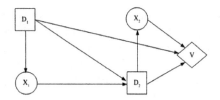

**Fig. 1.** An example of influence diagram.

**Table 1.** Initial possibility distributions associated to the PID of Fig. 1.

| $X_1$ | $D_1$ | $\pi_{ID}(X_1|D_1)$ | $X_2$ | $D_2$ | $\pi_{ID}(X_2|D_2)$ |
|---|---|---|---|---|---|
| $x_1$ | $d_1$ | 1 | $x_2$ | $d_2$ | .3 |
| $x_1$ | $\neg d_1$ | .4 | $x_2$ | $\neg d_2$ | 1 |
| $\neg x_1$ | $d_1$ | .2 | $\neg x_2$ | $d_2$ | 1 |
| $\neg x_1$ | $\neg d_1$ | 1 | $\neg x_2$ | $\neg d_2$ | .4 |

**Table 2.** Initial qualitative utilities associated to the PID of Fig. 1.

| $X_2$ | $D_1$ | $D_2$ | $\mu(X_2, D_1, D_2)$ | $X_2$ | $D_1$ | $D_2$ | $\mu(X_2, D_1)$ |
|---|---|---|---|---|---|---|---|
| $x_2$ | $d_1$ | $d_2$ | .2 | $\neg x_2$ | $d_1$ | $d_2$ | .3 |
| $x_2$ | $d_1$ | $\neg d_2$ | .4 | $\neg x_2$ | $d_1$ | $\neg d_2$ | .6 |
| $x_2$ | $\neg d_1$ | $d_2$ | 1 | $\neg x_2$ | $\neg d_1$ | $d_2$ | 0 |
| $x_2$ | $\neg d_1$ | $\neg d_2$ | .1 | $\neg x_2$ | $\neg d_1$ | $\neg d_2$ | .7 |

This influence diagram is decomposed into two qualitative possibilistic networks. The first one network $\Pi K_{min} = (G_K, \pi_k)$ describes agent's knowledge and the second one $\Pi P_{min} = (G_P, \mu)$ will express its preferences. The graphical component $G_K$ of $\pi K_{min}$ is given by Fig. 2. The initial possibility distributions $\pi_k$ are given by Tables 3 and 4.

The graphical component $G_P$ of $\pi P_{min}$ is given by Fig. 3. The initial possibility distributions associated are given by Tables 5 and 6.

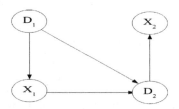

**Fig. 2.** Knowledge-based possibilistic network associated to the PID of Fig. 1.

**Table 3.** Initial possibility distributions associated to the network of Fig. 2.

| $D_1$ | $\pi(D_1)$ | $X_1$ | $D_1$ | $\pi_{ID}(X_1 \mid D_1)$ | $X_1$ | $D_1$ | $\pi_{ID}(X_1 \mid D_1)$ |
|---|---|---|---|---|---|---|---|
| $d_1$ | 1 | $x_1$ | $d_1$ | 1 | $\neg x_1$ | $d_1$ | .2 |
| $\neg d_1$ | 1 | $x_1$ | $\neg d_1$ | .4 | $\neg x_1$ | $\neg d_1$ | 1 |

**Table 4.** Initial possibility distributions associated to the network of Fig. 2.

| $D_2$ | $D_1$ | $X_1$ | $\pi(D_2 \mid D_1, X_1)$ | $D_1$ | $D_1$ | $x_1$ | $\pi(D_2 \mid D_1, X_1)$ | $X_2$ | $D_2$ | $\pi(X_2 \mid D_2)$ |
|---|---|---|---|---|---|---|---|---|---|---|
| $d_2$ | $d_1$ | $x_1$ | 1 | $\neg d_2$ | $d_1$ | $x_1$ | 1 | $x_2$ | $d_2$ | .3 |
| $d_2$ | $d_1$ | $\neg x_1$ | 1 | $\neg d_2$ | $d_1$ | $\neg x_1$ | 1 | $x_2$ | $\neg d_2$ | 1 |
| $d_2$ | $\neg d_1$ | $x_1$ | 1 | $\neg d_2$ | $\neg d_1$ | $x_1$ | 1 | $\neg x_2$ | $d_2$ | 1 |
| $d_2$ | $\neg d_1$ | $\neg x_1$ | 1 | $\neg d_2$ | $\neg d_1$ | $\neg x_1$ | 1 | $\neg x_2$ | $\neg d_2$ | .4 |

**Fig. 3.** Preference-based possibilistic network.

**Table 5.** Initial possibility distributions associated to the network of Fig. 3.

| $D_1$ | $\pi(D_1)$ | $D_2$ | $\pi(D_2)$ |
|---|---|---|---|
| $d_1$ | 1 | $d_2$ | 1 |
| $\neg d_1$ | 1 | $\neg d_2$ | 1 |

**Table 6.** Initial possibility distributions associated to the network of Fig. 3.

| $X_2$ | $D_1$ | $D_2$ | $\pi(X_2 \mid D_1, D_2)$ | $X_2$ | $D_1$ | $D_2$ | $\pi(X_2 \mid D_1, D_2)$ |
|---|---|---|---|---|---|---|---|
| $x_2$ | $d_1$ | $d_2$ | .2 | $\neg x_2$ | $d_1$ | $d_2$ | .3 |
| $x_2$ | $d_1$ | $\neg d_2$ | .4 | $\neg x_2$ | $d_1$ | $\neg d_2$ | .6 |
| $x_2$ | $\neg d_1$ | $d_2$ | 1 | $\neg x_2$ | $\neg d_1$ | $d_2$ | 0 |
| $x_2$ | $\neg d_1$ | $\neg d_2$ | 1 | $\neg x_2$ | $\neg d_1$ | $\neg d_2$ | .7 |

The union is free of cycles, then the result of merging $\Pi K_{min}$ and $\Pi P_{min}$ is the min-based possibilistic network $\Pi G_\oplus = (G_\oplus, \pi_\oplus)$, where $G_\oplus$ is given in Fig. 4.

The initial possibility distributions are given by Tables 7, 8 and 9, which are obtained using the minimum of local distributions $\pi_k$ and $\pi_P$.

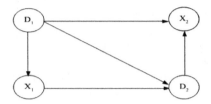

**Fig. 4.** Possibilistic network $G_\oplus$.

**Table 7.** The possibility distributions associated to the network of Fig. 4.

| $D_1$ | $\pi(D_1)$ | $X_1$ | $D_1$ | $\pi(X_1|D_1)$ | $X_1$ | $D_1$ | $\pi(X_1|D_1)$ |
|---|---|---|---|---|---|---|---|
| $d_1$ | 1 | $x_1$ | $d_1$ | 1 | $\neg x_1$ | $d_1$ | .2 |
| $\neg d_1$ | 1 | $x_1$ | $\neg d_1$ | .4 | $\neg x_1$ | $\neg d_1$ | 1 |

**Table 8.** The possibility distributions associated to the network of Fig. 4.

| $D_2$ | $D_1$ | $X_1$ | $\pi(D_2|D_1,X_1)$ | $D_1$ | $D_1$ | $x_1$ | $\pi(D_2|D_1,X_1)$ |
|---|---|---|---|---|---|---|---|
| $d_2$ | $d_1$ | $x_1$ | 1 | $\neg d_2$ | $d_1$ | $x_1$ | 1 |
| $d_2$ | $d_1$ | $\neg x_1$ | 1 | $\neg d_2$ | $d_1$ | $\neg x_1$ | 1 |
| $d_2$ | $\neg d_1$ | $x_1$ | 1 | $\neg d_2$ | $\neg d_1$ | $x_1$ | 1 |
| $d_2$ | $\neg d_1$ | $\neg x_1$ | 1 | $\neg d_2$ | $\neg d_1$ | $\neg x_1$ | 1 |

**Table 9.** The possibility distributions associated to the network of Fig. 4.

| $X_2$ | $D_1$ | $D_2$ | $\pi(X_2|D_1,D_2)$ | $X_2$ | $D_1$ | $D_2$ | $\pi(X_2|D_1,D_2)$ |
|---|---|---|---|---|---|---|---|
| $x_2$ | $d_1$ | $d_2$ | .2 | $\neg x_2$ | $d_1$ | $d_2$ | .3 |
| $x_2$ | $d_1$ | $\neg d_2$ | .4 | $\neg x_2$ | $d_1$ | $\neg d_2$ | .4 |
| $x_2$ | $\neg d_1$ | $d_2$ | .3 | $\neg x_2$ | $\neg d_1$ | $d_2$ | 0 |
| $x_2$ | $\neg d_1$ | $\neg d_2$ | .1 | $\neg x_2$ | $\neg d_1$ | $\neg d_2$ | .4 |

## 4.2   Computing Sequential Decisions Using Junction Trees

Computing the optimistic sequential decisions amounts to find the normalization degree of the junction tree resulting from the merging of the two possibilistic networks codifying knowledge of the agent and its preferences respectively. Note that the construction of the junction tree is done only once. However, the propagation and the initialization (which are both polynomial) are repeated for each decision $d_i^*$.

**Building Junction Tree $\mathcal{JT}$.** Min-based propagation algorithms begin by transforming the initial graph $G_\oplus$ into a junction tree in three steps [4]:

- *Moralization of the initial graph $G_\oplus$:* consists in creating an undirected graph from the initial one by adding links between the parents of each variable.
- *Triangulation of the moral graph:* allows to identify sets of variables that can be gathered as clusters or cliques denoted by $C_i$.

– *Construction of a junction tree $\mathcal{JT}$*: the junction tree is built by connecting the clusters identified in the previous step. Once adjacent clusters have been identified, between each pair of clusters $C_i$ and $C_j$, a separator $S_{ij}$ containing their common variables, is inserted.

**Initialization for a Conjunction of Decision $d_i$ and Evidence $\varepsilon_{i-1}$.** Once the junction tree built, we proceed to its quantification taking into account the decision $d_i$ and the evidence $\varepsilon_{i-1}$ as follows:

– for each cluster $C_i$ (resp. $S_{ij}$), $\pi_{C_i}^I \leftarrow 1$. (resp.$\pi_{S_{ij}}^I \leftarrow 1$)
– for each variable $A_i$, choose a cluster $C_i$ containing
  $A_i \cup U_{A_i}, \pi_{C_i} \leftarrow min(\pi_{C_i}, \pi_{\oplus}(A_i|U_{A_i})$
– encode the fact $d_i \wedge \varepsilon_{i-1}$ as likelihood $\Lambda_E(d_i \wedge \varepsilon_{i-1})$:

$$\Lambda_E(d_i \wedge \varepsilon_{i-1}) = \begin{cases} 1 \ E \text{ is instanciated as } d_i \wedge \varepsilon_{i-1} \\ 0 \text{ otherwise} \end{cases} \tag{14}$$

– identify a cluster $C_i$ containing $D \wedge \varepsilon_{i-1}$:

$$\pi_{C_i}^t \leftarrow min(\pi_{C_i}^t, \Lambda_E). \tag{15}$$

Note that Eq. 14 does not appear in standard initialization of junction trees associated with standard min-based possibilistic networks. It is proper to our frame-work by entering the fact $d_i \wedge \varepsilon_{i-1}$, the junction trees $JT$ encodes $\pi_{JT} = (\pi_{G_{\oplus}}(\omega), \pi_{d_i \wedge \varepsilon_{i-1}}(\omega))$. Then the qualitative utility associated to a decision $d_i$ taking into account a selected instantiation of decisions in previous steps is summarized by the following proposition:

**Proposition 4.** *Let $\Pi K_{\min} = (G_K, \pi_K)$ be a min-based possibilistic network representing agent's beliefs and $\Pi P_{\min} = (G_P, \mu)$ be a min-based possibilistic network representing agent's preferences. Let $\Pi G_{\oplus} = (G_{\oplus}, \pi_{\oplus})$ be the result of merging $\Pi K_{\min}$ and $\Pi P_{\min}$ using the min operator. Let $JT$ be the junction trees corresponding to $\Pi G_{\oplus}$ generated using the above initialization procedure. Then,*

$$U^*(\delta) = \max_{\omega \in \Omega} \pi_{JT}(\omega). \tag{16}$$

**Global Propagation.** The global propagation is performed in order to make it globally consistent. Namely: $\max\limits_{C_i \setminus S_{ij}} \pi_{C_i}^t = \pi_{S_{ij}}^t = \max\limits_{C_j \setminus S_{ij}} \pi_{C_j}^t$.

The global propagation is ensured via a message passing mechanism between clusters which starts by choosing an arbitrary cluster to be a pivot node, then follows two main phases concerning collection and distribution of the evidence:

– collect-evidence: each cluster passes a message to its adjacent cluster in the pivot direction.
– distribute-evidence: each cluster passes a message to its adjacent clusters away from the pivot direction beginning by the pivot itself until reaching the leaves of the graph.

If a cluster $C_i$ sends a message to its adjacent cluster $C_j$, then the potential of $C_j$ and their separator $S_{ij}$ are updated as follows:

(a) Update the potential of $S_{ij}$ : $\pi_{S_{ij}}^{t+1} \leftarrow \max\limits_{C_i \backslash S_{ij}} \pi_{C_i}^t$.

(b) Update the potential of $C_j$ : $\pi_{C_j}^{t+1} \leftarrow \min(\pi_{C_j}^t, \pi_{S_{ij}}^{t+1})$.

Once stability is reached, the computation of the qualitative utility relative to a decision $d$ can be achieved.

**Proposition 5.** *Let* $\Pi K_{min} = (G_K, \pi)$ *and* $\Pi P_{min} = (G_P, \mu)$ *be the min-based networks representing agent's beliefs and preferences. Let* $\Pi G_{\oplus} = (G_{\oplus}, \pi_{\oplus})$ *be the result of merging* $\Pi K_{min}$ *and* $\Pi P_{min}$ *using the min operator. Let* $\mathcal{JT}$ *be the junction tree associated with* $\Pi G_{\oplus}$ *generated using the above global propagation procedure. Then, the computation of optimistic decisions amounts to compute a normalization degree of* $\mathcal{JT}$ :

$$u^*(d) = h(\pi_{\mathcal{JT}}) = \max_{C_i} \pi_{C_i}. \tag{17}$$

The optimal optimistic decisions are those maximizing the qualitative utility. The computation of these optimal optimistic decisions is obtained using the Algorithm 4.

---

**Algorithm 4.** Graph-based computation of optimistic sequential decisions.

---

**Require:**
$\Pi ID_{min}(G_{ID}, \pi_{min}^{ID}, \mu_{min}^{ID})$, a min-based Influence Diagram,
$\mathcal{D} = \{D_1, ..., D_p\}$, set of decisions.
**Ensure:** strategies $\delta$.
$\Pi K_{min} = Algo\text{-}1\text{-}Building\_knowledge\text{-}based\_network\ (\Pi ID_{min})$
**if** Building Preference == without reducing **then**
    $\Pi P_{min} = Algo\text{-}3\text{-}preference\text{-}based\_possibilistic\_network(\Pi ID_{min})$
**else**
    $\Pi P_{min} = Algo\text{-}2\text{-}preference\text{-}based\_possibilistic\_network(\Pi ID_{min})$
**end if**
$Fusion(\Pi K_{min}, \Pi P_{min}, \Pi G_{\oplus})$
$Junction - Tree(\Pi G_{\oplus}, \mathcal{JT})$
$i \leftarrow 1$,
$Norm_1 \leftarrow 0$, /*normalisation degree*/,
$Norm_2 \leftarrow 0$, /*normalisation degree*/,
$\delta\emptyset$, /*optimal optimistic decisions*/,
**for** $i = 1..p$ **do**
    $Init(\mathcal{JT}, \delta \cup d_{i\_1})$,/*Initialization step for the instance $d_{i\_1}$*/
    $Norm_1 \leftarrow Prog(\mathcal{JT})$, /*global propagation*/
    $Init(\mathcal{JT}, \delta \cup d_{i\_2})$,/*Initialization step for the instance $d_{i\_2}$*/
    $Norm_2 \leftarrow Prog(\mathcal{JT})$, /*global propagation*/
    **if** $Norm_1 > Norm_2$ **then**
        $\delta \leftarrow \delta \cup d_{i\_1}$,
    **else**
        $\delta \leftarrow \delta \cup d_{i\_2}$,
    **end if**
**end for**

---

*Example 2.* Let us continue Example 1. Knowing that the temporal order associated to decisions $\{D_1, D_2\}$ is: $D_1 \prec D_2$. To compute a strategy $\delta$, we first start by constructing the junction tree, as depicted in Fig. 5 associated with the graph $G_\oplus$ representing the fusion of $\Pi K_{min}$ and $\Pi P_{min}$.

**Fig. 5.** The junction tree associated with $G_\oplus$.

For each decision value $D_2 = \{d_2, \neg d_2\}$, we must run the propagation algorithm is used in order to compute the normalization degree associated with the junction tree.

**Step 1:** $D = d_2$

the fact $D_2 = d_2$ is encoded as likelihood using Eq. 14. From the initialization procedure, we get:

$\pi C_1 = \min(1, \pi_{G_\oplus}(D_1)), \pi_{G_\oplus}(D_2|D_1 X_1), \pi_{G_\oplus}(X_1|D1)))$.

$\pi C_2 = \min(1, \pi_{G_\oplus}(X_2|D_1 D_2), \Lambda_{D2})$.

Once the junction tree is quantified, then the global propagation allows to compute the normalization degree of the junction tree which corresponds to the normalization degree of any cluster. Using this procedure, we obtain: $U^*(d_2) = \max_{C_1} \pi_{C_1} = \max_{C_2} \pi_{C_2} = 0.3$.

**Step 2:** $D_2 = \neg d_2$

We repeat the same procedure described in the previous step, with $D_2 = \neg d_2$. Then, we get: $U^*(\neg d_2) = \max_{C_1} \pi_{C_1} = \max_{C_2} \pi_{C_2} = 0.4$.

Thus, we can conclude that the optimal optimistic decision is $D_2 = \neg d_2$ with the maximal qualitative utility equal to 0.4.

The choice of $D_2$ is then fixed, so the set of evidence must be updated. Namely $E_1 = \{D_2 = \neg d_2\}$. In the same way it will be computed the optimal optimistic utility of decision $D_1$ taking into account the value of the decision $D_2$.

**Step 1:** $D = d_1$

In this case, the fact $d_1 \wedge \neg d_2$ is encoded as likelihood using Eq. 14. By applying the propagation process, we obtain: $U^*(d_1 \wedge \neg d_2) = 0.4$.

**Step 2:** $D_1 = \neg d_1$

We repeat the same procedure with the fact $\neg d_1 \wedge \neg d_2$ using Eq. 14. By applying the propagation process, we get: $U^*(\neg d_1 \wedge \neg d_2) = 0.4$.

Thus, we can conclude that the optimal optimistic strategy $\delta$ is defined by: $\delta = (D_1 = d_1, D_2 = \neg d_2)$ and $(D_1 = \neg d_1, D_2 = \neg d_2)$ with the maximal qualitative utility equal to 0.4.

## 5   Experimental Studies

In order to evaluate the performances of the proposed algorithms for the decomposition of an influence diagram, we conducted a set of experiments. Each experiment consists of generating four models representing qualitative possibilistic influences diagrams containing respectively:

– a single utility node with a single decision node,
– a single utility node with multiple decision nodes,
– a multiple nodes with multiple decision nodes,
– very complex PID.

For each model, the following steps are applied:

– generating a set of samples by varying the number of nodes corresponding to the associated description.
– decomposing the PID into two min-based possibilistic networks corresponding to the knowledge and the preferences using:
     1. Algorithm 2 (with reduction of the utility nodes),
     2. Algorithm 3 (without reduction of the utility nodes).
– computing the optimistic strategy using Algorithm 4.

Figure 6 illustrates the attitudes of the two algorithms used to compute the optimistic strategies.

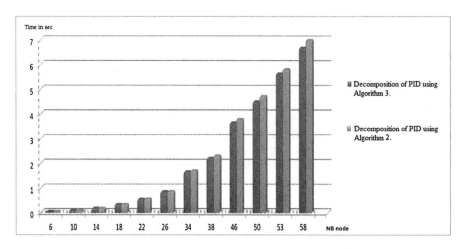

**Fig. 6.** Comparison of execution time for computing optimistic strategies using the Algorithms 2 and 3.

The results, depicted in Fig. 6, indicates that the computation of the optimistic strategies when the decomposition process is achieved without reducing the utility notes (Algorithm 2) is realized in a more optimal time when the reducing process is used (Algorithm 3). Indeed, reducing utilities nodes provides non compact representation of beliefs. It only increases the complexity of the graph.

# 6    Conclusions

This chapter first proposed a decomposition of a Possibilistic Influence Diagram into two possibilistic networks: the first expresses agents knowledge and the second encodes its preferences. This procedure allows a simple representation of decision problems under uncertainty. Indeed, the decomposition process described in this chapter offers a natural way to express knowledge and preferences of a agent separately in unified way using only one type of nodes. Also this chapter addressed a new approach for computing optimal optimistic sequential decisions (strategy) in a possibilistic graphical framework. Our approach first merges possibilistic networks associated with available uncertain knowledge and possibilistic networks associated with agents preferences. We then showed that computing optimistic sequential decisions comes down to compute a normalization degree of the junction tree associated to the resulting graph of merging agent's beliefs and preferences networks. This allows an efficient computation of optimal decisions.

**Acknowledgments.** This work has received supports from the french Agence Nationale de la Recherche, ASPIQ project reference ANR-12-BS02-0003. This work has also received support from the european project H2020 Marie Sklodowska-Curie Actions (MSCA) research and Innovation Staff Exchange (RISE): AniAge (High Dimensional Heterogeneous Data based Animation Techniques for Southeast Asian Intangible Cultural Heritage Digital Content), project number 691215.

# References

1. Ajroud, A., Omri, M., Youssef, H., Benferhat, S.: Loopy belief propagation in bayesian networks: origin and possibilistic perspectives. CoRR abs/1206.0976 (2012)
2. Amor, N.B., Benferhat, S., Mellouli, K.: Anytime propagation algorithm for min-based possibilistic graphs. Soft Comput. **8**(2), 150–161 (2003)
3. Benferhat, S., Khellaf, F., Zeddigha, I.: A possibilistic graphical model for handling decision problems under uncertainty. In: The 8th Conference of the European Society for Fuzzy Logic and Technology, EUSFLAT, Milano, Italy, September 2013
4. Darwiche, A.: Modeling and Reasoning with Bayesian Networks, 1st edn. Cambridge University Press, New York (2009)
5. Dubois, D., Godo, L., Prade, H., Zapico, A.: On the possibilistic decision model: from decision under uncertainty to case-based decision. Int. J. Uncertain. Fuzziness Knowl.-Based Syst. **7**(6), 631–670 (1999)
6. Dubois, D., Prade, H.: Possibility Theory: An Approach to Computerized Processing of Uncertainty. Plenum Press, New York (1988)
7. Dubois, D., Prade, H.: Possibility theory as a basis for qualitative decision theory. In: Proceedings of the 14th International Joint Conference on Artificial Intelligence, vol. 2, pp. 1924–1930. Morgan Kaufmann Publishers Inc., San Francisco (1995)
8. Dubois, D., Prade, H., Sabbadin, R.: Decision-theoretic foundations of qualitative possibility theory. Eur. J. Oper. Res. **128**(3), 459–478 (2001)
9. Titouna, F.: Fusion de réseaux causaux possibilistes. Ph.D. thesis, Université d'Artois (2009)

10. Garcia, L., Sabbadin, R.: Possibilistic influence diagrams. In: 17th European Conference on Artificial Intelligence (ECAI 2006), Riva del Garda, Italy, pp. 372–376. IOS Press, August 2006

11. Gebhardt, J., Kruse, R.: Background and perspectives of possibilistic graphical models. In: Gabbay, D.M., Kruse, R., Nonnengart, A., Ohlbach, H.J. (eds.) ECSQARU/FAPR -1997. LNCS, vol. 1244, pp. 108–121. Springer, Heidelberg (1997). doi:10.1007/BFb0035616

12. Giang, P., Shenoy, P.: Two axiomatic approaches to decision making using possibility theory. Eur. J. Oper. Res. 162(2), 450–467 (2005)

13. Guezguez, W., Amor, N.B., Mellouli, K.: Qualitative possibilistic influence diagrams based on qualitative possibilistic utilities. Eur. J. Oper. Res. 195(1), 223–238 (2009)

14. Sabbadin, R.: Une approche logique de la résolution de problèmes de décision sous incertitude basée sur les atms. In: Actes du 11ème Congrés Reconnaissance des Formes et Intelligence Artificielle (RFIA 1998), Clermont-Ferrand, pp. 391–400, 20–22 Janvier 1998

15. Sabbadin, R.: A possibilistic model for qualitative sequential decision problems under uncertainty in partially observable environments. In: The Fifteenth Conference on Uncertainty in Artificial Intelligence (UAI), pp. 567–574 (1999)

16. Tatman, J., Shachter, R.: Dynamic programming and influence diagrams. IEEE Trans. Syst. Man Cybern. 20(2), 365–379 (1990)

17. Zhang, N.: Probabilistic inference in influence diagrams. In: Computational Intelligence, pp. 514–522 (1998)

# Enhancing Visual Clustering Using Adaptive Moving Self-Organizing Maps (AMSOM)

Gerasimos Spanakis$^{(\boxtimes)}$ and Gerhard Weiss

Department of Data Science and Knowledge Engineering, Maastricht University,
6200MD Maastricht, Netherlands
{jerry.spanakis,gerhard.weiss}@maastrichtuniversity.nl,
https://project.dke.maastrichtuniversity.nl/RAI/

**Abstract.** Recent advancements in computing technology allowed both scientific and business applications to produce large datasets with increasing complexity and dimensionality. Clustering algorithms are useful in analyzing these large datasets but often fall short to provide completely satisfactory results. Integrating clustering and visualization not only yields better clustering results but also leads to a higher degree of confidence in the findings. Self-Organizing Map (SOM) is a neural network model which is used to obtain a topology-preserving mapping from the (usually high dimensional) input/feature space to an output/map space of fewer dimensions (usually two or three in order to facilitate visualization). Neurons in the output space are connected with each other but this structure remains fixed throughout training and learning is achieved through the updating of neuron reference vectors in feature space. Despite the fact that growing variants of SOM overcome the fixed structure limitation, they increase computational cost and also do not allow the removal of a neuron after its introduction. In this paper, a variant of SOM is presented called AMSOM (Adaptive Moving Self-Organizing Map) that on the one hand creates a more flexible structure where neuron positions are dynamically altered during training and on the other hand tackles the drawback of having a predefined grid by allowing neuron addition and/or removal during training. Experimental evaluation on different literature datasets with diverse characteristics improves SOM training performance, leads to a better visualization of the input dataset, and provides a framework for determining the optimal number and structure of neurons as well as the optimal number of clusters.

**Keywords:** Self-Organizing Maps · Clustering · Visualization · Unsupervised learning

## 1 Introduction

Clustering is one of the basic data analysis tasks: It is a process of organizing data into similar groups, without any prior knowledge or training. With the increasing graphics capabilities of the available computers, researchers realized

© Springer International Publishing AG 2017
J. van den Herik and J. Filipe (Eds.): ICAART 2016, LNAI 10162, pp. 189–211, 2017.
DOI: 10.1007/978-3-319-53354-4_11

[2,8] that integrating the visual component into the clustering process helps to improve the effectiveness of automated clustering algorithms. This synthesis of computational clustering methods and interactive visualization techniques not only yields better clustering results but allows exploration and refinement of the clustering structure. Designing such embedded algorithms is tricky mainly due to two limitations: (a) automated clustering algorithms are sensitive to input parameters and results may significantly vary and (b) large data spaces often have skewed distributions which are difficult to be approximated.

The Self-Organizing Map (SOM) [27] is an unsupervised neural network model which effectively maps high-dimensional data to a low-dimensional space (usually two-dimensional). The low-dimensional space (also called output space) consists of a grid of neurons connected with each other, according to a specific structure (can be hexagonal, rectangular, etc.). This structure allows the topology preservation of input data (i.e., similar input patterns are expected to be mapped to neighboring neurons in the output grid) [24]. By this way, SOM manages to achieve dimensionality reduction, abstraction, clustering and visualization of the input data and this is the reason that it has been applied successfully to many different domains and datasets like financial data [12], speech recognition [25], image classification [31], document clustering [29,40].

The SOM algorithm raises some issues and problems: (a) SOM's architecture is fixed and predefined in terms of number and arrangement of neurons. In case of largely unknown input data, it is difficult to determine apriori the correct structure that provides satisfactory results. There is some work in this area in order to how to add/remove neurons but none of current approaches adjusts neuron positions on the grid based on training progress. (b) Training a SOM comes with a large computation cost, especially in cases of large datasets and/or large maps. Many epochs might be needed in order for the SOM to converge and the map to reach a final state.

In this paper we study how an extension of the traditional SOM can effectively be used for visual clustering and handles both issues described above: First, it allows neurons to change positions during training which provides better visualization and faster training time. Second, number of neurons can be adjusted (neurons can be either added or removed) according to dataset requirements and training progress. Due to this enhanced training scheme, the number of epochs required for training is significantly reduced. The rest of the paper is organized as follows. Section 2 presents background work on SOM, extensions on the traditional algorithm and their limitations. The proposed method is presented in Sect. 3 while experimental setup is described in Sect. 4. Finally, Sect. 5 concludes the paper.

## 2     Related Work

### 2.1     SOM and Competitive Learning

The Self-Organizing Map (SOM) is a fully connected single-layer linear neural network. The SOM uses a set of neurons, often arranged in a 2-D rectangular or hexagonal grid, to form a discrete topological mapping of an input space, $\mathbf{X} \in R^D$. Input space consists of a set of vectors $\mathbf{x}_j \in R^D$:

$$\mathbf{x}_j = [x_{j1}, x_{j2}, \ldots, x_{jD}]^T \tag{1}$$

$\mathbf{w}_i$ is the weight vector associated to neuron $i$ and is a vector of the same dimension $(D)$ of the input space, $M$ is the total number of neurons. Obviously, these weights represent the synaptic connections of each neuron $i$ and can be denoted:

$$\mathbf{w}_i = [w_{i1}, w_{i2}, \ldots, w_{iD}]^T \tag{2}$$

The fundamental principle of SOM is the soft competition between the nodes in the output layer; not only the node (winner) but also its neighbors are updated [28].

A SOM architecture can be found in Fig. 1.

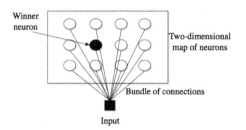

**Fig. 1.** The SOM (fully connected) architecture.

All the weights $\mathbf{w}_1, \mathbf{w}_2, \ldots, \mathbf{w}_M$ are initialized to random numbers, in the range of the corresponding input characteristics. We also introduce a discrete time index $t$ such that $\mathbf{x}(t), t = 0, 1, \ldots$ is presented to network at time $t$ and $\mathbf{w}_i(t)$ is the weight vector of neuron $i$ computed at time $t$. The available input vectors are recycled during the training (or learning) process: a single pass over the input data is called an epoch.

**On-Line Training of SOM.** In the conventional "on-line" or "flow-through" method, the weight vectors are updated recursively after the presentation of each input vector. As each input vector is presented, the Euclidean distance between the input vector and each weight vector is computed:

$$d_i(t) = ||\mathbf{x}(t) - \mathbf{w}_i(t)||^2 \tag{3}$$

Next, the winning or best-matching node (denoted by subscript $c$) is determined by:

$$c = \{i, min_i d_i(t)\} \tag{4}$$

Note that we suppress the implicit dependence of $c$ on discrete time $t$. The weight vectors are updated using the following rule:

$$\mathbf{w}_i(t+1) = \mathbf{w}_i(t) + \alpha(t) \cdot h_{ci}(t) \cdot [\mathbf{x}(t) - \mathbf{w}_i(t)] \tag{5}$$

where $\alpha(t)$ is the learning-rate factor and $h_{ci}(t)$ is the neighborhood function. The learning rate factor controls the overall magnitude of the correction to the weight vectors, and is reduced monotonically during the training phase. The neighborhood function controls the extent to which $\mathbf{w}_i(t)$ is allowed to adjust in response to an input most closely resembling $\mathbf{w}_c(t)$ and is typically a decreasing function of the distance on the 2-D lattice between nodes $c$ and $i$. We use the standard Gaussian neighborhood function:

$$h_{ci}(t) = exp\left(-\frac{||\mathbf{r}_i - \mathbf{r}_c||^2}{\sigma(t)^2}\right) \tag{6}$$

where $\mathbf{r}_i$ and $\mathbf{r}_c$ denote the coordinates of nodes $i$ and $c$, respectively, on the output space (usually two-dimensional grid). The width $\sigma(t)$ of the neighborhood function decreases during training, from an initial value comparable to the dimension of the lattice to a final value effectively equal to the width of a single cell. It is this procedure which produces the self-organization and topology preserving capabilities of the SOM: presentation of each input vector adjusts the weight vector of the winning node along with those of its topological neighbors to more closely resemble the input vector. The converged weight vectors approximate the input probability distribution function, and can be viewed as prototypes representing the input data.

**Batch Training of SOM.** The SOM update given by Eq. (5) is "on-line" in the sense that the weight vectors are updated after the presentation of each input record. In the batch SOM algorithm (proposed in [26]), the weights are updated only at the end of each epoch according to:

$$\mathbf{w}_i(t_f) = \frac{\sum_{t'=t_0}^{t'=t_f} \tilde{h}_{ci}(t') \cdot \mathbf{x}(t')}{\sum_{t'=t_0}^{t'=t_f} \tilde{h}_{ci}(t')} \tag{7}$$

where $t_0$ and $t_f$ denote the start and finish of the present epoch, respectively, and $w_i(t_f)$ are the weight vectors computed at the end of the present epoch. Hence, the summations are accumulated during one complete pass over the input data. The winning node at each presentation of new input vector is computed using:

$$\tilde{d}_i(t) = ||\mathbf{x}(t) - \mathbf{w}_i(t_0)||^2 \tag{8}$$
$$c = \{i, min_i \tilde{d}_i(t)\} \tag{9}$$

where $\mathbf{w}_i(t_0)$ are the weight vectors computed at the end of the previous epoch. The neighborhood functions $\tilde{h}_{ci}(t)$ are computed using Eq. (6), but with the winning nodes determined from Eq. (9). This procedure for computing the neighborhood function is identical to the Voronoi partitioning. As is in the on-line method, the width of the neighborhood function decreases monotonically over the training phase.

A more concrete explanation of the batch algorithm is given by the following equation:

$$\mathbf{w}_i = \frac{\sum_j n_j \cdot h_{ji} \cdot \tilde{x}_j}{\sum_j n_j \cdot h_{ji}} \tag{10}$$

where $n_j$ is the number of input items mapped into node $j$ and the index $j$ runs over the nodes in the neighborhood of node $i$. The basic idea is that for every node $j$ in the grid, the average $\tilde{x}_j$ of all those input items $x(t)$ is formed that have node $j$ (i.e., vector $\mathbf{w}_j$) as the closest node. The above equation is used for updating the node weight vectors and this is repeated for a few times, always using the same batch of input data items to determine the updated $\tilde{x}_j$.

The batch SOM offers several advantages over the conventional on-line SOM method. Since the weight updates are not recursive, there is no dependence upon the order in which the input records are presented. In addition to facilitating the development of data-partitioned parallel methods, this also eliminates concerns [34] that input records encountered later in the training sequence may overly influence the final results. The learning rate parameter $\alpha(t)$ does not appear in the batch SOM algorithm, thus eliminating a potential source of poor convergence [9] if this parameter is not properly specified.

The mathematical theory of SOM is very complicated and only the one-dimensional case has been analyzed completely [16], since SOM belongs to the "ill posed" problems in mathematics. The SOM can also be looked at as a "nonlinear projection" of the probability density function of high-dimensional input data onto the two-dimensional display.

Usually, the input is mapped onto a 1- or 2-dimensional map. Mapping onto higher dimensions is possible as well, but complicates the visualization. The neurons connected to adjacent neurons by a neighborhood relationship define the structure of the map. The two most common 2-dimensional grids are the hexagonal grid and the rectangular grid and are shown in Fig. 2.

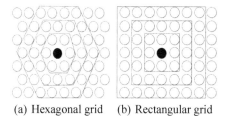

(a) Hexagonal grid    (b) Rectangular grid

**Fig. 2.** Typical SOM grids with different neighborhoods around the winner neuron.

The neighborhood function defines the correlation between neurons. The simplest neighborhood function is called *bubble*; it is constant over the neighborhood of the winner neuron and zero otherwise. The neighborhood of different sizes in rectangular and hexagonal maps can be seen in Fig. 2. A more flexible definition is the *gaussian neighborhood function* defined by Eq. (6).

The number of neurons, the dimensions of the map grid, the map lattice and shape must be specified before training. The more neurons the grid has, the more flexible the mapping becomes but the computation complexity of the training phase increases as well. The choice of the map structure and size is both related to the type of problem and the subjective choice of the user.

## 2.2  Flexible Structure in Neural Networks and SOM

The norm in artificial neural nets is that classic techniques involve simple and often fixed network topologies trained via stimulus-based methods such as back-propagation. However, there are cases in which the structural design of the network is strongly influenced by the environment and by utilizing constructive and pruning algorithms. Both these algorithmic categories deliver a network which is gradually adjusted in response to training data. There are many approaches which apply these algorithms in classic neural networks [6, 21, 23, 35, 46].

Also, there are many variations of SOM that allow a more flexible structure of the output map which can be divided into two categories: In the first type, we include growing grid (GG) [18], incremental GG [5], growing SOM (GSOM) [1] all coming with different variants. GG is the only variant which allows growing a new node from the interior of the grid (but this is a whole row or column of nodes). In the rest cases, new nodes are generated by a boundary node, despite the fact that the highest error could have been generated by an internal node. The idea is that the error will be propagated to the exterior to guarantee that growing can only be from the boundaries but this process can lead to a map structure with not perfect topology preservation. Therefore, map size becomes very wide after a limited number of insertions, with some additional nodes, which have no effect. MIGSOM [3] allows a more flexible structure by adding neurons both internally and from the boundary but still does not offer the ability to remove neurons if necessary.

In the second type of growing variants, the rectangular grid is replaced with some connected nodes. We distinguish growing cell structures (GCSs) [17], growing neural gas (GNG) [19] and growing where required [33]. These works just add the necessary nodes at the same time, to fine-tune the optimal map size. Nevertheless, GCS and GNG are facing many difficulties for visualizing high-dimensional data. Visualization in these cases is guaranteed only with low-dimensional data.

Limitations in growing and visualization led to hierarchical variants of the previous model like the Growing Hierarchical SOM (GHSOM) [39]. With GHSOM you can get an idea of the hierarchical structure of the map, but the growing parameter of the map has to be determined beforehand. Other approaches (like TreeGNG [13] or TreeGCS [22]) use dendrograms for representation but due to this tree structure they lose the topological properties.

Disadvantages of these approaches are: (a) the high computational cost due to the fact that structure starts from a very basic architecture and has to grow in order to reach an acceptable structure for the data and (b) the fact that after adding neurons there is not the possibility of removing a neuron if performance is not improving.

# 3   Expanding the Idea of Self-organization in Neuron Locations

During the classic SOM algorithm neuron positions remain unchanged and the grid is fixed from the beginning till the end of the training. This facilitates the process of learning (since neighborhood structure is known beforehand) but is restricting regarding the final result and ways of visualizing it. We propose a different and more flexible scheme in regard to position vectors $r_i$ of neurons, which allows a more adaptive form of the neuron grid and acts as an extension to the batch learning algorithm.

Starting from an already grown map size, AMSOM can adapt both its size and structure in order to better represent the data at a specific level of detail. After a specific number of steps, neurons are analyzed to see whether the level of representation is sufficient or adjustments are needed: removal and/or addition of neurons. Initially, connections between neurons are determined based on the grid structure but as training advances, these can change and adjust according to the way that neuron positions are also changed during the process. The algorithm flow is described in Fig. 3 and more details about the steps are presented in the following subsections.

## 3.1   Phase I: AMSOM Initialization

**Grid Structure and Size.** The first step of AMSOM algorithm is to define the initial grid structure (as the classic SOM). This process facilitates training time in contrast to starting from a small-size structure and building on that as other approaches do [43]. It is also in agreement with the neural development which suggests that nearly all neural cells used through human lifetime have been produced in the first months of life [14]. This overproduction of neuron cells is thought to have evolved as a competitive strategy for the establishment of efficient connectivity [10].

Having this in mind, the initial structure of SOM is determined. Several empirical rules [37] suggest that the number of neurons should be $5 \cdot \sqrt{N}$ where $N$ is the number of patterns in the dataset. In this case, the two largest eigenvalues of the training data are first calculated, then the ratio between side lengths of the map grid is set to the ratio between the two maximum eigenvalues. The actual side lengths are finally set so that their product is close to the number of map units determined according to [43] rule. The eigenvalues ratio shows how well the data is flattened and elongated [15]. At this point a more precise determination of the number of neurons is not essential, since this number will be fine tuned

---

**1. Initialization Phase**
1.1: Derive initial grid structure and size (number of neurons $M$) of the AMSOM
1.2: Initialize weight vectors ($\mathbf{w}_i$) to random values (according to the value range of features).
1.3: Initialize position vectors ($\mathbf{r}_i$) according to the initial grid structure
1.4: Initialize edge connectivity matrix ($\mathbf{E}$) values according to the grid connections
1.5: Initialize edge age matrix ($\mathbf{A}$) values to zero
1.6: Define growing threshold ($GT$) according to dimension of the data $D$ and a spreading factor ($SF$).
**2. Training phase**
**for** $t = 1 : maxepochs$ **do**
   **for** $i = 1 : P$ **do**
      2.1: Find winner neuron $N_a$ according to Equation (9) and increase times that neuron $N_a$ is winner by 1
      2.2: Find second best matching neuron $N_b$ (using Equation (9) and excluding $N_a$ from the search)
      2.3: Age of all edges between $N_a$ and its neighbors increased by one
      2.4: Connect $N_a$ with $N_b$ (if they were not already connected)
      2.5: Reset age between $N_a$ and $N_b$ to zero
   **end for**
   2.6: Use Equations 12-13 to update neuron weights.
   2.7: Use Equations 14-15 to update neuron positions.
   2.8:
   **if** neurons need to be added/removed (check $age_{max}$ and $t_{add}$) **then** add/remove neurons and update accordingly
   **end if**
   2.9:
   **if** error does not change significantly **then** end training phase
   **else**Continue
   **end if**
**end for**
**3. Smoothing phase**
3.1: Fine-tune weights and deliver the AMSOM neuron weight vectors and positions
3.2: Utilize edge connectivity matrix $\mathbf{E}$ and similarity between neuron weight vectors $\mathbf{w}_i$ in order to find the optimal number of clusters

---

**Fig. 3.** AMSOM algorithm overview.

during the training process. Initially, neurons are connected with their neighbors following the idea of Fig. 2 using a rectangular or hexagonal grid. For example, if the algorithm suggests that the initial grid of the AMSOM should be $5 \times 4$ (let's suppose rectangular), every neuron has 4 neighbors (except the marginal ones). Figure 4 demonstrates two different topologies, a rectangular and a hexagonal one with the corresponding connections between neurons.

**Vector, Matrix and Parameters Initialization.** For each neuron the following are defined and initialized accordingly:

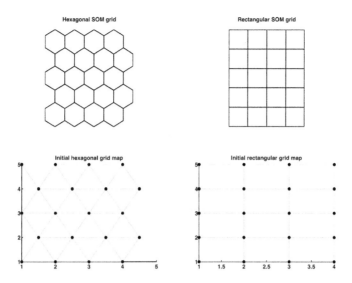

**Fig. 4.** Initial grid example (hexagonal and rectangular).

- Neuron vector (weight vector, $\mathbf{w}_i$): It is the same as the classic SOM (see Eq. (2)) and shows the representation of the neuron in the feature (input) space. Initialization of neuron vectors is random according to literature standards.
- Neuron position (position vector, $\mathbf{r}_i$): Depending on the output space (mostly it is two-dimensional), it's a vector that shows the position of the neuron. Initial position vectors are equal to the positions of the neurons in the grid, i.e., in Fig. 4 one can see the coordinates of neurons according to the structure (hexagonal or rectangular).

Since the structure of the grid is subject to changes during training, we need to keep track of the neighbors of each neuron. There is the possibility that some neurons which where connected in the initial grid become disconnected after some time (or vice versa). In order to keep track of these changes we introduce the orthogonal and symmetrical matrices $\mathbf{E}$ and $\mathbf{A}$ (both size $M \times M$) where $E(p,q)$ shows if neurons $p$ and $q$ are connected (0 translates to no connection, 1 translates to connected neurons) and $A(p,q)$ shows the age of edge (as implied by $E(p,q)$) between neurons $p$ and $q$: This will be used in order to determine which neurons had incidental connections to other neurons or strong connections as training moves forward. When $A(p,q)$ is 0 that means that neurons $p$ and $q$ were closest neighbors at current epoch but any other value (i.e., 2) implies that neurons $p$ and $q$ were closest neighbors some epochs before (i.e., 2). An example of matrices $\mathbf{E}$ and $\mathbf{A}$ is seen in Fig. 5.

In this example, neurons number ($M$) is 4 and connectivity matrix $\mathbf{E}$ shows how neurons are connected to each other (as implied by the graph). Age matrix $\mathbf{A}$ shows how many epochs an edge has "survived": Connection between neuron #1 and #2 has age 2 whereas connection between neuron #2 and #4 has age

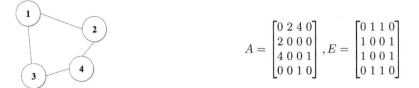

$$A = \begin{bmatrix} 0 & 2 & 4 & 0 \\ 2 & 0 & 0 & 0 \\ 4 & 0 & 0 & 1 \\ 0 & 0 & 1 & 0 \end{bmatrix}, E = \begin{bmatrix} 0 & 1 & 1 & 0 \\ 1 & 0 & 0 & 1 \\ 1 & 0 & 0 & 1 \\ 0 & 1 & 1 & 0 \end{bmatrix}$$

**Fig. 5.** Example of matrices $A$ and $E$ describing connections between AMSOM neurons.

0. Notice that age 0 can either mean that neurons are not connected, like neurons #1 and #4 or that neurons are connected at this current epoch (so their connection is "recent"), like neurons #2 and #4.

Also, at this stage the growing threshold $GT$ of the map is defined as a function of data dimension ($D$) and a spread factor ($SF$) defined by the user. Formula used is adapted from [1] and is the following:

$$GT = -ln(D) \times ln(SF) \tag{11}$$

Generally, a $SF$ value of 0.5 always yields good results but its fine tuning is up to the user requirements and the dataset structure.

### 3.2 Phase II: Training

**Weight and Position Updating.** For the weight learning of neurons, the SOM batch algorithm is utilized, as it was given in Eqs. 7–10, which are repeated here for clarity.

$$\mathbf{w}_i(t+1) = \frac{\sum_j n_j(t) \cdot h_{ji}(t) \cdot \tilde{\mathbf{x}}_j(t)}{\sum_j n_j(t) \cdot h_{ji}(t)} \tag{12}$$

$$h_{ji}(t) = exp\left(-\frac{||\mathbf{r}_j - \mathbf{r}_i||^2}{\sigma(t)^2}\right) \tag{13}$$

where:

- $\mathbf{w}_i(t+1)$ marks neurons $i$ updated weight (at epoch $t+1$),
- $t$ marks current epoch and $t+1$ marks the next epoch,
- $n_j(t)$ marks the number of patterns that are assigned to neuron $j$,
- $h_{ji}(t)$ marks the neighborhood function and is a measure of how close are neuron $j$ and neuron $i$,
- $\tilde{\mathbf{x}}_j(t)$ is the mean feature vector of all $x$ that are assigned to neuron $j$ at epoch $t$,
- $\mathbf{r}_j, \mathbf{r}_i$ are the position vectors (in the output space) for neurons $j$ and $i$,
- $\sigma(t)$ is the adaptation factor, decreasing through training.

Building on top of this, at the end of each epoch, the neuron position vectors are adjusted in a similar manner to the SOM training algorithm. In more detail, at the end of each epoch and after the neuron weight vectors update is over, the distances between the neuron vectors ($\mathbf{w}_i$) are computed. These distances show how close neurons are (in the input space) and can be used as a measure in order to update neuron positions (in the output space). This is achieved through the following equations:

$$\mathbf{r}_i(t+1) = \mathbf{r}_i(t) + \alpha(t) \cdot \frac{\sum_j n_j(t) \cdot \delta_{ji}(t)(\mathbf{r}_j(t) - \mathbf{r}_i(t))}{\sum_j n_j(t) \cdot \delta_{ji}(t)} \tag{14}$$

$$\delta_{ji}(t) = exp\left(-\frac{||\mathbf{w}_j - \mathbf{w}_i||^2}{\gamma \times \sigma(t)^2}\right) \tag{15}$$

where:

- $t$, $n_j(t)$ were defined in Eqs. 12 and 13,
- $\alpha(t)$ denotes the learning rate at epoch $t$ and controls the rate that positions of neurons are moving,
- $\delta_{ji}(t)$ is a neighborhood function denoting how close neurons $j$ and $i$ are (during time $t$ and is based on their distance in the input space (i.e., distance computed based on their vectors $w_i$),
- $\gamma$ is a parameter that controls the neighborhood shrinking as a fraction of $\sigma$ which was used in Eq. (13).

Notice the similarity of $\delta_{ji}$ with $h_{ji}$: both are neighborhood functions and are used to determine how close two neurons are but the first one does so using their distances in the feature (input) space while the latter does so using their distances in the output space (map).

Equation (14) will adjust neuron's $i$ position vector according to the neurons which proved winners for more patterns in its neighborhood and less (or even none) according to neurons which were winners for few patterns (or none). This process enhances the concept of neighborhood around the neurons that attract more patterns and also allows to cover any empty spaces in the data representation. It is expected to improve the training speed, since position updating will lead to more accurate position vectors that will be used for the next training epoch and leads to more insightful representations of the neurons in the output space.

Learning rate $\alpha(t)$ can also be set to a small value 0.01 since the neighborhood function controls well the percentage of change in the position vectors. It was selected to update the position vectors with this hybrid on-line-batch SOM rule, due to the fact that output space is much smaller (in most SOM applications) than the input space, so in many cases minor adjustments (rather than major repositioning of the neurons) are necessary in order to guarantee satisfactory training but also representation. Also notice that the parameter $\gamma$ which controls neighborhood shrinking for position can also control how fast the map will be updated and how neurons are going to affect each other.

**Adding and Removing Neurons.** During the weight updating process, for each input (pattern) the best matching neuron is determined ($N_a$) and also the second best matching ($N_b$). At this step the age of all edges between $N_a$ and its neighbors is increased. Afterwards, $N_a$ is connected to $N_b$. If both of the neurons were already connected then their age is reset to zero. This is another step that implements the competitive learning rule, since for each new pattern, a new edge connecting the two closest neurons is drawn. This process is repeated for all patterns as they are presented to the AMSOM. Finally, at the end of the epoch for each incident edge between neurons $(i, j)$, if $A(i, j) \geq age_{max}$, then this edge is removed. $age_{max}$ can be set to a value not small enough (so as to avoid many disconnections) but also not big enough (so as to avoid having a fully connected grid). In our experiments this value was 30. If either of the implicated neurons becomes isolated from the remainder of the structure, then it is removed from the grid. The aim here is to remove edges that are no longer useful because they are replaced by younger edges that are created during the AMSOM training. That is the reason that each time two neurons are connected by an edge, then its age is reset to zero. By this process, neurons that were connected incidentally -especially at the beginning of the training when the map is still under forming- are disconnected after some epochs. This process has two distinct advantages: (a) self-organization and competitive learning will allow (after some epochs) the removal of redundant number of neurons and (b) adjustment of connections between neurons so as to enhance topological properties of the dataset. An example of a removal of a neuron is shown in Fig. 6 along with the necessary adjustments to matrices **A** and **E**.

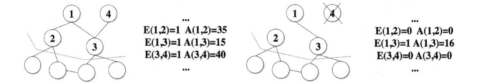

**Fig. 6.** The process of removing neurons in a part of AMSOM: With $age_{max}$ set to 30, neuron 4 is disconnected from neuron 3 and neuron 1 is disconnected from neuron 2 (notice that matrices $A$ and $E$ are updated accordingly). Neuron 4 is left with no connections so it is removed.

Also, there is the possibility that after some epochs ($t_{add}$), new neurons are added. The criterion is based on the training progress and when an addition happens, then new neurons can be added only after a number of epochs ($t_{add}$) in order to allow weight adaptation of the map, before evaluating current structure. First step is to spot the neuron $N_u$ with the largest quantization error. A new neuron will be added, if its quantization error is higher than $GT$, where $GT$ is the growing threshold of the map: A high value for $GT$ will result in less spread out map and a low $GT$ will produce a more spread map. If the quantization error satisfies the above condition then its Voronoi region is considered to be under-represented and therefore a new neuron has to be added to share the load of the high-error-valued neuron.

Regarding the new neuron that will be added, we follow the the biological process of "cell division" [36]. By this way the neuron with the highest quantization error is "splitted" to two new neurons (instead of just adding one new neuron somewhere at random with no connections at all). Both new neurons preserve the same connectivity (and also they are connected to each other) with the original neuron, thus we achieve a preservation of behavioral link between the parent and the offspring. Regarding the exact position of the two neurons the following process is followed: Neuron with the largest error among $N_u$'s neighbors is spotted (let it be $N_v$). One neuron will preserve $N_u$'s position and the other one will be placed in the middle between $N_u$ and $N_v$. In detail, weights and positions of the two new neurons ($u_1$ and $u_2$) are calculated using the following equations:

$$\mathbf{w}_{u1} = (1 + \beta) \times \mathbf{w}_u \tag{16}$$

$$\mathbf{w}_{u2} = -\beta \times \mathbf{w}_u \tag{17}$$

$$\mathbf{r}_{u1} = \mathbf{r}_u \tag{18}$$

$$\mathbf{r}_{u2} = \frac{\mathbf{r}_u + \mathbf{r}_v}{2} \tag{19}$$

where $\mathbf{w}_u$ refers to the weight vector of neuron $u$ (neuron that is splitted) and $\beta$ is a mutation parameter which can take either a fixed or random value according to a certain distribution rule (following [36]). In any case, value of $\beta$ has to be chosen small in order to avoid a large change both in network topology but also in the weight vectors. In this paper, $\beta$ takes a random value according to a Gaussian distribution with a mean of zero and variance of one. New neurons retain the same connectivity to other neurons as the parent neuron but age weights are zeroed. The process of adding a new neuron (along with any changes in matrices $\mathbf{E}$ and $\mathbf{A}$) is described in Fig. 7.

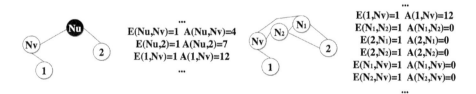

**Fig. 7.** The process of adding new neurons in a part of AMSOM: $N_u$ is highlighted as the neuron with the highest error and $N_v$ is the neuron among its neighbors with the largest error. Neurons $N_1$ and $N_2$ are added instead of $N_u$, matrices $E$ and $A$ are updated accordingly and weight/position vectors are determined by Eqs. 16–19.

It has to be pointed out that there is the possibility that a neuron would be removed from a region of the map and to be added in another region (removing and adding neurons are consecutive processes). This comes to agreement with several theories in neural organization, suggesting that cortical regions can adapt to their input sources and are somewhat interchangeable or "reusable" by other modalities, especially in vision- or hearing-impaired subjects [44].

**Architecture Adaptation and Termination Criterion.** As it is described before, initial structure of AMSOM is adapted through learning and training in order to find what is optimal for the number of neurons, their weights and their connections. The adaptation process starts by training the initial structure of AMSOM. When the criteria of adding or removing neurons are satisfied, then the network is adapted. In order to maintain (as possible) the initial structure (i.e., rectangular or hexagonal or any other lattice selected), after this adaptation process we re-evaluate all connections of all neurons and make sure that each neuron has at most $Q$ neighbors (where $Q$ is decided in the beginning, i.e., in the case of rectangular lattice, $Q = 4$): This can be ensured by checking edge matrix $E$ after each epoch and if a neuron is found to have more than $Q$ connections then only the $Q$-"recent" are kept (utilizing age of edges in matrix $A$). This process is presented in Fig. 8.

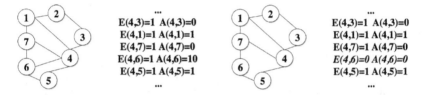

**Fig. 8.** Maintaining the structure of AMSOM: With $Q = 4$ (i.e., a rectangular grid) neuron 4 is connected to five neurons, so it's connection with neuron 6 (oldest connection) is removed.

By this training scheme, AMSOM simultaneously adapts the structure of the map (number of neurons and connections) and the weight vectors. Removing and adding neurons occur when different criteria are met, so they can be applied in any sequence, depending on when the criteria are satisfied. By applying these operations repeatedly, AMSOM is expected to find a near-optimal structure and representation of a given dataset.

Finally, like every SOM algorithm, AMSOM has an upper limit of epochs that training takes place. This number is set to 1000 but there is also a premature termination criterion depending on the mean quantization error change between two consecutive epochs. Thus, if $mqe(t) - mqe(t-1) < \epsilon_1$ where $\epsilon_1$ is a small value (like $1E-06$) then the map has reached the desired size (according to the $GT$ provided) and training is terminated.

## 3.3    Phase III: AMSOM Finalization and Clustering of the Map

Final phase of AMSOM begins when learning is complete and structure of the network is not any more changing. No neurons are added or removed at this phase and no connections between neurons are added or removed but weight and position vector adaptation is continued with a lower rate. Purpose of this process is to smooth out any quantization error and fine tune weights and positions of the neurons, especially for neurons added at the latter epochs. For this purpose, neighborhood function (both for Eqs. 12 and 14) is constrained only to the immediate neighborhood and learning rate $\alpha(t)$ in Eq. (14) is set to 0.001 (even smaller than in phase II). Phase III is concluded when there is no significant change in mean quantization error (i.e., when $mqe(t) - mqe(t-1) < \epsilon_2$), where $\epsilon_2$ is set to a smaller value than $\epsilon_1$ (like $1E - 10$).

In order to effectively compute the number of clusters that are discovered by the AMSOM algorithm, we take into account the graph structure that is created during training and is represented by matrix $\mathbf{E}$. The result is a segmented map that represents the clusters. Literature methods for SOM clustering involve the use of a clustering algorithm like $K$-means or Hierarhical Agglomerative Clustering (HAC) [42] or Spectral Clustering [41] but disadvantage of these approaches is that they require additional (sometimes time consuming) steps after the SOM training and additional parameters to be determined (e.g. number of clusters $K$ or a distance measure to be used [7,20,45]). These approaches accurately extract the clusters when they are well separated but that is not the case when cluster structure is not that direct. Finally, other approaches utilize graph theoretic methods for partitioning the map but these approaches also rely on extra steps after the end of SOM training [38]. On the other hand, our proposed approach has two distinct advantages over traditional SOM clustering algorithms: (a) The graph construction is inherent to the algorithm, since matrices $\mathbf{E}$ and $\mathbf{A}$ are computed during the training process and (b) involves a simple heuristic process with only one parameter which is automatically determined.

The map to be clustered is represented by an undirected adjacency graph $G(V, \mathbf{E})$; where $V$ represents the set of neurons after the end of training and $\mathbf{E}$ is the edge adjacency matrix as formed during training. In our proposed approach we also take into account the similarity between adjacent neurons in terms of the input space (weight vectors). The exact steps of the algorithm are the following:

- Given a trained AMSOM map and matrix $\mathbf{E}$, we compute the distance between any adjacent neurons $i$ and $j$ ($E(i,j) = 1$ for adjacent neurons and $dist(i,j) = ||w_i - w_j||^2$ as used in Eq. 15),
- For each adjacent neuron the edge is considered adjacent when $dist(i,j) \leq v$, where $v$ is a threshold,
- For each edge inconsistency ($dist(i,j) > v$), a null connection is considered in position $(i,j)$ of the graph ($E(i,j)$ is set to 0), otherwise we retain 1,
- A different class code is assigned to each connected neuron set.

The threshold $v$ is automatically set to the mean value of distance between all neurons $(i,j) \in V$, so it is not mandatory to be determined, unless there are specific user requirements: a larger value of $v$ will to less clusters whereas a smaller value will lead to more clusters. The result is a partitioned map, which indicates the number of clusters. Obviously, after this process the input patterns can be projected on the map (by finding the best matching neuron) and the label of the neuron can be assigned to each input.

## 4   Experiments

AMSOM performance has been tested with several literature datasets in order to evaluate both map quality (in terms of topology preservation) and the number of epochs needed to converge. Quantization Error (QE) and Topographic Error (TE) were used as intrinsic measures of evaluation (for more details readers are encouraged to read [4]). All (non-textual) datasets were provided by the UCI repository[1], except the CLUSTER dataset which is a simple and random but large two-dimensional dataset with four groups. In order to test the scalability of the approach for larger datasets, we also tested AMSOM to a large textual dataset[2]. This dataset involves 4 classes from the RCV1 dataset and counts 9625 documents with 29992 discrete features (which correspond to different words, since we are using the bag-of-words model). All datasets used with their characteristics are presented in Table 1.

**Table 1.** Quality of AMSOM compared to classic SOM and number of neurons for different datasets.

| Dataset name | Characteristics | | | QE | | TE | | # of neurons | |
|---|---|---|---|---|---|---|---|---|---|
| | Instances | Features | Classes | AMSOM | SOM | AMSOM | SOM | AMSOM | SOM |
| CLUSTER | 1000 | 3 | 4 | 0.108 | 0.1090 | 0.028 | 0.063 | 121 | 154 |
| IRIS | 150 | 4 | 3 | 0.1047 | 0.3930 | 0.009 | 0.013 | 40 | 66 |
| WINE | 178 | 13 | 3 | 1.7394 | 1.8830 | 0.008 | 0.017 | 42 | 66 |
| IONOSPHERE | 351 | 35 | 2 | 2.5697 | 2.9418 | 0.0026 | 0.0057 | 78 | 91 |
| CANCER | 699 | 9 | 2 | 0.7941 | 0.9456 | 0.0145 | 0.0286 | 103 | 132 |
| GLASS | 214 | 10 | 7 | 0.9797 | 1.1178 | 0.0041 | 0.0093 | 43 | 72 |
| RCV1-4 | 9625 | 29992 | 4 | 1.6937 | 2.3251 | 0.0864 | 0.1232 | 431 | 500 |

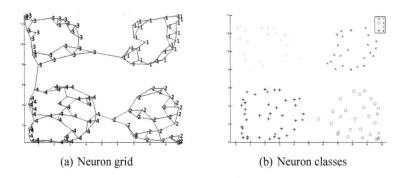

(a) Neuron grid                    (b) Neuron classes

**Fig. 9.** Visualization results for CLUSTER dataset (4 classes).

---

[1] http://archive.ics.uci.edu/ml/.
[2] http://www.cad.zju.edu.cn/home/dengcai/Data/TextData.html.

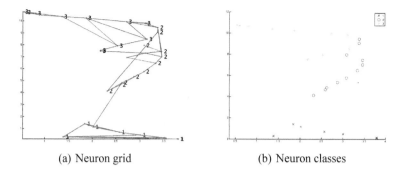

(a) Neuron grid                                    (b) Neuron classes

**Fig. 10.** Visualization results for IRIS dataset (3 classes).

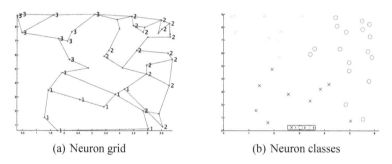

(a) Neuron grid                                    (b) Neuron classes

**Fig. 11.** Visualization results for WINE dataset (3 classes).

Each dataset is shuffled and split to training, testing and validation set (60%, 20% and 20% respectively). Each experiment was performed 20 times and the results presented here are average over these runs (deviations were small and are not presented here). Results for AMSOM QE and TE (compared to classic SOM) along with the number of neurons used by each model are presented in Table 1. From this table it is obvious that AMSOM's performance is much better than classic SOM. AMSOM starts from the same number of neurons as classic SOM but by removing and adding neurons when necessary reaches a number which is suitable to represent the dataset. Both QE and TE are improved using AMSOM algorithm and this improvement is more significant in TE because of the neuron position changing which allows the map to better adjust to the dataset.

Visualization results for the six small-scale datasets are presented in Figs. 9, 10, 11, 12, 13, 14. In these Figures final positions of the neurons and their connections are represented. For each neuron the process described in Sect. 3.3 was followed in order to determine the optimal number of clusters but also the class that each neuron belongs to. For the simple CLUSTER dataset it is obvious that the four classes are identified and the grid structure can effectively represent their relations. For the IRIS dataset one class is completely identified whereas the other two (which are more similar) are also highlighted. Also notice that neurons which belong to the same class are mostly connected with each other on the grid

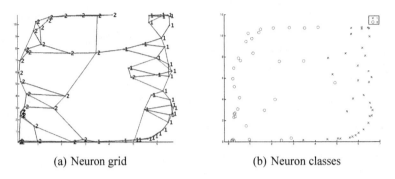

| (a) Neuron grid | (b) Neuron classes |

**Fig. 12.** Visualization results for IONOSPHERE dataset (2 classes).

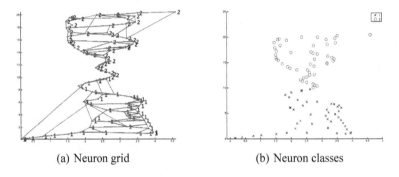

| (a) Neuron grid | (b) Neuron classes |

**Fig. 13.** Visualization results for CANCER dataset (2 classes).

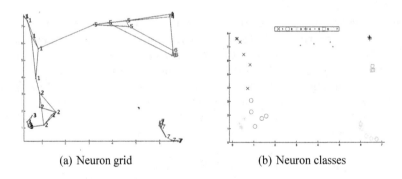

| (a) Neuron grid | (b) Neuron classes |

**Fig. 14.** Visualization results for GLASS dataset (7 classes).

and only some spontaneous connections between different classes exist. Same observations can be drawn for the WINE dataset where also the role of "dead" neurons (neurons that do not represent any input pattern) can be highlighted: They act as intermediate neurons between classes (see Fig. 11a). Dead neurons is a well known problem for SOMs [11,30] but as it can be seen in all Figures, the percentage of dead units is significantly small, which is an improvement

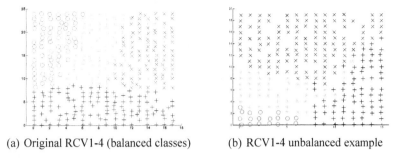

(a) Original RCV1-4 (balanced classes)          (b) RCV1-4 unbalanced example

**Fig. 15.** Visualization results for RCV1-4 dataset (4 classes).

to the classic SOM algorithm and (like in the WINE dataset) these neurons act as a border between the different classes. For the more demanding dataset of IONOSPHERE (see the relatively higher QE), AMSOM manages to differentiate in a great degree the two classes. Ability of AMSOM when it comes to multiple class can be seen in GLASS dataset where it successfully manages to highlight all seven classes and separate the corresponding neurons accordingly. Finally, visualization of the results on the RCV1-4 dataset is presented in Fig. 15(a). Due to the high complexity of the dataset (high dimensionality) it was expected that there would be not many significant changes in the neuron positions or a great reduction in the neurons' number. Graph structure is not presented due to the many connections which make the graph not viewable in such a format, but the clustering process reveals that the four classes are clearly identifiable and separable. Moreover, we also conducted a series of experiments in order to determine how AMSOM can handle unbalanced classes. We used uneven number of patterns per class and experimental results for different combinations (very dense and very sparse classes) were also promising. An example of these experiments where one class is under-represented and one is over-represented can be seen in Fig. 15(b).

Parameters to be set for AMSOM are the following:

- Spread Factor ($SF$) controls the growing threshold ($GT$) of the map. For the experiments presented here a value 0.5 was chosen since it always leads to satisfactory results and visualizations. In general, provided there is no prior knowledge on the data examined, a low value of $SF$ (up to 0.3) will allow high-lighting of the most significant clusters. The formula for computing $GT$ (see Eq. 11) also involves the dimensionality $D$ of the dataset so that an increasing dimensionality will allow a more spread map.
- $\gamma$ parameter is present in Eq. 14 for the neuron position updating. It was found to effectively control the spreading or shrinking of neuron neighborhood and by this way can create either more isolated or more connected clusters. Several experiments were conducted and showed that small values of gamma (1 till 10) produce the best results for all datasets. The higher the $\gamma$, the better topographic preservation (reduced TE) but the quantization error (QE) rises.

Also, high values of $\gamma$ tend to increase the number of neurons that remain unused (dead units) whereas values close to 100 tend to approach the classic SOM algorithm (position updating is minimal).

- $t_{add}$, $age_{max}$: Two more parameters that need to be adjusted are $age_{max}$ and $t_{add}$. For both parameters, 30 epochs were found to be optimal, which is sound given the fact that 30 epochs is enough time to check whether current structure performs well (reduced QE) or if adjustments are needed (adding/removing neurons). Increasing these values will lead to less flexible structures (since not many opportunities will be given to the AMSOM to adjust itself) while decreasing their values to fewer epochs will increase instability in terms of both structure and performance.

Complexity of the developed algorithm is slightly increased due to the need for updating matrices $\mathbf{A}$ and $\mathbf{E}$ and also due to the more flexible structure. The use of batch algorithm (compared to the on-line algorithm) and the use of compressed representations for all similarity/distance matrices facilitates training but still introduces an overhead (CPU usage increase of around 10%) is counterbalanced by the faster training process (in all experiments there was a decrease in epochs number around 20%) since updating neuron positions clearly improves training time (requires less epochs) and for memory intensive tasks like the processing of textual datasets algorithm performed fast enough. Boosting with optimization techniques [32] can however assist handling scalability issues.

## 5    Conclusion

In this paper we presented AMSOM, a novel algorithm to perform visual clustering which extends SOM competitive learning in the output space. Neuron positions may change during this "double" training process and the number of neurons can be adjusted (addition of new neurons or removal of existing ones). These innovations allow a more flexible structure grid which has the ability to represent the dataset more efficiently. Experimental results on different datasets (with different characteristics in regard to dimensionality, number of latent classes and origin of the data) show improvement in the performance of AMSOM against classic SOM algorithm. AMSOM produces better reference vectors by reducing the Quantization Error, topology is preserved through the neuron moving by significantly reducing the Topographic Error and the visualization result matches as much as possible the original dataset partitions. Also, AMSOM produces fewer nodes with no significant effect while at the same time it reduces the required number of training epochs. Finally, AMSOM provides a framework to directly estimate the optimal number of clusters in the dataset with accurate quantitative and qualitative results.

AMSOM provides new insights on how to handle large volumes of otherwise incomprehensible data covering a wide range of human endeavor (science, business, medicine, healthcare, etc.). Obtained results highlight the effective use of competitive learning and self-organization in neural networks and demonstrate that AMSOM can be used with a big variety of datasets. Further work involves work in the following directions: firstly, evaluate the visualization result and its ability to facilitate discovery process, secondly, evaluate the algorithm in even larger datasets and more specifically explore whether statistical properties of the original data are preserved and finally, explore ways to improve performance in terms of time and space requirements.

# References

1. Alahakoon, D., Halgamuge, S.K., Srinivasan, B.: Dynamic self-organizing maps with controlled growth for knowledge discovery. IEEE Trans. Neural Netw. **11**(3), 601–614 (2000)
2. Andrienko, G., Andrienko, N., Rinzivillo, S., Nanni, M., Pedreschi, D., Giannotti, F.: Interactive visual clustering of large collections of trajectories. In: IEEE Symposium on Visual Analytics Science and Technology, VAST, pp. 3–10. IEEE (2009)
3. Ayadi, T., Hamdani, T.M., Alimi, A.M.: MIGSOM: multilevel interior growing self-organizing maps for high dimensional data clustering. Neural Process. Lett. **36**(3), 235–256 (2012)
4. Bauer, H.-U., Herrmann, M., Villmann, T.: Neural maps and topographic vector quantization. Neural Netw. **12**(4), 659–676 (1999)
5. Blackmore, J., Miikkulainen, R.: Incremental grid growing: encoding high-dimensional structure into a two-dimensional feature map. In: IEEE International Conference on Neural Network, pp. 450–455 (1993)
6. Bortman, M., Aladjem, M.: A growing and pruning method for radial basis function networks. IEEE Trans. Neural Netw. **20**(6), 1039–1045 (2009)
7. Brugger, D., Bogdan, M., Rosenstiel, W.: Automatic cluster detection in Kohonen's SOM. IEEE Trans. Neural Netw. **19**(3), 442–459 (2008)
8. Bruneau, P., Otjacques, B.: An interactive, example-based, visual clustering system. In: 17th International Conference on Information Visualisation, pp. 168–173. IEEE (2013)
9. Ceccarelli, M., Petrosino, A., Vaccaro, R.: Competitive neural networks on message-passing parallel computers. Concurrency Pract. Exp. **5**(6), 449–470 (1993)
10. Changeux, J.P., Danchin, A.: Selective stabilisation of developing synapses as a mechanism for the specification of neuronal networks. Nature **264**(5588), 705–712 (1976)
11. Chaudhary, V., Bhatia, R.S., Ahlawat, A.K.: An efficient self-organizing map (E-SOM) learning algorithm using group of neurons. Int. J. Comput. Intell. Syst. **7**(5), 963–972 (2014)
12. Deboeck, G., Kohonen, T.: Visual Explorations in Finance: With Self-Organizing Maps. Springer Science & Business Media, Heidelberg (2013)
13. Doherty, K., Adams, R., Davey, N.: TreeGNG-hierarchical topological clustering. In: ESANN, pp. 19–24 (2005)
14. Dowling, J.E.: Debate, The Great Brain : Nature or Nurture?. Princeton University Press, Princeton (2007)
15. Estévez, P.A., Príncipe, J.C., Zegers, P.: Advances in Self-Organizing Maps: 9th International Workshop, WSOM Santiago, Chile, December 12–14, Proceedings. Springer Science & Business Media (2012)
16. Fort, J.-C.: SOMS mathematics. Neural Netw. **19**(6), 812–816 (2006)

17. Fritzke, B.: Growing cell structuresa self-organizing network for unsupervised and supervised learning. Neural Netw. **7**(9), 1441–1460 (1994)
18. Fritzke, B.: Growing grida self-organizing network with constant neighborhood range and adaptation strength. Neural Process. Lett. **2**(5), 9–13 (1995)
19. Fritzke, B., et al.: A growing neural gas network learns topologies. Adv. Neural Inf. Proc. Syst. **7**, 625–632 (1995)
20. Halkidi, M., Vazirgiannis, M.: A density-based cluster validity approach using multi-representatives. Pattern Recogn. Lett. **29**(6), 773–786 (2008)
21. Han, H.-G., Qiao, J.-F.: A structure optimisation algorithm for feedforward neural network construction. Neurocomputing **99**, 347–357 (2013)
22. Hodge, V.J., Austin, J.: Hierarchical growing cell structures: TreeGCS. IEEE Trans. Knowl. Data Eng. **13**(2), 207–218 (2001)
23. Islam, M., Sattar, A., Amin, F., Yao, X., Murase, K.: A new adaptive merging and growing algorithm for designing artificial neural networks. IEEE Trans. Syst. Man Cybern. Part B: Cybern. **39**(3), 705–722 (2009)
24. Kohonen, T.: Self-organized formation of topologically correct feature maps. Biol. Cybern. **43**(1), 59–69 (1982)
25. Kohonen, T.: The 'neural' phonetic typewriter. Computer **21**(3), 11–22 (1988)
26. Kohonen, T.: Things you haven't heard about the self-organizing map. In: IEEE International Conference on Neural Networks, pp. 1147–1156. IEEE (1993)
27. Teuvo, K.: Self-organizing Maps. Springer Series in Information Sciences. Springer, Berlin (2001)
28. Kohonen, T.: Self-organization and Associative Memory, vol. 8. Springer, Heidelberg (2012)
29. Krista, L., Timo, H., Samuel, K., Teuvo, K.: WEBSOM for textual data mining. Artif. Intell. Rev. **13**(5–6), 345–364 (1999)
30. Li, Z., Eastman, J.R.: The nature and classification of unlabelled neurons in the use of Kohonen's self organizing map for supervised classification. Trans. GIS **10**(4), 599–613 (2006)
31. Lu, S.Y.: Pattern classification using self-organizing feature maps. In: IJCNN International Joint Conference on 1990, pp. 471–480 (1990)
32. Maiorana, F., Mastorakis, NE., Poulos, M., Mladenov, V., Bojkovic, Z., Simian, D., Kartalopoulos, S., Varonides, A., Udriste, C.: Performance improvements of a Kohonen self organizing classification algorithm on sparse data sets. In: Proceedings of WSEAS International Conference on Mathematics and Computers in Science and Engineering, vol. 10. WSEAS (2008)
33. Marsland, S., Shapiro, J., Nehmzow, U.: A self-organising network that grows when required. Neural Netw. **15**(8), 1041–1058 (2002)
34. Mulier, F., Cherkassky, V.: Learning rate schedules for self-organizing maps. In: Proceedings of the 12th IAPR International. Conference on Pattern Recognition, vol. 2-Conference B: Computer Vision and Image Processing, vol. 2, pp. 224–228. IEEE (1994)
35. Narasimha, P.L., Delashmit, W.H., Manry, M.T., Li, J., Maldonado, F.: An integrated growing-pruning method for feedforward network training. Neurocomputing **71**(13), 2831–2847 (2008)
36. Odri, S.V., Petrovacki, D.P., Krstonosic, G.A.: Evolutional development of a multilevel neural network. Neural Netw. **6**(4), 583–595 (1993)
37. Park, Y.S., Tison, J., Lek, S., Giraudel, J.L., Coste, M., Delmas, F.: Application of a self-organizing map to select representative species in multivariate analysis: a case study determining diatom distribution patterns across France. Ecol. Inf. **1**(3), 247–257 (2006). 4th International Conference on Ecological Informatics

38. Phuc, D., Hung, MX.: Using SOM based graph clustering for extracting main ideas from documents. In: IEEE International Conference on Research, Innovation and Vision for the Future, RIVF, pp. 209–214. IEEE (2008)
39. Rauber, A., Merkl, D., Dittenbach, M.: The growing hierarchical self-organizing map: exploratory analysis of high-dimensional data. IEEE Trans. Neural Netw. **13**(6), 1331–1341 (2002)
40. Spanakis, G., Siolas, G., Stafylopatis, A.: DoSO: a document self-organizer. J. Intell. Inf. Syst. **39**(3), 577–610 (2012)
41. Taşdemir, K.: Spectral clustering as an automated SOM segmentation tool. In: Laaksonen, J., Honkela, T. (eds.) WSOM 2011. LNCS, vol. 6731, pp. 71–78. Springer, Heidelberg (2011). doi:10.1007/978-3-642-21566-7_7
42. Vesanto, J., Alhoniemi, E.: Clustering of the self-organizing map. IEEE Trans. Neural Netw. **11**(3), 586–600 (2000)
43. Vesanto, J., Himberg, J., Alhoniemi, E., Parhankangas, J.: SOM toolbox for Matlab 5. Citeseer (2000)
44. Wedeen, V.J., Rosene, D.L., Wang, R., Dai, G., Mortazavi, F., Hagmann, P., Kaas, J.H., Tseng, W.I.: The geometric structure of the brain fiber pathways. Science **335**(6076), 1628–1634 (2012)
45. Sitao, W., Chow, T.W.S.: Clustering of the self-organizing map using a clustering validity index based on inter-cluster and intra-cluster density. Pattern Recogn. **37**(2), 175–188 (2004)
46. Yang, S.-H., Chen, Y.-P.: An evolutionary constructive and pruning algorithm for artificial neural networks and its prediction applications. Neurocomputing **86**, 140–149 (2012)

# Discrete Multi-agent Plan Recognition: Recognizing Teams, Goals, and Plans from Action Sequences

Chris Argenta[✉] and Jon Doyle

North Carolina State University, Raleigh, NC, USA
{cfargent, jon_doyle}@ncsu.edu

**Abstract.** Multi-agent Plan Recognition (MPAR) infers teams and their goals from observed actions of individual agents. The complexity of creating a priori plan libraries significantly increases to account for diversity of action sequences different team structures may exhibit. A key challenge in MPAR is effectively pruning the joint search space of agent to team compositions and goal to team assignments. Here, we describe discrete Multi-agent Plan Recognition as Planning (MAPRAP), which extends Ramirez and Geffner's Plan Recognition as Planning (PRAP) approach to multi-agent domains. Instead of a plan library, MAPRAP uses the planning domain and synthesizes plans to achieve hypothesized goals with additional constraints for suspected team composition and previous observations. By comparing costs of plans, MAPRAP identifies feasible interpretations that explain the teams and plans observed. We establish a performance profile for discrete MAPRAP in a multi-agent blocks-world domain. We evaluated precision, accuracy, and recall after each observation. We compare two pruning strategies to dampen the explosion of hypotheses tested. Aggressive pruning averages 1.05 plans synthesized per goal per time step for multi-agent scenarios vice 0.56 for single agent scenarios.

**Keywords:** Multi-agent systems · Plan recognition

## 1 Introduction

Recognizing the plans of multi-agent teams from remote observation of their actions enables people and intelligent systems to make sense of complex behaviors, identify collaborations pursuing goals of interest, and better predict the future actions and states of the world. The process of identifying cooperative plans and the composition of teams pursuing them is called Multi-agent Plan Recognition (MPAR) [1]. MAPR attempts to identify plans underlying the observable actions of a collection of agents, which are organized into teams that share a common goal and perform coordinated planning. An online recognizer observes actions conducted by agents over time and at each time step infers a set of interpretations for the scene. These interpretations including which agents are working together as a team, what goal(s) each team is pursuing, and how they may intend to achieve their goal(s) in the form of a multi-agent plan.

© Springer International Publishing AG 2017
J. van den Herik and J. Filipe (Eds.): ICAART 2016, LNAI 10162, pp. 212–228, 2017.
DOI: 10.1007/978-3-319-53354-4_12

In this paper, we describe two variants of discrete Multi-agent Plan Recognition as Planning (MAPRAP), which extends Ramirez and Geffner's [2, 3] Plan Recognition as Planning (PRAP) approach into multi-agent domains. PRAP (and MAPRAP) differs from most plan recognition approaches in that it generates potential hypothesized plans given observations and evaluates if the observations support or refute the hypotheses. We outline the core challenges and present our framework for evaluating recognition on key metrics. Finally, we give results using a version of the well-established Blocks World domain [2, 4, 5]. These results demonstrate the complexity of the discrete recognition problem and serve as a baseline for on-going research exploring alternative strategies (e.g., probabilistic), application to other benchmark multi-agent domain, and comparing recognition performance under less ideal conditions (e.g., missing observations or competing teams).

We designed MAPRAP for general purpose plan recognition, meaning that we can apply it to any domain in which necessary inputs and stated assumptions are met. We have been inspired by the approach used in General Game Playing (GPP) [6] and International Planning Competition (IPC) communities, and have attempted to avoid depending on domain-specific knowledge and a priori base rates. In MAPRAP, the planning domain is based on Plan Domain Description Language (PDDL) [7] annotated for multiple agents (similar to MA-PDDL [8] conversion via [9]). Our domain includes a complete initial state, list of agents, list of potential goals, and action model – all of are intended to describe the problem rather than the specifics of any solution.

In contrast, most plan recognition techniques match observables to patterns within a plan library (often human generated). Where a plan library represents what to watch for if a plan is being attempted, a plan domain is designed for creating plans to accomplish goals. As a result, MAPRAP does not depend on human expertise to identify domain-specific recognition strategies. Likewise, this approach does not require a training set of labeled traces or a priori base rates.

Figure 1 shows our high level architecture for staging and evaluating MAPRAP (and other recognizers). We simulate a given scenario to produce a full action trace and

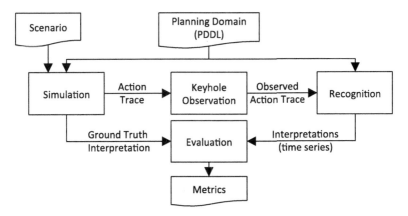

**Fig. 1.** Our research framework uses a general planning domain to simulate and recognize multi-agent actions, enabling reliable performance evaluation.

ground truth interpretation of goals and team composition. Under the keyhole observer model [10] used here, the recognizer has no interaction with the observed agents. The results in this paper reflect an ideal observer model with a serialized trace. Our online recognizer (MAPRAP) then infers team goals and compositions after every observation (not required). Finally, we evaluate the performance of recognition using precision, recall, and accuracy by comparing the recognizer's interpretation with the simulator's ground truth interpretation.

We position this work with related research in plan recognition in Sect. 2. We describe our recognizer in Sect. 3, and our evaluation approach in Sect. 4. Section 5 provides baseline results for efficiency and recognition performance. This is followed by future work and conclusions.

## 2  Related Research

Multi-agent Plan Recognition (MAPR) solutions attempt to make sense of a temporal stream of observables generated by a set of agents. The recognizer's goal is to infer both the organization of agents that are collaborating on a plan, and the plan each team is pursuing. (While not addressed here, some have also included identifying dynamic teams that change over time [11, 12].) To accomplish this goal, solutions must address two challenges noted by Intille and Bobick [13]. First, the combination of agents significantly inflates state and feature spaces making exhaustive comparisons infeasible. Second, detecting coordination patterns in temporal relationships of actions is critical for complex multi-agent activities.

One approach is to use domain knowledge to identify activities indicative of team relationships. For example, Sadilek and Kautz [14] recognized tagging events in a capture-the-flag game by detecting co-location followed by an expected effect (tagged player must remain stationary until tagged again). Sukthankar and Sycara [15] detected physical formations in a tactical game domain and inferred cooperation to prune the search space. While practical and effective for the given domains, discovering exploitable characteristics has been a human process and similar patterns may not exist in other domains.

Generalized MAPR solutions use domain-independent recognition algorithms along with a description of the domain. Most commonly, a plan library is created that provides patterns for which a recognizer searches. For example, Banerjee et al. [11] matched patterns in synchronized observables, for all combination of agents, to a flattened plan library. Sukthankar and Sycara [15] detected coordinated actions and used them to prune the multi-agent plan library using a hash table that mapped key observerable sequences for distinguishing sub-plans (i.e., last action of parent and first of sub-plan). However, it may be difficult to build a full plan library for complex domains, so others use a planning domain to guide the recognizer. Zhuo et al. [4] used MAX-SAT to solve hard (observed or causal) and soft (likelihood of various activities) constraints derived from the domain (action-model). In an effort to replicate the spirit of general game playing and IPC planning competitions where the algorithm is only given a general description of the problem at run-time, we use no a priori domain-specific knowledge or manually tuned libraries.

Plan Recognition as planning (PRAP) was introduced by Ramirez and Geffner in [2] as a generative approach to single agent plan recognition that uses off the shelf planners and does not require a plan library. They convert observations to interim subgoals that the observed agent has accomplished. They synthesize plans for each goal with and without the observed subgoals, if the costs are equal then observations could be interpreted as pursuing that goal. In [3] they extended PRAP to probabilistic recognition. In the case of uniform priors, the most likely goals are those that minimize the cost difference for achieving the goal with and without explicitly meeting the observed subgoals. This research builds on PRAP for creating a generalized MAPR given a planning domain.

# 3   Multi-agent Plan Recognition as Planning

We had three key objectives for MAPRAP:

1. Perform recognition from a standardized planning domain (in PDDL) and action trace, vice a plan library. This removes the quality of the plan library as a factor in recognition performance.
2. Prune the search space intelligently for any generalized domain (without domain-specific tricks) and scale efficiently (i.e., closer to a single agent solution).
3. Accuracy of MAPR as characterized by precision, recall, and accuracy measures over time and across a wide range of randomly generated recognition instances. This provides a baseline for performance comparison.

## 3.1   Recognizing Multi-agent Plans

We consider a set of $n$ agents, $A = \{A_0, A_1, \ldots, A_{n-1}\}$ partitioned into $m$ teams from a set $T = \{T_0, T_1, \ldots, T_{m-1}\}$ possible teams such that each $|T_x| \geq 1$. Agents perform actions in pursuit of a team goal $G_x \in G$ for all $T$, where $G$ is the set of all possible goals. In this paper, each team has one goal. Agents perform actions over time, $(1, \ldots, t)$ to achieve goals. These actions, M, and environment state, E, are defined in PDDL. We define the planning domain as a tuple $D = \{A, G, M, E\}$. We define a scenario as a set of team assignments $\{(A_x, T_x) \ldots (A_z, T_z)\}$ and team goals $\{(G_x, T_x) \ldots (G_z, T_z)\}$ with each agent assigned to a single team and each team having a unique goal.

Our simulation component accepts both the domain and scenario, plans actions for teams, and generates a trace file. A trace consists of time-stamped observations $O = \{O_1, \ldots, O_t\}$ where each includes a grounded action from $D$ parameterized by the acting agent $a \in A$. We refer to observable actions performed by a specific agent $a$ at time $t$ as $O_t^a$. Actions that can take place concurrently (same $t$) are randomly ordered in the serial trace.

Our keyhole observer component interleaves the actions of all agents while maintaining action dependencies within the teams. This is also where adding noise and observation filtering can be performed, if desired. In this paper, all actions in the domain are observable, such that $O^a_{1...t}$ includes all actions performed by the agent from time 1 to time $t$, but this is not a requirement. Our system does not add "noop" actions when no action is observed for an agent at any time unless this is an action explicit in the PDDL.

The recognition component takes the domain as input and accepts a stream of observables. For each observable (alternatively each simulation time step) the recognition component outputs a set of interpretations. An interpretation is the tuple $I = (t, A_x, T_y, G_{z,}, p, P_{T_v})$ where p is the probability (in this discrete case 0 or 1) that at time $t$ the scenario $\{(A_x, T_v), (T_v, G_z)\}$ is true and $P_{T_v}$ is the team plan trace on which the interpretation is based. $P_{T_v}$ includes observerables $O^{A_x}_{1...t}$, and predicts future actions necessary to achieve the goal $G_z$.

Finally, the evaluation component compares the ground truth scenario against each of the recognizer's interpretations. It scores accuracy, precision, and recall of each agent/goal combination for interpretation at each time step. We do not penalize interpretations for agents that with no observed actions up to that time step.

## 3.2    Extending PRAP to Teams

The single agent PRAP method of plan recognition compares the utility cost $C$ (e.g., number of actions) of two plans for each possible goal $G_x \in G$. The first reflects only the goal $G_x$, the second incorporates a sequence of observations $O_{1...t}$ (from initial to the current time step $t$) expressed as subgoals that are achieved by performing the observed actions, $G_x \cap O_{1...t}$. When $C(G_x) < C(G_x \cap O_{1...t})$, the goal $G_x$ is not supported by the observations because the observed actions increased the cost of achieving the goal. See Ramirez and Geffner's [2] single agent PRAP for complete explanation and implementation.

We summarize performance simply as the number of plans synthesized, because CPU and clock time for planning varies greatly with domain and planner used. The worst-case number of plans synthesized for a single agent scenario ($|A| = 1$) with interpretations at every time step is $|G| \cdot (t+1)$. If we directly apply this to any partitioning of agents into teams, the worst case is $|G| \cdot (t+1) \cdot b(|A|) \cdot |A|^2$ where $b(|A|)$ is the Bell number [17] of number of agents (representing an exponential number of possible team combinations). By accepting the domain assumption that team activities are independent of other team compositions, we can reduce the worst case to $|G| \cdot (t+1) \cdot (2^{|A|} - 1)$. In either case, considerable pruning is required to contain this explosion in the number of plans synthesized and make this approach tractable.

MAPRAP manages the potential agent to team assignments $\sigma$ for each goal $G^\sigma_x$. We start by hypothesizing all teams compositions are pursuing all goals, until observations indicate otherwise. We then synthesize multi-agent plans using team compositions to get a base utility cost $C(G^\sigma_x)$ without observations. At each time step, $C(G^\sigma_x) < C(G^\sigma_x \cap O^\sigma_{1...t})$ identifies that the last observed action is inconsistent with the plan and MAPRAP then prunes the search space. Two variants of this algorithm (Conservative and Aggressive) are outlined below, where an off-the-shelf planner is called to compute $C(G^a_x \cap O^a_{1...t})$ by the function "plan (goal, previously observed actions, hypothesized team composition)". The plan function internally prunes cases where no agents are hypothesized for a particular team/goal combination. The "obs (step, goal, team)" function returns the appropriate previously observed actions of the hypothesized team as subgoals. The function "report(step)" outputs the inferred agent/goal interpretations for external scoring.

In the discrete MAPRAP case, we can prune planning instances that cannot effect the interpretation. These include: any hypothesized team in time steps with no new observables for agents on the team (i.e., no explaining away alternatives), and all team/goal combinations that have been previously eliminated. Our conservative pruning solution (MAPRAP A) implements this as outlined here.

```
// Step 1: Initialize all possible
// interpretations are feasible
#compositions=2^#agents // all agent combos
hypotheses[#compositions][#goals] = true

// Step 2: Baseline cost of plans
// for goals given no observables
for each goal in all goals
  for each team composition
    baseCost[team][goal] = plan(goal, null, team)

// Step 3: Process observations
// comparing costs to baseline
step=0
for each new observable action
  step++
  agent=agentFromAction(observable)
  for each goal in all goals
    for each team composition
      if(hypotheses [team][goal]==true)
        cost = plan(goal, obs(step,goal,team), team)

// Step 4: Prune compositions when
// observed actions counter plan
        if(cost > baseCost[team][goal])

          hypotheses [team][goal]=false
// Step 5: report metrics for time step
  report(step)
```

MAPRAP A with Conservative Pruning eliminates team composition/goal combinations when plan given observables has a higher cost than without observables.

MAPRAP B with Aggressive Pruning further reduces the worst-case bounds by starting with a single team (composed of all agents) for each goal, and removing agents from compositions when their individual actions cause the utility cost to increase. While this will not work for all domains (there is a requirement for independence between the actions of agents on separate teams), the worst-case performance for Aggressive Pruning (in terms of plans synthesized) is bound by $|G| \cdot (t+1) + |G| \cdot (|A| - 1)$. The second term counts updating the baseline plan after eliminating an agent from a goal/team combination. In the code below the baseline cost never goes down, if reducing the number of agents in a domain could reduce cost, this strategy would fail. However, Aggressive Pruning effectively reduces the number of planning jobs run closer to single agent PRAP speed.

```
// Step 1: Initialize all possible
// interpretations are feasible
#teams = #agents // worst case
compositions[#teams][#agents] = true
hypotheses [#teams][#goals] = true

// Step 2: Baseline cost of plans
// given no observables
for each goal in all goals
  for each team composition
    baseCost[team][goal] = plan(goal, null, team)

// Step 3: Process observations
// comparing costs to baseline
Step = 0
for each new observable action
  step++
  agent = agentFromAction(observable)
  for each goal in all goals
    for each team composition
      if (hypotheses[team][goal]==true)
        cost = plan(goal,obs(step,goal,team),team)

// Step 4: Prune agents from teams when
// their actions reduce performance
        if (cost > baseCost[team][goal])
          compositions[team][agent] = false
          baseCost[team][goal] = plan(goal, null, team)

// Step 5: report metrics for time step
  report(step)
```

MAPRAP B with Aggressive Pruning eliminates agents from teams when their actions increase the utility cost.

### 3.3   Assumptions and Limitations

There are several aspects of MAPRAP research that we do not address here, for example, alternative domains and planners, probabilistic recognition, and imperfect observer models. We will address in future papers.

Our initial discrete implementation of MAPRAP relies on two related assumptions about the domain that we will resolve in future research. The first assumption is the requirement that every agent is performing towards a goal optimally and is never impeded by agents on other teams. Since team plans are synthesized independently, this also requires that the actions of different teams be independent of each other. This limitation excludes competitive domains, which are important for many applications.

A second assumption, is that more agents on a team achieve a goal at least as efficiently as fewer agents, even if this means some agents simply do nothing. This may not be true for domains where communication or sequential action requirements introduce a burden for larger teams. MAPRAP with Aggressive Pruning (B) relies on this condition when comparing the cost of its initial hypothesis to alternatives.

Other PRAP assumptions, such as finite and enumerable goals, and purposeful actions are also true of MAPRAP.

## 4   MAPRAP Evaluation

MAPRAP is designed to be independent of any particular domain or planner. For this evaluation, we selected the Team Blocks domain because it is simple multi-agent adaption is well established within the MAPR community. Similarly, we chose an open source implementation of GraphPlan because it is well known, relatively fast, easy to adapt to multiple agents, and emphasizes the use of an off-the-shelf planner.

### 4.1   A Team Blocks World Domain

Team Blocks World is a multi-agent adaptation of the Blocks World domain. In this domain there are a series of lettered blocks randomly stacked on a table. Each agent operates a robot gripper that can pick up one block at a time as shown in Fig. 2. Teams are composed of 1 to |A| agents that are planning together and act collaboratively towards the same goal. Actions are atomic and include: pickup, unstack (pickup from atop another block), put down (on table), stack (put down atop another block); each action is parameterized by the block(s) acted on and agent performing the action.

We added several domain predicates to prevent agents from picking up blocks held by other agents. Since we plan teams independently, we also partitioned the blocks and goals to avoid conflicting plans. However, no information about teams (count or sizes), partitioning of blocks, or goals assignments are accessible to the recognizer.

The goal of Team Blocks World is for each team to rearrange blocks into a stack in a specified sequence. Goals are random letter sequences of various lengths interpreted from bottom (on table) to up (clear). Letters are not repeated in a goal. For example, (and (ontable A) (on B A) (on C B) (clear C)) specifies the goal "ABC" pursued by Team0 in Fig. 2.

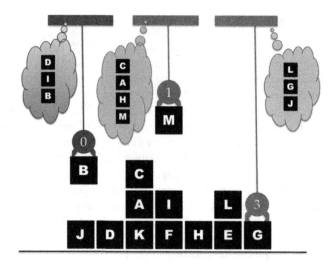

**Fig. 2.** In Team Blocks, agents (numbered grippers) are controlled by a team (indicated by color) to achieve a stacking. Teams, goals, and plans are inferred by the recognizer. (Color figure online)

### 4.2  Multi-agent Plan Synthesis

We used PDDL to specify our plan domain, which enables the use of a wide range of off-the-shelf planners (e.g., those used in the IPC Planning Competitions). For this research we used an instance of GraphPlan [16] with post-planning multi-agent scheduling logic. Because PDDL was not designed for multi-agent planning, every action in our domain includes a parameter of type "agent" which allows the planner to treat all available agents as a resource (i.e., it plans for the entire team). We synthesize plans for each team independently, including only agents on, or hypothesized to be on, that team. The trace outputs for all teams are interleaved by time step, and concurrent actions are shuffled to mitigate ordering effects.

We randomly generated 5180 different Team Blocks World scenarios (280 were used to evaluate the less efficient MAPRAP A) with stacks of 6–8 blocks per team ($\mu = 6.5$). We generated 1–2 teams with 1–5 agents that did not need to be balanced, but had at least one agent per team. Goals were all permutations of selected stacking orders of 4–7 blocks ($\mu = 4.5$). The number of potential goals averaged 64 for single team and 873 for two team scenarios. In the two team case, each team's partition was full sized, and possible goals included permutations across the partitions. During the generation process, we stored the ground truth team and goal assignments as a key for evaluation, but these were not available to the recognizer.

We simulated each scenario and recorded an action trace. Each trace consists of a serialized sequence of observed actions identifying the action, time step (1 to t), agent performing, and other action parameters. Our traces ranged from 5 to 16 actions ($\mu = 9.2$ for single and $\mu = 8.6$ for two team scenarios). The average action parallelism (multiple agents acting in the same time step) for multi-agent scenarios was 1.4 concurrent actions. We used the action trace from initial simulation as the observables for plan recognition.

# 5  Results

## 5.1  Efficiency of Pruning

Efficiency of MAPRAP pruning is measured in terms of the count of plans synthesized, which we normalized to average number of runs per goal per time step (Fig. 3). Actual wall clock time for each plan synthesis run is dependent on hardware resources, planner, and domain, which do not change here, so we focus on the quantity.

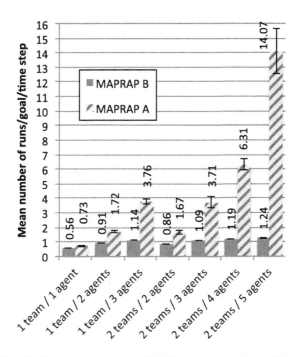

**Fig. 3.** MAPRAP with Conservative Pruning (A) effectively prunes the multi-agent search space well below the exponential worst case. MAPRAP with Aggressive Pruning (B) reduces the average runs/goal/time for scenarios to near the single agent worst-case (1.0). Single agent scenarios also benefitted from pruning.

Overall, performance of MAPRAP performance for multi-agent scenarios trailed single agent. MAPRAP with Conservative Pruning (A) averaged 4.38 plans synthesized for each goal and time step for multi-agent, and 0.73 for single agents. MAPRAP with Aggressive Pruning (B) averaged 1.05 plans synthesized for each goal and time step for multi-agent, compared to an exponential worst case at the high end and 0.56 for single agents as a lower bound. Aggressive Pruning (B) clearly scales with agent and team counts better than Conservative Pruning (A) which increases by ~2x for each additional agent.

## 5.2   Precision of Recognition

Precision at each time step indicates how well recognition eliminates interpretations of the scenario that do not match ground truth. In MAPRAP, all interpretations are hypothesized correct until demonstrated to be incorrect by conflicting observations. As shown in Fig. 4, single agent scenarios require fewer observations to converge on interpretations than multi-agent scenarios.

Notice, because there is only one correct interpretation, so any feasible interpretation are counted as false positives. Since Precision is the ratio of true positives to all positives, a large number of false positives severely impacts precision. For our examples of Team Blocks World, our list of potential goals included all stacking orders of blocks (without knowing simulation partitioning), so there are many goals that are only distinguished late in there stacking order. Figure 5 separates out the two key drivers of precision showing a plot for each of four team compositions. Each line (colored) in the plots represents the average of traces of a specific number of observations (i.e., the left most point of each line represents the state after the goal has been successfully achieved for all teams).

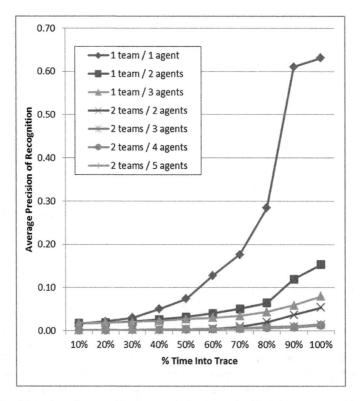

**Fig. 4.** Precision plots show multi-agent scenarios have significantly more possible interpretations, so many more observations are required to eliminate interpretations that are consistent with observations up to that time, but incorrect.

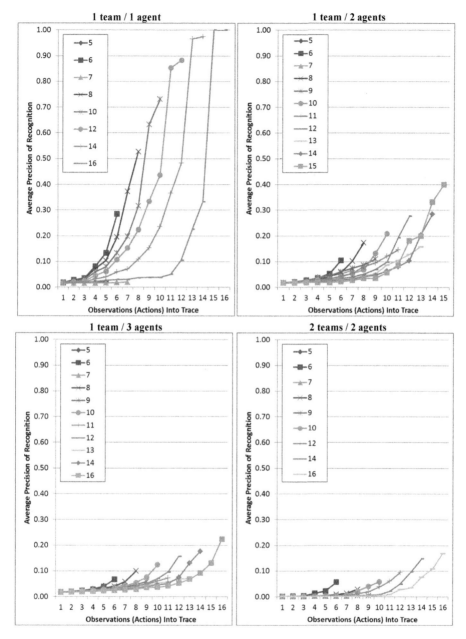

**Fig. 5.** The recognizer is unaware of the team composition and total trace size, but precision goes up when it sees more observations for each agent and as teams get closer to accomplishing their goal. Early stage MAPR has fewer observations on which to make decisions. (Color figure online)

We observed that reduced precision in the multi-agent cases reflects both fewer observations per individual agent at any time, and a large number of potential team compositions. In essence, the explanatory power of each observation is diluted across the pool of agents. As a result, it takes more observations to rule-out all feasible, but ultimately incorrect, interpretations. In fact, unlike the single agent case, most multi-agent traces ended before the recognizer converged to a single correct interpretation. We did not reduce the goal count or ensure goals diversity, which would improve precision. Since MAPRAP is an online recognizer, it is not aware does not observe the ending of a trace.

### 5.3   Accuracy of Recognition

Accuracy is the ratio of correct classifications to total classifications. As shown in Fig. 6, the mean accuracy of MAPRAP trails the single agent case, but demonstrates correct classifications of potential interpretations for observables over time.

Figure 7 breaks out accuracy by team composition and the number of observations in the trace. Additional observations improve accuracy nearly linearly in most cases.

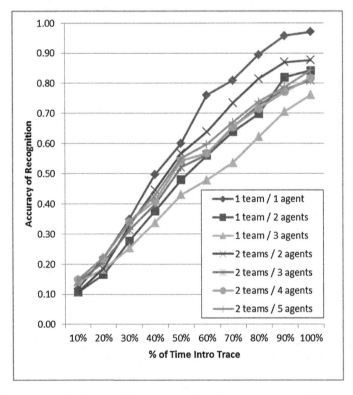

**Fig. 6.** Accuracy metric shows single agent scenarios converge on correct interpretation faster than multi-agent scenarios.

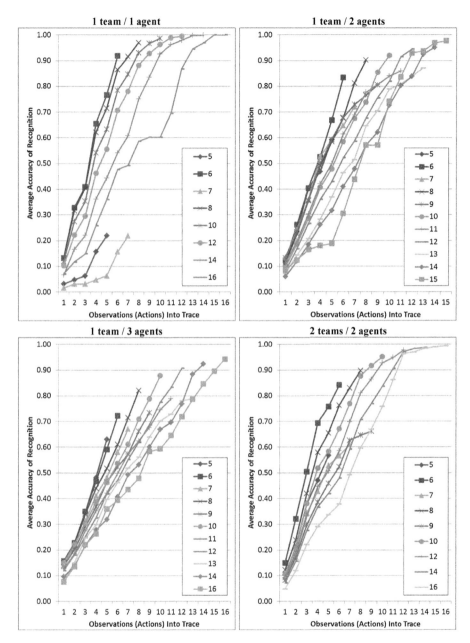

**Fig. 7.** Accuracy increases somewhat consistently in all team organizations, which suggests that the number of feasible interpretations is being reduced with almost every observation. Note that the recognizer is not given either the team composition or plan length when performing online recognition.

MAPRAP recognizes multi-agent scenarios with reasonable accuracy, which is driven by the ability to quickly eliminate many incorrect interpretations (true negatives). However, the difference in precision between single and multi-agent scenarios reflects the large number of team composition possibilities. This indicates that few multi-agent recognition jobs converged to a single interpretation, meaning that some interpretations simply cannot be discarded given the observations up to that point.

### 5.4   Recall of Recognition

Recall is the measure of how well the recognizer positively classifies correct interpretations. Discrete MAPRAP, when pruning assumptions are met, has complete recall (value of 1) at every time step because it only eliminates candidate interpretations when contradicted by observables. This results in no false negative interpretations. This was expected given that we did not implement erroneous observations, suboptimal agent action, or probabilistic recognition in this experiment.

## 6   Future Work

These discrete implementations of MAPRAP expose several potential areas for improvement. We are adapting additional planning domains for multi-agent benchmarking. New domains challenge the limitations of the current approach and enforce generality. One key consideration is to select/build domains that sample the relevant domain characteristic space. Also, the ability to scale from 1 agent on 1 team to n agents on n teams, ensures we the domain does not artificially limit the team composition search space, and allows us to compare performance. Similarly, Ramirez and Geffner [2] demonstrated that satisficing and specialized planners improved speed at little cost to PRAP accuracy, making it useful for investigating larger parameter spaces. We intend to examine the use of other planners as well.

Secondly, in this paper discuss discrete MAPRAP. Like Ramirez and Geffner [2], we are extending this to a probabilistic solution. Moving away from discrete decisions introduces new efficiency challenges for which we are developing new pruning strategies. Critically, this will better enable recognition in cases of less optimal action traces, not currently addressed in the discrete version. Probabilistic MAPRAP allows us to prioritize interpretations instead of just eliminating them. This allows us to return to interpretations when it is the best explanation, even when some observations conflict with it. In less optimal actions sequences, this may result in recall occasionally dipping to less than one.

In addition we intend to reduce our current limitations, show the effects of observation error/loss, and reduce restrictions on inter-team interaction (e.g., competition) in future research.

## 7   Conclusions

In this paper we introduced a discrete version of MAPRAP, our MAPR system based on an extension of PRAP. Discrete MAPRAP meets our key objective of working from a planning domain vice plan library. This enforces generalization and eliminates the dependency on human expertise in designating what actions to watch in a domain. Because producing plan libraries for varied team compositions is difficult, a MAPR solution that depends only on the planning domain information is valuable, particularly for problems where the physics of the world are well known, but there are many possible methods for achieving goals.

We show that recognizing team compositions and goals/plans from an online action sequence, without domain-specific tricks, greatly expands the search space of feasible interpretations of observed actions. We evaluated the efficiency and performance of two MAPRAP pruning strategies on a range of Team Blocks World scenarios, and established (with stated domain limitations) efficiencies nearing single agent solutions. We found we can effectively prune the search space to improve run-time independent of the planner used. There is a high degree of parallelism in MAPRAP because all plan synthesis for the same time step can be executed currently.

We evaluated recognition performance on a multi-agent version of the well-known Blocks World domain. We assessed precision, accuracy, and recall measures over time. This is particularly relevant as observations in multi-agent scenarios have many more potentially feasible interpretations than the single agent case. This in turn requires more observations to limit potentially feasible interpretations down to the single correct interpretation. However, we observed that when observations consist of actions being executed by varied agents, potentially on different teams, the ability to eliminate interpretation is reduced. For the Team Blocks World domain, we showed how precision and accuracy increases with additional observations and how sensitive this growth is to the composition of the team being observed.

Our precision and accuracy measures over time help quantify this difference. Precision of multi-agent scenarios was significantly lower than single-agent because it was challenged by a high false positive rate. Because there is only one correct interpretation and many possible interpretations (some of which only vary in later stage actions) false positives drives the precision metric. However, accuracy was reasonably high, as MAPRAP was able to consistently identify and eliminated infeasible interpretations with each observation.

Discrete MAPRAP sustained a consistent recall of 1.0. This is critical to support effective pruning for discrete interpretations because once eliminated an interpretation are never revisited. For the case where there is only one correct interpretation, recall is either 1 or 0 at any time. For on-line applications, we do not want to discard the correct interpretation, so we prioritize recall over precision.

# References

1. Sukthankar, G., Goldman, R.P., Geib, C., Pynadath, D.V., Bui, H.H.: Plan, Activity, and Intent Recognition Theory and Practice. Morgan Kaufmann, Burlington (2014)
2. Ramirez, M., Geffner, H.: Plan recognition as planning. In: Proceedings of the 21st International Joint Conference on Artificial Intelligence (2009)
3. Ramirez, M., Geffner, H.: Probabilistic plan recognition using off-the-shelf classical planners. In: Proceedings of the AAAI 2010 (2010)

4. Zhuo, H.H., Yang, Q., Kambhampati, S.: Action-model based multi-agent plan recognition. In: Advances in Neural Information Processing Systems 25 (2012)
5. Banerjee, B., Kraemer, L., Lyle, J.: Multi-agent plan recognition: formalization and algorithms. In: AAAI 2010 (2010)
6. Genersereth, M., Love, N.: General game playing: overview of the AAAI competition. AI Mag. **26**(2), 62 (2005)
7. McDermott, D., AIPS-98 Planning Competition Committee: PDDL–the planning domain definition language (1998)
8. Kovacs, D.: A multi-agent extension of PDDL3.1. In: WS-IPC 2012, p. 19 (2012)
9. Muise, C., Lipovetzky, N., Ramirez, M.: MAP-LAPKT: omnipotent multi-agent planning via compilation to classical planning. In: Competition of Distributed and Multi-agent Planners (CoDMAP 2015) (2014)
10. Cohen, P.R., Perrault, C.R., Allen, J.F.: Beyond question answering. In: Strategies for Natural Language Processing, pp. 245–274. Hillsdale, NJ (1981)
11. Banerjee, B., Lyle, J., Kraemer, L.: New algorithms and hardness results for multi-agent plan recognition. In: AAAI 2011 (2011)
12. Sukthankar, G., Sycara, K.: Simultaneous team assignment and behavior recognition from spatio-temporal agent traces. In: Proceedings of the Twenty-First National Conference on Artificial Intelligence (AAAI 2006) (2006)
13. Intille, S.S., Bobick, A.F.: Recognizing planned, multi-person action. Comput. Vis. Image Underst. **81**, 414–445 (2001)
14. Sadilek, A., Kautz, H.: Recognizing multi-agent activities from GPS data. In: Twenty-Fourth AAAI Conference on Artificial Intelligence (2010)
15. Sukthankar, G., Sycara, K.: Efficient plan recognition for dynamic multi-agent teams. In: Proceedings of 7th International Conference on Autonomous Agents and Multi-agent Systems (AAMAS 2008) (2008)
16. Pellier, D.: PDDL4J and GraphPlan open source implementation (2014). http://sourceforge.net/projects/pdd4j
17. "Bell Numbers" Wikipedia. The Free Encyclopedia. Wikimedia Foundation, Inc. (2014). https://en.wikipedia.org/wiki/Bell_number

# Keeping Secrets in $\mathcal{EL}^+$ Knowledge Bases

Gopalakrishnan Krishnasamy Sivaprakasam$^{(\boxtimes)}$ and Giora Slutzki

Department of Computer Science, Iowa State University, Ames, USA
{sgk,slutzki}@iastate.edu

**Abstract.** In this paper we study Secrecy-Preserving Query Answering problem under Open World Assumption (OWA) for $\mathcal{EL}^+$ Knowledge Bases (KBs). First we compute some consequences of ABox ($\mathcal{A}$) and TBox ($\mathcal{T}$) denoted by $\mathcal{A}^*$ and $\mathcal{T}^*$ respectively. A secrecy set of a querying agent is subset $\mathbb{S}$ of $\mathcal{A}^* \cup \mathcal{T}^*$ which the agent is not allowed to access. Next we compute envelopes which provide logical protection to the secrecy set against the reasoning of the querying agent. Once envelopes are computed, they are used to efficiently answer assertional and GCI queries without compromising the secret information in $\mathbb{S}$. When the querying agent asks a query $q$, the reasoner answers "Yes" if KB $\models q$ and $q$ does not belong to the envelopes; otherwise, the reasoner answers "Unknown". Being able to answer "Unknown" plays a key role in protecting secrecy under OWA. Since we are not computing all the consequences of the KB, answers to the queries based on just $\mathcal{A}^*$ and $\mathcal{T}^*$ could be erroneous. To fix this problem, we further augment our algorithms to make the query answering procedure foolproof.

**Keywords:** Knowledge representation and reasoning · Ontologies · Privacy and security · Semantic web

## 1 Introduction

The explosive growth in online banking activities, social networks, web based travel services and other internet based business and homeland security applications contain massive amounts of private details of users, administrators, service providers and governmental agencies. This contributes, on one hand, to unprecedented levels of information sharing and, on the other hand, to grave concerns about privacy and confidentiality of communication between WWW users. It will be an indispensable aspect of future web based service industry that private information while being shared must remain inviolate. In literature, most of the approaches dealing with "information protection" are based on access control mechanisms. For semantic web applications, the authors of [11] have proposed policy languages to represent obligation and delegation policies based on access control approach. Biskup et al. in [5,6] studied secrecy in incomplete databases using controlled query evaluation (CQE). Since description logics (DLs) underlie web ontology languages (OWLs), recently researchers have shown an interest in studying secrecy-preserving reasoning in DL knowledge bases (KBs).

© Springer International Publishing AG 2017
J. van den Herik and J. Filipe (Eds.): ICAART 2016, LNAI 10162, pp. 229–246, 2017.
DOI: 10.1007/978-3-319-53354-4_13

In [4, 15, 16], the authors have developed a secrecy framework that attempts to satisfy the following competing goals: (a) it protects secret information and (b) queries are answered as informatively as possible (subject to satisfying property (a)). The notion of an *envelope* to hide secret information against logical inference was first defined and used in [15]. Further, in [16], Tao et al., introduced a more elaborate conceptual framework for secrecy-preserving query answering (SPQA) under Open World Assumption (OWA) with multiple querying agents. So far it has been restricted to instance-checking queries. Specifically, in [14–16] the main idea was to utilize the secret information within the reasoning process, but then answering "Unknown" whenever the answer is truly unknown or in case the true answer could compromise confidentiality.

In this paper we extend the work of Krishnasamy Sivaprakasam and Slutzki reported in [14], to the $\mathcal{EL}^+$ language. Note that the language $\mathcal{EL}^+$ is defined by adding role inclusions whose left hand side can be a composition of role names to the RBox. The reason for this restriction is that an unrestricted use of composition leads to intractability and even undecidability, see [2,3]. The new contributions in this paper are (a) we have expanded the rule system to allow for composition of role names to generate new assertions and GCIs and (b) a different approach was required to prove the completeness of tableau algorithms that compute sets of assertional and GCI consequences. This in turn necessitated an extensive adaptation of canonical interpretation definition [9]. Moreover, the tableau algorithms to compute envelopes have been modified accordingly as where query answering algorithms. As a first step in constructing SPQA system, we design two tableau algorithms to compute finite sets $\mathcal{T}^*$ and then $\mathcal{A}^*$, of consequences of the TBox $\mathcal{T} \cup \mathcal{R}^*$ and the KB $\Sigma = \langle \mathcal{A}, \mathcal{T}^*, \mathcal{R}^* \rangle$ respectively, restricted to individuals and concepts that actually occur in the given KB $= \langle \mathcal{A}, \mathcal{T}, \mathcal{R} \rangle$ and an extra "auxiliary" set of concepts defined over the signature of $\Sigma$. The approach to constructing SPQA system presented in this paper is quite different from [15]. In [15], the KB and envelope are expanded with new queries. This makes the subsequent query answering step more and more complicated. In general, the sets of all assertional consequences and GCI consequences of a given $\Sigma = \langle \mathcal{A}, \mathcal{T}, \mathcal{R} \rangle$ may be infinite. By forcing the tableau algorithms to compute the consequences (both assertions and GCIs) of KB restricted to individuals and subconcepts that occur in a given prescribed set, we obtain finite $\mathcal{A}^*$ and $\mathcal{T}^*$ that in fact can be computed efficiently in polynomial time. These sets, once computed, remain fixed and are not modified. The two tableau algorithms are sound and complete under the restrictions stated above, see Sects. 3.1 and 3.2. Since the sets $\mathcal{A}^*$ and $\mathcal{T}^*$ do not contain all the consequences of the KB, in order to answer user queries we have designed recursive algorithms which break the queries into smaller assertions or GCIs all the way until the information in the sets $\mathcal{A}^*$ and $\mathcal{T}^*$ can be used. In effect, we have split the task of query answering into two parts: in the first part we compute all the consequences of $\Sigma$ restricted to concepts and individuals that occur in $\Sigma$, in the second part we use a recursive algorithm to evaluate more complex queries with the base case that has been computed in the first part.

As for computing the envelopes, we start from the secrecy sets $\mathbb{S}_{\mathcal{A}}$ (of assertions) and $\mathbb{S}_{\mathcal{T}}$ (of GCIs), and compute finite supersets of assertions and GCIs, viz., the *envelopes* $\mathbb{E}_{\mathcal{A}} \subseteq \mathcal{A}^*$ of $\mathbb{S}_{\mathcal{A}}$ and $\mathbb{E}_{\mathcal{T}} \subseteq \mathcal{T}^*$ of $\mathbb{S}_{\mathcal{T}}$ respectively. These envelopes are computed by two tableau algorithms based on the idea of inverting the expansion rules of two tableau algorithms listed in Figs. 1 and 2. The idea behind the envelope concept is that no expression in the envelope can be logically deduced from information outside the envelope. Once such envelopes are computed, the answers to the queries are censored whenever the queries belong to the envelopes. Since, generally, an envelope for a given secrecy set is not unique, the developer can force the algorithm to output a specific envelope from the available choices satisfying the needs of application domain, company policy, social obligations and user preferences.

Next, we discuss query answering procedures which allow us answer queries without revealing secrets. Usually in SPQA framework queries are answered by checking their membership in $\mathcal{A}^* \backslash \mathbb{E}_{\mathcal{A}}$ (if the query is an assertion) or in $\mathcal{T}^* \backslash \mathbb{E}_{\mathcal{T}}$ (if the query is a GCI). Since $\mathcal{A}^*$ and $\mathcal{T}^*$ do not contain all the statements entailed by $\Sigma$, we need to extend the query answering procedure from just membership checking. Towards that end we designed two recursive algorithms to answer more complicated assertion and GCI queries. To answer an assertion query $q$, the algorithm first checks if $q \in \mathcal{A}^* \backslash \mathbb{E}_{\mathcal{A}}$ in which case the answer is "Yes"; otherwise, the given query is broken into subqueries based on the constructors, and the algorithm is applied recursively on the subqueries, see Sect. 5. This query answering procedure runs in polynomial time in the size of the KB and the query $q$. Similar approach is used to answer GCI queries.

## 2    Syntax and Semantics of $\mathcal{EL}^+$

A vocabulary of $\mathcal{EL}^+$ is a triple $<N_O, N_C, N_R>$ of countably infinite, pairwise disjoint sets. The elements of $N_O$ are called *objects* or *individual names*, the elements of $N_C$ are called *concept names* and the elements of $N_R$ are called *role names*. The set of $\mathcal{EL}^+$ *concepts* is denoted by $\mathcal{C}$ and is defined by the following rules

$$C ::= A \mid \top \mid C \sqcap D \mid \exists r.C$$

where $A \in N_C$, $r \in N_R$, $\top$ denotes the *"top concept"*, and $C, D \in \mathcal{C}$. *Assertions* are expressions of the form $C(a)$ or $r(a, b)$, *general concept inclusions (GCIs)* are expressions of the form $C \sqsubseteq D$ and *role inclusions* are expressions of the form $r \sqsubseteq s$ or $r \circ s \sqsubseteq t$ where $C, D \in \mathcal{C}$, $r, s, t \in N_R$ and $a, b \in N_O$, and $\circ$ denotes the composition operator. The semantics of $\mathcal{EL}^+$ concepts is specified, as usual, by an *interpretation* $\mathcal{I} = \langle \Delta, \cdot^{\mathcal{I}} \rangle$ where $\Delta$ is the *domain* of the interpretation, and $\cdot^{\mathcal{I}}$ is an *interpretation function* mapping each $a \in N_O$ to an element $a^{\mathcal{I}} \in \Delta$, each $A \in N_C$ to a subset $A^{\mathcal{I}} \subseteq \Delta$, and each $r \in N_R$ to a binary relation $r^{\mathcal{I}} \subseteq \Delta \times \Delta$. The interpretation function $\cdot^{\mathcal{I}}$ is extended inductively to all $\mathcal{EL}^+$ concepts in the usual manner:

$$\top^{\mathcal{I}} = \Delta; \quad (C \sqcap D)^{\mathcal{I}} = C^{\mathcal{I}} \cap D^{\mathcal{I}}; \quad (\exists r.C)^{\mathcal{I}} = \{d \in \Delta \mid \exists e \in C^{\mathcal{I}} : (d, e) \in r^{\mathcal{I}}\}.$$

An Abox $\mathcal{A}$ is a finite, non-empty set of assertions. A TBox $\mathcal{T}$ is a finite set of GCIs and an RBox $\mathcal{R}$ is a finite set of role inclusions. An $\mathcal{EL}^+$ KB is a triple $\Sigma = \langle \mathcal{A}, \mathcal{T}, \mathcal{R} \rangle$ where $\mathcal{A}$ is an ABox, $\mathcal{T}$ is a TBox and $\mathcal{R}$ is an RBox. Let $\mathcal{I} = \langle \Delta, \cdot^{\mathcal{I}} \rangle$ an interpretation, $C, D \in \mathcal{C}$, $r \in N_R$ and $a, b \in N_O$. We say that $\mathcal{I}$ satisfies $C(a)$, $r(a, b)$, $C \sqsubseteq D$, $r \sqsubseteq s$ or $r \circ s \sqsubseteq t$, notation $\mathcal{I} \models C(a)$, $\mathcal{I} \models r(a, b)$, $\mathcal{I} \models C \sqsubseteq D$, $\mathcal{I} \models r \sqsubseteq s$ or $\mathcal{I} \models r \circ s \sqsubseteq t$ if, respectively, $a^{\mathcal{I}} \in C^{\mathcal{I}}$, $(a^{\mathcal{I}}, b^{\mathcal{I}}) \in r^{\mathcal{I}}$, $C^{\mathcal{I}} \subseteq D^{\mathcal{I}}$, $r^{\mathcal{I}} \subseteq s^{\mathcal{I}}$ or $r^{\mathcal{I}} \circ s^{\mathcal{I}} \subseteq t^{\mathcal{I}}$[1]. $\mathcal{I}$ is a *model* of $\Sigma$, notation $\mathcal{I} \models \Sigma$, if $\mathcal{I}$ satisfies all the assertions in $\mathcal{A}$, all the GCIs in $\mathcal{T}$ and all the role inclusions in $\mathcal{R}$. Let $\alpha$ be an assertion, a GCI or a role inclusion. We say that $\Sigma$ *entails* $\alpha$, notation $\Sigma \models \alpha$, if all models of $\Sigma$ satisfy $\alpha$.

## 3    Computation of $\mathcal{A}^*$ and $\mathcal{T}^*$

Let $\Sigma = \langle \mathcal{A}, \mathcal{T}, \mathcal{R} \rangle$ be an $\mathcal{EL}^+$ KB. In this section, we give two tableau algorithms that compute $\mathcal{A}^*$, a set of assertional consequence of $\Sigma$, and $\mathcal{T}^*$ a set of GCI consequences of $\Sigma$, both restricted to concepts that occur in $\Sigma$. Before computing $\mathcal{T}^*$ and $\mathcal{A}^*$, we compute $\mathcal{R}^* = \mathcal{R}^+ \cup \mathcal{R}^\dagger$, where $\mathcal{R}^+$ is the transitive closure of $\mathcal{R}$ with respect to role inclusion and $\mathcal{R}^\dagger = \{r \sqsubseteq r \mid r \text{ occurs in } \Sigma\}$. As an example, consider a KB $\Sigma = \langle \mathcal{A}, \mathcal{T}, \mathcal{R} \rangle$ where ABox $\mathcal{A} = \{A(a), \exists m.B(c)\}$, TBox $\mathcal{T} = \{A \sqsubseteq \exists n.D\}$ and RBox $\mathcal{R} = \{r \sqsubseteq s, p \sqsubseteq q, u \sqsubseteq v, r \circ p \sqsubseteq w, s \circ q \sqsubseteq u\}$. Then, $\mathcal{R}^* = \mathcal{R} \cup \{s \circ q \sqsubseteq v\} \cup \{m \sqsubseteq m, n \sqsubseteq n, r \sqsubseteq r, s \sqsubseteq s, p \sqsubseteq p, q \sqsubseteq q, u \sqsubseteq u, v \sqsubseteq v, w \sqsubseteq w\}$. Note that $r \circ p \sqsubseteq u \notin \mathcal{R}^*$ even though the role inclusion $r \circ p \sqsubseteq u$ holds true in any model of the RBox $\mathcal{R}$. $\mathcal{R}^*$ is easily computed in polynomial time and we omit the details.

### 3.1    Computation of $\mathcal{T}^*$

Denote by $N_\Sigma$ the set of all concept names and role names occurring in $\Sigma$ and let $\mathbb{S}$ be a finite set of concepts over the symbol set $N_\Sigma$. Let $\mathcal{C}_{\Sigma, \mathbb{S}}$ be the set of all subconcepts of concepts that occur in either $\mathbb{S}$ or $\Sigma$. Given $\Sigma$ and $\mathcal{C}_{\Sigma, \mathbb{S}}$, we describe a procedure that computes $\mathcal{T}^*$, a set of GCI consequences of the given KB $\Sigma$ (restricted to concepts in $\mathcal{C}_{\Sigma, \mathbb{S}}$). That is, $\mathcal{T}^* = \{C \sqsubseteq D \mid C, D \in \mathcal{C}_{\Sigma, \mathbb{S}}$ and $\Sigma \models C \sqsubseteq D\}$. This procedure is similar to the calculus presented in [12].

Let $AX_\mathcal{T} = \{C \sqsubseteq C, C \sqsubseteq \top, \top \sqsubseteq \top \mid C \in \mathcal{C}_{\Sigma, \mathbb{S}}\}$. $\mathcal{T}^*$ is initialized as $AX_\mathcal{T}$ and then expanded by exhaustively applying expansion rules listed in Fig. 1. The $T_\sqsubseteq$-rule derives a GCI based on transitivity of subsumption. $T_\sqcap^-$-rule derives new GCIs by decomposing conjunction concepts into its two conjuncts. To derive GCIs whose right side involves concept expressions which occur in $\mathcal{C}_{\Sigma, \mathbb{S}}$, we use the $T_\sqcap^+$-rule. Similarly, $T_H^+$ and $T_\circ^+$-rules derive GCIs based on monotonicity property of GCIs and role inclusions.

A TBox is *completed* if no expansion rule in Fig. 1 is applicable to it. We denote by $\Lambda_\mathcal{T}$ the *algorithm* which, given $\Sigma$ and $\mathcal{C}_{\Sigma, \mathbb{S}}$, non-deterministically applies expansion rules in Fig. 1 until no further applications are possible. Since

---

[1] $r^{\mathcal{I}} \circ s^{\mathcal{I}}$ denotes composition of two binary relations $r^{\mathcal{I}}$ and $s^{\mathcal{I}}$.

$T_\sqsubseteq$ – rule : if $C \sqsubseteq D \in \mathcal{T}^*$, $D \sqsubseteq E \in \mathcal{T}$ and $C \sqsubseteq E \notin \mathcal{T}^*$,
           then $\mathcal{T}^* := \mathcal{T}^* \cup \{C \sqsubseteq E\}$;

$T_\sqcap^-$ – rule : if $C \sqsubseteq D \sqcap E \in \mathcal{T}^*$, and $C \sqsubseteq D \notin \mathcal{T}^*$ or $C \sqsubseteq E \notin \mathcal{T}^*$,
           then $\mathcal{T}^* := \mathcal{T}^* \cup \{C \sqsubseteq D, C \sqsubseteq E\}$;

$T_\sqcap^+$ – rule : if $C \sqsubseteq D$, $C \sqsubseteq E \in \mathcal{T}^*$, $D \sqcap E \in \mathcal{C}_{\Sigma,\mathbb{S}}$ and
           $C \sqsubseteq D \sqcap E \notin \mathcal{T}^*$, then $\mathcal{T}^* := \mathcal{T}^* \cup \{C \sqsubseteq D \sqcap E\}$;

$T_H^+$ – rule : if $C \sqsubseteq \exists r.D$, $D \sqsubseteq E \in \mathcal{T}^*$, $r \sqsubseteq s \in \mathcal{R}^*$, $\exists s.E \in \mathcal{C}_{\Sigma,\mathbb{S}}$ and
           $C \sqsubseteq \exists s.E \notin \mathcal{T}^*$, then $\mathcal{T}^* := \mathcal{T}^* \cup \{C \sqsubseteq \exists s.E\}$;

$T_\circ^+$ – rule : if $C \sqsubseteq \exists u.D$, $D \sqsubseteq \exists v.E$, $E \sqsubseteq F \in \mathcal{T}^*$, $u \sqsubseteq r, v \sqsubseteq s$,
           $r \circ s \sqsubseteq t \in \mathcal{R}^*$, $\exists t.F \in \mathcal{C}_{\Sigma,\mathbb{S}}$ and $C \sqsubseteq \exists t.F \notin \mathcal{T}^*$,
           then $\mathcal{T}^* := \mathcal{T}^* \cup \{C \sqsubseteq \exists t.F\}$.

**Fig. 1.** TBox Tableau expansion rules.

$\Lambda_\mathcal{T}$ has been restricted to derive GCIs whose left and right hand side concept expressions occur in $\mathcal{C}_{\Sigma,\mathbb{S}}$, the size of the $\mathcal{T}^*$ is at most a polynomial in the size of its input. Hence, the running time of $\Lambda_\mathcal{T}$ is polynomial in $\mid \Sigma \mid + \mid \mathcal{C}_{\Sigma,\mathbb{S}} \mid$. The correctness of $\Lambda_\mathcal{T}$ can be shown by proving soundness and completeness of $\Lambda_\mathcal{T}$. The soundness proof is obvious.

To prove the completeness of $\Lambda_\mathcal{T}$, we define a *canonical interpretation* $\mathcal{J} = \langle \Delta, \cdot^\mathcal{J} \rangle$ for a completed TBox $\mathcal{T}^*$ as follows:

$$\Delta = \{a_C \mid C \in \mathcal{C}_{\Sigma,\mathbb{S}}\};$$
$$\top^\mathcal{J} = \Delta;$$
$$\text{for } A \in N_C, \; A^\mathcal{J} = \{a_C \mid C \sqsubseteq A \in \mathcal{T}^*\};$$
$$\text{for } r \in N_R, \; r^\mathcal{J} = \{(a_C, a_D) \mid C \sqsubseteq \exists s.D \in \mathcal{T}^*, \; s \sqsubseteq r \in \mathcal{R}^*\} \cup$$
$$\{(a_C, a_D) \mid C \sqsubseteq \exists u.E, \; E \sqsubseteq \exists v.D \in \mathcal{T}^*, \; u \circ v \sqsubseteq r \in \mathcal{R}^*\}.$$

The interpretation function $\cdot^\mathcal{J}$ is extended to concept expressions as usual. To prove that $\mathcal{J}$ is a model of $\mathcal{T}^*$, we need the following technical lemma. The proof of Lemma 1 is by an easy induction argument and therefore it is omitted.

**Lemma 1.** *Let $B$, $C \in \mathcal{C}_{\Sigma,\mathbb{S}}$. Then,*

*(a) $a_C \in C^\mathcal{J}$.*
*(b) $a_C \in B^\mathcal{J}$ if and only if $C \sqsubseteq B \in \mathcal{T}^*$.*

We next argue that $\mathcal{J}$ satisfies $\mathcal{T}^*$ and $\mathcal{R}^*$.

**Lemma 2.** $\mathcal{J} \models \mathcal{T}^* \cup \mathcal{R}^*$.

*Proof.* It follows immediately from the definition of $\mathcal{J}$ that $\mathcal{J} \models \mathcal{R}^*$.

– Let $F \sqsubseteq G \in T^*$. Then, $F$, $G \in \mathcal{C}_{\Sigma,\mathbb{S}}$. Assume that $a_C \in F^{\mathcal{J}}$. By part (b) of Lemma 1, $C \sqsubseteq F \in T^*$. By the $T_{\sqsubseteq}$-rule, we get $C \sqsubseteq G \in T^*$. Again by part (b) of Lemma 1, we have $a_C \in G^{\mathcal{J}}$. Hence, $\mathcal{J} \models F \sqsubseteq G$.     □

The completeness of $\Lambda_T$ now follows by an easy argument.

**Theorem 1.** *Let $\Sigma$ be a $\mathcal{EL}^+$ KB and let $T^*$ be the completed TBox. For any concepts $C$, $D \in \mathcal{C}_{\Sigma,\mathbb{S}}$, if $\Sigma \models C \sqsubseteq D$ then $C \sqsubseteq D \in T^*$.*

*Proof.* Suppose $C \sqsubseteq D \notin T^*$, i.e., by part (b) of Lemma 1, $a_C \notin D^{\mathcal{J}}$. On the other hand by part (a) of Lemma 1, $a_C \in C^{\mathcal{J}}$ and this implies that $\mathcal{J} \not\models C \sqsubseteq D$. Since by Lemma 2, $\mathcal{J} \models T^*$, and since $T \subseteq T^*$, we obtain $T \not\models C \sqsubseteq D$.     □

## 3.2   Computation of $\mathcal{A}^*$

Let $\Sigma = \langle \mathcal{A}, T, \mathcal{R} \rangle$ be an $\mathcal{EL}^+$ KB, $\mathcal{R}^*$ be defined as at the beginning of this section and $T^*$ be the completed TBox as computed in Sect. 3.1. Also, let $\mathcal{O}_\Sigma$ be the set of individual names that occur in $\Sigma$ and define $AX_{\mathcal{A}} = \{\top(a) \mid a \in \mathcal{O}_\Sigma\}$. Now we outline the procedure that computes $\mathcal{A}^*$, the set of assertional consequences of $\Sigma^* = \langle \mathcal{A}, T^*, \mathcal{R}^* \rangle$, restricted as follows:

$$\mathcal{A}^* = \{C(a) \mid C \in \mathcal{C}_{\Sigma,\mathbb{S}} \text{ and } \Sigma^* \models C(a)\} \cup$$
$$\{r(a,b) \mid r \text{ occurs in } \Sigma \text{ and } \Sigma^* \models r(a,b)\}.$$

$\mathcal{A}^*$ is initialized as $\mathcal{A} \cup AX_{\mathcal{A}}$ and is expanded by exhaustively applying expansion rules listed in Fig. 2. A$_{\sqcap}^-$-rule decomposes conjunctions, and the A$_{\sqsubseteq}$-rule derives assertions based on the GCIs present in $T^*$. To build new concept assertions whose concept expressions already occur in $\mathcal{C}_{\Sigma,\mathbb{S}}$, we use the A$_{\sqcap}^+$ and A$_{\exists}^+$-rules. Similarly, the A$_{\exists H}^+$ and A$_{\exists o}^+$-rules derive concept assertions based on role inclusions. An important property of this procedure is that it does not introduces any fresh individual names into $\mathcal{A}^*$. This implies that some assertions of the form $\exists r.C(a)$ may not have "syntactic witnesses". Finally, the A$_H$ and A$_o$-rules derive role assertions based on role inclusions and role compositions respectively.

An ABox is *completed* if no expansion rule in Fig. 2 is applicable to it. We denote by $\Lambda_{\mathcal{A}}$ the *algorithm* which, given $\mathcal{A}$, $\mathcal{R}^*$, $T^*$ and $\mathcal{C}_{\Sigma,\mathbb{S}}$, non-deterministically applies expansion rules in Fig. 2 until no further applications are possible. Since $\Lambda_{\mathcal{A}}$ derives only assertions involving concept expressions that occur in $\mathcal{C}_{\Sigma,\mathbb{S}}$, it is easy to see that the running time of $\Lambda_{\mathcal{A}}$ is polynomial in $\mid \Sigma \mid + \mid \mathcal{C}_{\Sigma,\mathbb{S}} \mid$.

The correctness of $\Lambda_{\mathcal{A}}$ can be shown by proving its soundness and completeness. The soundness is obvious. To prove the completeness of $\Lambda_{\mathcal{A}}$, we first define a *canonical interpretation* $\mathcal{K} = \langle \Delta, \cdot^{\mathcal{K}} \rangle$ for a completed ABox $\mathcal{A}^*$, cf. [8]. Define the witness set, $\mathcal{W} = \{w_C \mid C \in \mathcal{C}_{\Sigma,\mathbb{S}}\}$.

$$\Delta = \mathcal{O}_\Sigma \cup \mathcal{W}; \ a^{\mathcal{K}} = a, \text{where } a \in \mathcal{O}_\Sigma; \ \top^{\mathcal{K}} = \Delta;$$
$$\text{for } A \in N_C, \ A^{\mathcal{K}} = \{a \in \mathcal{O}_\Sigma \mid A(a) \in \mathcal{A}^*\} \cup \{w_C \in \mathcal{W} \mid C \sqsubseteq A \in T^*\};$$

$A_{\sqcap}^{-}$ – rule : if $C \sqcap D(a) \in \mathcal{A}^*$, and $C(a) \notin \mathcal{A}^*$ or $D(a) \notin \mathcal{A}^*$,
then $\mathcal{A}^* := \mathcal{A}^* \cup \{C(a), D(a)\}$;

$A_{\sqcap}^{+}$ – rule : if $C(a)$, $D(a) \in \mathcal{A}^*$, $C \sqcap D \in \mathcal{C}_{\Sigma,\mathbb{S}}$ and
$C \sqcap D(a) \notin \mathcal{A}^*$, then $\mathcal{A}^* := \mathcal{A}^* \cup \{C \sqcap D(a)\}$;

$A_{\exists}^{+}$ – rule : if $r(a,b)$, $C(b) \in \mathcal{A}^*$, $\exists r.C \in \mathcal{C}_{\Sigma,\mathbb{S}}$ and
$\exists r.C(a) \notin \mathcal{A}^*$, then $\mathcal{A}^* := \mathcal{A}^* \cup \{\exists r.C(a)\}$;

$A_{\sqsubseteq}$ – rule : if $C(a) \in \mathcal{A}^*$, $C \sqsubseteq D \in \mathcal{T}^*$, and $D(a) \notin \mathcal{A}^*$,
then $\mathcal{A}^* := \mathcal{A}^* \cup \{D(a)\}$;

$A_{\exists H}^{+}$ – rule : if $\exists r.C(a) \in \mathcal{A}^*$, $r \sqsubseteq s \in \mathcal{R}^*$, $C \sqsubseteq D \in \mathcal{T}^*$, $\exists s.D \in \mathcal{C}_{\Sigma,\mathbb{S}}$ and
$\exists s.D(a) \notin \mathcal{A}^*$, then $\mathcal{A}^* := \mathcal{A}^* \cup \{\exists s.D(a)\}$;

$A_{\exists \circ}^{+}$ – rule : if $\exists u.C(a) \in \mathcal{A}^*$, $C \sqsubseteq \exists v.D$, $D \sqsubseteq E \in \mathcal{T}^*$,
$u \sqsubseteq r$, $v \sqsubseteq s$, $r \circ s \sqsubseteq t \in \mathcal{R}^*$, $\exists t.E \in \mathcal{C}_{\Sigma,\mathbb{S}}$ and $\exists t.E(a) \notin \mathcal{A}^*$,
then $\mathcal{A}^* := \mathcal{A}^* \cup \{\exists t.E(a)\}$;

$A_{H}$ – rule : if $r(a,b) \in \mathcal{A}^*$, $r \sqsubseteq s \in \mathcal{R}^*$, and $s(a,b) \notin \mathcal{A}^*$,
then $\mathcal{A}^* := \mathcal{A}^* \cup \{s(a,b)\}$;

$A_{\circ}$ – rule : if $r(a,b), s(b,c) \in \mathcal{A}^*$, $r \circ s \sqsubseteq t \in \mathcal{R}^*$, and $t(a,c) \notin \mathcal{A}^*$,
then $\mathcal{A}^* := \mathcal{A}^* \cup \{t(a,c)\}$.

**Fig. 2.** ABox Tableau expansion rules.

for $r \in N_R$, $r^{\mathcal{K}} = \{(a,b) \in \mathcal{O}_{\Sigma} \times \mathcal{O}_{\Sigma} \mid s(a,b) \in \mathcal{A}^*,\ s \sqsubseteq r \in \mathcal{R}^*\}$
$\cup \{(a,b) \in \mathcal{O}_{\Sigma} \times \mathcal{O}_{\Sigma} \mid$ for some $c \in \mathcal{O}_{\Sigma},\ u(a,c),$
$v(c,b) \in \mathcal{A}^*,\ u \circ v \sqsubseteq r \in \mathcal{R}^*\}$
$\cup \{(a, w_C) \in \mathcal{O}_{\Sigma} \times \mathcal{W} \mid \exists s.C(a) \in \mathcal{A}^*,\ s \sqsubseteq r \in \mathcal{R}^*\}$
$\cup \{(a, w_C) \in \mathcal{O}_{\Sigma} \times \mathcal{W} \mid \exists u.D(a) \in \mathcal{A}^*,\ D \sqsubseteq \exists v.C \in \mathcal{T}^*,$
$u \circ v \sqsubseteq r \in \mathcal{R}^*\}$
$\cup \{(w_C, w_D) \mid C \sqsubseteq \exists s.D \in \mathcal{T}^*,\ s \sqsubseteq r \in \mathcal{R}^*\}$
$\cup \{(w_C, w_D) \mid C \sqsubseteq \exists u.E,\ E \sqsubseteq \exists v.D \in \mathcal{T}^*,$
$u \circ v \sqsubseteq r \in \mathcal{R}^*\}.$

$\mathcal{K}$ is extended to compound concepts in the usual way. We argue that $\mathcal{K}$ is a model of $\mathcal{A}^*$, $\mathcal{T}^*$ and $\mathcal{R}^*$. In the following, we shall prove several technical lemmas to show that $\mathcal{K}$ is indeed a canonical model of $\langle \mathcal{A}^*, \mathcal{T}^*, \mathcal{R}^* \rangle$.

**Lemma 3.** *Let $a, b \in \mathcal{O}_{\Sigma}$ and suppose that the role name $r$ occurs in $\Sigma$. If $(a,b) \in r^{\mathcal{K}}$, then $r(a,b) \in \mathcal{A}^*$.*

*Proof.* Assume the hypotheses. We argue by cases.

– Let $s(a,b) \in \mathcal{A}^*$ and $s \sqsubseteq r \in \mathcal{R}^*$. Then by applying $A_H$-rule, $r(a,b) \in \mathcal{A}^*$.
– Let $u(a,c), v(c,b) \in \mathcal{A}^*$ and $u \circ v \sqsubseteq r \in \mathcal{R}^*$. By the $A_{\circ}$-rule, $r(a,b) \in \mathcal{A}^*$. □

The following two lemmas are proved by using the definition of $\mathcal{K}$ and, in the case of Lemma 5, by an easy induction on the structure of concept $B$.

**Lemma 4.** *If $r(a, b) \in \mathcal{A}^*$, then $(a, b) \in r^{\mathcal{K}}$.*

**Lemma 5.** *Let $B$, $C \in \mathcal{C}_{\Sigma,\mathbb{S}}$. Then,*

*(a) $w_C \in C^{\mathcal{K}}$.*
*(b) $w_C \in B^{\mathcal{K}}$ if and only if $C \sqsubseteq B \in \mathcal{T}^*$.*

The following lemma is useful in proving the completeness of $\Lambda_{\mathcal{A}}$.

**Lemma 6.** *Let $a \in \mathcal{O}_\Sigma$ and $B \in \mathcal{C}_{\Sigma,\mathbb{S}}$. If $a \in B^{\mathcal{K}}$, then $B(a) \in \mathcal{A}^*$.*

*Proof.* The proof is by induction on the structure of $B$.

- When $B \in N_C$, the claim follows directly from the definition of $\mathcal{K}$.
- When $B = \top$, the claim follows from the definition of $AX_{\mathcal{A}}$.
- $B = C \sqcap D$. Then, $a \in (C \sqcap D)^{\mathcal{K}} \Rightarrow a \in C^{\mathcal{K}}$ and $a \in D^{\mathcal{K}} \Rightarrow C(a), D(a) \in \mathcal{A}^*$, by inductive hypothesis. Since $C \sqcap D$ occurs in $\mathcal{C}_{\Sigma,\mathbb{S}}$, by the $A_\sqcap^+$-rule, we have $C \sqcap D(a) = B(a) \in \mathcal{A}^*$.
- $B = \exists r.C$. Then, $a \in (\exists r.C)^{\mathcal{K}} \Rightarrow$ there is an element $b \in \Delta$ such that $(a, b) \in r^{\mathcal{K}}$ and $b \in C^{\mathcal{K}}$. There are two cases.
  - $b \in \mathcal{O}_\Sigma$. Since $r$ occurs in $\Sigma$ and $C$ occurs in $\mathcal{C}_{\Sigma,\mathbb{S}}$, by Lemma 3, we have $r(a, b) \in \mathcal{A}^*$ and by the inductive hypothesis, $C(b) \in \mathcal{A}^*$. Since $\exists r.C$ occurs in $\mathcal{C}_{\Sigma,\mathbb{S}}$, by the $A_\exists^+$-rule, we have $\exists r.C(a) = B(a) \in \mathcal{A}^*$.
  - $b = w_D \in \mathcal{W}$ for some $D \in \mathcal{C}_{\Sigma,\mathbb{S}}$. Then, we have $(a, w_D) \in r^{\mathcal{K}}$ and $w_D \in C^{\mathcal{K}}$. By part (b) of Lemma 5, $D \sqsubseteq C \in \mathcal{T}^*$. Now, we have two subcases.
    - $\exists s.D(a) \in \mathcal{A}^*$ and $s \sqsubseteq r \in \mathcal{R}^*$. Since $D \sqsubseteq C \in \mathcal{T}^*$ and $\exists r.C \in \mathcal{C}_{\Sigma,\mathbb{S}}$, by the $A_{\exists H}^+$-rule, we have $\exists r.C(a) = B(a) \in \mathcal{A}^*$.
    - $\exists u.E(a) \in \mathcal{A}^*$, $E \sqsubseteq \exists v.D \in \mathcal{T}^*$ and $u \circ v \sqsubseteq r \in \mathcal{R}^*$. Since $D \sqsubseteq C \in \mathcal{T}^*$, $\exists r.C \in \mathcal{C}_{\Sigma,\mathbb{S}}$ and $u \sqsubseteq u, v \sqsubseteq v \in \mathcal{R}^*$ by the $A_{\exists H}^+$-rule, we have $\exists r.C(a) = B(a) \in \mathcal{A}^*$.     □

To prove $\mathcal{K}$ is a model of $\mathcal{A}^*$, $\mathcal{T}^*$ and $\mathcal{R}^*$, we need the following technical lemma.

**Lemma 7.** *If $B(a) \in \mathcal{A}^*$, then $a \in B^{\mathcal{K}}$.*

*Proof.* We prove the claim by induction on the structure of $B$.

- $B = A \in N_C$. Then, $A(a) \in \mathcal{A}^* \Rightarrow a \in A^{\mathcal{K}} = B^{\mathcal{K}}$.
- $B = \top$. The claim follows from the definition of $\mathcal{K}$.
- $B = C \sqcap D$. Then, $C \sqcap D(a) \in \mathcal{A}^*$. By $A_\sqcap^-$-rule, we have $C(a), D(a) \in \mathcal{A}^* \Rightarrow a \in C^{\mathcal{K}}$ and $a \in D^{\mathcal{K}} \Rightarrow a \in (C \sqcap D)^{\mathcal{K}}$, by inductive hypothesis.
- $B = \exists r.D$. Then, $\exists r.D(a) \in \mathcal{A}^*$. By the definition of $\mathcal{K}$, $(a, w_D) \in r^{\mathcal{K}}$. By Lemma 1, $w_D \in D^{\mathcal{K}}$. Hence, by the semantics of $\exists$, $a \in (\exists r.D)^{\mathcal{K}} = B^{\mathcal{K}}$.     □

In the following we prove that $\mathcal{K}$ satisfies $\mathcal{A}^*$, $\mathcal{T}^*$ and $\mathcal{R}^*$.

**Lemma 8.** $\mathcal{K} \models \mathcal{A}^* \cup \mathcal{T}^* \cup \mathcal{R}^*$.

*Proof.* It follows immediately from the definition of $\mathcal{K}$ that $\mathcal{K} \models \mathcal{R}^*$. Next, we show that $\mathcal{K}$ satisfies $\mathcal{A}^*$.

- $C(a) \in \mathcal{A}^*$. By Lemma 7, $a \in C^{\mathcal{K}}$, i.e., $\mathcal{K} \models B(a)$.
- $r(a, b) \in \mathcal{A}^*$. By Lemma 4, $\mathcal{K} \models r(a, b)$.

Hence $\mathcal{K} \models \mathcal{A}^*$.

Now, we show that $\mathcal{K}$ satisfies $\mathcal{T}^*$. Let $F \sqsubseteq G \in \mathcal{T}^*$ and $a \in F^{\mathcal{K}}$. We have two cases.

- $a \in \mathcal{O}_\Sigma$. Then, by Lemma 6, $F(a) \in \mathcal{A}^*$. Since $\mathcal{A}^*$ is completed, by the $A_\sqsubseteq$-rule, we get $G(a) \in \mathcal{A}^*$. By Lemma 7, $a \in G^{\mathcal{K}}$. Hence, $\mathcal{K} \models F \sqsubseteq G$.
- $w_C \in \mathcal{W}$ for some $C \in \mathcal{C}_{\Sigma,\mathbb{S}}$. This implies, by the definition of $\mathcal{K}$, $C \sqsubseteq F \in \mathcal{T}^*$. Since $\mathcal{T}^*$ is completed, we have $C \sqsubseteq G \in \mathcal{T}^*$. Again by the definition of $\mathcal{K}$, $a \in G^{\mathcal{K}}$ which implies $\mathcal{K} \models F \sqsubseteq G$. □

Now, we are ready to prove the completeness of $\Lambda_{\mathcal{A}}$.

**Theorem 2.** *Let $\Sigma^* = \langle \mathcal{A}, \mathcal{T}^*, \mathcal{R}^* \rangle$ be a $\mathcal{EL}^+$ KB as defined in Sect. 3.2. Also, let $\mathcal{T}^*$ and $\mathcal{A}^*$ be the completed TBox and ABox respectively. Suppose that $B \in \mathcal{C}_{\Sigma,\mathbb{S}}$ and $r$ occurs in $\Sigma$. Then, for any $a, b \in \mathcal{O}_\Sigma$,*

- $\Sigma^* \models B(a) \;\Rightarrow\; B(a) \in \mathcal{A}^*$.
- $\Sigma^* \models r(a, b) \;\Rightarrow\; r(a, b) \in \mathcal{A}^*$.

*Proof.* Proof by contrapositive argument. Since $\mathcal{A} \subseteq \mathcal{A}^*$ and by Lemma 8, we have $\mathcal{K} \models \Sigma^*$. We show that $\mathcal{K} \not\models B(a)$ and $\mathcal{K} \not\models r(a, b)$.

- Assume that $B(a) \notin \mathcal{A}^*$ for some $B \in \mathcal{C}_{\Sigma,\mathbb{S}}$. Therefore, $a \notin B^{\mathcal{K}}$ by Lemma 6. Hence $\mathcal{K} \not\models B(a)$.
- Assume that $r(a, b) \notin \mathcal{A}^*$ for some $r$ that occurs in $\Sigma$. Therefore, $(a, b) \notin r^{\mathcal{K}}$ by Lemma 3. Hence $\mathcal{K} \not\models r(a, b)$. □

## 4   Secrecy-Preserving Reasoning in $\mathcal{EL}^+$ KBs

Let $\Sigma = \langle \mathcal{A}, \mathcal{T}, \mathcal{R} \rangle$ be a $\mathcal{EL}^+$ KB. Also let $\mathbb{S}_{\mathcal{A}} \subseteq \mathcal{A}^* \backslash AX_{\mathcal{A}}$ and $\mathbb{S}_{\mathcal{T}} \subseteq \mathcal{T}^* \backslash AX_{\mathcal{T}}$ be the "secrecy sets". Given $\Sigma$, $\mathbb{S}_{\mathcal{A}}$ and $\mathbb{S}_{\mathcal{T}}$, the objective is to answer assertion or GCI queries while preserving secrecy. Our approach is to compute two sets $\mathbb{E}_{\mathcal{A}}$ and $\mathbb{E}_{\mathcal{T}}$, where $\mathbb{S}_{\mathcal{A}} \subseteq \mathbb{E}_{\mathcal{A}} \subseteq \mathcal{A}^* \backslash AX_{\mathcal{A}}$ and $\mathbb{S}_{\mathcal{T}} \subseteq \mathbb{E}_{\mathcal{T}} \subseteq \mathcal{T}^* \backslash AX_{\mathcal{T}}$, called the *secrecy envelopes* for $\mathbb{S}_{\mathcal{A}}$ and $\mathbb{S}_{\mathcal{T}}$ respectively, so that protecting $\mathbb{E}_{\mathcal{A}}$ and $\mathbb{E}_{\mathcal{T}}$, the querying agent cannot logically infer any assertion in $\mathbb{S}_{\mathcal{A}}$ and any GCI in $\mathbb{S}_{\mathcal{T}}$. The role of OWA in answering the queries is the following: When answering a query with "Unknown", the querying agent should not be able to distinguish between the case that the answer to the query is truly unknown to the KB reasoner and the case that the answer is being protected for reasons of secrecy.

Now we explain the secrecy-reasoning framework. We envision a situation in which once the ABox $\mathcal{A}^*$ and TBox $\mathcal{T}^*$ are computed, a reasoner $\mathfrak{R}$ is associated with it. $\mathfrak{R}$ is designed to answer queries as follows: If a query cannot be inferred from $\Sigma$, the answer is "Unknown". If it can be inferred and it is not in $\mathbb{E}_\mathcal{A} \cup \mathbb{E}_\mathcal{T}$, the answer is "Yes"; otherwise, the answer is "Unknown". We make the following assumptions about the capabilities of the querying agent:

(a) does not have direct access to the KB $\Sigma = \langle \mathcal{A}, \mathcal{T}, \mathcal{R} \rangle$, but is aware of the underlying vocabulary,
(b) can ask queries in the form of assertions or GCIs, and
(c) cannot ask queries in the form of role inclusions.

We formally define the notion of an envelope in the following.

**Definition 1.** *Let $\Sigma = \langle \mathcal{A}, \mathcal{T}, \mathcal{R} \rangle$ be a $\mathcal{EL}^+$ KB, and let $\mathbb{S}_\mathcal{A}$ and $\mathbb{S}_\mathcal{T}$ be two finite secrecy sets. The secrecy envelopes $\mathbb{E}_\mathcal{A}$ and $\mathbb{E}_\mathcal{T}$ of $\mathbb{S}_\mathcal{A}$ and $\mathbb{S}_\mathcal{T}$ respectively, have the following properties:*

- $\mathbb{S}_\mathcal{A} \subseteq \mathbb{E}_\mathcal{A} \subseteq \mathcal{A}^* \backslash AX_\mathcal{A}$,
- $\mathbb{S}_\mathcal{T} \subseteq \mathbb{E}_\mathcal{T} \subseteq \mathcal{T}^* \backslash AX_\mathcal{T}$,
- *for every $\alpha \in \mathbb{E}_\mathcal{T}$, $\mathcal{T}^* \backslash \mathbb{E}_\mathcal{T} \not\models \alpha$ and*
- *for every $\alpha \in \mathbb{E}_\mathcal{A}$, $\mathcal{A}^* \backslash \mathbb{E}_\mathcal{A} \not\models \alpha$.*

The intuition for the above definition is that no information in $\mathbb{E}_\mathcal{A}$ and $\mathbb{E}_\mathcal{T}$ can be inferred from the corresponding sets $\mathcal{A}^* \backslash \mathbb{E}_\mathcal{A}$ and $\mathcal{T}^* \backslash \mathbb{E}_\mathcal{T}$. To compute envelopes, we use the idea of inverting the rules of Figs. 1 and 2 (see [15], where this approach was first utilized for membership assertions). Induced by the TBox and ABox expansion rules in Figs. 1 and 2, we define the corresponding "inverted" ABox and TBox expansion rules in Figs. 3 and 4, respectively. These inverted expansion rules are denoted by prefixing Inv- to the name of the corresponding expansion rules.

From now on, we assume that $\mathcal{A}^*$, $\mathcal{T}^*$ and $\mathcal{R}^*$ have been computed and readily available for computing the envelopes. The computation of envelopes consists of two steps. In the first step, we compute $\mathbb{E}_\mathcal{A}$ by initializing it to $\mathbb{S}_\mathcal{A}$ and then expanding it using the inverted expansion rules listed in Fig. 3 until no further applications of rules are possible. We denote by $\Lambda_\mathcal{A}^S$ the algorithm which computes the set $\mathbb{E}_\mathcal{A}$. Due to non-determinism in applying the rules Inv-$A_\sqcap^+$, Inv-$A_\exists^+$ and Inv-$A_\circ$, different executions of $\Lambda_\mathcal{A}^S$ may result different output. Since $\mathcal{A}^*$ is finite, the computation of $\Lambda_\mathcal{A}^S$ terminates. Let $\mathbb{E}_\mathcal{A}$ be the output of $\Lambda_\mathcal{A}^S$. Since the size of $\mathcal{A}^*$ is polynomial in $|\Sigma| + |\mathcal{C}_{\Sigma,\mathbb{S}}|$, and each application of inverted expansion rule moves some assertions from $\mathcal{A}^*$ into $\mathbb{E}_\mathcal{A}$, the size of $\mathbb{E}_\mathcal{A}$ is at most the size of $\mathcal{A}^*$. Therefore $\Lambda_\mathcal{A}^S$ takes polynomial time in $|\Sigma| + |\mathcal{C}_{\Sigma,\mathbb{S}}|$ to compute the envelope $\mathbb{E}_\mathcal{A}$.

In step two, we compute $\mathbb{E}_\mathcal{T}$ by initializing it to $\mathbb{S}_\mathcal{T}$ and then expanding it using the inverted TBox expansion rules listed in Fig. 4 until no further applications of rules are possible. We denote by $\Lambda_\mathcal{T}^S$ the algorithm which computes the set $\mathbb{E}_\mathcal{T}$. Due to non-determinism in applying Inv-$T_\sqcap^+$ and Inv-$T_\circ^+$-rules, different executions of $\Lambda_\mathcal{T}^S$ may result different output. Since $\mathcal{T}^*$ is finite, the computation

---

Inv-A$_\sqcap^-$ – rule : if $\{C(a), D(a)\} \cap \mathbb{E}_\mathcal{A} \neq \emptyset$ and $C \sqcap D(a) \in \mathcal{A}^* \setminus \mathbb{E}_\mathcal{A}$,
  then $\mathbb{E}_\mathcal{A} := \mathbb{E}_\mathcal{A} \cup \{C \sqcap D(a)\}$;

Inv-A$_\sqcap^+$ – rule : if $C \sqcap D(a) \in \mathbb{E}_\mathcal{A}$, $C \sqcap D \in \mathcal{C}_{\Sigma,\mathrm{s}}$ and
  $\{C(a), D(a)\} \subseteq \mathcal{A}^* \setminus \mathbb{E}_\mathcal{A}$,
  then $\mathbb{E}_\mathcal{A} := \mathbb{E}_\mathcal{A} \cup \{C(a)\}$ or $\mathbb{E}_\mathcal{A} := \mathbb{E}_\mathcal{A} \cup \{D(a)\}$;

Inv-A$_\exists^+$ – rule : if $\exists r.C(a) \in \mathbb{E}_\mathcal{A}$, $r(a,b), C(b) \in \mathcal{A}^* \setminus \mathbb{E}_\mathcal{A}$ and $\exists r.C \in \mathcal{C}_{\Sigma,\mathrm{S}}$,
  then $\mathbb{E}_\mathcal{A} := \mathbb{E}_\mathcal{A} \cup \{r(a,b)\}$ or $\mathbb{E}_\mathcal{A} := \mathbb{E}_\mathcal{A} \cup \{C(b)\}$;

Inv-A$_\sqsubseteq$ – rule : if $D(a) \in \mathbb{E}_\mathcal{A}$, $C \sqsubseteq D \in \mathcal{T}^*$, and $C(a) \in \mathcal{A}^* \setminus \mathbb{E}_\mathcal{A}$,
  then $\mathbb{E}_\mathcal{A} := \mathbb{E}_\mathcal{A} \cup \{C(a)\}$;

Inv-A$_{\exists H}^+$ – rule : if $\exists s.D(a) \in \mathbb{E}_\mathcal{A}$, $C \sqsubseteq D \in \mathcal{T}^*$, $r \sqsubseteq s \in \mathcal{R}^*$, $\exists s.D \in \mathcal{C}_{\Sigma,\mathrm{S}}$
  and $\exists r.C(a) \in \mathcal{A}^* \setminus \mathbb{E}_\mathcal{A}$, then $\mathbb{E}_\mathcal{A} := \mathbb{E}_\mathcal{A} \cup \{\exists r.C(a)\}$;

Inv-A$_{\exists\circ}^+$ – rule : if $\exists t.E(a) \in \mathbb{E}_\mathcal{A}$, $C \sqsubseteq \exists v.D, D \sqsubseteq E \in \mathcal{T}^*$, $u \sqsubseteq r, v \sqsubseteq s$,
  $r \circ s \sqsubseteq t \in \mathcal{R}^*$, $\exists t.E \in \mathcal{C}_{\Sigma,\mathrm{S}}$ and $\exists u.C(a) \in \mathcal{A}^* \setminus \mathbb{E}_\mathcal{A}$,
  then $\mathbb{E}_\mathcal{A} := \mathbb{E}_\mathcal{A} \cup \{\exists u.C(a)\}$;

Inv-A$_H$ – rule : if $s(a,b) \in \mathbb{E}_\mathcal{A}$, $r \sqsubseteq s \in \mathcal{R}^*$, and $r(a,b) \in \mathcal{A}^* \setminus \mathbb{E}_\mathcal{A}$,
  then $\mathbb{E}_\mathcal{A} := \mathbb{E}_\mathcal{A} \cup \{r(a,b)\}$;

Inv-A$_\circ$ – rule : if $t(a,c) \in \mathbb{E}_\mathcal{A}$, $r \circ s \sqsubseteq t \in \mathcal{R}^*$, and
  $\{r(a,b), s(b,c)\} \subseteq \mathcal{A}^* \setminus \mathbb{E}_\mathcal{A}$,
  then $\mathbb{E}_\mathcal{A} := \mathbb{E}_\mathcal{A} \cup \{r(a,b)\}$ or $\mathbb{E}_\mathcal{A} := \mathbb{E}_\mathcal{A} \cup \{s(b,c)\}$.

---

**Fig. 3.** Inverted ABox Tableau expansion rules: we use the same conventions as in Fig. 2.

---

Inv-T$_\sqsubseteq$ – rule : if $C \sqsubseteq E \in \mathbb{E}_\mathcal{T}$, $D \sqsubseteq E \in \mathcal{T}$ and $C \sqsubseteq D \in \mathcal{T}^* \setminus \mathbb{E}_\mathcal{T}$,
  then $\mathbb{E}_\mathcal{T} := \mathbb{E}_\mathcal{T} \cup \{C \sqsubseteq D\}$;

Inv-T$_\sqcap^-$ – rule : if $\{C \sqsubseteq D, C \sqsubseteq E\} \cap \mathbb{E}_\mathcal{T} \neq \emptyset$ and $C \sqsubseteq D \sqcap E \in \mathcal{T}^* \setminus \mathbb{E}_\mathcal{T}$,
  then $\mathbb{E}_\mathcal{T} := \mathbb{E}_\mathcal{T} \cup \{C \sqsubseteq D \sqcap E\}$;

Inv-T$_\sqcap^+$ – rule : if $C \sqsubseteq D \sqcap E \in \mathbb{E}_\mathcal{T}$, $D \sqcap E \in \mathcal{C}_{\Sigma,\mathrm{s}}$ and
  $\{C \sqsubseteq D, C \sqsubseteq E\} \subseteq \mathcal{T}^* \setminus \mathbb{E}_\mathcal{T}$,
  then $\mathbb{E}_\mathcal{T} := \mathbb{E}_\mathcal{T} \cup \{C \sqsubseteq D\}$ or $\mathbb{E}_\mathcal{T} := \mathbb{E}_\mathcal{T} \cup \{C \sqsubseteq E\}$;

Inv-T$_H^+$ – rule : if $C \sqsubseteq \exists s.E \in \mathbb{E}_\mathcal{T}$, $r \sqsubseteq s \in \mathcal{R}^*$,
  $\exists s.E \in \mathcal{C}_{\Sigma,\mathrm{s}}$ and $\{C \sqsubseteq \exists r.D, D \sqsubseteq E\} \subseteq \mathcal{T}^* \setminus \mathbb{E}_\mathcal{T}$,
  then $\mathbb{E}_\mathcal{T} := \mathbb{E}_\mathcal{T} \cup \{C \sqsubseteq \exists r.D\}$ or $\mathbb{E}_\mathcal{T} := \mathbb{E}_\mathcal{T} \cup \{D \sqsubseteq E\}$;

Inv-T$_\circ^+$ – rule : if $C \sqsubseteq \exists t.F \in \mathbb{E}_\mathcal{T}$, $u \sqsubseteq r, v \sqsubseteq s, r \circ s \sqsubseteq t \in \mathcal{R}^*$,
  $\exists t.F \in \mathcal{C}_{\Sigma,\mathrm{s}}$ and $\{C \sqsubseteq \exists u.D, D \sqsubseteq \exists v.E, E \sqsubseteq F\} \subseteq \mathcal{T}^* \setminus \mathbb{E}_\mathcal{T}$,
  then $\mathbb{E}_\mathcal{T} := \mathbb{E}_\mathcal{T} \cup \{C \sqsubseteq \exists u.D\}$ or $\mathbb{E}_\mathcal{T} := \mathbb{E}_\mathcal{T} \cup \{D \sqsubseteq \exists v.E\}$
  or $\mathbb{E}_\mathcal{T} := \mathbb{E}_\mathcal{T} \cup \{E \sqsubseteq F\}$.

---

**Fig. 4.** Inverted TBox Tableau expansion rules: we use the same conventions as in Fig. 1.

of $\Lambda_{\mathcal{T}}^S$ terminates. Let $\mathbb{E}_{\mathcal{T}}$ be the output of $\Lambda_{\mathcal{T}}^S$. Since the size of $\mathcal{T}^*$ is polynomial in the size of $\Sigma$ and $\mathcal{C}_{\Sigma,\mathbb{S}}$, and each application of inverted TBox expansion rule moves some GCIs from $\mathcal{T}^*$ into $\mathbb{E}_{\mathcal{T}}$, the size of $\mathbb{E}_{\mathcal{T}}$ is at most the size of $\mathcal{T}^*$. Therefore $\Lambda_{\mathcal{T}}^S$ takes polynomial time in $\mid \Sigma \mid + \mid \mathcal{C}_{\Sigma,\mathbb{S}} \mid$ to compute the envelope $\mathbb{E}_{\mathcal{T}}$.

Before proving the main results on envelopes, we prove the following auxiliary lemmas. First, we show that no assertions in $\mathbb{E}_{\mathcal{A}}$ is "logically reachable" from $\mathcal{A}^*\backslash\mathbb{E}_{\mathcal{A}}$.

**Lemma 9.** *Let $\mathcal{A}^*$ be a completed ABox obtained from $\mathcal{A}$ by applying the tableau expansion rules in Fig. 2. Also, let $\mathbb{E}_{\mathcal{A}}$ be a set of assertions which is completed by applying the tableau expansion rules in Fig. 3 starting with the secrecy set $\mathbb{S}_{\mathcal{A}}$. Then, the ABox $\mathcal{A}^*\backslash\mathbb{E}_{\mathcal{A}}$ is completed.*

*Proof.* We have to show that no rule in Fig. 2 is applicable to $\mathcal{A}^*\backslash\mathbb{E}_{\mathcal{A}}$. The proof is by contradiction according to cases.

- If $\mathsf{A}_{\sqcap}^-$-rule is applicable, then there is an assertion $C \sqcap D(a) \in \mathcal{A}^*\backslash\mathbb{E}_{\mathcal{A}}$ such that $C(a) \notin \mathcal{A}^*\backslash\mathbb{E}_{\mathcal{A}}$ or $D(a) \notin \mathcal{A}^*\backslash\mathbb{E}_{\mathcal{A}}$. Since $\mathcal{A}^*$ is completed, $\{C(a), D(a)\} \subseteq \mathcal{A}^*$. Hence, $\{C(a), D(a)\} \cap \mathbb{E}_{\mathcal{A}} \neq \emptyset$. This makes the Inv-$\mathsf{A}_{\sqcap}^-$-rule applicable, contrary to the assumption that $\mathbb{E}_{\mathcal{A}}$ is completed.
- If $\mathsf{A}_{\sqcap}^+$-rule is applicable, then there are assertions $C(a), D(a) \in \mathcal{A}^*\backslash\mathbb{E}_{\mathcal{A}}$ and $C \sqcap D \in \mathcal{C}_{\Sigma,\mathbb{S}}$ such that $C \sqcap D(a) \notin \mathcal{A}^*\backslash\mathbb{E}_{\mathcal{A}}$. Since $\mathcal{A}^*$ is completed, $C \sqcap D(a) \in \mathcal{A}^*$. Hence, $C \sqcap D(a) \in \mathbb{E}_{\mathcal{A}}$. This makes the Inv-$\mathsf{A}_{\sqcap}^+$-rule applicable, contrary to the assumption that $\mathbb{E}_{\mathcal{A}}$ is completed.
- If $\mathsf{A}_{\exists}^+$-rule is applicable, then there are assertions $r(a, b), C(b) \in \mathcal{A}^*\backslash\mathbb{E}_{\mathcal{A}}$ and $\exists r.C \in \mathcal{C}_{\Sigma,\mathbb{S}}$ such that $\exists r.C(a) \notin \mathcal{A}^*\backslash\mathbb{E}_{\mathcal{A}}$. Since $\mathcal{A}^*$ is completed, $\exists r.C(a) \in \mathcal{A}^*$. Hence, $\exists r.C(a) \in \mathbb{E}_{\mathcal{A}}$. This makes the Inv-$\mathsf{A}_{\exists}^+$-rule applicable, contrary to the assumption that $\mathbb{E}_{\mathcal{A}}$ is completed.
- If $\mathsf{A}_{\sqsubseteq}$-rule is applicable, then there is an assertion $C(a) \in \mathcal{A}^*\backslash\mathbb{E}_{\mathcal{A}}$ and a GCI $C \sqsubseteq D \in \mathcal{T}^*$ such that $D(a) \notin \mathcal{A}^*\backslash\mathbb{E}_{\mathcal{A}}$. Since $\mathcal{A}^*$ is completed, $D(a) \in \mathcal{A}^*$. Hence, $D(a) \in \mathbb{E}_{\mathcal{A}}$. This makes the Inv-$\mathsf{A}_{\sqsubseteq}$-rule applicable, contrary to the assumption that $\mathbb{E}_{\mathcal{A}}$ is completed.
- If $\mathsf{A}_{\exists H}^+$-rule is applicable, then there is an assertion $\exists r.C(a) \in \mathcal{A}^*\backslash\mathbb{E}_{\mathcal{A}}$, a GCI $C \sqsubseteq D \in \mathcal{T}^*$, a role inclusion $r \sqsubseteq s \in \mathcal{R}^*$ and $\exists s.D \in \mathcal{C}_{\Sigma,\mathbb{S}}$ such that $\exists s.D(a) \notin \mathcal{A}^*\backslash\mathbb{E}_{\mathcal{A}}$. Since $\mathcal{A}^*$ is completed, $\exists s.D(a) \in \mathcal{A}^*$. Hence, $\exists s.D(a) \in \mathbb{E}_{\mathcal{A}}$. This makes the Inv-$\mathsf{A}_{\exists H}^+$-rule applicable, contrary to the assumption that $\mathbb{E}_{\mathcal{A}}$ is completed.
- If $\mathsf{A}_{\exists o}^+$-rule is applicable, then there is an assertion $\exists u.C(a) \in \mathcal{A}^*\backslash\mathbb{E}_{\mathcal{A}}$, GCIs $C \sqsubseteq \exists v.D, D \sqsubseteq E \in \mathcal{T}^*$, role inclusions $u \sqsubseteq r, v \sqsubseteq s, r \circ s \sqsubseteq t \in \mathcal{R}^*$ and $\exists t.E \in \mathcal{C}_{\Sigma,\mathbb{S}}$ such that $\exists t.E(a) \notin \mathcal{A}^*\backslash\mathbb{E}_{\mathcal{A}}$. Since $\mathcal{A}^*$ is completed, $\exists t.E(a) \in \mathcal{A}^*$. Hence, $\exists t.E(a) \in \mathbb{E}_{\mathcal{A}}$. This makes the Inv-$\mathsf{A}_{\exists o}^+$-rule applicable, contrary to the assumption that $\mathbb{E}_{\mathcal{A}}$ is completed.
- If $\mathsf{A}_H$-rule is applicable, then there is an assertion $r(a, b) \in \mathcal{A}^*\backslash\mathbb{E}_{\mathcal{A}}$ and a role inclusion $r \sqsubseteq s \in \mathcal{R}^*$ such that $s(a, b) \notin \mathcal{A}^*\backslash\mathbb{E}_{\mathcal{A}}$. Since $\mathcal{A}^*$ is completed, $s(a, b) \in \mathcal{A}^*$. Hence, $s(a, b) \in \mathbb{E}_{\mathcal{A}}$. This makes the Inv-$\mathsf{A}_H$-rule applicable, contrary to the assumption that $\mathbb{E}_{\mathcal{A}}$ is completed.

– If $A_\circ$-rule is applicable, then there are assertions $r(a,b), s(b,c) \in \mathcal{A}^* \backslash \mathbb{E}_\mathcal{A}$ and a role inclusion $r \circ s \sqsubseteq t \in \mathcal{R}^*$ such that $t(a,c) \notin \mathcal{A}^* \backslash \mathbb{E}_\mathcal{A}$. Since $\mathcal{A}^*$ is completed, $t(a,c) \in \mathcal{A}^*$. Hence, $t(a,c) \in \mathbb{E}_\mathcal{A}$. This makes the Inv-$A_\circ$-rule applicable, contrary to the assumption that $\mathbb{E}_\mathcal{A}$ is completed. $\qquad \square$

The next lemma is an analog of Lemma 9 for $\mathcal{T}^*$. Its proof is omitted.

**Lemma 10.** *Let $\mathcal{T}^*$ be a completed TBox obtained from $\Sigma$ and $\mathcal{C}_{\Sigma,\mathbb{S}}$ by applying the tableau expansion rules in Fig. 1. Also, let $\mathbb{E}_\mathcal{T}$ be a set of GCIs which is completed by using tableau expansion rules in Fig. 4 starting with the secrecy set $\mathbb{S}_\mathcal{T}$. Then, the TBox $\mathcal{T}^* \backslash \mathbb{E}_\mathcal{T}$ is completed.*

We now show that the completed sets $\mathbb{E}_\mathcal{A}$ and $\mathbb{E}_\mathcal{T}$ are in fact envelopes.

**Theorem 3.** *$\mathbb{E}_\mathcal{A}$ and $\mathbb{E}_\mathcal{T}$ are envelopes for $\mathbb{S}_\mathcal{A}$ and $\mathbb{S}_\mathcal{T}$ respectively.*

*Proof.* We must show that the sets $\mathbb{E}_\mathcal{A}$ and $\mathbb{E}_\mathcal{T}$ satisfy the properties of Definition 1. Properties 1 and 2 are obvious.

To prove property 3, let us suppose $\mathcal{A}^* \backslash \mathbb{E}_\mathcal{A} \models \alpha$, for some $\alpha \in \mathbb{E}_\mathcal{A}$. Since $\mathcal{A}^* \backslash \mathbb{E}_\mathcal{A}$ is completed, by Theorem 2, we have $\alpha \in (\mathcal{A}^* \backslash \mathbb{E}_\mathcal{A})^*$ and by Lemma 9, $\alpha \in (\mathcal{A}^* \backslash \mathbb{E}_\mathcal{A})^* \Rightarrow \alpha \in \mathcal{A}^* \backslash \mathbb{E}_\mathcal{A}$. This is a contradiction.

Now we prove property 4. Let us suppose $\mathcal{T}^* \backslash \mathbb{E}_\mathcal{T} \models \alpha$, for some $\alpha \in \mathbb{E}_\mathcal{T}$. Since $\mathcal{T}^* \backslash \mathbb{E}_\mathcal{T}$ is completed, by Theorem 1, we have $\alpha \in (\mathcal{T}^* \backslash \mathbb{E}_\mathcal{T})^*$ and by Lemma 10, $\alpha \in (\mathcal{T}^* \backslash \mathbb{E}_\mathcal{T})^* \Rightarrow \alpha \in \mathcal{T}^* \backslash \mathbb{E}_\mathcal{T}$. This is a contradiction. $\qquad \square$

## 5   Query Answering

In Sect. 4, we have described briefly how the reasoner $\mathfrak{R}$ responds to queries. In this section we provide a few more details. At this point we assume that $\mathcal{A}^*$, $\mathbb{E}_\mathcal{A}$, $\mathcal{T}^*$, $\mathbb{E}_\mathcal{T}$ and $\mathcal{R}^*$ have all been precomputed and are considered as global parameters. Define the set $R_\mathcal{R} = \{r \mid r$ is a role name that occurs in $\mathcal{R}\}$. The recursive procedures for answering the assertional queries and the GCI queries are given in Figs. 5 and 6 respectively. These procedures primarily based on case arguments. In line 2 of Fig. 5, we consider the case where we check the membership of $q$ in $\mathcal{A}^* \backslash \mathbb{E}_\mathcal{A}$ and answer "Yes" if $q \in \mathcal{A}^* \backslash \mathbb{E}_\mathcal{A}$. From line 5 onwards we discuss several cases in which we break the query $q$ into subqueries based on the constructors defined in the language $\mathcal{EL}^+$ and apply the procedure recursively.

The following theorem proves the correctness claim of the algorithm given in Fig. 5.

**Theorem 4.** *Let $\Sigma = \langle \mathcal{A}, \mathcal{T}, \mathcal{R} \rangle$ be a given KB and $q$ an assertional query. Assume that the sets $\mathcal{A}^*$, $\mathcal{T}^*$, $\mathcal{R}^*$ and $\mathbb{E}_\mathcal{A}$ are precomputed and are global parameters for the recursive procedure EvalA(q). Then,*

– *Soundness: EvalA(q) outputs "Yes" $\Rightarrow \langle \mathcal{A}^* \backslash \mathbb{E}_\mathcal{A}, \mathcal{T}^*, \mathcal{R}^* \rangle \models q$*
– *Completeness: EvalA(q) outputs "Unknown" $\Rightarrow \langle \mathcal{A}^* \backslash \mathbb{E}_\mathcal{A}, \mathcal{T}^*, \mathcal{R}^* \rangle \not\models q$.*

EvalA($q$)

> 1: **case** $q \in \mathcal{A}^* \setminus \mathbb{E}_\mathcal{A}$
> 2:     **return** "Yes"
> 3: **case** $q = C \sqcap D(a)$
> 4:     **if** EvalA($C(a)$) = "Yes"  and  EvalA($D(a)$) = "Yes" **then**
> 5:         **return** "Yes"
> 6:     **else**
> 7:         **return** "Unknown"
> 8: **case** $q = \exists r.C(a)$
> 9:     **if** for some $d \in \mathcal{O}_\Sigma$ [ $r(a,d) \in \mathcal{A}^* \setminus \mathbb{E}_\mathcal{A}$  and
>             EvalA($C(d)$) = "Yes"]  **then**
> 10:         **return** "Yes"
> 11:     **else**
> 12:         **if** for some $E \in \mathcal{C}_{\Sigma,\mathbb{S}}$ [$E \sqsubseteq C \in \mathcal{T}^*$ and
>                 EvalA($\exists r.E(a)$) = "Yes" ] **then**
> 13:             **return** "Yes"
> 14:         **else**
> 15:             **if**  for some $s \in R_\mathcal{R}$ [$s \sqsubseteq r \in \mathcal{R}^*$ and
>                     EvalA($\exists s.C(a)$) = "Yes" ] **then**
> 16:                 **return** "Yes"
> 17:             **else**
> 18:                 **if** for some $u, v \in R_\mathcal{R}$, for some
>                         $D \in \mathcal{C}_{\Sigma,\mathbb{S}}$ [$D \sqsubseteq \exists v.C \in \mathcal{T}^*, u \circ v \sqsubseteq r \in \mathcal{R}^*$ and
>                         EvalA($\exists u.D(a)$) = "Yes" ] **then**
> 19:                     **return** "Yes"
> 20:                 **else**
> 21:                     **return** "Unknown"

**Fig. 5.** Query answering algorithm for assertional queries.

*Proof.* First let us prove the soundness part. Assume the hypothesis. Let $\mathcal{I}$ be an arbitrary model of $\langle \mathcal{A}^* \setminus \mathbb{E}_\mathcal{A}, \mathcal{T}^*, \mathcal{R}^* \rangle$ and $q$ be a query. Now, we prove the claim by induction on the structure of $q$. The base case: Let $q \in \mathcal{A}^* \setminus \mathbb{E}_\mathcal{A}$. Then, $\mathcal{I} \models q$ because $\Lambda_\mathcal{A}$ is sound. The inductive hypothesis is, for each assertion $\alpha$, if EvalA($\alpha$) = "Yes", then $\mathcal{I} \models \alpha$. Let $q \notin \mathcal{A}^* \setminus \mathbb{E}_\mathcal{A}$.

- $q = C \sqcap D(a)$. Then, EvalA($C(a)$) = EvalA($D(a)$) = "Yes" and by inductive hypothesis, $\mathcal{I} \models C(a)$ and $\mathcal{I} \models D(a)$. Hence, $a \in C^\mathcal{I} \cap D^\mathcal{I} = (C \sqcap D)^\mathcal{I}$, i.e., $\mathcal{I} \models C \sqcap D(a)$.
- $q = \exists r.C(a)$. There are several subcases:
  - for some $d \in \mathcal{O}_\Sigma$ [ $r(a,d) \in \mathcal{A}^* \setminus \mathbb{E}_\mathcal{A}$ and EvalA($C(d)$) = "Yes"]. By the base case $\mathcal{I} \models r(a,d)$ and by inductive hypothesis $\mathcal{I} \models C(d)$. This immediately proves $\mathcal{I} \models \exists r.C(a)$.

- for some $E \in \mathcal{C}_{\Sigma,\mathbb{S}}$ $[E \sqsubseteq C \in \mathcal{T}^*$ and $\mathrm{EvalA}(\exists r.E(a)) = $ "Yes"]. Since $\mathcal{I} \models \mathcal{T}^*$, we have $\mathcal{I} \models E \sqsubseteq C$. By inductive hypothesis, $\mathcal{I} \models \exists r.E(a)$, whence $\mathcal{I} \models \exists r.C(a)$.
- Let for some $s \in R_{\mathcal{R}}$ $[s \sqsubseteq r \in \mathcal{R}^*$ and $\mathrm{EvalA}(\exists s.C(a)) = $ "Yes"]. Then, $\mathcal{I} \models s \sqsubseteq r$, and by inductive hypothesis, $\mathcal{I} \models \exists s.C(a)$ implying $\mathcal{I} \models \exists r.C(a)$.
- Let for some $u, v \in R_{\mathcal{R}}$, for some $D \in \mathcal{C}_{\Sigma,\mathbb{S}}$ $[D \sqsubseteq \exists v.C \in \mathcal{T}^*, u \circ v \sqsubseteq r \in \mathcal{R}^*$ and $\mathrm{EvalA}(\exists u.D(a)) = $ "Yes"]. Then, $\mathcal{I} \models D \sqsubseteq \exists v.C$, $\mathcal{I} \models u \circ v \sqsubseteq r$, and by inductive hypothesis, $\mathcal{I} \models \exists u.D(a)$ implying $\mathcal{I} \models \exists r.C(a)$.

We prove the completeness part using a contrapositive argument. Assume that $\langle \mathcal{A}^* \backslash \mathbb{E}_{\mathcal{A}}, \mathcal{T}^*, \mathcal{R}^* \rangle \models q$. We have to show that $\mathrm{EvalA}(q) = $ "Yes". Let $\mathcal{K}$ be the canonical interpretation restricted to $\mathcal{A}^* \backslash \mathbb{E}_{\mathcal{A}}$ as defined in Sect. 3.2. By Lemma 8, $\mathcal{K}$ satisfies $\mathcal{A}^* \backslash \mathbb{E}_{\mathcal{A}}$, $\mathcal{T}^*$ and $\mathcal{R}^*$ and hence $\mathcal{K}$ satisfies $q$. We argue that: if $\mathcal{K} \models q$ then $\mathrm{EvalA}(q) = $ "Yes", by induction on the structure of $q$. The base case: If $q \in \mathcal{A}^* \backslash \mathbb{E}_{\mathcal{A}}$, then by Line 1 in Fig. 5, the claim follows immediately. Next, consider the case $q \notin \mathcal{A}^* \backslash \mathbb{E}_{\mathcal{A}}$. There are several cases:

- $q = C \sqcap D(a)$. To answer this query the algorithm computes $\mathrm{EvalA}(C(a))$ and $\mathrm{EvalA}(D(a))$. Now, the assumption $\mathcal{K} \models C \sqcap D(a)$ implies $\mathcal{K} \models C(a)$ and $\mathcal{K} \models D(a)$ which, by inductive hypothesis, implies that $\mathrm{EvalA}(C(a)) = \mathrm{EvalA}(D(a)) = $ "Yes". Hence, by Lines 4 and 5 in Fig. 5, $\mathrm{EvalA}(C \sqcap D(a)) = $ "Yes".
- $q = \exists r.C(a)$. By the assumption, $\mathcal{K} \models \exists r.C(a)$. This implies, for some $b \in \Delta$ $[(a,b) \in r^{\mathcal{K}}$ and $b \in C^{\mathcal{K}}]$. There are two subcases:
  - $b \in \mathcal{O}_\Sigma$. Again, there are two cases:
    - $s(a,b) \in \mathcal{A}^* \backslash \mathbb{E}_{\mathcal{A}}$ and $s \sqsubseteq r \in \mathcal{R}^*$. Then, $A_H$-rule is applicable. Since, by Lemma 9 $\mathcal{A}^* \backslash \mathbb{E}_{\mathcal{A}}$ is completed, $r(a,b) \in \mathcal{A}^* \backslash \mathbb{E}_{\mathcal{A}}$. By inductive hypothesis $\mathrm{EvalA}(C(b)) = $ "Yes". Hence, by Lines 9 and 10 in Fig. 5, $\mathrm{EvalA}(\exists r.C(a)) = $ "Yes".
    - $u(a,c), v(c,b) \in \mathcal{A}^* \backslash \mathbb{E}_{\mathcal{A}}$ and $u \circ v \sqsubseteq r \in \mathcal{R}^*$. Then, $A_\circ$-rule is applicable. Since, by Lemma 9, $\mathcal{A}^* \backslash \mathbb{E}_{\mathcal{A}}$ is completed, $r(a,b) \in \mathcal{A}^* \backslash \mathbb{E}_{\mathcal{A}}$. By inductive hypothesis $\mathrm{EvalA}(C(b)) = $ "Yes". Hence, by Lines 9 and 10 in Fig. 5, $\mathrm{EvalA}(\exists r.C(a)) = $ "Yes".
  - $b = w_D \in \mathcal{W}$ for some $D \in \mathcal{C}_{\Sigma,\mathbb{S}}$. By Lemma 5, $D \sqsubseteq C \in \mathcal{T}^*$. Now we have three cases:
    - $\exists r.D(a) \in \mathcal{A}^* \backslash \mathbb{E}_{\mathcal{A}}$ and $r \sqsubseteq r \in \mathcal{R}^*$. By the inductive hypothesis $\mathrm{EvalA}(\exists r.D(a)) = $ "Yes". Hence, by Lines 12 and 13 in Fig. 5, $\mathrm{EvalA}(\exists r.C(a)) = $ "Yes".
    - $\exists s.D(a) \in \mathcal{A}^* \backslash \mathbb{E}_{\mathcal{A}}$ and $s \sqsubseteq r \in \mathcal{R}^*$. By the inductive hypothesis $\mathrm{EvalA}(\exists s.D(a)) = $ "Yes". Hence, by Lines 15 and 16 in Fig. 5, $\mathrm{EvalA}(\exists r.C(a)) = $ "Yes".
    - $\exists u.D(a) \in \mathcal{A}^* \backslash \mathbb{E}_{\mathcal{A}}$, $D \sqsubseteq \exists v.C \in \mathcal{T}^*$ and $u \circ v \sqsubseteq r \in \mathcal{R}^*$. By the inductive hypothesis $\mathrm{EvalA}(\exists u.D(a)) = $ "Yes". Hence, by Lines 18 and 19 in Fig. 5, $\mathrm{EvalA}(\exists r.C(a)) = $ "Yes". $\qquad \square$

---

EvalT($q$)

  1: **case** $q \in \mathcal{T}^* \setminus \mathbb{E}_{\mathcal{T}}$
  2:     **return** "Yes"
  3: **case** $q = C \sqsubseteq D \sqcap E$
  4:     **if** EvalT($C \sqsubseteq D$) ="Yes" and EvalT($C \sqsubseteq E$) ="Yes" **then**
  5:         **return** "Yes"
  6:     **else**
  7:         **return** "Unknown"
  8: **case** $q = C \sqsubseteq \exists r.D$
  9:     **if** for some $E \in \mathcal{C}_{\Sigma,\mathbb{S}}$ $[E \sqsubseteq D \in \mathcal{T}^* \setminus \mathbb{E}_{\mathcal{T}}$ and
              EvalT($C \sqsubseteq \exists r.E$) ="Yes"] **then**
10:         **return** "Yes"
11:     **else**
12:         **if** for some $s \in R_{\mathcal{R}}$ $[s \sqsubseteq r \in \mathcal{R}^*$ and
              EvalT($C \sqsubseteq \exists s.D$) ="Yes"] **then**
13:             **return** "Yes"
14:         **else**
15:             **if** for some $u, v \in R_{\mathcal{R}}$, for some
              $E \in \mathcal{C}_{\Sigma,\mathbb{S}}$ $[E \sqsubseteq \exists v.D \in \mathcal{T}^* \setminus \mathbb{E}_{\mathcal{T}}, u \circ v \sqsubseteq r \in \mathcal{R}^*$
              and EvalT($C \sqsubseteq \exists u.E$) ="Yes"] **then**
16:             **return** "Yes"
17:             **else**
18:                 **return** "Unknown"

---

**Fig. 6.** Query answering algorithm for GCI queries.

Since the algorithm given in Fig. 5 runs in polynomial time in the size of $\mathcal{A}^* \setminus \mathbb{E}_{\mathcal{A}}$, the assertional query answering can be done in polynomial time as a function of the size of $\mathcal{A}^*$.

Next, suppose that the querying agent poses a GCI query $q$. In response, the reasoner $\mathfrak{R}$ invokes the query answering algorithm EvalT($q$) given in Fig. 6 and returns the answer as output of the EvalT($q$). Now we prove the correctness of the recursive algorithm given in Fig. 6.

**Theorem 5.** *Let $\Sigma = \langle \mathcal{A}, \mathcal{T}, \mathcal{R} \rangle$ be a given KB and $q$ a GCI query. Assume that the sets $\mathcal{T}^*$, $\mathcal{R}^*$ and $\mathbb{E}_{\mathcal{T}}$ are precomputed and are global parameters for the recursive procedure EvalT($q$). Then,*

- *Soundness: EvalT($q$) outputs "Yes"* $\Rightarrow \langle \mathcal{T}^* \setminus \mathbb{E}_{\mathcal{T}}, \mathcal{R}^* \rangle \models q$
- *Completeness: EvalT($q$) outputs "Unknown"* $\Rightarrow \langle \mathcal{T}^* \setminus \mathbb{E}_{\mathcal{T}}, \mathcal{R}^* \rangle \not\models q.$

*Proof.* We omit the proof of soundness.

We prove the completeness part using a contrapositive argument. Assume that $\langle \mathcal{T}^* \setminus \mathbb{E}_{\mathcal{T}}, \mathcal{R}^* \rangle \models q$. We have to show that EvalT($q$) ="Yes". Let $\mathcal{J}$ be the canonical interpretation restricted to $\mathcal{T}^* \setminus \mathbb{E}_{\mathcal{T}}$ as defined in Sect. 3.1. By Lemma 2, $\mathcal{J}$ satisfies $\mathcal{T}^* \setminus \mathbb{E}_{\mathcal{T}}$ and $\mathcal{R}^*$ and $q$. We argue by induction on the structure of $q$.

The inductive hypothesis is, if $\mathcal{J} \models q$ then EvalT($q$) = "Yes". The base case: Let $q \in \mathcal{T}^* \backslash \mathbb{E}_\mathcal{T}$. Then, by Lines 1 and 2 in Fig. 6, the claim is obvious. Next, consider the case $q \notin \mathcal{T}^* \backslash \mathbb{E}_\mathcal{T}$. There are several cases:

- $q = C \sqsubseteq D \sqcap E$. The algorithm in Fig. 6 computes EvalT($C \sqsubseteq D$) and EvalT($C \sqsubseteq E$). Now, the assumption $\mathcal{J} \models C \sqsubseteq D \sqcap E$ implies $\mathcal{J} \models C \sqsubseteq D$ and $\mathcal{J} \models C \sqsubseteq E$ which, by inductive hypothesis, implies that EvalT($C \sqsubseteq D$) = EvalT($C \sqsubseteq E$) = "Yes". Hence, by Lines 4 and 5 in Fig. 6, EvalT($C \sqsubseteq D \sqcap E$)="Yes".
- $q = C \sqsubseteq \exists r.D$. By the assumption, $\mathcal{J} \models C \sqsubseteq \exists r.D$. This implies, $C, D \in \mathcal{C}_{\Sigma,\mathbb{S}}$. By Lemma 1, $a_C \in C^\mathcal{J}$ and hence $a_c \in (\exists r.D)^\mathcal{J}$. By the semantics of $\exists$, for some $a_E \in \Delta$, $(a_C, a_E) \in r^\mathcal{J}$ and $a_E \in D^\mathcal{J}$. By part (b) of Lemma 1, $E \sqsubseteq D \in \mathcal{T}^* \backslash \mathbb{E}_\mathcal{T}$. There are three cases:
    - $C \sqsubseteq \exists r.E \in \mathcal{T}^* \backslash \mathbb{E}_\mathcal{T}$ and $r \sqsubseteq r \in \mathcal{R}^*$. By induction hypothesis EvalT($C \sqsubseteq \exists r.E$) = "Yes". Since $E \sqsubseteq D \in \mathcal{T}^* \backslash \mathbb{E}_\mathcal{T}$, by Lines 9 and 10, EvalT($C \sqsubseteq \exists r.D$) = "Yes".
    - $C \sqsubseteq \exists s.E \in \mathcal{T}^* \backslash \mathbb{E}_\mathcal{T}$ and $s \sqsubseteq r \in \mathcal{R}^*$. By induction hypothesis EvalT($C \sqsubseteq \exists s.E$) = "Yes". Since $E \sqsubseteq D \in \mathcal{T}^* \backslash \mathbb{E}_\mathcal{T}$, by Lines 12 and 13, EvalT($C \sqsubseteq \exists r.D$) = "Yes".
    - $C \sqsubseteq \exists u.E, E \sqsubseteq \exists v.D \in \mathcal{T}^* \backslash \mathbb{E}_\mathcal{T}$ and $u \circ v \sqsubseteq r \in \mathcal{R}^*$. By induction hypothesis EvalT($C \sqsubseteq \exists u.E$) = "Yes". Hence, by Lines 15 and 16, EvalT($C \sqsubseteq \exists r.D$) = "Yes". $\qquad\square$

Since the algorithm runs in polynomial time in the size of $\mathcal{T}^* \backslash \mathbb{E}_\mathcal{T}$, the GCI query answering can be done in polynomial time as a function of the size of $\mathcal{T}^*$.

## 5.1   Conclusions

In this paper we have studied the problem of secrecy-preserving query answering in $\mathcal{EL}^+$ KBs. $\mathcal{EL}^+$ language allows composition constructor on the role names in such way that reasoning tasks can be done efficiently. We take advantage of this fact and we extend our previous work [14] in which we considered both assertions and GCIs in the secrecy set to $\mathcal{EL}^+$ language. The main contribution in this work is in the way that we compute the consequences and preserve secrecy while answering queries. We break the process into two parts, first one precomputes all the consequences for concepts and individuals that occur in the given KB. For this we use four separate (but related) tableau procedures. As for the actual query answering, we parse the query all the way to constituents that occur in the previously precomputed set of consequences. Then, the queries are answered based on the membership of the constituents of the query in $\mathcal{A}^* \backslash \mathbb{E}_\mathcal{A}$ and $\mathcal{T}^* \backslash \mathbb{E}_\mathcal{T}$. All the algorithms are efficient and can be implemented in polynomial time.

# References

1. Baader, F., Lutz, C., Suntisrivaraporn, B.: Efficient reasoning in EL. In: 2006 International Workshop on Description Logics DL 2006, pp. 15–26 (2006)
2. Baader, F., Brandt, S., Lutz, C.: Pushing the EL envelope. In: IJCAI, vol. 5, pp. 364–369

3. Baader, F.: Terminological cycles in a description logic with existential restrictions. In: IJCAI, vol. 3, pp. 325–330 (2003)
4. Bao, J., Slutzki, G., Honavar, V.: Privacy-preserving reasoning on the semantic web. In: Web Intelligence, pp. 791–797. IEEE Computer Society (2007)
5. Biskup, J., Weibert, T.: Keeping secrets in incomplete databases. Int. J. Inf. Secur. **7**(3), 199–217 (2008)
6. Biskup, J., Tadros, C.: Revising belief without revealing secrets. In: Lukasiewicz, T., Sali, A. (eds.) FoIKS 2012. LNCS, vol. 7153, pp. 51–70. Springer, Heidelberg (2012). doi:10.1007/978-3-642-28472-4_4
7. Delaitre, V., Kazakov, Y.: Classifying ELH ontologies in SQL databases. In: OWLED (2009)
8. Lutz, C., Toman, D., Wolter, F.: Conjunctive query answering in $\mathcal{EL}$ using a database system. In: OWLED (2008)
9. Lutz, C., Toman, D., Wolter, F.: Conjunctive query answering in the description logic EL using a relational database system. In: IJCAI, vol. 9, pp. 2070–2075 (2009)
10. Cuenca Grau, B., Kharlamov, E., Kostylev, E.V., Zheleznyakov, D.: Controlled query evaluation over OWL 2 RL ontologies. In: Alani, H., et al. (eds.) ISWC 2013. LNCS, vol. 8218, pp. 49–65. Springer, Heidelberg (2013). doi:10.1007/978-3-642-41335-3_4
11. Kagal, L., Finin, T., Joshi, A.: A policy based approach to security for the semantic web. In: Fensel, D., Sycara, K., Mylopoulos, J. (eds.) ISWC 2003. LNCS, vol. 2870, pp. 402–418. Springer, Heidelberg (2003). doi:10.1007/978-3-540-39718-2_26
12. Kazakov, Y., Krotzsch, M., Simancik, F.: The incredible ELK. J. Autom. Reason. **53**(1), 1–61 (2014)
13. Knechtel, M., Hladik, J., Dau, F.: Using OWL DL reasoning to decide about authorization in RBAC. In: OWLED (2008)
14. Krishnasamy Sivaprakasam, G., Slutzki, G.: Secrecy-preserving query answering in ELH knowledge bases. In: Proceedings of 8th International Conference on Agents and Artificial Intelligence (2016)
15. Tao, J., Slutzki, G., Honavar, V.: Secrecy-preserving query answering for instance checking in $\mathcal{EL}$. In: Proceedings of 4th International Conference on Web Reasoning and Rule Systems, pp. 195–203 (2010)
16. Tao, J., Slutzki, G., Honavar, V.: A conceptual framework for secrecy-preserving reasoning in knowledge bases. TOCL **16**(1), 3:1–3:32 (2014)

# An Automatic Approach for Generation of Fuzzy Membership Functions

Hossein Pazhoumand-Dar, Chiou Peng Lam$^{(\boxtimes)}$, and Martin Masek

School of Science, Edith Cowan University, Perth, Australia
{h.pazhoumanddar, c.lam, m.masek}@ecu.edu.au

**Abstract.** Eliciting representative membership functions is one of the fundamental steps in applications of fuzzy theory. This paper investigates an unsupervised approach that incorporates variable bandwidth mean-shift and robust statistics for generating fuzzy membership functions. The approach automatically learns the number of representative functions from the underlying data distribution. Given a specific membership function, the approach then works out the associated parameters of the specific membership function. Our evaluation of the proposed approach consists of comparisons with two other techniques in terms of (i) parameterising MFs for attributes with different distributions, and (ii) classification performance of a fuzzy rule set that was developed using the parameterised output of these techniques. This evaluation involved its application using the trapezoidal and the triangular membership functions. Results demonstrate that the generated membership functions can better separate the underlying distributions and classifiers constructed using the proposed method of generating membership function outperformed three other classifiers that used different approaches for parameterisation of the attributes.

**Keywords:** Fuzzy membership functions · Variable bandwidth mean-shift · Fuzzy logic · Activities of daily living · Abnormality detection · Robust statistics

## 1 Introduction

Eliciting representative membership functions (MFs) for data is one of the fundamental steps in applications of fuzzy theory as the success of many fuzzy approaches depends on the membership functions used. However, there are no simple rules, guidelines, or even consensus among the community on how to choose the number, type, and parameters of membership functions for any application or domain [1]. Several methods for the automatic generation of MFs have been proposed in the literature and the choice of function has been linked to the problem and the type of data available. However, in most of these techniques, the number of fuzzy sets has to be provided empirically. Furthermore, the range for membership functions generated by many existing techniques does not address the impact of outliers and noisy measurements in data.

In this paper, we propose a hybrid approach that incorporates variable bandwidth mean-shift (VBMS) and robust statistics for automatic generation of representative

© Springer International Publishing AG 2017
J. van den Herik and J. Filipe (Eds.): ICAART 2016, LNAI 10162, pp. 247–264, 2017.
DOI: 10.1007/978-3-319-53354-4_14

MF(s) for an attribute. The analysis of the underlying data distribution is unsupervised as the proposed approach first determines the number of modes from the probability density function (PDF) and then uses this value as the number of clusters for a multimodal data distribution. The approach overcomes the problems associated with some of the existing approaches by

- determining the number of representative MFs for the attribute from the underlying data distribution automatically
- automatically handling noise and outliers in the attribute feature space.

The rest of this paper is organised as follow: Sect. 2 briefly reviews relevant literature on MF generation techniques. Section 3 describes the proposed approach. The experimental evaluation of our technique is presented in Sect. 4 followed by conclusions in Section 5.

## 2 Background

Many techniques have been proposed to generate fuzzy membership functions from an attribute. Three questions that have to be addressed are: (1) how many fuzzy sets should be defined to represent the attribute, (2) what type of membership function can represent the attribute better, and (3) how to determine the parameters associated with the adopted membership functions.

Typically, techniques have used manual partitioning of attributes, mostly based on expert knowledge, and adopted a pre-determined number of membership functions [2] to partition the data space for the attribute by (usually evenly-spaced) MFs. However, manual approaches suffer from the deficiency that they rely on subjective interpretations from human experts.

Given a labelled dataset, evolutionary methods can also be utilized to generate MFs. Moeinzadeh et al. [3] applied genetic algorithm (GA) and particle swarm optimization for the adjustment of MF parameters to increase degree of membership of data to their classes for classification problems. Authors in [4] applied GA for evolving parameters associated with MFs in a fuzzy logic controller for a helicopter. Initial guesses for the MFs are made by the expert and the GA adjusts the MF parameters to minimise the movement of a hovering helicopter. In the classification method proposed by Tang et al. [5], a fitness function quantifies how well the crisp values of attributes are classified into MFs and the GA process evolves over time by searching the best set of MF parameters which optimises result of the fitness function.

Takagi and Hayashi [6] also proposed the use of artificial neural networks (ANN) for the construction of membership functions. Once raw data are clustered into a specific number of groups, ANN is applied to the clustered data to determine the parameters associated with membership functions.

However, for situations where the training data is not labelled, MF generation techniques generally involve unsupervised clustering of data using a specific distance measure and then the parameters of detected clusters (mean, variance, etc.) are used to generate MFs. For example, techniques [7] have used the Fuzzy C-Means (FCM) clustering algorithm [8] to cluster a particular attribute into specific number of clusters. Cluster boundaries and the location of the centre were then used to determine the cluster membership function parameters. Doctor et al. [9] presented a fuzzy approach to model an occupant behaviour in a residential environment. They used a double clustering technique [10] combining FCM and agglomerative hierarchical clustering for extracting a predefined number of MFs from the user's recorded input/output data.

The disadvantage associated with most of these methods is that the number of fuzzy sets must be predefined. However, we usually do not know an optimal number of representative MFs for a particular attribute. In addition, outliers in data are included in range of MFs generated by many of these techniques. New robust techniques that can determine number of representative MFs automatically would address some of these limitations.

## 3 The Proposed Approach

For each attribute the approach automatically defines a number of associated MFs as linguistic variables. Let an attribute take a series of crisp numerical values $x_n$ $(n = 1, \ldots, N)$ and these data points belong to an unknown probability density function (PDF) f. The two-step procedure of the proposed approach for generating MFs for the attribute is as follows

Step 1.    use VBMS to find modes (local maxima) of f representing the attribute and cluster of data points associated with each mode

Step 2.    use skewness adjusted boxplot (SAB) technique [11] to obtain the normal range of data for each cluster (where there are no outliers), and subsequently determine the parameters associated with a specific MF for the cluster.

VBMS proposed by Comaniciu et al. [12] is a nonparametric clustering technique which does not require the number of clusters to be defined. It takes multidimensional data with an unknown density f and estimates the density at each point by taking the average of locally-scaled kernels centered at each of the data points, and tries to map each data point to its corresponding mode. The output of this technique is locations of modes detected in f and the cluster of data associated with each mode. Usually the kernel $K$ is taken to be a radially symmetric, nonnegative function centered at zero such that $K(x) = k(\|x^2\|)$. Details associated with this technique can be found in [13].

The SAB technique is a graphical tool (with a robust measure of skewness) used in robust statistics (RS) for the purpose of outlier detection [14]. Given a continuous unimodal data, SAB first calculates a robust measure of skewness (i.e., medcouple (MC) [15]) of the underlying data distribution. Then it outputs a normal range for the data which excludes possible outliers from the normal data. Details associated with its use in this approach can be found in [13].

When an attribute has a multimodal PDF and each mode may be associated with a different density distribution, one fixed global bandwidth is not optimal for estimating the location of modes in PDF, and thus local bandwidths should be computed [12]. Using VBMS, we determine a local bandwidth for each data point in a way that points corresponding to tails of the data distributions receive a bigger bandwidth than data points lying in large density region of distributions and hence the estimated density function for tails of the distributions is smoothed more. The output of Step 1 is the location of modes of $f$ denoted as $m_{i(1 \leq i \leq N)}$ and the cluster of data associated with each mode.

In Step 2, we use the output from Step 1, the number of modes as the number of required MFs representing the attribute and for each cluster of data associated with a mode, we define a MF. We first use the SAB technique to determine the normal range (NR) for the cluster and we denoted this as $[l, h]$. The output of Step 2 for each attribute is a tuple $(X, m_1, m_2, \ldots, m_{nc})$ as linguistic variables, where X stands for the attribute name and $m_i$ stands for an MF defined over the universe of discourse for the attribute and $nc$ stands for the number of modes identified in Step 1.

The proposed approach can be employed to determine the parameters associated with different forms of MFs to characterise the identified clusters. In this paper we demonstrate how the approach can be applied on two different types of MF, namely the triangular and trapezoidal membership functions. These two MFs are selected because of their simplicity of calculation and ability to represent skewed distributions.

## 3.1   Generating Triangular Membership Functions

As shown in Fig. 1, parameters of triangular MFs are defined by a triad $(A, B, C)$, with point A representing the left foot of triangular MF, B is the location of the center, and C is the location of the right foot.

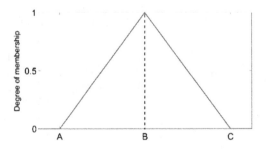

**Fig. 1.**   An example of a triangular membership function defined by a triad $(A, B, C)$.

To define a triangular MF for a detected cluster we use NR $[l, h]$ ($l$ is the lower and $h$ is the higher limit for the normal range, respectively) associated with the cluster, and the cluster mode, $m$, to determine its parameters $(A, B, C)$.

This is illustrated using an example shown in Fig. 2. Figure 2(a) showed the histogram associated with the cluster, with the detected mode $m$ and normal range $[l, h]$. A probability density distribution (PDF) is first obtained from this histogram. Please note that histograms in this paper are obtained using the plug-in rule technique with the bin size of the histogram equal to the bandwidth calculated from the plug-in rule [16].

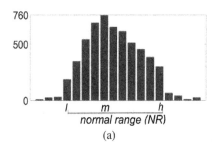 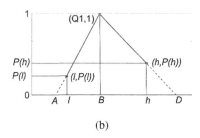

(a)  (b)

**Fig. 2.** (a) The histogram of a detected data cluster from Step 1. The vertical axis shows the number of observations. (b) The corresponding MF defined for the cluster.

Figure 2(b) shows the corresponding triangular MF defined for the cluster with $m$ as the center point $B$ for the triangular MF.

Next, using the generated PDF, we calculate the probability density of lower bound ($l$) and higher bound ($h$) of the cluster, denoted by $P(l)$ and $P(h)$ in Fig. 2(b), respectively. Then, we find the parameter $A$ for the triangular MF by extrapolating the two points $(m, 1)$ and $(l, P(l))$. In the same manner, we find the parameter $C$ by extrapolating the two points $(h, P(h))$ and $(m, 1)$. Now, triangular MF is defined using Eq. (1).

$$\mu^i(x) = \begin{cases} 0 & if\ x \leq A_i \\ \frac{x-A_i}{B_i-C_i} & if\ A_i < x \leq B_i \\ \frac{C_i-x}{C_i-B_i} & if\ B_i < x \leq C_i \\ 0 & if\ C_i \leq x \end{cases} \qquad (1)$$

More details associated with employing the approach for generating triangular MFs can be found in [13].

## 3.2 Generating Trapezoidal Membership Functions

A trapezoidal MF is characterized by four parameters $A, B, C, D$ (with $A < B \leq C < D$) as shown in Fig. 3. These determine the x coordinates of the four corners of the

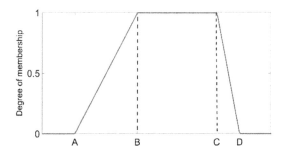

**Fig. 3.** An example of a trapezoidal membership function defined by a quad $(A, B, C, D)$.

underlying trapezoidal defined over the attribute space. Specifically, points A and D specify the left and right feet. Parameters $B$ and $C$ specify the shoulders for the trapezoidal.

To obtain the parameters $(A, B, C, D)$ associated with the trapezoidal MF for a cluster, $NR\ [l, h]$ associated with the cluster, and the first and third quartiles for the cluster are used. Figure 4(a) shows the histogram for an example cluster obtained from Step 1. In this example Q1 and Q3 denote the location of the first and third quartiles, respectively, and the normal range for the cluster is shown as $[l, h]$. The following operations are performed to define the respective trapezoidal MF, shown in Fig. 4(b), to represent the cluster.

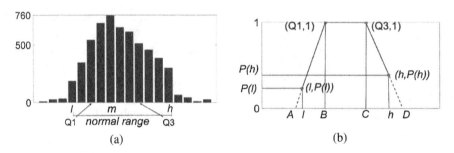

(a)                                                (b)

**Fig. 4.** (a) An example of a histogram of a data cluster obtained from Step 1. The vertical axis shows the number of data points in each bin. (b) The corresponding trapezoidal MF defined for the cluster.

1. Calculate the probability density of lower bound ($l$) and higher bound ($h$) of the cluster, denoted by $P(l)$ and $P(h)$, respectively (see Fig. 4(b)).
2. Find the parameter $A$ for the trapezoidal MF by extrapolating the two points $(Q1, 1)$ and $(l, P(l))$.
3. Set $B$ and $C$ as the location of Q1 and Q3, respectively.
4. Find the parameter $D$ by extrapolating the two points $(h, P(h))$ and $(Q3, 1)$.

Define the trapezoidal MF using Eq. (2).

$$
\mu^i(x) = \begin{cases}
0 & if\ x \leq A \\
\frac{x-A}{B-C} & if\ A < x < B \\
1 & if\ B \leq x \leq C \\
\frac{C-x}{C-B} & if\ C < x \leq D \\
0 & if\ C \leq x
\end{cases}
\tag{2}
$$

Here, data between Q1 and Q3 are assigned with full membership as they represent the middle 50% of cluster values. Accordingly, in the extrapolating performed in operations 2 and 4, $(Q1, 1)$, and $(Q3, 1)$ represent the coordinates for the location of shoulders.

### 3.3   Impact of the Shape of Cluster on Support of MFs

Depending on the shape of data distribution for a cluster obtained from Step 1, the support for the generated triangular MF can be greater than the support for the trapezoidal MFs. Figure 5(a) shows an example data distribution with different colours indicating the range for clusters obtained from Step 1 of the proposed approach. Figure 5(b) shows the characteristics of the triangular and trapezoidal MFs generated for the cluster shown in red color. As can be observed, since this cluster is located in the middle of the data distribution, the tail end of this cluster has been truncated. When the extrapolations are performed to obtain parameters of the triangular and trapezoidal MFs, it is clearly evident that the range for the triangular MF is greater than that for the trapezoidal MF. This means that generated triangular MFs generally offer more perturbation of normal data without labelling them as abnormal.

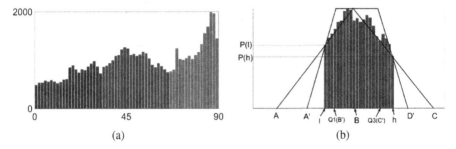

**Fig. 5.** An example data distribution - different colours indicate range for clusters obtained using Step 1. (b) The characteristics of the triangular and trapezoidal MFs generated for the cluster shown in red color. (Color figure online)

## 4   Experimental Results

Our evaluation consists of comparison between the proposed approach and two other techniques in terms of (i) parameterising MFs for attributes with different distributions, and (ii) classification performance of a fuzzy rule set that was developed using the parameterised output of each of the 3 techniques.

### 4.1   Dataset

We evaluated the effectiveness of the proposed approach using attributes associated with a dataset for classification activities of daily living (ADLs), as previously used in [7]. This dataset is collected via multiple Kinect cameras, each installed in a different area of a single monitored house. The system used for the gathering of data consisted of Windows 8.1 notebook PCs, with one notebook per Kinect device. Custom data collection code was written in C# under the Microsoft.Net framework. Data analysis was subsequently performed in MATLAB™.

Data was collected from this house for a period of five weeks, during which a single occupant undertook activities typical of a retired elderly person. From each Kinect, observations for activities undertaken are taken at one-second intervals and ones in which a person is detected are stored. The entire dataset consisted of more than two million observations. The attributes we extracted from this dataset were the occupant's Centre of Gravity pixel location ($Xc, Yc$), Aspect Ratio ($AR$) of the 3D axis-aligned bounding box, and Orientation ($O$).

The dataset for each location was partitioned into a training set and an unseen test set. The training set for each location consisted of nearly one million observations of behaviour patterns associated to typical (or normal) ADLs of the occupant. The test set holds some sequences of normal behaviour (i.e. typical ADLs) and abnormal events (e.g. occupant lying on the floor of the kitchen).

## 4.2 Comparison of Techniques for Parameterizing Attributes with Different Characteristics

Attributes with different data distribution were used to compare the parameterisation results between the proposed approach (VBMS–RS) and two other techniques: (i) using MS (instead of VBMS) in Step 1 of the proposed approach followed by the procedure of robust statistics in Step 2 (MS-RS), and (ii) using the Fuzzy-C-Means (FCM) clustering algorithm [17] to generate a fixed number of membership functions over the domain of a particular attribute without the use of robust statistics. For each particular attribute, we empirically set this number for FCM according to the number of modes in the attribute probability density function, as discussed in the following sections. In each case, comparisons are made through the clusters and MFs produced by each of the 3 techniques.

**Attribute with Separated Distributions.** One example with well separated distributions is for the attribute $Xc$ associated with the living room dataset, as shown in Fig. 6. The reason is that, as shown in Fig. 7, the living room was occupied mainly for sitting at a computer desk (the left distribution) and using the sofa for watching TV (the distribution to the right) and as a result, values for $Xc$ are mostly concentrated around two separate regions in feature space of $Xc$ (i.e., 150 and 325), respectively.

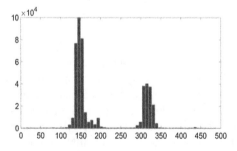

**Fig. 6.** A bimodal distribution for the $Xc$ attribute associated with the living room dataset. Note that the base distributions are well separated.

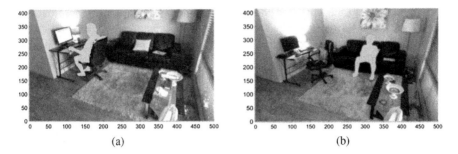

**Fig. 7.** (a) Sitting at a computer desk, and (b) watching TV while sitting on a sofa in the living room. The body of the occupant is masked by its binary silhouette obtained from the Kinect SDK and the numbers in the vertical and horizontal axis indicate pixel location.

Figure 8(a) illustrates the results of using VBMS–RS for parameterising distributions of $Xc$ from the living room. Each underlying distribution of data associated with a detected mode is shown with a different colour.

VBMS–RS could separate correctly this attribute feature space into two main underlying distributions. The distribution to the right in Fig. 8(a) is in the shape of

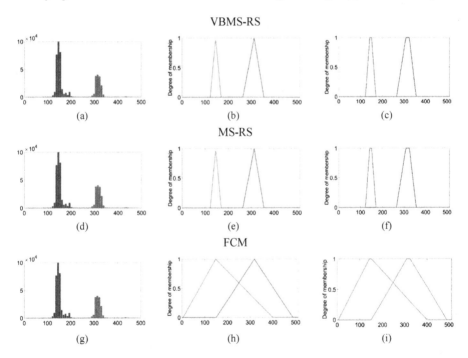

**Fig. 8.** Results for different techniques for parameterising the two base distributions shown in Fig. 6. The different colours in each of (a), (D), and (G) show range for clusters obtained using different techniques. (B), (E), and (H) show the respective triangular Mfs, resulted from the output of the 3 techniques, respectively. (C), (F) and (I) show the corresponding trapezoidal Mfs resulted from the output of the 3 techniques, respectively. (Color figure online)

reverse-J (skewed to the left), and the corresponding triangular and trapezoidal MFs defined by VBMS–RS (parts (b) and (c)) represents only the range for the normal data points associated with this distribution. Note that since the normal range obtained for both clusters in Fig. 8(a) is small, the shoulder of trapezoidal MFs in Fig. 8(c) is small and thus both trapezoidal MFs nearly have the same shape and cover the same area in the feature space.

To further evaluate VBMS-RS, VBMS was replaced with MS in Step 1 of the proposed approach and the experiment was repeated. By comparing the results, it was observed that where the distributions in the attribute feature space are separated distinctly, both methods work equally well. However, MS–RS requires an empirical input, the bandwidth parameter, whereas for VBMS in the proposed approach, the initial bandwidth is derived from the data automatically [13].

In the comparison using the FCM technique, the number of membership functions was empirically set to 2 (as this is obvious from a visual examination of the data). As shown with blue and red colours, Fig. 8(g) demonstrates that this technique correctly separated the attribute into two distributions in the attribute feature space. As a result, MFs in Fig. 8(h) and (i) were generated to represent the two distributions detected in the attribute feature space via triangular and trapezoidal shapes, respectively. Since this technique does not use robust statistics, the resulting parameterization of the MFs is not the same as the proposed approach. More specifically, MFs generated by this technique have a wider support and hence represent a wider area outside the normal range for the two main distributions in Fig. 6. As a result, the MFs generated by this technique will also encompass many rare observations (outliers) around the main distributions. For example, triangular MFs generated by FCM give membership degrees 0.17 and 0.83 to the outlier point $Xc = 380$ so that the sum of memberships of this point becomes one. This is in contrast to triangular MFs generated by VBMS-RS which give zero membership to this outlier point.

**Attribute with a Unimodal Distribution.** One example of the attributes that have unimodal skewed distribution is the *AR* attribute from the dining room, as illustrated in images on the left hand side of Fig. 9 (i.e., (a), (d), and (g)). The overall distribution shown in those images illustrates the skewed distribution for *AR*. Different colors in each of the images indicate the distributions related to the clusters that have been obtained using different techniques. Figure 9(b), (e), and (h) illustrate triangular MFs generated using the 3 techniques. Figure 9(c), (f), and (i) show results of generating trapezoidal MFs for the distribution of the *AR* attribute using the 3 techniques. As shown in Fig. 9(a), VBMS-RS correctly associated all data points with the only mode in the distribution. However, as shown in Fig. 9(d), MS-RS has broken the distribution into two clusters. This difference is mainly because in VBMS, points that correspond to the tails of the underlying density will get a broader neighbourhood and a smaller importance. Therefore, they will be included to main structures and hence, tail of distributions will not be broken into pieces. This is unlike MS, where it assigns a fixed global bandwidth to all data points and hence all points receive the same importance when estimating the PDF of data.

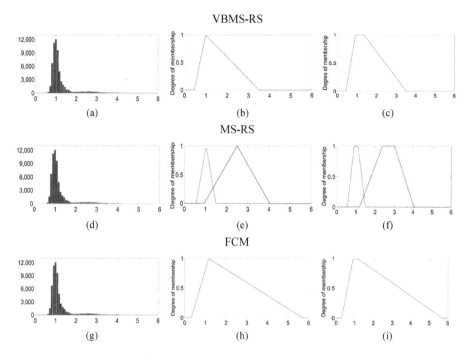

**Fig. 9.** Using different techniques for parameterising distribution of *AR* attribute for the dining room dataset. (a), (d), and (g) show the range for clusters obtained using the 3 different techniques. (b), (e), and (h) show the respective triangular MFs resulted from the output of 3 techniques. (c), (f) and (i) show the corresponding trapezoidal MFs resulted from the output of 3 techniques. (Color figure online)

As the distribution is unimodal, input value for the number of clusters in FCM was set to 1. From Fig. 9(g) we can see that although this technique has grouped all data points in the distribution into the stipulated one cluster, the supports of the generated MFs in Fig. 9(h) and (i) are much broader than corresponding MFs generated by VBMS-RS which might lead to non-specific responses for classification of the attribute values (i.e., every point is considered to be in the set). Also, when the application of generating MFs is for classification of outliers, the generated MFs by this technique represents many rare observations (outliers) located between *AR* = 4 and *AR* = 6, and thus will be not able to correctly classify a new abnormal observation within that range. However, both triangular and trapezoidal MFs from the proposed approach does not represent any data point for outside the normal range [0.5, 3.5] and therefore, VBMS-RS method can obtain better classification results for normal points and better accuracy for handling outlier observations.

**Attribute with Multimodal Distribution.** An example of an attribute with multimodal distribution is *Xc* from the kitchen dataset. From the ground truth in examining the video data for this attribute there were three distinct places for *Xc* where the occupant performed most of the activities in the kitchen. As a result, PDF for this attribute has 3 modes, each associated with a particular distribution and the 3 distributions overlap.

Results of parameterising this attribute using the different techniques are shown in Fig. 10. Input value for the number of clusters to be created by FCM was set to 3. It is clear from the results in Fig. 10 that, VBMS-RS partitions the feature space into the right number of membership functions whereas using other techniques were unable to separate the mixed distributions correctly. The difference between results for VBMS-RS and MS-RS is due to the fact that, using VBMS, the data points lying in large density regions will get a narrower neighbourhood since the kernel bandwidth is smaller, but are given a larger importance. So when base distributions are mixed in the attribute feature space, VBMS can better separate those structures than MS. This finding is consistent with Comaniciu et al. [12].

As observed in Fig. 10, the range of triangular MFs generated by 3 techniques, in general, is greater than their respective trapezoidal MFs. For instance, the wider data distribution associated with the right-hand-side cluster (ranging from pixel location 220 to 500) in Fig. 10(a) and (d) causes the respective trapezoidal MFs in Fig. 10(c) and

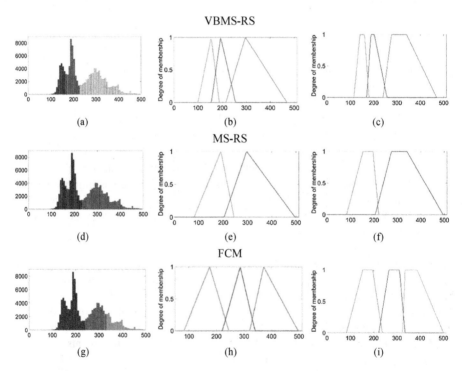

**Fig. 10.** Results for using the 3 different techniques for parameterising distribution of $Xc$ associated with the kitchen dataset. (a), (d), and (g) show the range for clusters obtained using the 3 different techniques. (b), (e), and (h) show the respective triangular MFs resulted from the output of 3 techniques. (c), (f) and (i) show the corresponding trapezoidal MFs resulted from the output of 3 techniques. (Color figure online)

(f) to have a relatively wider shoulder, which in turn has resulted in those MFs to receive steeper descending foots upon performing extrapolation in Step 2 of the approach. Accordingly, they cover less area when compared to their respective triangulate MFs in Fig. 10(b) and (e). As already pointed out in Sect. 3.3, at the stage of classification, the wider support of triangular MFs allows more variations for normal data for each cluster.

From Fig. 10(g) FCM has partitioned the attribute feature space to be represented by three MFs. However, the parameters for these three MFs are different to those of the results from VBMS-RS. The reason is that this technique aims to minimise the distance of data points from their respective cluster centres. As a result, the locations of centre of clusters are not always corresponding to the modes in distribution of data. Furthermore, as seen in Fig. 10(h) and (i), distributions with their modes located on pixel locations 150 and 200, respectively, are represented by the same MF. Hence, MFs generated by this technique are not accurately representing data distributions in this attribute feature space.

### 4.3 Results on Classification Accuracy Using MFs Produced by Different Techniques

The characteristics of MFs generated by a particular technique have a direct impact on performance of the corresponding fuzzy rule set for classification purposes. In other words, a better technique to estimate the base distributions for attributes can lead to more representative MFs and hence a better classification accuracy of the corresponding fuzzy rule set. To investigate this, we conducted experiments in which we applied the output of the 3 different MF generation techniques, including the proposed approach, to obtain a fuzzy rule set for the application of detecting abnormal activities in ADLs. As we had data from 5 rooms and each room was associated with 4 attributes with different number of modes in their corresponding PDF, we empirically set the number of clusters for FCM to a specific number (i.e., 3) to suite across all situations, a technique used typically by existing fuzzy approaches [18]. To obtain the classifier, we extracted the attributes (described in Sect. 4.1) from the training dataset associated with each location and developed the fuzzy system using the approach from [7]. A brief description of this approach is described below:

The unsupervised ADLs monitoring approach proposed by [7] uses a set of attributes derived from Kinect camera observations and consists of two phases: training and classification (monitoring).

During the training phase, the system learns "normal" behaviour patterns of the occupant as a set of fuzzy rules. More specifically, for each monitored location, epochs of activity are first determined and for each epoch, normal behaviour patterns are then learnt by finding frequent occurrences of attributes via the use of a fuzzy association rule mining algorithm [8]. Hence, for each monitored location a fuzzy rule set is obtained. The antecedent part of each rule in a fuzzy rule set represents a combination of fuzzy linguistic values describing a frequent behaviour of the occupant along with their expected epoch of activity. The normal duration of the frequent behaviour is specified in the consequent part of the rule. Also, for each monitor location, the duration of infrequent behaviours is estimated.

The monitoring phase takes the fuzzy rule set obtained from the training phase as input, and for each location, it classifies the current behaviour of the occupant as abnormal if it is not in the set of frequent behaviours. For more detail, we refer the reader to [7].

Table 1 shows the total number of rules obtained from the output of each technique. Variations in performing activities typically create a number of base distributions for an attribute. Hence, each particular activity can be typically represented by a specific combination of base distributions over different attributes. Since MFs generated by VBMS-RS for an attribute represent the normal range for base distributions, different versions of a particular activity are usually represented by the same combination of fuzzy attributes, and thus one fuzzy rule. When each frequent activity is modelled by one fuzzy rule, the total number of fuzzy rules for a location becomes considerably less than situations where multiple rules are developed to represent versions of the same activity. For example, from the generated rules by VBMS-RS, it was observed that, for each of the four activity epochs detected for the living room, two fuzzy rules were generated to represent frequent activities of sitting behind the computer desk, and sitting on the sofa, respectively, forming eight (out of nine) rules for the living room rule set. Also, for the afternoon epoch, a rule represents the activity of sleeping on the sofa as it was occasionally carried out by the occupant during that period.

**Table 1.** The number of fuzzy rules obtained from the output of different MF generation techniques.

| Dataset | | Kitchen | Living room | Dining room | Bedroom | Overall |
|---|---|---|---|---|---|---|
| Technique | | | | | | |
| FCM | Triangular | 30 | 28 | 22 | 5 | 85 |
| | Trapezoidal | 33 | 29 | 23 | 5 | 90 |
| MS-RS | Triangular | 24 | 8 | 6 | 2 | 40 |
| | Trapezoidal | 26 | 8 | 6 | 2 | 42 |
| VBMS-RS | Triangular | 15 | 9 | 6 | 2 | 32 |
| | Trapezoidal | 16 | 9 | 6 | 2 | 33 |

From Table 1 it can be seen that using the output of other MF generation techniques (e.g., FCM and MS-RS) resulted in a higher number of rules. This is because MFs obtained from the output of those techniques do not necessarily represent data distributions over space of attributes well, and therefore, the values of an attribute for different versions of an activity might be represented by different MFs defined over the attribute. This results in different fuzzy rules with a different combination of fuzzy attributes to be generated for modelling slightly different versions of the same activity, hence a higher number of rules.

It is also observed that when using FCM and MS-RS techniques, the number of rules obtained by trapezoidal MFs is slightly more than those obtained from using triangular MFs. As already mentioned, MFs generated by these techniques do not necessarily represent base distributions well and, as the support of trapezoidal MFs are less in comparison with triangular MFs, more combinations of MFs are required to represent variations of attributes during activities. However, since triangular or trapezoidal MFs generated by VBMS-RS represent base distributions well, variation of attributes during activities have been represented by almost the equal number of rules.

Table 2 quantitatively compares classification accuracy for fuzzy rules obtained using the output of the 3 different MF generation techniques with different MFs. More specifically, 40 sequences of different scenarios for normal and abnormal behaviour in the unseen test set (20 sequences for each category of normal and abnormal behaviour, respectively) were used to evaluate the accuracy of the fuzzy rule set obtained using the output of a particular technique with a particular type of MF (i.e., triangular and trapezoidal) and the resulting classification accuracy is reported in Table 2.

**Table 2.** Results of using the output of different MF generation techniques to obtain a fuzzy rule set for the application of detecting abnormal activities in ADLs.

| Method | | Normal behaviour | Abnormal behaviour | Overall accuracy |
|---|---|---|---|---|
| FCM (3 clusters) | Triangular | 70.0% | 85.0% | 77.5% |
| | Trapezoidal | 60.0% | 85.0% | 72.5% |
| MS-RS | Triangular | 90.0% | 80.0% | 85.0% |
| | Trapezoidal | 85.0% | 80.0% | 82.5% |
| VBMS | Triangular | 100.0% | 35.0% | 67.5% |
| | Trapezoidal | 100.0% | 40.0% | 70.0% |
| VBMS-RS | Triangular | 100.0% | 85.0% | 92.5% |
| | Trapezoidal | 95.0% | 85.0% | 90.0% |

From Table 2 it can be observed that when we use MS-RS to obtain triangular MFs for fuzzy rules, 6 of the test sequences, mostly representing an abnormal behaviour, were classified incorrectly. This is mainly because MS couldn't distinctly separate overlapped distributions in feature space of attributes. Therefore, for some attributes two or more behaviour patterns belonging to different overlapped distributions were represented by the same MF and hence represented by the same fuzzy rule. For example, distributions of $AR$ for crouching on the kitchen floor (to pick up an object) and bending down (to manipulate objects inside the kitchen cabinet), while belonging to different main distributions in the attribute feature space, considered as belonging to the same cluster, and hence, the corresponding fuzzy rule set was not able to label a sequence for spending a long time sitting on the kitchen floor as abnormal behaviour. Using MS-RS to obtain trapezoidal MFs results in misclassification of 7 test sequences, resulting in a classification accuracy of 82.5%. Specifically, as the support of trapezoidal MFs is less in comparison with their respective triangular ones, one another test sequence for normal behavior that was slightly different from the training samples was misclassified as being abnormal.

Classification that results from using FCM to generate triangular MFs produced accuracy of 77.5%. This is mostly because the test sequences involving normal behaviour patterns that were slightly different from their corresponding training patterns were misclassified by this classifier as abnormal. This was mainly because FCM broke main distributions for some attributes into pieces, and consequently, for a particular activity, when most of training values belonged to a particular part of the distribution and the values for test sequences fell into another part of the distribution, the corresponding fuzzy rule for the activity could not be able to trigger and hence less accuracy of the classifier. Using FCM to generate trapezoidal MFs produced an accuracy of 72.5%.

We also evaluated the classification accuracy of the fuzzy rules obtained by applying the proposed approach without robust statistics and results are shown Table 2 denoted by VBMS. When using triangular MFs, we observed that many test sequences for abnormal behaviour have been labelled as normal. In those sequences, the values of attributes were well outside of the normal range for the main distributions in the feature space of attributes. However, since the range of generated triangular MFs was wider than the range of main distributions, they included many outlier observations, and hence, outlier observations in each of those test sequences triggered a corresponding rule for a normal behaviour in the rule base to be fired and resulted in the test sequence being labelled normal. The generated trapezoidal MFs cover less area (less outliers) in attributes space and hence caused slightly less test sequences for abnormal behaviour to be labelled as normal.

From the last two rows of Table 2 we see that the rule set obtained from the results of VBMS-RS with triangular MFs could classify 37 test sequences correctly and hence an accuracy of 92.5%. We observed that for almost all attributes, using the combination of VBMS and robust statistics yields in the resulting triangular MFs representing only the normal range for the base distributions in the attributes. Therefore, while outlier observations for abnormal behaviours were classified correctly, attribute values during most of sequences for normal behaviour were within the bounds associated with the generated MFs, and hence, those sequences triggered a rule corresponding to a normal behaviour to fire. However, it is observed that using trapezoidal MFs caused one test sequence for normal behaviour to be misclassified as abnormal, resulting in an overall accuracy of 90% for the classifier.

Note that although, in average, using trapezoidal MFs resulted in slightly less classification accuracy, we observed that they assign higher degrees of membership to normal data points during the classification stage. Specifically, trapezoidal MFs assign the maximum membership degree to those data points that fall between the two shoulders in the trapezoidal shape whereas triangular MFs give the maximum membership value just to those data points correspond to the centroid of the triangular shape.

## 5  Conclusion

In this paper, we presented an unsupervised approach that incorporates variable bandwidth mean-shift and robust statistics for generating fuzzy membership functions. The approach automatically learns the number of representative functions from the underlying data distribution and then works out the associated parameters of a given membership function. We examined the proposed approach using the trapezoidal and the triangular membership functions and compared its performance against two other techniques. Results in Sect. 4.2 demonstrated that, from perspective of partitioning an attribute, the generated membership functions generated by VBMS-RS can better separate the underlying distributions. As a better technique to estimate the base distributions for attributes can lead to more representative MFs and hence a better classification accuracy of the corresponding fuzzy rule set, we examined classifiers constructed using the proposed method of generating membership function and 3 other methods for both the trapezoidal and the triangular membership functions. Results were examined from the perspectives of number of fuzzy rules and classification accuracy associated with each classifier. Results in Tables 1 and 2 showed that classifiers associated with VBMS-RS outperformed three other classifiers that used different approaches for parameterisation of the attributes.

# References

1. Medasani, S., Kim, J., Krishnapuram, R.: An overview of membership function generation techniques for pattern recognition. Int. J. Approx. Reason. **19**(3), 391–417 (1998)
2. Seki, H.: Fuzzy inference based non-daily behavior pattern detection for elderly people monitoring system. In: 2009 Annual International Conference of the IEEE Engineering in Medicine and Biology Society, EMBC 2009, pp. 6187–6192. IEEE (2009)
3. Moeinzadeh, H., et al.: Improving classification accuracy using evolutionary fuzzy transformation. In: Proceedings of the 11th Annual Conference Companion on Genetic and Evolutionary Computation Conference: Late Breaking Papers. ACM (2009)
4. Amaral, T.G., Crisóstomo, M.M.: Automatic helicopter motion control using fuzzy logic. In: 2001 The 10th IEEE International Conference on Fuzzy Systems. IEEE (2001)
5. Tang, K., Man, K., Chan, C.: Fuzzy control of water pressure using genetic algorithm. In: Proceedings of the Safety, Reliability and Applications of Emerging Intelligent Control Technologies (2014)
6. Takagi, H., Hayashi, I.: NN-driven fuzzy reasoning. Int. J. Approx. Reason. **5**(3), 191–212 (1991)
7. Pazhoumand-Dar, H., Lam, C.P., Masek, M.: A novel fuzzy based home occupant monitoring system using kinect cameras. In: IEEE 27th International Conference on Tools with Artificial Intelligence, Vietri sul Mare, Italy (2015)
8. Kuok, C.M., Fu, A., Wong, M.H.: Mining fuzzy association rules in databases. ACM Sigmod Rec. **27**(1), 41–46 (1998)
9. Doctor, F., Iqbal, R., Naguib, R.N.: A fuzzy ambient intelligent agents approach for monitoring disease progression of dementia patients. J. Ambient Intell. Humaniz. Comput. **5**(1), 147–158 (2014)
10. Castellano, G., Fanelli, A., Mencar, C.: Generation of interpretable fuzzy granules by a double-clustering technique. Arch. Control Sci. **12**(4), 397–410 (2002)
11. Hubert, M., Vandervieren, E.: An adjusted boxplot for skewed distributions. Comput. Stat. Data Anal. **52**(12), 5186–5201 (2008)
12. Comaniciu, D., Ramesh, V., Meer, P.: The variable bandwidth mean shift and data-driven scale selection. In: Proceedings of the Eighth IEEE International Conference on Computer Vision, ICCV 2001. IEEE (2001)

13. Pazhoumand-Dar, H., Lam, C.P., Masek, M.: Automatic generation of fuzzy membership functions using adaptive mean-shift and robust statistics. In: Proceedings of the 8th International Conference on Agents and Artificial Intelligence, Italy (2016)
14. Rousseeuw, P.J., Hubert, M.: Robust statistics for outlier detection. Wiley Interdisc. Rev. Data Mining Knowl. Discov. **1**(1), 73–79 (2011)
15. Brys, G., Hubert, M., Struyf, A.: A robust measure of skewness. J. Comput. Graphical Stat. **13**(4), 996–1017 (2004)
16. Sheather, S.J., Jones, M.C.: A reliable data-based bandwidth selection method for kernel density estimation. J. R. Stat. Soc. Ser. B (Methodol.) **53**, 683–690 (1991)
17. Bezdek, J.C., Ehrlich, R., Full, W.: FCM: The fuzzy c-means clustering algorithm. Comput. Geosci. **10**(2), 191–203 (1984)
18. Tajbakhsh, A., Rahmati, M., Mirzaei, A.: Intrusion detection using fuzzy association rules. Appl. Soft Comput. **9**(2), 462–469 (2009)

# Facilitating Multi-agent Coalition Formation in Self-interested Environments

Ted Scully[1]([⊠]) and Michael G. Madden[2]

[1] Cork Institute of Technology, Cork, Ireland
ted.scully@cit.ie
[2] National University of Ireland, Galway, Ireland
michael.madden@nuigalway.ie

**Abstract.** This paper considers the problem of facilitating coalition formation in self-interested multi-agent environments. To successfully form a coalition, agents must collectively agree on the monetary amount to charge for completion of a task as well as the distribution of subtasks within the coalition. The problem is accentuated as different subtasks have various degrees of difficulty and the agents do not possess perfect information. That is, an agent is uncertain of the true monetary requirement of other agents for completing subtasks. These complexities, coupled with the self-interested nature of agents, can inhibit or even prevent the formation of coalitions in such a real-world setting. As a solution we present an auction-based protocol called *ACCORD*. *ACCORD* facilitates coalition formation by promoting the adoption of cooperative behaviour amongst agents as a means of overcoming the complexities outlined above. Through extensive empirical analysis we analyse two variations of the *ACCORD* protocol and demonstrate that cooperative and fair behaviour is dominant and any agents deviating from this behaviour suffer a degradation in performance.

## 1 Introduction

We consider the problem of coalition formation in a dynamic real-world context. The real-world problem domain that we address consists of a marketplace populated by self-interested agents, where each agent represents an individual firm. In this marketplace, a task consisting of multiple subtasks is proposed to all agents. We assume that no agent is capable of individually performing an entire task. Therefore, in order to successfully perform a task, agents must cooperate by forming a coalition.

We provide a context for our problem domain by considering a simplified model of a real world transport marketplace. Each agent represents a transportation firm, and the ability of an agent relates to the routes its firm can service. As an example, consider a transportation task, $Tr(A, D)$. This task requires the delivery of an item from point $A$ to $D$. Each task can be broken into subtasks. In our model, subtasks correspond to the sub-routes that constitute the complete journey. A transportation subtask, $Sr(A, B)$, requires the transportation

© Springer International Publishing AG 2017

J. van den Herik and J. Filipe (Eds.): ICAART 2016, LNAI 10162, pp. 265–282, 2017.
DOI: 10.1007/978-3-319-53354-4_15

of an item from point $A$ to $B$. For the purpose of illustration, we subdivide the example transportation task $Tr(A, D)$ into three subtasks, $Sr(A, B)$, $Sr(B, C)$ and $Sr(C, D)$.

To ensure the practical applicability of the work we assume that agents do not possess perfect information about one another; rather, each agent is unsure of the value (monetary or otherwise) that other agents place on specific subtasks. However, we also assume that the values maintained by agents for a particular subtask are not widely distributed. For example, a transportation firm cannot precisely predict the value another firm will charge for completion of $Sr(A, B)$, however, it can make a reasonable estimate, based on details such as distance. An emergent difficulty is that agents may artificially inflate the financial reward they require for performing a subtask within a coalition.

We incorporate an additional real-world complexity into our problem domain with the assumption that subtasks may have various levels of difficulty or require different levels of expertise. It is realistic that the more challenging subtasks may yield a higher financial reward. This may lead to an increased level of competition for these subtasks, which in turn could lead to a scenario where agents are unable to reach agreement on the distribution of tasks within a coalition. We refer to the occurrence of such a scenario as deadlock.

We propose that the occurrence of deadlock and the artificial inflation of financial rewards can be avoided if the agents involved were to act in a fair and cooperative manner. In the context of this work, an agent exhibits fair behaviour if it honestly calculates the financial reward for all member agents of a coalition (including itself) on the basis of its personal beliefs. Agents behaving fairly will not artificially inflate the financial rewards they expect for performing subtasks. An agent is cooperative if it agrees to participate in any coalition proposal irrespective of the subtask it is asked to perform, assuming the financial reward it receives for performing that subtask is adequate. Cooperation allows us to avoid deadlock as an agent will participate in a coalition, even though it may not be optimal from that agent's perspective. While the adoption of cooperative and fair behaviour would allow agents to successfully form coalitions, the difficulty remains that such agents are self-interested and have to be motivated to adopt these behaviours.

As a solution to this problem, we have recently proposed two coalition formation protocols. One called Public $ACCORD$ [1] and the second called Private $ACCORD$ [3]: This paper describes the details of both protocols and presents a detailed empirical evaluation that demonstrates that cooperative and fair behaviour is dominant.

## 2    Related Research

A fundamental challenge encountered in many multi-agent systems is the capability of agents to form coalitions. Agents may need to dynamically join together in a coalition in order to complete a complex task, which none of them may be able to complete independently [5]. Within the area of MASs the issue of coalition formation has generally been approached from either a macroscopic or microscopic perspective [6].

The macroscopic perspective adopts a system-level view of the entire agent population; it describes the system from the viewpoint of an external observer. Typically, the macroscopic perspective assumes that each agent within the environment has a number of tasks to perform and that coalition formation is utilised to enhance the ability of the agents to perform these tasks. Research work in this area has focused on calculating the optimal coalition structure, which is the division of all agents in the environment into exhaustive and disjoint coalitions [7–11]. When adopting the macroscopic perspective, it is typically assumed that each coalition has a fixed associated value, which is universally known and accepted by all agents [12].

The microscopic perspective adopts an agent-level view of the system. Each agent will reason about the process of forming a coalition based on its personal information and its perspective of the system. The work in this area can be broadly categorised into cooperative and self-interested multi-agent environments. A number of distributed coalition formation protocols have been proposed for cooperative agent environments [5,13,14]. However, given the self-interested nature of our environment these protocols cannot be directly applied to our problem domain.

Microscopic coalition formation has recently been examined in the context of hedonic games. In a hedonic game agents are self-interested and their level of coalition satisfaction is dependent on the composition of the coalition they join. A number of distributed protocols have been proposed to facilitate coalition formation in such self-interested environments [15–17]. While hedonic games adopt a macroscopic perspective in a self-interested environment the context of the problem is quite different to our proposed scenario. The solution to a hedonic game is the exhaustive decomposition of all agents in an environment into coalitions.

## 3   ACCORD

Our definition of a coalition formation protocol is: a set of public rules that govern the behaviour of agents by specifying how they may form coalitions. In this section, we describe the $ACCORD$(An Auction Integrated Coalition Formation Protocol For Dynamic Multi-Agent Environments) protocol, which will enable agents to form coalitions while simultaneously governing agent behaviour by promoting the adoption of cooperative and fair behaviour. We consider two variants, *Public ACCORD* and *Private ACCORD*.

### 3.1   Problem Description

The $ACCORD$ environment contains a set of self-interested service agents $A = \{a_1, a_2, \ldots, a_m\}$ and an auctioneer agent. The set $S = \{s_1, s_2, \ldots, s_h\}$ consists of all valid subtasks that can be performed in this market. Any agent $a_i \in A$

is capable of performing a certain set of subtasks $S_{a_i}$, such that $S_{a_i} \subseteq S$. In addition, $a_i$ maintains a set of private valuations for all possible subtasks. The function $mn()$ denotes the monetary valuation that $a_i$ places on any subtask. For example, $a_i$'s private valuation of subtask $s_g$ is $mn(i, s_g)$.

In order to perform a task, $a_i$ must cooperate with one or more agents in the form of a coalition. A coalition is represented by the tuple $\langle C, salloc, palloc \rangle$. The members of the proposed coalition are contained in the set $C$, such that $C \subseteq A$. In order for a coalition to form successfully, the agents in $C$ must reach an agreement on the distribution of subtasks and finances within the coalition. The subtask distribution is specified by the allocation function $salloc()$. For any agent $a_i \in C$, $salloc(a_i)$ returns the subtask(s) within the coalition that $a_i$ is to perform. The financial distribution is specified by the allocation function $palloc()$. Therefore, the monetary amount that $a_i$ would receive for performing its specified subtask(s) within the coalition is $palloc(a_i)$.

### 3.2   Protocol Description of Public ACCORD

*Public ACCORD* can be subdivided into the following eight stages:

1. **Task Submission:** A customer submits a task $T$ consisting of multiple subtasks to the auctioneer, such that $T \subseteq S$. Subsequently, the auctioneer will send notification of $T$ to each agent $a_i$.
2. **Bidder Participation:** Each agent $a_i$ will inform the auctioneer of whether or not it is willing to participate in the protocol. It is logical that $a_i$ will participate iff:

$$\exists \, s_x \; : \; s_x \in S_{a_i} \, \wedge \, s_x \in T$$

   In order for $a_i$ to indicate its willingness to participate in the protocol it must submit its offers to the auctioneer. The subtask and monetary offers from $a_i$ in relation to $T$ are denoted by the set $B_{a_i}^T = \{S_{a_i}^T, P_{a_i}^T\}$. The set $S_{a_i}^T = \{s_1', s_2', \ldots, s_q'\}$ contains the subtasks in $T$ that $a_i$ is capable of performing. The set $P_{a_i}^T$ contains $a_i$'s private monetary valuation for each subtask specified in $S_{a_i}^T$. Therefore,
   $P_{a_i}^T = \{mn(i, s_1'), \ldots \, mn(i, s_q')\}$.
3. **Auction Commencement:** The auctioneer maintains a record, $B^T$, of the subtask and monetary capabilities of all agents willing to participate in the protocol. When the auctioneer receives a reply, $B_{a_i}^T$, from $a_i$ it adds it to the record $B^T$.

   Once all replies have been collected the auctioneer will commence a first-price sealed bid auction for $T$. Subsequently, the auctioneer sends notification of the auction deadline coupled with $B^T$ to each agent $a_i$ that is willing to participate in the protocol.

4. **Coalition Proposal:** Agents participating in the protocol will propose coalitions to each other in a peer-to-peer manner. Therefore, an $a_i$ will initially perform coalition calculation in order to determine the optimal coalition proposal $CP_{a_i} = \langle C, salloc, palloc \rangle$. In order to construct such a coalition proposal, $a_i$ must consider both the monetary demands and subtask capabilities of all agents. Fortunately, on receipt of $B^T$, $a_i$ is aware of the subtasks in $T$ that all other agents can perform as well as the monetary amount each agent will charge for completion of these subtasks.

We also assume that $a_i$ maintains a private estimation of the level of cooperation exhibited by other agents. It is reasonable to expect that $a_i$ will incorporate these cooperation ratings into its coalition calculation process. For example, it would be less likely to include an agent that constantly refuses all coalition proposals compared to an agent that regularly demonstrates a high willingness to accept proposals.

Once $a_i$ has determined the optimal member agents $C = \{a'_1, a'_2, \ldots, a'_n\}$ it can construct and send $CP_{a_i}$ to each member agent in $C$.

5. **Proposal Response:** An agent $a_v$ will assess any coalition proposal $CP_{a_i}$ that it receives. It will issue either an accept or reject notice to the proposing agent. $ACCORD$ does not control the means by which $a_v$ evaluates a coalition proposal. However, it is reasonable to assume that $a_v$ will consider both the subtask(s) and the monetary award it is offered in $CP_{a_i}$. It is also reasonable to expect that $a_v$ will assess the value of participating in a coalition with the other member agents in $C$.

6. **Coalition Proposal Result:** After sending a proposal $a_i$ must await the replies from the potential member agents of the coalition. The two possible outcomes of this stage are:

   – The failure to form the proposed coalition $CP_{a_i}$. If $a_i$ receives one or more rejections from the member agents in $C$ the coalition cannot be formed. It must subsequently inform all agents in $C$ of the unsuccessful completion of coalition formation. If adequate time remains before the auction deadline expires $a_i$ can recommence the coalition proposal stage and attempt to form another coalition.

   – The successful formation of the proposed coalition $CP_{a_i}$. If $a_i$ receives an acceptance from each of the potential member agents then the coalition formation process has been successful. It subsequently notifies each member agent that the proposed coalition has been successfully formed.

7. **Bid Submission:** If $a_i$ successfully forms the proposed coalition $CP_{a_i}$ it will subsequently enter the coalition as a bid in the auction. Each agent is limited to submitting a single bid. Therefore, after $a_i$ has submitted a bid, it can only participate in the proposal response stage. That is, it can only accept or reject coalitions proposed by other agents.

Once the auctioneer receives $CP_{a_i}$, it calculates the total monetary reward required by the coalition to perform $T$ as $\sum_{d=1}^{n} palloc(a'_d)$. Subsequently, the auctioneer records this as a sealed-price bid in the auction.

8. **Winner Notification:** Once the auction deadline expires, the auctioneer calculates the lowest monetary bid. The member agents of the corresponding coalition are notified that they have been successful in obtaining the contract to collectively perform $T$.

## 3.3   Protocol Description of Private ACCORD

*Private ACCORD* facilitates agent-based coalition formation while also placing emphasis on the retention of private information. *Private ACCORD* can be subdivided into the same eight stages used to illustrate *Public ACCORD*. However, only two of these stages differ from the formal description of *Public ACCORD*. We confine our description of *Private ACCORD* to these two stages.

(2) **Bidder Participation:** In order for an agent $a_i$ to indicate its willingness to participate in the *Private ACCORD* protocol it must submit a list of its subtask capabilities to the auctioneer. The agent does not provide it's private monetary valuation to the auctioneer.
The subtask capabilities of $a_i$ for $T$ are denoted by $B_{a_i}^T = \{S_{a_i}^T\}$. As before, the set
$$S_{a_i}^T = \{s_1', s_2', \ldots, s_q'\}$$
denotes the subtasks that $a_i$ can perform.

(4) **Coalition Proposal:** Agents participating in the protocol will propose coalitions to each other in a peer-to-peer manner. Each agent $a_i$, must first perform coalition calculation in order to determine its optimal coalition proposal $CP_{a_i} = \langle C, salloc, palloc \rangle$.
In order to construct such a coalition proposal, $a_i$ will need to consider both the monetary demands and subtask capabilities of other agents. On receipt of $B^T$, $a_i$ is aware of the subtasks in $T$ that all other agents can perform. However, because perfect information is not available, $a_i$ is uncertain of the monetary amount each agent will require as payment for performing a given subtask.
Each agent $a_i$ must maintain a matrix of expected payments for each subtask for each agent. Initially $a_i$ may base the monetary price of a sub-task to other agents as equal to its own cost for performing that sub-task. However, we also assume that $a_i$ has basic learning abilities that allow it to improve the accuracy of its estimations through repeated interaction with other agents. It is also reasonable to assume that $a_i$ will maintain a private estimation of the level of cooperation exhibited by other agents. Therefore, the cooperation rating of all participating agents is also considered when performing coalition calculation.
Once $a_i$ has determined the optimal member agents $C = \{a_1', a_2', \ldots, a_n'\}$ it can construct and send $CP_{a_i}$ to each member agent in $C$.

# 4    Empirical Evaluation

The objective of this empirical evaluation is to undertake a comparative analysis between *Public* and *Private ACCORD* as well as determining whether the *ACCORD* protocols promote cooperative and fair behaviour amongst agents. We have developed a simulation testbed to evaluate the protocols. Each experiment measures the performance of agents adopting different behaviours in the *ACCORD* simulation environment. Sections 4.2 and 4.3 analyse the effects of uncooperative and selfish behaviour in *Public ACCORD*, while Sects. 4.4 and 4.5 assess the impact of adopting uncooperative and selfish behaviour in *Private ACCORD*.

## 4.1    Experimental Methodology

Each experiment is run on 10 randomly generated datasets. A dataset is comprised of 50 tasks, which are auctioned in sequential order. Each task consists of 8 subtasks, chosen randomly from a set of 20 possible subtasks. The duration of each auction is 4 minutes. If two bids of equal value are submitted, a winner is chosen randomly.

For each new dataset a population of 20 service agents is generated. Each agent is capable of performing 8 subtasks. For the purpose of these experiments it is necessary to simulate a marketplace where deadlock regularly occurs. By allowing each agent to perform 8 out of the possible 20 subtasks, a high level of competition and consequently deadlock regularly occurs in our simulation environment.

The monetary amount each agent will charge for subtask completion must also be generated. For each subtask $s_z \in S$ (where $S$ is the set of all possible subtasks), we have randomly selected a mean cost, $V_{s_z}$, with a uniform distribution between 10 and 99. To simulate uncertainty of information, each agent chooses the monetary amount it will charge for completion of $s_z$ by using a Normal distribution with a standard deviation of 2 and a mean equal to $V_{s_z}$.

For each of the 10 datasets generated, the performance of 4 differing behaviour types (described later) is contrasted. Within the simulated marketplace of 20 agents, each agent will exhibit 1 of the 4 behaviours (5 agents for each behaviour). The subtask capabilities are also represented equally amongst agents exhibiting differing behaviours. This allows us to compare the performance of different behaviour types in an unbiased manner.

The result of a single experiment is arrived at by combining the results obtained from 10 randomly generated datasets. After each task in a dataset is auctioned, the accummulated financial reward obtained by each agent type is recorded. Therefore, the results of a single experiment are derived by summing the accumulated financial reward received by each agent type across the 10 datasets. For example, in Fig. 1 the maximum financial reward obtained by the best performing agent type is derived by summing the maximum reward obtained by that agent type in each of the 10 datasets.

We characterise each agent with a function accepting two parameters, $\lambda(\alpha, \beta)$. The level of cooperation exhibited by an agent is denoted by $\alpha$, such that $0 \leq \alpha \leq 1$, $\alpha \in \mathbb{R}$. The level of selfishness displayed by an agent is defined by $\beta$, such that $0 \leq \beta \leq 4$, $\beta \in \mathbb{Z}$.

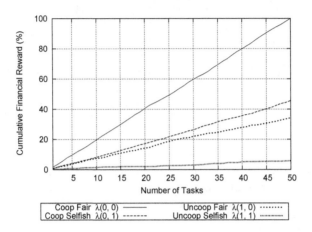

**Fig. 1.** Experiment 1: a comparison between the performance of fair ($\beta = 0$) and selfish ($\beta = 1$) behaviour for $ACCORD$.

A fair coalition proposal offers an agent an adequate financial reward for performing a specific subtask. An adequate financial reward is greater than or equal to the minimum reward the agent would expect to receive for performing the subtask. If an agent receives a fair coalition proposal, it must subsequently decide whether it will cooperate and join the proposed coalition. It bases this decision on its value of $\alpha$. The parameter $\alpha$ represents the minimum fraction of the most financially rewarding subtask that an agent is willing to accept. For example, consider our transportation model where the transportation task $Tr(A, D)$ consists of the sub-routes $Sr(A, B)$, $Sr(B, C)$ and $Sr(C, D)$. Assume that agent $t_1$ with an $\alpha$ value of 0.5 expects a monetary reward of 15 units for performing $Sr(A, B)$ and 40 units for performing $Sr(C, D)$. Therefore, its $\alpha$ value dictates that it will not accept a coalition proposal that offers less than 20 ($0.5 * 40$). Higher values of $\alpha$ imply lower cooperation. If $t_1$ in our above example had an $\alpha$ value of 0.8 then it would only accept a coalition proposal that offered it greater than or equal to 32 ($0.8 * 40$).

An agent can exhibit selfish behaviour by artificially inflating its own financial rewards. The value of $\beta$ signifies the amount by which an agent increases its financial reward. For example, assume the agent $t_1$ with $\beta = 0$ expects a financial reward of 40 units for performing $Sr(C, D)$. If the configuration of $t_1$ is changed so that it has $\beta = 1$ it would now expect a financial reward of 41 units for performing $Sr(C, D)$. Agents with $\beta = 0$ exhibit fair behaviour because they do not artificially inflate their own financial rewards.

## 4.2 Fair/Selfish Behaviour in *Public ACCORD*

To investigate the effect of different levels of selfishness ($\beta$) in *Public ACCORD*, we perform 4 experiments that contrast the performance of fair ($\beta = 0$) and selfish ($\beta > 0$) agents. In Experiment 1 we contrast the performance of selfish agents where $\beta = 1$ with fair agents ($\beta = 0$). The 4 agent types that populate the market-place are Cooperative Fair ($\lambda(0,0)$), Cooperative Selfish ($\lambda(0,1)$), Uncooperative Fair ($\lambda(1,0)$) and Uncooperative Selfish ($\lambda(1,1)$).

The details for Experiments 2–4 are the same, except that selfish agents use $\beta = 2$ in Experiment 2, $\beta = 3$ in Experiment 3 and $\beta = 4$ in Experiment 4.

The results obtained from Experiment 1 are presented in Fig. 1. The Cooperative Fair $\lambda(0,0)$ agent type is dominant and obtains the maximum earned reward, which is depicted as 100% in Fig. 1. The cumulative financial reward of all 4 agent types is measured as a percentage of this maximum financial reward. The Cooperative Fair $\lambda(0,0)$ agent type outperforms their selfish equivalent, $\lambda(0,1)$. Likewise, the Uncooperative Fair $\lambda(1,0)$ agent type outperforms their selfish equivalent $\lambda(1,1)$.

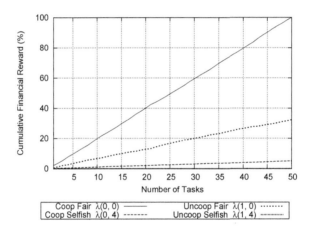

**Fig. 2.** Comparing performance of fair ($\beta = \mathbf{0}$) and selfish ($\beta = \mathbf{4}$) behaviour for *Public ACCORD*.

The results obtained from Experiment 4 are depicted in Fig. 2. As with Experiment 1 the cumulative financial reward of all 4 agent types is measured as a percentage of the maximum financial reward obtained by the dominant Cooperative Fair $\lambda(0,0)$ agent type. When the results of Experiment 4 are compared with those of Experiment 1, it can be seen that an increase in $\beta$ to 4 has resulted in a degradation in the performance of the selfish agent types.

An overview of the results obtained by cooperative agents in the Experiments 1–4 are presented in Fig. 3. The performance of the Cooperative Fair $\lambda(0,0)$ agent type over Experiments 1–4 is normalised as 100%. Figure 3 measures the performance of the Cooperative Selfish agent types ($\lambda(0,1)$, $\lambda(0,2)$,

$\lambda(0,3)$, $\lambda(0,4)$) in the Experiments 1–4 as a percentage of the performance of the Cooperative Fair agent type. The Cooperative Fair $\lambda(0,0)$ agent type exhibits the best performance in Fig. 3. It is evident from the results depicted that an increase in the value of $\beta$ corresponds to a decrease in performance. It should be noted that agents experience a short period of instability at the commencement of the experiments. This instability corresponds to the period in which each agent attempts to learn about the other service agents with whom it shares the market-place. While this instability is an undesirable property of our coalition formation protocol it is necessary in order to allow agents to accurately identify coalition partners.

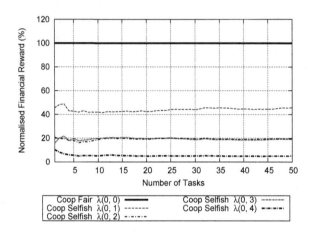

**Fig. 3.** Overview of fair ($\beta = 0$) and selfish ($\beta > 0$) behaviour for *Public ACCORD*.

## 4.3   Cooperative/Uncooperative Behaviour in *Public ACCORD*

To investigate the effect of different levels of cooperation ($\alpha$), Experiments 5–8 are performed. The objective of these experiments is to contrast the performance of cooperative ($\alpha = 0$) and uncooperative ($0 < \alpha \le 1$) agents. In Experiment 5, we examine the performance of uncooperative agents that use $\alpha = 0.25$ with cooperative agents ($\alpha = 0$). The 4 agent types that populate the market-place for Experiment 5 are Cooperative Fair $\lambda(0,0)$, Cooperative Selfish $\lambda(0,2)$, Uncooperative Fair $\lambda(0.25,0)$ and Uncooperative Selfish $\lambda(0.25,2)$. The details for Experiments 6–8 are the same, except that uncooperative agents use $\alpha = 0.5$ in Experiment 6, $\alpha = 0.75$ in Experiment 7 and $\alpha = 1$ in Experiment 8.

Figure 4 contains the results of Experiment 5. Again the Cooperative Fair $\lambda(0,0)$ agent type performs best, outperforming its uncooperative equivalent $\lambda(0.25,0)$. The cooperative selfish $\lambda(0,2)$ agent type also outperforms its uncooperative equivalent $\lambda(0.25,2)$.

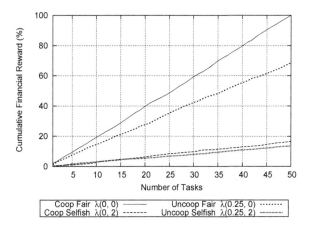

**Fig. 4.** Comparing performance of cooperative ($\alpha = \mathbf{0}$) and uncooperative ($\alpha = \mathbf{0.25}$) behaviour for *Public ACCORD*.

Experiment 8 contrasts the performance of cooperative agents using $\alpha = 0$ and uncooperative agents using $\alpha = 1$. The results are presented in Fig. 5. Again the Cooperative Fair $\lambda(0, 0)$ agent type is dominant. It is interesting to compare the results of Experiment 5 and 8. The uncooperative agent types in Experiment 5 ($\lambda(0.25, 0)$ and $\lambda(0.25, 2)$) perform better than the uncooperative agent types in Experiment 8 ($\lambda(1, 0)$ and $\lambda(1, 2)$). This indicates that by increasing its value of $\alpha$, an agent experiences a loss in performance.

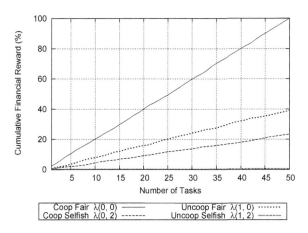

**Fig. 5.** Comparing performance of cooperative ($\alpha = \mathbf{0}$) and uncooperative ($\alpha = \mathbf{1}$) behaviour for *Public ACCORD*.

This conclusion is further supported by Fig. 6, which contains an overview of the results obtained by fair agents in the Experiments 5–8. As a fair agent reduces its value of $\alpha$ it experiences a corresponding degradation in performance. This result demonstrates the dominance of cooperative behaviour ($\alpha = 0$) in *Public ACCORD*.

The period of instability present in Fig. 3 is repeated in Fig. 6. However, it takes longer to stabilise in Fig. 6. This suggests that it is more difficult for agents to accurately identify uncooperative agents as opposed to selfish agents. This effect can be attributed to the fact that agents participating in *Public ACCORD* are made immediately aware of the financial demands of the participating agents. Therefore, the identification of selfish behaviour is a relatively straight forward process. However, the level of cooperative behaviour possessed by various agents is not known in advance and must be learned through interaction. This effect manifests itself in the form of increased initial instability.

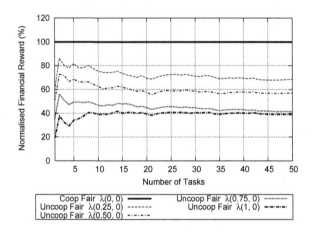

**Fig. 6.** Overview of cooperative ($\alpha = 0$) and uncooperative ($0 < \alpha \leq 1$) behaviour for *Public ACCORD*.

### 4.4   Fair/Selfish Behaviour in *Private ACCORD*

The experiments undertaken in this section investigate the effect of different levels of selfish behaviour ($\beta$) amongst agents participating in *Private ACCORD*. Experiments 9–12 are executed in the *Private ACCORD* environment. As in Sect. 4.2 these experiments contrast the performance of fair ($\beta = 0$) and selfish ($\beta > 0$) agents. The agent population setup for Experiments 9–12 is the same as the setup used for Experiments 1–4 respectively. For example, selfish agents use $\beta = 1$ in Experiment 9, $\beta = 2$ in Experiment 10, $\beta = 3$ in Experiment 11 and $\beta = 4$ in Experiment 12.

The results obtained from Experiment 9 are depicted in Fig. 7. The Cooperative Fair ($\lambda(0,0)$) agent type significantly outperforms all other agent types. The results from Experiment 12 are presented in Fig. 8. Again the Cooperative Fair ($\lambda(0,0)$) agent type is dominant. The 2 selfish agent types (($\lambda(1,4)$) and ($\lambda(0,4)$)) perform badly, coming second last and last respectively.

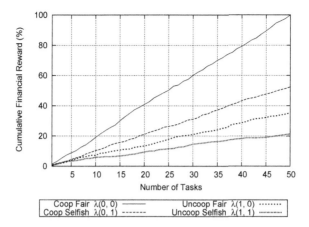

**Fig. 7.** Comparing performance of fair ($\beta = 0$) and selfish ($\beta = 1$) behaviour for *Private ACCORD*.

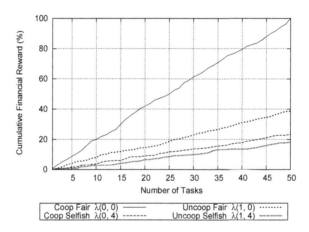

**Fig. 8.** Comparing performance of fair ($\beta = 0$) and selfish ($\beta = 4$) behaviour for *Private ACCORD*.

Figure 9 presents an overview of the results obtained by cooperative agents in Experiments 9–12. The results confirm that the performance of an agent type decreases as it increases its value of $\beta$. It is also interesting to compare the overview of selfish variation in *Private ACCORD* (Fig. 9) with that of selfish variation in *Public ACCORD* (Fig. 3). The selfish agent types in *Private ACCORD* outperform their equivalent agents in *Public ACCORD*, confirming that selfish behaviour is more severely punished in *Public ACCORD* than in *Private ACCORD*. It can also be observed that the initial period of instability experienced by agents in Fig. 3 is also present in Fig. 9. However, not only is the duration of the instability experienced in Fig. 9 longer than that experienced in Fig. 3 but the degree of variance present is also more severe. As mentioned in

Sect. 4.3 this period of instability is attributed to the learning process that each agent must undergo. That is, each agent must learn about the other agents with whom they share the market-place. However, in *Public ACCORD* each agent is already aware of the price other agents require for performing specific subtasks. Therefore, an agent need only learn about the level of cooperation exhibited by other agents. However, agents participating in *Private ACCORD* are unaware of the financial demands of other agents and consequently face a more complicated and time consuming learning task. This is reflected in the increased instability present in Fig. 9.

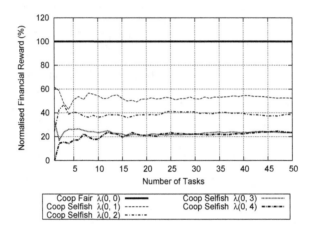

**Fig. 9.** Overview of fair $(\beta = 0)$ and selfish $(1 \leq \beta \leq 4)$ behaviour for *Private ACCORD*.

### 4.5   Cooperative/Uncooperative Behaviour in *Private ACCORD*

In order to assess the impact of varying levels of uncooperative behaviour in *Private ACCORD*, 4 experiments (numbered 13–16) are performed. The agent population setup for these experiments is the same as for Experiments 5–8. The only difference is that Experiments 13–16 are run on the *Private ACCORD* simulation environment instead of the *Public ACCORD* environment. Uncooperative agents use, $\alpha = 0.25$ in Experiment 13, $\alpha = 0.5$ in Experiment 14, $\alpha = 0.75$ in Experiment 15 and $\alpha = 1$ in Experiment 16.

The results obtained from Experiment 13 are depicted in Fig. 10. As with the previous experiments the Cooperative Fair $(\lambda(0,0))$ agent type outperforms all other agent types. It is interesting to contrast the results of this experiment with those obtained from the equivalent experiment (Experiment 5) performed on the *Public ACCORD* simulation environment. The uncooperative agent types $(\lambda(0.25,0)$ and $\lambda(0.25,2))$ perform better when participating in *Private ACCORD* (Experiment 13) than they do in *Public ACCORD* (Experiment 5). This indicates that uncooperative behaviour is less advantageous in *Public ACCORD* than it is in *Private ACCORD*.

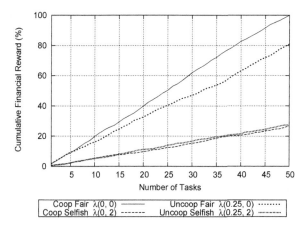

**Fig. 10.** Comparing performance of cooperative ($\alpha = \mathbf{0}$) and uncooperative ($\alpha = \mathbf{0.25}$) behaviour for *Private ACCORD*.

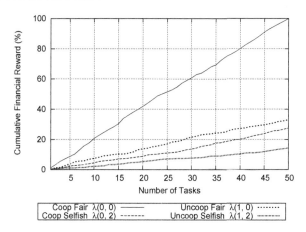

**Fig. 11.** Comparing performance of cooperative ($\alpha = \mathbf{0}$) and uncooperative ($\alpha = \mathbf{1}$) behaviour for *Private ACCORD*.

The results of Experiment 16 are presented in Fig. 11. The cooperative agent types outperform their uncooperative equivalents. When comparing the results of Experiment 13 and 16 it is noticeable that an increase in the level of uncooperative behaviour has resulted in a corresponding drop in the performance of the uncooperative agent types. In particular the uncooperative fair ($\lambda(1,0)$) agent type has experienced a performance drop of almost 50%. It is interesting to contrast the results of Experiment 16 and its equivalent *Public ACCORD* experiment (Experiment 8). The results prove to be quite similar; the only notable difference is that the Uncooperative Selfish ($\lambda(1,2)$) agent type performs much better when participating in *Private ACCORD* (Experiment 16) than it does when participating in *Public ACCORD* (Experiment 8). Again this indicates that *Private ACCORD* does not punish uncooperative behaviour as severely as *Public ACCORD*.

An overview of the results obtained by fair agents in the Experiments 13–16 are presented in Fig. 12.

On examination of Fig. 12 it is apparent that a significant period of instability occurs at the commencement of each of the experiments. The Cooperative Fair ($\lambda(0,0)$) agent type is outperformed briefly by the Uncooperative Fair ($\lambda(0.25,0)$) agent type at the beginning of Experiment 13. The performance of each agent type stabilises over the duration of the experiment. While the initial instability in Fig. 12 is an undesirable attribute of *Private ACCORD*, it is still necessary in order for each agent to learn about the other agents in the marketplace and identify potential partners. Apart from initially being outperformed the Cooperative Fair ($\lambda(0,0)$) agent type still proves to be dominant. The instability present in Fig. 12 is more severe than that present in Fig. 6, which presents an overview of uncooperative behaviour in *Public ACCORD*. This is consistent with our previous observation that *Private ACCORD* experiences greater initial instability than *Public ACCORD* (Sect. 4.4). This was attributed to the increased complexity of learning about other agents in *Private ACCORD*.

It is also interesting to compare the instability that occurs in Fig. 12 and in Fig. 9, which presents an overview of selfish behaviour in *Private ACCORD*. The instability present in Fig. 9 is visibly less severe than that encountered in Fig. 12. This indicates that learning to identify uncooperative agents represents a more difficult task than learning to identify selfish agents. This is to be expected because of the inherent inconsistency of uncooperative behaviour. While a selfish agent behaves selfishly all the time, uncooperative agents may only exhibit uncooperative behaviour occasionally. An uncooperative agent will only adopt uncooperative behaviour if the monetary amount it expects to receive from a

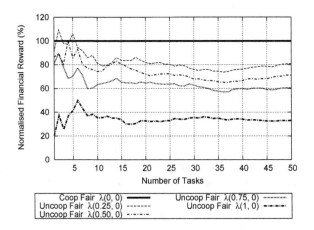

**Fig. 12.** Overview of cooperative ($\alpha = 0$) and uncooperative ($0 < \alpha \leq 1$) behaviour for *Private ACCORD*.

coalition proposal fails to exceed its threshold value. Therefore, an agent with $\alpha = 0.25$ may rarely adopt uncooperative behaviour. As a result of the this inconsistency, uncooperative agents are more difficult to identify than selfish agents.

As expected, Fig. 12 demonstrates that as an agent increases its level of uncooperative behaviour its performance degrades. By comparing the results of Figs. 12 and 6, which assesses the impact of uncooperative behaviour in *Public ACCORD*, we can conclude that agents adopting uncooperative behaviour achieve a higher level of performance when participating in *Private ACCORD* than they do in *Public ACCORD*. This confirms that uncooperative behaviour is less severely punished in *Private ACCORD* than in *Public ACCORD*.

## 5 Conclusions

This paper has presented the *Public* and *Private ACCORD* coalition formation protocols. Specifically, it has presented detailed empirical results for both protocols. The results demonstrate that cooperative and fair behaviour is dominant, thus enabling us to overcome the issues of deadlock and artificial inflation of financial rewards. This solves the problems of deadlock and the artificial inflation of financial rewards because both *Public* and *Private ACCORD* motivate agents to act in a cooperative and fair manner.

The empirical results clearly show that the cooperative and fair behaviour obtains better results in *Public ACCORD* as agents are required to reveal their monetary valuations for subtasks. The results also consistently showed a period of instability in both *Public* and *Private ACCORD*, which corresponds to the duration of the agent learning process. The revelation of subtask values means the instability experienced in *Public ACCORCD* is significantly less than that encountered in *Private ACCORD*.

We hypothesize that the incorporation of a reputation-based mechanism would help mitigate this initial period of instability. Previous work in this area has demonstrated that the exploitative tendency of selfish agents could be effectively curbed with the incorporation of reputation mechanism [2].

## References

1. Scully, T., Madden, M.G.: Forming coalitions in self-interested multi-agent environments through the promotion of fair and cooperative behaviour. In: Bulling, N. (ed.) EUMAS 2014. LNCS (LNAI), vol. 8953, pp. 144–158. Springer, Heidelberg (2015). doi:10.1007/978-3-319-17130-2_10
2. Sen, S., Dutta, P.: Searching for optimal coalition structures. In: Proceedings Fourth International Conference on MultiAgent Systems, pp. 287–292 (2000)
3. Scully, T., Madden, M.G.: Promoting cooperation and fairness in self-interested multi-agent systems. In: Proceedings of the 8th International Conference on Agents and Artificial Intelligence, pp. 172–180 (2016)

4. Sun, Q., Yu, W., Kochurov, N., Hao, Q., Hu, F.: A multi-agent-based intelligent sensor and actuator network design for smart house and home automation. J. Sens. Actuator Netw. **2**(3), 557–588 (2013)

5. Ye, D., Zhang, M., Sutanto, D.: Self-adaptation-based dynamic coalition formation in a distributed agent network: a mechanism and a brief survey. Parallel Distrib. Syst. **24**(5), 1042–1051 (2013)

6. Vassileva, J., Breban, S., Horsch, M.: Agent reasoning mechanism for long-term coalitions based on decision making and trust. Comput. Intell. **18**(4), 583–595 (2002)

7. Bachrach, Y., Kohli, P., Kolmogorov, V., Zadimoghaddam, M.: Optimal coalition structure generation in cooperative graph games finding the optimal coalitional structure. In: Twenty-Seventh AAAI Conference on Artificial Intelligence, pp. 81–87 (2013)

8. Rahwan, T., Ramchurn, S.: An anytime algorithm for optimal coalition structure generation. J. Artif. Intell. **34**, 521–567 (2009)

9. Iwasaki A., Ueda S., Yokoo M.: Finding the core for coalition structure utilizing dual solution. In: IEEE/WIC/ACM International Joint Conferences on Web Intelligence (WI), Intelligent Agent Technologies (IAT), pp. 114–121 (2013)

10. Dan, W., Cai, Y., Zhou, L., Wang, J.: A cooperative communication scheme based on coalition formation game in clustered wireless sensor networks. IEEE Trans. Wireless Commun. **11**(3), 1190–1200 (2012)

11. Xu, B., Zhang, R., Yu, J.: Improved multi-objective evolutionary algorithm for multi-agent coalition formation. J. Softw. **8**, 2991–2995 (2013)

12. Sandholm, T., Lesser, V.: Coalitions among computationally bounded agents. Artif. Intell. Spec. Issue Econ. Principles Multi-Agent Syst. **94**, 99–137 (1997)

13. Tošić, P.T., Ordonez, C.: Distributed protocols for multi-agent coalition formation: a negotiation perspective. In: Huang, R., Ghorbani, A.A., Pasi, G., Yamaguchi, T., Yen, N.Y., Jin, B. (eds.) AMT 2012. LNCS, vol. 7669, pp. 93–102. Springer, Heidelberg (2012). doi:10.1007/978-3-642-35236-2_10

14. Smirnov, A., Sheremetov, L.: Models of coalition formation among cooperative agents: the current state and prospects of research. Sci. Tech. Inf. Process. **39**, 283–292 (2012)

15. Ghaffarizadeh, A., Allan, V.: History based coaliton formation in hedonic conext using trust. Int. J. Artif. Intell. Appl. **4** (2013)

16. Aziz, H., Brandt, F., Seedig, H.: Stable partitions in additively separable hedonic games. Auton. Agents Multiagent Syst. **1**, 183–190 (2011)

17. Genin, T., Aknine, S.: Constraining self-interested agents to guarantee pareto optimality in multiagent coalition formation problem. In: IEEE/WIC/ACM International Conferences on Web Intelligence, Intelligent Agent Technology, pp. 369–372 (2011)

# Modeling the Directionality of Attention During Spatial Language Comprehension

Thomas Kluth[1(✉)], Michele Burigo[1], and Pia Knoeferle[2]

[1] Language & Cognition Group, CITEC (Cognitive Interaction Technology
Excellence Cluster), Bielefeld University, Inspiration 1, 33619 Bielefeld, Germany
{tkluth,mburigo}@cit-ec.uni-bielefeld.de
[2] Department of German Language and Linguistics, Humboldt University,
Unter den Linden 6, 10099 Berlin, Germany
pia.knoeferle@hu-berlin.de

**Abstract.** It is known that the comprehension of spatial prepositions
involves the deployment of visual attention. For example, consider the
sentence "The salt is to the left of the stove". Researchers [29,30] have
theorized that people must shift their attention from the stove (the reference object, RO) to the salt (the located object, LO) in order to compre-
hend the sentence. Such a shift was also implicitly assumed in the Attentional Vector Sum (AVS) model by [35], a cognitive model that computes
an acceptability rating for a spatial preposition given a display that contains an RO and an LO. However, recent empirical findings showed that
a shift from the RO to the LO is not necessary to understand a spatial
preposition ([3], see also [15,38]). In contrast, these findings suggest that
people perform a shift in the reverse direction (i.e., from the LO to the
RO). Thus, we propose the reversed AVS (rAVS) model, a modified version of the AVS model in which attention shifts from the LO to the RO.
We assessed the AVS and the rAVS model on the data from [35] using
three model simulation methods. Our simulations show that the rAVS
model performs as well as the AVS model on these data while it also integrates the recent empirical findings. Moreover, the rAVS model achieves
its good performance while being less flexible than the AVS model. (This
article is an updated and extended version of the paper [23] presented
at the 8th International Conference on Agents and Artificial Intelligence
in Rome, Italy. The authors would like to thank Holger Schultheis for
helpful discussions about the additional model simulation.)

**Keywords:** Spatial language · Spatial prepositions · Cognitive modeling · Model flexibility · Visual attention

## 1   Introduction

Imagine a household robot that helps you in the kitchen. You might want the
robot to pass you the salt and instruct it as follows: "Could you pass me the
salt? It is to the left of the stove". Here, the salt is the located object (LO),

© Springer International Publishing AG 2017
J. van den Herik and J. Filipe (Eds.): ICAART 2016, LNAI 10162, pp. 283–301, 2017.
DOI: 10.1007/978-3-319-53354-4_16

because it should be located relative to the reference object (RO, the stove). To find the salt, the robot should interpret this sentence the way you intended it. In the interaction with artificial systems, humans often instruct artificial systems to interact with objects in their environment. To this end, artificial systems must interpret spatial language, i.e., language that describes the locations of the objects of interest. To make the interaction as natural as possible, artificial systems should understand spatial language the way humans do. The implementation of psychologically validated computational models of spatial language into artificial systems might thus prove useful. With these kind of models, artificial systems could begin to interpret and generate human-like spatial language.

[30] were the first to outline a computational framework of the processes that are assumed to take place when humans understand spatial language. Their framework consists of "four different kinds of processes: spatial indexing, reference frame adjustment, spatial template alignment, and computing goodness of fit" [30, p. 500].

*Spatial indexing* is required to bind the perceptual representations of the RO and the LO to their corresponding conceptual representations. According to [30, p. 499], "the viewer's attention should move from the reference object to the located object". *Reference frame adjustment* consists of imposing a *reference frame* on the RO and setting its parameters (origin, orientation, direction, scale). "The reference frame is a three-dimensional coordinate system [...]" [30, p. 499]. *Spatial template alignment* is the process of imposing a *spatial template* on the RO that is aligned with the reference frame. A spatial template consists of regions of acceptability of a spatial relation. Every spatial relation is assumed to have its own spatial template. Finally, *computing goodness of fit* is the evaluation of the location of the LO in the aligned spatial template.

Trying to identify possible nonlinguistic mechanisms that underlie the rating of spatial prepositions, [35] developed a cognitive model: the Attentional Vector Sum (AVS) model.[1] This model – based on the assumption that goodness-of-fit ratings for spatial prepositions against depicted objects reflect language processing – accounts for a range of empirical findings in spatial language processing. A central mechanism in the AVS model concerns the role of attention for the understanding of spatial relations.

*Direction of the Attentional Shift.* Previous research has shown that visual attention is needed to process spatial relations ([28–30]; see [7] for a review). The AVS model has formalized the role of visual attention. Although [35] do not explicitly talk about attentional shifts, the AVS model can be interpreted as assuming a shift of attention from the RO to the LO. [35] motivate the implementation of attention based on studies conducted by [28] and [29, p. 115]: "The linguistic distinction between located and reference objects specifies a direction for attention to move – from the reference object to the located object." (See also [30, p. 499]: "the viewer's attention should move from the reference object to

---

[1] Apart from the AVS model, a range of other computational models of spatial language processing were also proposed, e.g., [5, 16, 19, 36, 39].

the located object".) But are humans actually shifting their attention in this direction while they are understanding a spatial preposition?

Evidence for shifts of covert attention comes from studies in the field of cognitive neuroscience by Franconeri and colleagues [15,38]. Using EEG, [15] showed that humans shift their covert attention when they process spatial relations. In their first experiment, they presented four objects of which two had the same shape but different colors. Two objects were placed to the right and two objects were placed to the left of a fixation cross such that two different shapes appeared on each side of the cross. Participants had to fixate the fixation cross and judge whether, say, the orange circle was left or right of the cyan circle. After the stimulus display was shown, participants chose one spatial relation out of two possible arrangements on a response screen (cyan circle left of orange circle or orange circle left of cyan circle). During the experiment, event-related potentials were recorded. All experiments reported in [15] revealed that participants shifted their attention from one object to the other object, although they had been instructed to attend to both objects simultaneously. However, the role of the *direction* of these shifts remained unclear in [15].

In another experiment, [38] presented questions like "Is red left of green?" to participants. Subsequently, either a red or a green object appeared on the screen, followed shortly afterwards (0–233 ms) by a green or a red object respectively. By manipulating the presentation order of the objects, a shift of attention was cued. Participants were faster to verify the question if the presentation order was the same as the order in the question. [38] interpreted this as evidence that the perceptual representation of a spatial relation follows its linguistic representation.

Evidence that a shift of attention from the RO to the LO as suggested in the AVS model is not necessary for understanding spatial language has been recently reported by [3], who conducted a visual world study. Here, participants inspected a display and listened to spoken utterances while their eye movements were recorded. Note that [3] investigated *overt* attention ([15,38] studied *covert* attention). [3] presented sentences with two German spatial prepositions (*über* [*above*] and *unter* [*below*]) across four different tasks. The RO and the LO of the sentence as well as a competitor object (not mentioned in the sentence) were presented on a computer screen. In their first experiment, participants verified the spatial sentence as quickly as possible, even before the sentence ended. In their second experiment, participants also verified the sentence, but they had to wait until the sentence was over. The third experiment consisted of a passive listening task, i.e., no response was required from the participants. Finally, in the fourth experiment, a gaze-contingent trigger was used: the competitor object and either the LO or the RO were removed from the display after participants had inspected the LO at least once.

The results from this study revealed that participants shifted their overt attention from the RO to the LO, as predicted by the AVS model. However, the task modulated the presence of these shifts. These shifts were only frequent in the post-sentence verification experiment (experiment 2), but infrequent in the other experiments. Crucially, if participants did not shift their attention from the RO to the LO, they performed equally well (as accuracy was not affected) – i.e., they were able to understand the sentence without shifting their attention overtly from the RO to the LO.

By contrast, participants frequently shifted gaze overtly from the LO towards the RO (in line with the incremental interpretation of the spoken sentence). This suggested that people may be able to apprehend a spatial relation with an overt attentional shift from the LO to the RO (and not from the RO to the LO as suggested by the AVS model).

Thus, the direction of the attentional shift as implemented in the AVS model conflicts with recent empirical findings. We propose a modified version of the AVS model: the reversed AVS (rAVS) model, for which the attentional shift has been reversed. Instead of a shift from the RO to the LO, we implemented a shift from the LO to the RO. We designed the rAVS model otherwise to be as similar as possible to the AVS model. By doing so, we can isolate the influence of the reversed shift on the performance of the two models.

## 2   The Models

In this section, we first describe the AVS model, since the proposed rAVS model is based on the structure of the AVS model and modifies some parts of it. Next, we introduce the rAVS model.

### 2.1   The AVS Model

[35] proposed a cognitive model of spatial term comprehension: the Attentional Vector Sum (AVS) model. The AVS model takes the 2D-location and the 2D-shape of a RO, the 2D-location of a LO, and a spatial preposition as input and computes an acceptability rating (i.e., how well the preposition describes the location of the LO relative to the RO). In the following, we are presenting how the AVS model processes the spatial relation between the RO and the LO and how it computes the acceptability rating. The AVS model consists of two components: The angular component and the height component. Figures 1a–c depict the angular component which we describe first. Figure 1d visualizes the height component that we describe thereafter.

*Angular Component.* First, the AVS model defines the focus $F$ of a distribution of visual attention as the point on top of the RO "that is vertically aligned with the trajector [LO] or closest to being so aligned"[2] [35, p. 277]. Next, the model defines the distribution of attention on every point $i$ of the RO as follows (see Fig. 1a for visualization):

$$a_i = \exp\left(\frac{-d_i}{\lambda \cdot \sigma}\right) \qquad (1)$$

---

[2] In the case of other prepositions, the corresponding part of the RO is chosen for the location of the focus (e.g., the focus lies on the bottom of the RO for *below*).

Here, $d_i$ is the euclidean distance between point $i$ of the RO and the attentional focus $F$, $\sigma$ is the euclidean distance between the attentional focus $F$ and the LO, and $\lambda$ is a free parameter. The resulting distribution of attention is highest at the focal point F and declines exponentially with greater distance from F (see Fig. 1a). Furthermore, the distance $\sigma$ of the LO to the RO as well as the free parameter $\lambda$ affect the width of the attentional distribution: A close LO results in a more focused attentional distribution (a large decline of attention from point F) whereas a distant LO results in a more broad attentional distribution (a small decline of attention from point F).

In the next step, vectors $v_i$ are rooted at every point $i$ of the RO. All vectors are pointing to the LO and are weighted with the amount of attention $a_i$ that was previously defined (see Fig. 1b). All these vectors are summed up to obtain a final vector:

$$\overrightarrow{direction} = \sum_{i \in RO} a_i \cdot \vec{v}_i \tag{2}$$

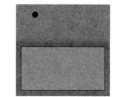

(a) Attentional Distribution. Darker color means higher amount of attention. Attention is maximal at the focal point $F$. $\sigma$ denotes the distance of the LO to point $F$.

(b) Population of vectors weighted with attention as shown in Figure 1a. On every point of the RO one vector is rooted. Every vector points to the LO.

(c) Deviation $\delta$ of the final vector from canonical upright (dashed line). The final vector does not necessarily point to the LO, because it is the weighted sum of all vectors in Figure 1b.

(d) Height Component. Red means a value of 1 and blue means a value of 0. The height component is multiplied with the outcome of the angular component.

**Fig. 1.** Schematized steps of the AVS model developed by [35]. (Color figure online)

The deviation $\delta$ of this final vector to canonical upright (in the case of *above*) is measured (see Fig. 1c) and used to obtain a rating with the help of the linear function $g(\delta)$ that maps high deviations to low ratings and low deviations to high ratings:

$$g(\delta) = slope \cdot \delta + intercept \tag{3}$$

Both, *slope* and *intercept*, are free parameters and $\delta$ is the angle between the sum of the vectors and canonical upright (in the case of *above*):

$$\delta = \angle(\overrightarrow{direction}, upright) \tag{4}$$

*Height Component.* $g(\delta)$ is the last step of the angular component. This value is then multiplied with the height component. The height component modulates the final outcome with respect to the elevation of the LO relative to the top of the RO: A height component of 0 results in a low rating, whereas a height component of 1 does not change the output of the angular component. The height component is defined as follows:

$$\text{height}(y_{LO}) = \frac{\text{sig}(y_{LO} - hightop, highgain) + \text{sig}(y_{LO} - lowtop, 1)}{2} \quad (5)$$

Here, *highgain* is a free parameter, *hightop* (or *lowtop*) is the y-coordinate of the highest (or lowest) point on top of the RO, and the $\text{sig}(\cdot, \cdot)$ function is defined as:

$$\text{sig}(x, gain) = \frac{1}{1 + \exp\left(gain \cdot (-x)\right)} \quad (6)$$

The AVS model has four free parameters in total: $\lambda, slope, intercept,$ *highgain*. Taken together, the final acceptability rating is computed by the AVS model with the following formula:

$$\text{above}(LO, RO) = g\left(\delta\right) \cdot \text{height}(y_{LO}) \quad (7)$$

## 2.2    The rAVS Model

Although [35] do not explicitly mention shifts of attention, the AVS model can be interpreted as assuming a shift of attention from the RO to the LO: This shift is implemented by the location of the attentional focus and in particular by the direction of the vectors (see Figs. 1a–c). As discussed before, this direction of the attentional shift conflicts with recent empirical findings [3,15,38]. This is why our modified version of the AVS model, the reversed AVS (rAVS) model, implements a shift from the LO to the RO.

To this end, the rAVS model reverses the direction of the vectors in the vector sum in the following way: Instead of pointing from every point in the RO to the LO, the vectors are pointing from every point in the LO to the RO. Since the LO is simplified as a single point in the AVS model, the vector sum in the rAVS model consists of only one vector. The end point of this vector, however, must be defined, since the RO has a mass.

In the rAVS model, the vector end point $D$ lies on the line between the center-of-mass $C$ of the RO and the proximal point $F$ (see Fig. 2a). Here, $F$ is the same point as the attentional focus in the AVS model. Depending on the relative distance of the LO, the vector end point $D$ is closer to $C$ (for distant LOs) or closer to $F$ (for close LOs). Thus, the center-of-mass orientation is more important for distant LOs, whereas the proximal orientation becomes important for close LOs, which corresponds to the rating pattern found by [35, experiment 7]. The width of the attentional distribution in the AVS model has a similar effect.

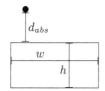

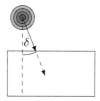

| **(a)** Vector destination $D$ lies always on the line that connects the center-of-mass of the RO (C) and F. | **(b)** Relative distance: Absolute distance $d_{abs}$ divided by the width $w$ and height $h$ of the RO. | **(c)** Deviation $\delta$ of the vector $\overrightarrow{LO, D}$ from canonical downwards (dashed line). | **(d)** The attentional distribution does not change the deviation $\delta$. |
|---|---|---|---|

**Fig. 2.** Schematized steps of the rAVS model.

In the rAVS model, the distance of a LO is considered in relative terms, i.e., the width and height of the RO change the relative distance of a LO, even if the absolute distance remains the same (see Fig. 2b). The relative distance is computed as follows:

$$d_{rel.}(LO, RO) = \frac{|LO, P|_x}{RO_{width}} + \frac{|LO, P|_y}{RO_{height}} \tag{8}$$

Here, $P$ is the proximal point in the intuitive sense: The point on the RO that has the smallest absolute distance to the LO. $F$ is guaranteed to lie on top of the RO, whereas $P$ can also be at the left, right, or bottom of the RO. If $P$ is on top of the RO, $P$ equals $F$.

Furthermore, the computation of the vector end point $D$ is guided with an additional free parameter $\alpha$ (with $\alpha \geq 0$). The new parameter $\alpha$ and the relative distance interact within the following linear function to obtain the new vector destination $D$:

$$D = \begin{cases} \overrightarrow{LO, C} + (-\alpha \cdot d_{rel.} + 1) \cdot \overrightarrow{CF} & \text{if } (-\alpha \cdot d_{rel.} + 1) > 0 \\ C & \text{else} \end{cases} \tag{9}$$

The direction of the vector $\overrightarrow{LO, D}$ is finally compared to canonical downwards instead of canonical upright (in the case of *above*, see Fig. 2c) – similar to the angular component of the AVS model:

$$\delta = \angle(\overrightarrow{LO, D}, \ downwards) \tag{10}$$

As in the AVS model, this angular deviation is then used as input for the linear function $g(\delta)$ (see Eq. 3) to obtain a value for the angular component. Note that a comparison to downwards is modeled, although the preposition is *above*. [38, p. 7] also mention this "counterintuitive, but certainly not computationally difficult" flip of the reference direction in their account.

In the rAVS model, the attentional focus lies on the LO. In fact, however, the location of the attentional focus as well as the attentional distribution do not matter for the rAVS model, because its weighted vector sum consists of only one single vector (due to the simplified LO). Since the length of the vector sum is not considered in the computation of the angle (neither in the AVS[3] nor in the rAVS model), the amount of attention at the vector root is not of any importance for the final rating (as long as it is greater than zero, see Fig. 2d).[4]

The height component of the AVS model is not changed in the rAVS model. So, it still takes the $y$-value of the LO as input and computes the height according to the grazing line of the RO (see Eq. 5). As in the AVS model the final rating is obtained by multiplying the height component with the angular component (see Eq. 7).

## 3   Model Comparison

In the previous section, we have presented the AVS model by [35] and proposed the rAVS model, since the AVS model conflicts with recent empirical findings regarding the direction of the attentional shift [3, 15, 38]. But how does the rAVS model perform in comparison to the AVS model?

[35] conducted seven acceptability rating experiments and showed that the AVS model was able to account for all empirical data from these experiments. These data consist of acceptability ratings for $n = 337$ locations of the LO above 10 different types of ROs. We evaluated the rAVS model on the same data set[5] to assess its performance using three different model simulation methods: Goodness-Of-Fit (GOF, Sect. 3.1), Simple Hold-Out (SHO, Sect. 3.2), and Model Flexibility Analysis (MFA, Sect. 3.3). We introduce each of these simulation methods before we present its results.

Both models and all simulation methods were implemented in C++ with the help of the Computational Geometry Algorithms Library [11]. The C++ source code is available under an open source license from [21]. For all simulations, we constrained the range of the model parameters in the following way:

$$\frac{-1}{45} \le slope \le 0 \tag{11}$$

$$0.7 \le intercept \le 1.3 \tag{12}$$

$$0 \le highgain \le 10 \tag{13}$$

$$0 < \lambda \le 5 \tag{14}$$

$$0 < \alpha \le 5 \tag{15}$$

---

[3] [35, p. 276]: "A central feature of this [angular] characterization of spatial term acceptability is that it is dependent only on the direction, not the length, of the vector connecting the landmark [RO] to the trajector [LO]."

[4] Therefore, the rAVS model does not need to compute a vector *sum* nor does it rely on an underlying attentional distribution and thus has a lower computational complexity. This lower computational complexity, however, originates from the simplification of the LO. Accordingly, these considerations are also only valid for simplified LOs.

[5] We thank Terry Regier and Laura Carlson for sharing these data.

## 3.1   Goodness-Of-Fit (GOF)

**Method.** The Goodness-Of-Fit (GOF) measures how well a model fits given data. We fitted both models to the $n$ rating data points from [35] by minimizing the normalized Root Mean Square Error (nRMSE):

$$nRMSE = \frac{\sqrt{\frac{1}{n} \sum_i^n (data_i - modelOutput_i)^2}}{rating_{max} - rating_{min}} \tag{16}$$

To this end, we used a method known as simulated annealing, a variant of the Metropolis algorithm [31]. This method estimates the free parameters of the model in order to minimize the nRMSE and has the advantage to not get stuck in local minima. The nRMSE gives us a Goodness-Of-Fit (GOF) value. In contrast to the non-normalized RMSE, the normalized RMSE can be compared throughout rating experiments with different rating scales, because it always has a range from 0 to 1: An nRMSE of 0.0 means best performance (the model is able to exactly reproduce the empirical data), an nRMSE of 1.0 means worst performance (model output and data are maximally different).

**Results.** Figure 3 shows the GOF results for fitting both models to all data from [35]. The model parameters for the plotted GOFs can be found in Table 1. First of all, both models are able to account for the data very closely as is evident from the overall low nRMSE ($<0.08$ for both models). The rAVS model has a slightly worse GOF value than the AVS model but the difference to the GOF value of the AVS model is very low (difference $<0.005$) which renders this difference inconclusive. Also, the GOF values change slightly with each new estimation due to the random nature of the parameter estimation method. The most important conclusion one can draw from the GOF values is whether the models are able to fit the data at all and this is the case for the models and the data under consideration. Assessing the relative performance of more than one model solely with their GOF, however, should be done very carefully.

[37] provide a thorough discussion of the theoretical problems of using GOF as the only measure of model performance. Related to the problems discussed by [37], [34] focus on the specific problem of *overfitting*: A more flexible model might obtain a better GOF just because it is more flexible. *Model flexibility*[6] is the ability of a model to produce arbitrary output: The more different the possible output of a model, the more flexible the model. A more flexible model might fit the noise in the given data better than a less flexible model. Although this results in a better GOF, it does not add anything to the explanatory power of the model in question. We tried to overcome the problem of overfitting by applying the Simple Hold-Out (SHO) method as outlined in the next section.

---

[6] Following [41] we favor the term *model flexibility* over *model complexity* (used by, e.g., [34]). Both terms mean the same.

## 3.2    Simple Hold-Out (SHO)

**Method.** To control for the problem of overfitting, we applied a cross-validation method that takes model flexibility into account: the Simple Hold-Out (SHO) method described in [40]. [40] showed that this method performs very well in comparison to other model comparison methods. In the SHO method, the data set is split into a training and a test set. Model parameters are estimated on the training set and used to compute an nRMSE on the test set. This nRMSE is also called prediction error, because it is the error the model makes for predicting "unseen" data (the test set).[7] This procedure is repeated several times with different, random splits of the data. The median of the prediction errors is the final outcome of the SHO method.

The results presented here were computed with 101 iterations of the SHO method. In each iteration 70% of the data was used as training data and 30 % was used as test data. Moreover, we computed 95% confidence intervals of the SHO median by using 100,000 bootstrap samples with the help of the `boot` package for R [6].

**Results.** The SHO results are plotted next to the GOF results in Fig. 3. These results reveal that the slightly better GOF of the AVS model might be the result of a light overfitting, because both models obtain similar SHO values with overlapping confidence intervals for the SHO values. That is, both models perform equally well and cannot be distinguished on these data using the SHO method.

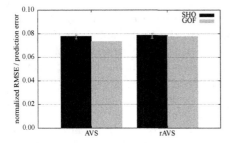

**Fig. 3.** GOF and SHO results for the AVS and the rAVS model for fitting all data from [35]. Error bars show 95% confidence intervals computed with 100,000 bootstrap samples.

**Table 1.** Values of the model parameters to achieve the GOFs shown in Fig. 3. The $\lambda$ parameter of the rAVS model does not change the output of the rAVS model, see Fig. 2d.

|           | AVS    | rAVS    |
|-----------|--------|---------|
| *slope*     | −0.005 | −0.004  |
| *intercept* | 0.973  | 0.943   |
| *highgain*  | 0.083  | 7.497   |
| $\lambda$   | 0.189  | (1.221) |
| $\alpha$    | –      | 0.322   |
| nRMSE     | 0.0735 | 0.0776  |

---

[7] The prediction error is also a measure of *model generalizability*, the property of a model to account for new empirical data, see [34].

## 3.3    Model Flexibility Analysis (MFA)

**Method.** The Model. Flexibility Analysis (MFA) proposed by [41] tries to account for another problem of using GOFs as a criterion for model evaluation stated by [37]: A model that achieves a good fit to empirical data might also fit other (possibly non-empirical) data very well. Put differently, the fact that a model fits data well does not exclude the possibility that the model might predict outcomes that humans would never generate. If the model also fits non-empirical data[8], its good fit to empirical data becomes less impressive.

Note that this problem is different from the problem for which we applied the SHO method. The SHO method accounts for overfitting, i.e., if a model fits too much noise, it will obtain a good GOF, but a worse SHO result (because predicting unseen data does not benefit from a closer fit to noisy data). Although the SHO method operates with predicting unseen data, it cannot be used for claims about all possible model predictions. This is because the SHO method uses (random) subsets of the same data set. All these subsets are in the same region of the space of possible data, namely, the region of empirically observed data. That is, a model can obtain good SHO values although it has a high flexibility (i.e., although it can generate a great range of different, possibly non-empirical data).

The MFA, however, was explicitly designed to quantify the size of the space of all possible outcomes a model can generate – regardless of whether these outcomes were empirically observed or not. This information can then be used as a measure to "know how impressed to be that theory and observation are consistent" [37, p. 359]. A good fit of a model is more impressive if the model generates (almost) only empirically observed data. A good fit is less impressive if the model also generates a great range of non-empirical data.

Given input to a model (in our case ROs and LOs), the MFA computes all possible model outputs (in our case acceptability ratings) by enumerating the whole space of the free parameters of the model. The outcome of the MFA is the proportion $\phi$ of these outputs to the size of the data space, where the data space contains all hypothetical possible data:

$$\phi = \frac{\text{number of different model outputs}}{\text{number of all possible data points}} \qquad (17)$$

If $\phi$ is low, the model is only able to compute (and thus fit) a small proportion of theoretically possible data. The lower $\phi$, the more strongly the model constrains its possible outcomes, i.e., the less flexible is the model. If $\phi$ is high, the model can compute a great range of possible data. With a high $\phi$ the model only weakly constrains its output, i.e., the model is highly flexible. As an example consider one RO with two LOs and a rating scale from 0 to 9. The space

---

[8] Note that it is difficult to call data "non-empirical". You can tell what people do, but it is harder to tell what people do not do. Given the right study design, previously considered "non-empirical" data might become empirical. Nevertheless, the greater the range of model predictions, the higher the probability that some of these predictions are at least implausible (or conflict with other generated predictions).

of theoretically possible data is then two-dimensional (two ratings) and each dimension ranges from 0 to 9. Thus, there are $10 \cdot 10 = 100$ theoretically possible data points, if we only consider integer ratings. If a model is able to compute 20 of these rating patterns, it will get the proportion $\phi = \frac{20}{100} = 0.2$, a model that can compute 80 rating patterns results in $\phi = 0.8$.

We computed the MFA proportions on the stimuli that [35] used. The dimension of the data space and each model output is 337, because [35] used 337 locations of the LO in total. We split the range of each of the four free parameters of both models into 50 intervals and computed the model output for each of these $50^4$ parameter sets (with a rating scale from 0 to 1). This gave us all outputs the models can generate with these parameter sets. Then, we divided the number of different model outputs by the number of all possible data points (see Eq. 17). To determine whether two model outputs are equal, the MFA uses a grid over the data space. If two model outputs are in the same cell of the grid, they are considered equal. [41] suggest to split each dimension of the data space into $\sqrt[n]{j^k}$ cells, where $n$ is the number of dimensions of the data space (in our case 337), $k$ is the number of free parameters (in our case 4) and $j$ is the number of intervals for each parameter (in our case 50). Accordingly, for our simulations each dimension of the data space should be split into 1.047528 cells. Since we used a rating scale from 0 to 1 for the computation of the MFA, this means that every rating between 0 and 0.954628 is mapped to the first cell and every rating between 0.954628 and 1 is mapped to the second cell. That is, almost all ratings are considered to be equal. This might not be be meaningful in our context, thus, we also considered a different splitting of the data space: Since [35] used a rating scale from 0 to 9 resulting in 10 possible, distinct ratings for each LO, we also computed the MFA with 10 cells for each dimension of the data space without changing the number of the model predictions.[9]

**Results.** The results of the MFA are shown in Table 2. The worst possible $\phi$ value is 1.0 (a model that generates all possible data), the lowest possible $\phi$ value is 0.0 (a model that generates no data). Since all $\phi$ values in Table 2 are relatively low, both models have a relatively low flexibility. However, regardless of the number of cells in the potential data space, the AVS model obtains higher $\phi$ values than the rAVS model. Thus, the AVS model is more flexible than the rAVS model which makes the good performance of the AVS model less impressive than the good performance of the rAVS model.

---

[9] One could argue that we did not compute enough model predictions to define 10 cells on each dimension of the data space. However, if we want to follow the suggestion from [41] and use $\sqrt[n]{j^k}$ cells, we would need more model predictions due to the high-dimensional data space ($n = 337$), namely $j^k = 10^{337}$, i.e. $j = 10^{\frac{337}{4}}$. Unfortunately, splitting each parameter range into $j = 100$ instead of $j = 50$ intervals already resulted in an unmanageable amount of data.

**Table 2.** Results of the Model Flexibility Analysis (MFA). The lower the $\phi$ value, the less flexible the model.

| Number of cells for each dimension of the data space | AVS | rAVS |
|---|---|---|
| $\sqrt[n]{j^k} = 1.047528$ | $\phi = 0.00041952$ | $\phi = 0.00029248$ |
| 10 | $\phi = 3.22139 \times 10^{-332}$ | $\phi = 2.7116 \times 10^{-332}$ |

## 3.4   Discussion

With the GOF and SHO simulations, we showed that both models are able to account equally well for the data from [35] and that this good performance is not the result of overfitting. Considering only these results, both attentional shifts are equally well supported. However, the AVS model also showed a greater flexibility in the MFA: the AVS model computes a greater range of possible outputs than the rAVS model. The lower flexibility of the rAVS model thus makes the good performance of the rAVS model more impressive than the good performance of the AVS model. This is because the rAVS model achieves the same performance while it also more strongly constrains the space of the model output. The rAVS model thus can be more easily falsified than the AVS model.

We asked where the greater flexibility of the AVS model originates. Computationally, the biggest difference of the two models is the computation of the final vector: The AVS model uses a weighted vector sum whereas the rAVS model only uses a linear function.[10] Thus, the vector sum seems to be the main source of the greater flexibility of the AVS model. Our results suggest that the vector sum is more flexible than is needed for the empirical data. This does not necessarily mean that the shift from the RO to the LO as assumed in the AVS model is less supported than the reversed shift. Rather, the way the shift is implemented in the AVS model might be more complex than needed.[11] However, [35] motivated the implementation of the vector sum as a possible non-linguistic mechanism underlying the linguistic process. More specifically, they used the vector sum, because it seems to be a widely used representation of direction in the brain (see discussion below). Accordingly, the vector sum is a crucial part of the model. Our results show that the AVS model has an overall low flexibility but they also show that the weighted vector sum is more flexible than the linear function used by the rAVS model. However, we did not present a model that performs better, just a model that performs equally well – with a lower flexibility. Moreover, the rAVS model does not offer a competing explanation of how the vector is

---

[10] Conceptually, the rAVS model also uses a vector sum on the LO. However, since the LO is simplified as a single point for the current model input, the rAVS model in fact does not compute a vector sum.

[11] A model that implements a shift from the RO to the LO without using a vector sum could be a modified rAVS model: One could change the direction of the vector and the reference direction. Computationally, this model computes the same output as the rAVS model.

computed (mainly because its motivation was different). At the neuronal level, this computation could still be done with a vector sum but the rAVS model does not provide details about the neuronal level.

Although our model simulations do not result in the support of one of the two shifts in question, they raise the question to which degree the attentional shift from the RO to the LO as proposed by [29] and [30] is the only shift that is implicated in the processing of spatial relations. The results from [3] suggest that humans perform both shifts, but that an overt shift from the LO to the RO alone (as in the rAVS model) can be enough to apprehend the spatial relation between the objects. The shift back (from the RO to the LO) could be a way to double-check the goodness-of-fit of the spatial preposition. Our results support this by showing that the rAVS model – that assumes only the shift from the LO to the RO – can account for the data from [35].

## 4    Conclusion

We proposed a new cognitive model for spatial language understanding: the rAVS model. This model is based on the AVS model by [35] but integrates recent psycholinguistic and neuroscientific findings [3,15,38] that conflict with the assumption of the direction of the attentional shift in the AVS model. In the AVS model, attention shifts from the RO to the LO; in the rAVS model, attention shifts from the LO to the RO. We assessed both models using the data from [35] and found that both models perform equally well, while the rAVS model is less flexible than the AVS model. Accordingly, our model simulations favor the rAVS model. Since the lower flexibility of the rAVS model originates from the lack of using a vector sum, however, the advantage of the rAVS model does not result in the favor of any of the two directionalities of the attentional shift. However, we showed that both directionalities can account for the empirical data.

*Theoretical Contribution.* [35] developed the AVS model with the goal to identify possible nonlinguistic mechanisms that underlie spatial term rating. To this end, they implemented two independent observations in the AVS model: First, the importance of attention to understand spatial relations and second, the neuronal representation of a motor movement as a vector sum. So, the main goal of the AVS model was not to examine the direction of the shift of attention but rather to describe linguistic processes with nonlinguistic mechanisms.

Although the focus of the AVS model was not on the direction of the attentional shift, the model implies a shift from the RO to the LO. [35] motivated the use of a vector sum because it seems to be a widely used representation of direction in the brain. [17] found that the direction of an arm movement of a rhesus monkey can be predicted by a vector sum of orientation tuned neurons. [27] provide evidence for a similar representation for saccadic eye movements. Eye movements (overt attention) are motor movements that are closely connected to covert visual attention: "Many studies have investigated the interaction of overt and covert attention, and the order in which they are deployed. The consensus is that covert attention precedes eye movements [...]." [10, p. 1487] Although the authors of the AVS model do not explicitly speak about which movement the vector sum in their model represents nor clearly specify the kind of attention in the model, it seems reasonable to interpret the direction of the vector sum in the AVS model as the direction of a shift of attention that goes from the RO to the LO.

Our aim was to implement the most recent findings of attentional mechanisms into the AVS model. To this end, we designed the rAVS model as similar as possible to the AVS model. So, the rAVS model follows the same basic concepts while it integrates the most recent findings. We do not claim that the nonlinguistic mechanisms proposed in the AVS model do not happen – rather, we propose an alternative way of how they might take place. That is, on the neuronal level, the orientation of the vector in the rAVS model that points from the LO to the RO could still be computed by a weighted population of neurons (similar to the attentional vector sum) but the rAVS model does not provide such details. Its focus lies on a more abstract level that concerns the *direction* of the attentional shift and not the detailed computation of this shift. Keeping the same basic concepts as the AVS model, the rAVS model accounts for the same data equally well – and also for the recent empirical findings regarding the direction of the attentional shift.

## 4.1   Future Work

*Modeling Both Shifts.* The success of both the rAVS model and the AVS model support the existence of *both* directionalities of the attentional shift. It might well be that people shift their attention in both directions during the processing of spatial relations – depending on the task and the linguistic input. Accordingly, a model that implements both attentional shifts might fit more data than the AVS or the rAVS model alone.[12]

It might be interesting to investigate this possibility by creating a model that allows both shifts of attention. Such a model should be applicable to more types of experimental data than the AVS model and the rAVS model (which both can only account for acceptability rating data). In particular, the model with both shifts should also specify when in time what type of attentional shift occurs and how long the computation takes. This model could then be fitted to a greater range of data, like real-time eye movement data from visual world studies (e.g., [3]) or reaction time data (e.g., [38]). Modeling different tasks would give more insight into the role of the attentional shift.

*Modeling the LO.* The main reason for the lower flexibility as well as the lower computational complexity of the rAVS model is the simplification of the LO as a single point. There is evidence, however, that geometric features of the LO also affect acceptability ratings [1,2,4]. A comprehensive model of spatial language thus should also model the LO in more detail. Accordingly, we are planning to extend the representation of the LO in the rAVS model by giving a mass to it. This would give us the opportunity to see first how the rAVS model

---

[12] We thank an anonymous reviewer for suggesting this idea.

deals with the situation where the computation of a vector sum is necessary to determine the angular deviation. Second, an extended LO might affect the role of the attentional distribution in the rAVS model.

We are also interested in modifying the use of the height component in the rAVS model. At the moment, the rAVS model applies the same computation as the AVS model for the height component: the y-coordinate of the LO is compared relative to the top of the RO (see Fig. 1d). In the rAVS model, the attentional focus is located on the LO. So, it would be more consistent if the location of the LO were taken as the baseline for the comparison with the location of the RO. Thus, we want to reverse the computation of the height component such that the grazing line lies on the bottom of the LO.

*Model Distinction.* To tease apart the two models and evaluate the accuracy of their predictions, we are currently analyzing the models with two more model simulation methods: the *landscaping* analysis proposed by [32,42] and an algorithm called *Parameter Space Partitioning* (PSP) proposed by [20,33].

Landscaping provides an overview how data and models behave to each other and how informative a specific data set is in distinguishing two models. The main idea of landscaping is the following: Given model input (i.e., ROs and LOs in our case), each model is used to generate sets of artificial data (i.e., ratings in our case) and then both models fit these data. Landscaping provides a measure of what is called *model mimicry* by [42]: The ability of a model to account for data generated by another model. Each model should fit the self-generated data quite well – without added noise this fit should be almost perfect. If, however, one model is also able to closely fit the data generated by another model, this model mimics the other model, i.e., this model is able to behave like the other model. We are currently applying the landscaping method on the stimuli from [35]. On a different set of stimuli, a landscaping analysis confirmed the greater flexibility of the AVS model (i.e., the AVS model mimics the rAVS model but not vice versa, see [24,25]).

The PSP algorithm is a Markov chain Monte Carlo (MCMC) based method and searches in the parameter space of the models for regions of patterns that are qualitatively different. First results confirm the high flexibility of the AVS model (i.e., the AVS model is able to generate many patterns that are qualitatively different by using different sets of parameters). The rAVS model, however, generates fewer patterns with a qualitative difference (see [22] for details). To test the predictions revealed by the PSP analysis we conducted an empirical rating study with the same stimuli. More on the results of this study can be found in [24,25].

*Functionality.* The AVS model does not account for any effects of the functionality of objects on spatial language comprehension, although there is evidence that – beside purely geometric effects – functional interactions between objects also affect the use of spatial prepositions [8,9,12–14,18].

For instance, [9] conducted an object placement task, where participants had to place a toothpaste tube above a toothbrush. They showed that the toothpaste tube was not placed above the center-of-mass of the toothbrush, but rather above the bristles of the toothbrush – that is, at the location where both objects can functionally interact. Objects with a smaller amount of functional interaction (here, a tube of oil paint) were placed more above the center-of-mass of the toothbrush instead of above the bristles.

Despite this evidence, the AVS model (and thus also our rAVS model) only considers geometric representations of the RO and the LO. For the AVS model, however, a range of extensions that integrate functionality were already proposed [8,26]. Since the rAVS model is designed to be as similar as possible to the AVS model, these functional extensions might also be applicable for the rAVS model.

*Implementing the Models in Artificial Systems.* In order to implement these models into artificial systems, additional steps are necessary. The models were designed to model spatial language *understanding*. The models thus produce an acceptability rating given a RO, a LO, and a preposition. As part of an artificial system that *interprets* spatial language, the models can be used straightforwardly: Given a spatial utterance and a visual scene, the models can be used to compute acceptability ratings for all points around the RO (i.e., a spatial template). The artificial system then starts the search for the LO at the point with the highest rating. To *generate* spatial language with the help of these models, one could imagine the following steps: Compute the acceptability ratings of different spatial prepositions (e.g., above, below, to the left of, in front of, ...) and subsequently pick the one with the highest rating.

Simulating the models showed that the computation of the attentional vector sum is computationally more expensive than the linear function that is used by the rAVS model. Thus, the rAVS model provides a shortcut for the computation of the final vector. In particular, this is interesting for the implementation of the model in real-time robotic systems that often have constrained computational resources.

In conclusion, we proposed a modified version of the AVS model: the rAVS model. The rAVS model accounts for the same empirical data as the AVS model while integrating additional recent findings regarding the direction of the attentional shift that conflict with the assumptions of the AVS model.

**Acknowledgments.** This research was supported by the Cluster of Excellence Cognitive Interaction Technology 'CITEC' (EXC 277) at Bielefeld University, which is funded by the German Research Foundation (DFG). The authors would also like to thank two anonymous reviewers for their useful comments and suggestions.

# References

1. Burigo, M.: On the role of informativeness in spatial language comprehension. Ph.D. thesis, School of Psychology, University of Plymouth (2008)
2. Burigo, M., Coventry, K.R., Cangelosi, A., Lynott, D.: Spatial language and converseness. Q. J. Exp. Psychol. **69**(12), 2319–2337 (2016). doi:10.1080/17470218. 2015.11248942016
3. Burigo, M., Knoeferle, P.: Visual attention during spatial language comprehension. PLoS ONE **10**(1), e0115758 (2015)

4. Burigo, M., Sacchi, S.: Object orientation affects spatial language comprehension. Cogn. Sci. **37**(8), 1471–1492 (2013)
5. Cangelosi, A., Coventry, K.R., Rajapakse, R., Joyce, D., Bacon, A., Richards, L., Newstead, S.N.: Grounding language in perception: a connectionist model of spatial terms and vague quantifiers. Prog. Neural Process. **16**, 47 (2005)
6. Canty, A., Ripley, B.: Boot: Bootstrap R (S-Plus) Functions (2015). R package version 1.3-15
7. Carlson, L.A., Logan, G.D.: Attention and spatial language. In: Itti, L., Rees, G., Tsotsos, J.K. (eds.) Neurobiology of Attention, pp. 330–336. Elsevier, Amsterdam (2005). Chap. 54
8. Carlson, L.A., Regier, T., Lopez, W., Corrigan, B.: Attention unites form and function in spatial language. Spat. Cogn. Comput. **6**(4), 295–308 (2006)
9. Carlson-Radvansky, L.A., Covey, E.S., Lattanzi, K.M.: "What" effects on "where": functional influences on spatial relations. Psychol. Sci. **10**(6), 516–521 (1999)
10. Carrasco, M.: Visual attention: the past 25 years. Vis. Res. **51**(13), 1484–1525 (2011)
11. CGAL: Computational geometry algorithms library. http://www.cgal.org
12. Coventry, K.R., Garrod, S.C.: Saying, Seeing, and Acting: The Psychological Semantics of Spatial Prepositions. Essays in Cognitive Psychology, Psychology Press, Taylor and Francis, Hove and New York (2004)
13. Coventry, K.R., Lynott, D., Cangelosi, A., Monrouxe, L., Joyce, D., Richardson, D.C.: Spatial language, visual attention, and perceptual simulation. Brain Lang. **112**(3), 202–213 (2010)
14. Coventry, K.R., Prat Sala, M., Richards, L.: The interplay between geometry and function in the comprehension of over, under, above, and below. J. Mem. Lang. **44**(3), 376–398 (2001)
15. Franconeri, S.L., Scimeca, J.M., Roth, J.C., Helseth, S.A., Kahn, L.E.: Flexible visual processing of spatial relationships. Cognition **122**(2), 210–227 (2012)
16. Gapp, K.-P.: An empirically validated model for computing spatial relations. In: Wachsmuth, I., Rollinger, C.-R., Brauer, W. (eds.) KI 1995. LNCS, vol. 981, pp. 245–256. Springer, Heidelberg (1995). doi:10.1007/3-540-60343-3_41
17. Georgopoulos, A.P., Schwartz, A.B., Kettner, R.E.: Neuronal population coding of movement direction. Science **233**, 1416–1419 (1986)
18. Hörberg, T.: Influences of form and function on the acceptability of projective prepositions in Swedish. Spat. Cogn. Comput. **8**(3), 193–218 (2008)
19. Kelleher, J.D., Kruijff, G.J.M., Costello, F.J.: Proximity in context: an empirically grounded computational model of proximity for processing topological spatial expressions. In: Proceedings of the 21st International Conference on Computational Linguistics and the 44th annual meeting of the Association for Computational Linguistics, pp. 745–752. Association for Computational Linguistics (2006)
20. Kim, W., Navarro, D.J., Pitt, M.A., Myung, I.J.: An MCMC-based method of comparing connectionist models in cognitive science. Adv. Neural Inf. Process. Syst. **16**, 937–944 (2004)
21. Kluth, T.: A C++ implementation of the reversed Attentional Vector Sum (rAVS) model. Bielefeld University (2016). doi:10.4119/unibi/2900103
22. Kluth, T., Burigo, M., Knoeferle, P.: Investigating the parameter space of cognitive models of spatial language comprehension. In: 5. Interdisziplinärer Workshop Kognitive Systeme, Bochum (2016)
23. Kluth, T., Burigo, M., Knoeferle, P.: Shifts of attention during spatial language comprehension: a computational investigation. In: Proceedings of the 8th International Conference on Agents and Artificial Intelligence, vol. 2, pp. 213–222. SCITEPRESS (2016). doi:10.5220/0005851202130222

24. Kluth, T., Burigo, M., Schultheis, H., Knoeferle, P.: Distinguishing cognitive models of spatial language understanding. In: Proceedings of the International Conference on Cognitive Modeling (2016). Poster presented at the ICCM 2016

25. Kluth, T., Burigo, M., Schultheis, H., Knoeferle, P.: Testing the predictions of cognitive models of spatial language comprehension (in preparation)

26. Kluth, T., Schultheis, H.: Attentional distribution and spatial language. In: Freksa, C., Nebel, B., Hegarty, M., Barkowsky, T. (eds.) Spatial Cognition 2014. LNCS (LNAI), vol. 8684, pp. 76–91. Springer, Heidelberg (2014). doi:10.1007/978-3-319-11215-2_6

27. Lee, C., Rohrer, W.H., Sparks, D.L.: Population coding of saccadic eye movements by neurons in the superior colliculus. Nature **332**, 357–360 (1988)

28. Logan, G.D.: Spatial attention and the apprehension of spatial relations. J. Exp. Psychol. Hum. Percept. Perform. **20**(5), 1015 (1994)

29. Logan, G.D.: Linguistic and conceptual control of visual spatial attention. Cogn. Psychol. **28**(2), 103–174 (1995)

30. Logan, G.D., Sadler, D.D.: A computational analysis of the apprehension of spatial relations. In: Bloom, P., Peterson, M.A., Nadel, L., Garrett, M.F. (eds.) Language and Space, pp. 493–530. The MIT Press, Cambridge (1996). Chap. 13

31. Metropolis, N., Rosenbluth, A.W., Rosenbluth, M.N., Teller, A.H., Teller, E.: Equation of state calculations by fast computing machines. J. Chem. Phys. **21**(6), 1087–1092 (1953)

32. Navarro, D.J., Pitt, M.A., Myung, I.J.: Assessing the distinguishability of models and the informativeness of data. Cogn. Psychol. **49**(1), 47–84 (2004)

33. Pitt, M.A., Kim, W., Navarro, D.J., Myung, J.I.: Global model analysis by parameter space partitioning. Psychol. Rev. **113**(1), 57–83 (2006)

34. Pitt, M.A., Myung, I.J.: When a good fit can be bad. Trends Cogn. Sci. **6**(10), 421–425 (2002)

35. Regier, T., Carlson, L.A.: Grounding spatial language in perception: an empirical and computational investigation. J. Exp. Psychol.: Gen. **130**(2), 273–298 (2001)

36. Richter, M., Lins, J., Schneegans, S., Sandamirskaya, Y., Schöner, G.: Autonomous neural dynamics to test hypotheses in a model of spatial language. In: Bello, P., Guarini, M., Mc-Shane, M., Scassellati, B. (eds.) Proceedings of the 36th Annual Conference of the Cognitive Science Society, pp. 2847–2852. Cognitive Science Society, Austin (2014)

37. Roberts, S., Pashler, H.: How persuasive is a good fit? A comment on theory testing. Psychol. Rev. **107**(2), 358–367 (2000)

38. Roth, J.C., Franconeri, S.L.: Asymmetric coding of categorical spatial relations in both language and vision. Front. Psychol. **3**, Article No. 464 (2012)

39. Schultheis, H., Carlson, L.A.: Mechanisms of reference frame selection in spatial term use: computational and empirical studies. Cogn. Sci. (2015). doi:10.1111/cogs.12327

40. Schultheis, H., Singhaniya, A., Chaplot, D.S.: Comparing model comparison methods. In: Proceedings of the 35th Annual Conference of the Cognitive Science Society, pp. 1294–1299. Cognitive Science Society, Austin (2013)

41. Veksler, V.D., Myers, C.W., Gluck, K.A.: Model flexibility analysis. Psychol. Rev. **122**(4), 755–769 (2015)

42. Wagenmakers, E.J., Ratcliff, R., Gomez, P., Iverson, G.J.: Assessing model mimicry using the parametric bootstrap. J. Math. Psychol. **48**(1), 28–50 (2004)

# Detecting Hidden Objects Using Efficient Spatio-Temporal Knowledge Representation

Joanna Isabelle Olszewska$^{(\boxtimes)}$

University of Gloucestershire, Cheltenham, UK
`joanna.olszewska@ieee.org`

**Abstract.** Detecting visible as well as invisible objects of interest in real-world scenes is crucial in new-generation video-surveillance. For this purpose, we design a fully intelligent system incorporating semantic, symbolic, and grounded information. In particular, we conceptualize temporal representations we use together with spatial and visual information in our multi-view tracking system. It uses them for automated reasoning and induction of knowledge about the multiple views of the studied scene, in order to automatically detect salient or hidden objects of interest. Tests on standard datasets demonstrated the efficiency and accuracy of our proposed approach.

**Keywords:** Surveillance application · Visual scene analysis · Automated scene understanding · Knowledge representation · Spatio-temporal visual ontology · Symbolic reasoning · Computer vision · Pattern recognition

## 1 Introduction

The newest generation of video-surveillance applications [1] requires multi-view, intelligent systems with robust semantic information extraction [13]. Hence, it has led to the development of automatic systems for multiple-object tracking [6], suspicious object detection [11], or unusual activity recognition [7], in a recorded scene [8].

In particular, the efficient detection and tracking of objects of interest in a multi-camera environment (Fig. 1) is still a challenging task. Indeed, it implies the understanding of the camera network in terms of visual coverage of the cameras [19], calibration of the cameras [27], etc. It also requires the design of computer vision techniques being robust to varying lighting conditions, or to objects occlusions of different nature such as object-to-object occlusions and object-to-scene occlusions [32]. Moreover, it usually involves the modelling of the knowledge about the scene, e.g. the number of the persons evolving in the scene, their location within the scene, or the direction of their trajectory.

In the computer-vision literature, works performing multi-object tracking in multi-camera environment apply techniques such as synergy map [9], probabilistic occupancy maps [12], or K-shortest path [4] to model such knowledge. Despite

© Springer International Publishing AG 2017
J. van den Herik and J. Filipe (Eds.): ICAART 2016, LNAI 10162, pp. 302–313, 2017.
DOI: 10.1007/978-3-319-53354-4_17

being widely used, these statistical methods are limited in terms of scalability with respect to the number of considered, contextual data [28].

On the other hand, symbolic representation has been used to codify knowledge about visual scenes in context of video content analysis [3], video summarization [26], or video annotation [15,20], especially modelling the video-surveillance domain [31]. In these works, ontologies have been developed to describe the studied visual scenes, but not to deduce new information.

Recently, some papers propose to integrate structured symbolic knowledge into computer-vision systems for activity recognition [29], event recognition [30], event prediction [18] or tracking estimation [14]. These approaches have been proven to be efficient. However, these context-aware methods are mainly deductive rather than inductive, and are designed for single camera views only.

In this paper, we propose to incorporate symbolic description of the scene together with ontological reasoning into a vision system to infer knowledge about the scene in order to detect and track objects of interest which may be hidden in some/most of the views. Hence, the system incorporates visual, spatial and temporal knowledge. In particular, this paper studies efficient temporal conceptualization for new-generation, video-surveillance applications. Hence, the designed system features a multi-camera, knowledge-based, detector and tracker of both visible and non-visible objects of the scene, and generates a complete, semantic description of the scene as well as its visual annotation in all views.

The analysed scene is assumed to be acquired in outdoor or indoor environment, captured by multiple, synchronized cameras with overlapping field of views (FOVs). Our system supports both static or mobile cameras, and does not require the specific knowledge of the parameters of the cameras.

Objects evolving in the scene could present occlusions in one or several views. Occlusions could be of object-to-object type, when two or more objects of interest overlap each other in a ratio from 0.1 to 1 (or full occlusion); or of object-to-scene type, when an object of interest is partially or totally not visible due to objects present in the background.

The developed intelligent vision system allows a computationally efficient and accurate analysis of objects of interest evolving in one or multiple views of a scene. It provides both qualitative and quantitative answers to the following questions: How much objects are in the scene? Where are the objects in each view? Is there a hidden object in a view? Which object is hidden in that view? Where about it is hidden in that view? When is the object in the scene/in a view? How long is the object in the scene/in a view?

Hence, the contributions of this paper are two folds:

- the design of an automated vision system which is based on the combined grounded and symbolic, spatio-temporal reasoning in order to detect both visible and invisible objects of interest evolving in real-world scenes captured by multiple, synchronized cameras;
- the efficient conceptualization of temporal knowledge for information induction rather than deduction, in context of automated detection and tracking of salient as well as hidden objects of interest in multi-view scenes.

The paper is structured as follows. In Sect. 2, we describe our system for multi-camera stream analysis (see Fig. 2) based on both computer-vision techniques to compute quantitative data, and on artificial intelligence methods to process qualitative data in order to generate a description of the observed scene and to induce information about its objects of interest. In addition, we present our conceptualization of the spatio-temporal knowledge used in this intelligent system. Our approach performance have been assessed on standard, real-world video-surveillance dataset as reported and discussed in Sect. 3. Conclusions are drawn up in Sect. 4.

## 2    Proposed Approach

The proposed approach to detect salient and hidden objects of interest in multi-camera, synchronized video streams consists of seven steps [25].

At first, frames of the different views of the scene are extracted from the videos acquired by cameras which could have the same or different calibration parameters.

Secondly, these visual views are processed in order to be synchronized both in time and space. The temporal synchronization consists in matching the time stamp of each of the video frame with this of a frame related to another view. Spatial matching [10] of temporally synchronized views is performed by matching local descriptors extracted in both frames of each of the background view. If there is more than two views, the matching process is repeated for each of the pair of views. It is worth to note that this second step could be done offline or partially skipped in case of synchronized videos or previously aligned views.

Thirdly, the visible objects of interest are detected in each of the visual views as described in [23] by means of active contours. Active contours are initialized based on blobs obtained by combining both frame difference and background subtraction techniques. Considering a color image $I(x, y)$ with M and N, its width and height, respectively, and RGB, its color space, blobs are computed in parallel by, on one hand, the difference between a current frame $I_k^v(x, y)$ in the view $v$ and the precedent one $I_{k-1}^v(x, y)$, and by, on the other hand, the difference between the current frame $I_k^v(x, y)$ and a background model of the view $v$, and afterwards, by adding both results in order to extract the foreground in the corresponding view. The background itself is modeled using the running Gaussian average (RGA), characterized by the mean $\mu_b^v$ and the variance $(\sigma_b^v)^2$, as the RGA method suits well for real-time tracking.

Hence, the foreground is determined by [23]

$$F^v(x, y) = \begin{cases} 1 & \text{if } \left| F_f^v(x, y) \cup F_b^v(x, y) \right| = 1, \\ 0 & \text{otherwise,} \end{cases} \tag{1}$$

with

$$F_f^v(x, y) = \begin{cases} 1 & \text{if } \left| I_k^v(x, y) - I_{k-1}^v(x, y) \right| > tf, \\ 0 & \text{otherwise,} \end{cases} \tag{2}$$

and

$$F_b^v(x, y) = \begin{cases} 1 & \text{if } |I_k^v(x, y) - \mu_b^v| > n \cdot \sigma_b^v, \\ 0 & \text{otherwise,} \end{cases} \tag{3}$$

where $tf$, is the threshold, and $n \in \mathbb{N}_0$.

To compute a final blob defined by labeled connected regions, morphological operations such as opening and closure are applied to the extracted foreground $F^v$, in order to exploit the existing information on the neighboring pixels, in a view $v$,

$$f^v(x, y) = Morph(F^v(x, y)). \tag{4}$$

Then, an active contour is computed for each frame $k$ in each view $v$ separately, and for each targeted object. In this work, an active contour [21] is a parametric curve $\mathcal{C}(s) : [0, 1] \rightarrow \mathbb{R}^2$, which evolves from its initial position computed by means of Eq. (4) to its final position, guided by internal and external forces as follows:

$$\mathcal{C}_t(s, t) = \alpha \, \mathcal{C}_{ss}(s, t) - \beta \, \mathcal{C}_{ssss}(s, t) + \Xi, \tag{5}$$

where $\mathcal{C}_{ss}$ and $\mathcal{C}_{ssss}$ are respectively the second and the fourth derivative with respect to the curve parameter $s$; $\alpha$ is the elasticity; $\beta$ is the rigidity; and $\Xi$ is the multi-feature vector flow [22].

After the detection of the visible objects of interest in the different views is performed using active contours as explained above, the symbolic description of the visual views is extracted automatically using the framework and repeated for each of the view.

In particular, we define the spatial relation $isInScene(P_p)$ with logic notations as follows:

$$\begin{aligned} isInScene(S, P_p) &\sqsubseteq Scene\_Property \\ &\sqcup isInView(V_1, P_p) \\ &\sqcup \dots \\ &\sqcup isInView(V_N, P_p), \end{aligned} \tag{6}$$

where $hasInView$ is a sub-property of $hasInScene$; $S$ is the analysed scene containing $N \in \mathbb{N}$ views; $P_p$ is the $pth$ object of interest within the scene; and $V_v$ is the $vth$ view of the scene, with $v = [1, N]$.

Furthermore, we extend this property (Eq. 6) to incorporate temporal relations we conceptualize as follows:

$$\begin{aligned} isInScene(S, P_p, t_i) &\sqsubseteq Scene\_Property \\ &\sqcup isInView(V_1, P_p, t_i) \\ &\sqcup \dots \\ &\sqcup isInView(V_N, P_p, t_i), \end{aligned} \tag{7}$$

where $t_i$ is the time of the event, i.e. of the observation, and thus $i$ corresponds to the frame $i$ of the videostream. Hence, Eq. 7 modifies point-based linear temporal

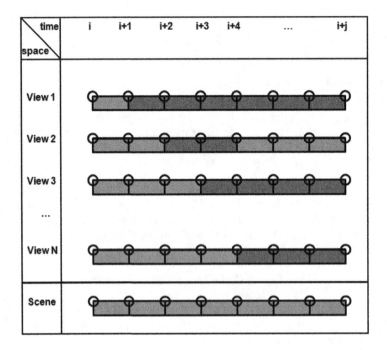

**Fig. 1.** Example of a space-time scenario computed based on the process of multi-view, synchronized videostreams where an object of interest is evolving in. The green notation is used in case the object of interest is visible in a view, while the red notation is used in case the object is non-visible in a view. The space-time scenario of the scene is induced from the scenarios extracted in the different views. Best viewed in color. (Color figure online)

relations, such as [17], to take into account the intrinsic time granularity of the scene which is dictated by the acquisition frame rate of 25 $f/s$. Indeed, $\Delta t = t_{i+1} - t_i$ is set to be equal to $1/25 = 0.04\,s$.

In order to further conceptualize the temporal relations within the scene (see Fig. 1), we define the following relation:

$$
\begin{aligned}
isInScene(S, P_p, [t_i, t_{i+j}]) \sqsubseteq\ & Scene\_Property \\
& \sqcup\, isInView(V_1, P_p, [t_i, t_{i+j}]) \\
& \sqcup\, ... \\
& \sqcup\, isInView(V_N, P_p, [t_i, t_{i+j}]),
\end{aligned}
\tag{8}
$$

where $t_i, t_{i+j}$ are the time interval of the observation, with $j \neq i$ and $j \in \mathbb{N}_0$, and

$$isInScene(S, P_p, [t_i, t_{i+j}]) \sqsubseteq Scene\_Property$$
$$\sqcup\, isInView(V_1, P_p, t_i)$$
$$\sqcup\, isInView(V_1, P_p, t_{i+1})$$
$$\sqcup\, ...$$
$$\sqcup\, isInView(V_1, P_p, t_{i+j})$$
$$\sqcup\, ...$$
$$\sqcup\, isInView(V_N, P_p, t_i)$$
$$\sqcup\, isInView(V_N, P_p, t_{i+1})$$
$$\sqcup\, ...$$
$$\sqcup\, isInView(V_N, P_p, t_{i+j}). \tag{9}$$

Equation 8 is based on interval temporal relations [2], while it naturally extends the point-based temporal concepts as shown in Eq. 9. Thus, this new formulation is well-adapted to the context of automated analysis of video streams.

The generation of the semantic scene description, followed by the generation of the views' knowledge-based descriptions, is automatically induced by the reasoner.

Then, the detection of the hidden objects in the visual views is based on this induced knowledge, since each view is related to another one because of the overlapping fields of view of the same scene and because of views' synchronisation. Moreover, qualitative spatial relations such as RCC-8 and the o'clock model [24] applied to objects of each of the views allow the definition of the potential regions where could appear hidden objects. Finally, the non-visible objects detected in the last step as well as the visible objects detected in the third step are all localized in the views by means of bounding boxes. The latter ones are computed to surround the detected objects in order to use standard metrics for sake of comparison with other methods, when tracking over the time the target objects, as detailed in Sect. 3.

# 3   Experiments and Discussion

To validate our approach, we have applied our system on the publicly available CVLAB dataset [4] called *Passageway*. It contains four video-surveillance sequences, recorded each by one of the four corresponding DV cameras at a rate of 25 fps, and encoded with Indeo 5. All cameras were synchronized and located about 2 m from the ground. They were filming the same area under different angles, and their fields of view were overlapping (Fig. 2). The resulting four videos are made of 2500 frames each, with a frame resolution of $360 \times 288$ pixels. The chosen location for the data acquisition was an outdoor environment consisting of a dark underground passageway to a train station, where were evolving objects of interests, i.e. pedestrians.

This database of 10,000 images in total owns challenges such as handling variations of the persons in quantity, pose, motion, size, appearance, and scale.

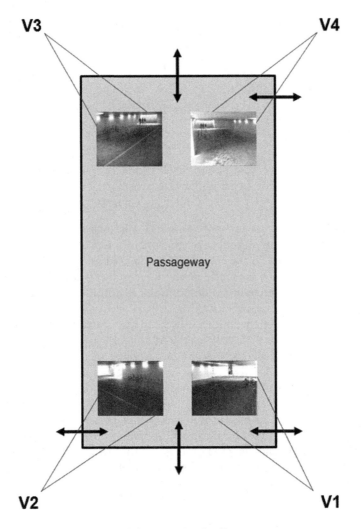

**Fig. 2.** Overview of the scene in the *Passageway* sequence.

In particular, the area covered by the system is wide, and people get very small on the far end of the scene, making their precise localization challenging.

This series of multi-camera video sequences involving several people passing through a public underground passageway also presents large lighting variations, which is typical in real-world surveillance situations. Indeed, scene's lighting conditions are very poor, since a large portion of the images is either underexposed or saturated.

Most importantly, this dataset requires the processing of multi-view video streams where many parts of the scenario were filmed by only two or even a single camera, with some people partially occluded or not visible over significant

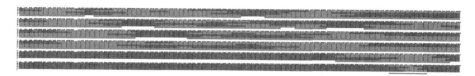

**Fig. 3.** Detected objects of interest in the four views of the scene in the *Passageway* sequence. The green notation is used for visible objects of interest, the red notation is used for non-visible objects, while the yellow notation is used for induced detection of object of interst in the scene. Best viewed in color. (Color figure online)

**Fig. 4.** Samples of results obtained with our approach for a scene captured by four synchronized cameras with overlapping field of views. First column: view 1; Second column: view 2; Third column: view 3; Fourth column: view 4. First row: raw visual data in each of the camera view. Second row: detected persons in all views (yellow bounding boxes), including the hidden persons (red bounding boxes). Best viewed in color. (Color figure online)

numbers of frames in the related views. All these difficulties make the dataset challenging and interesting to test our approach.

All the experiments have been run on a computer with Intel Core 2 Duo Pentium T9300, 2.5 GHz, 2 Gb RAM, using MatLab and OWL languages as well as HermiT reasoner.

To evaluate the performance of our system, we adopt the standard CLEAR metrics, i.e. Multiple Object Detection Accuracy (MODA) and Multiple Object Detection Precision (MODP), as well as Multiple Object Tracking Accuracy (MOTA) and Multiple Object Tracking Precision (MOTP). These metrics are standard for the evaluation of detection and tracking algorithms, and are convenient to compare our approach with other works such as [4]. The detection precision metric (MODP) assesses the quality of the bounding box alignment in case of correct detection, while its accuracy counterpart (MODA) evaluates the relative number of false positives and missed detections [16]. The tracking precision metric (MOTP) measures the alignment of tracks compared against ground truth, while the tracking accuracy metric (MOTA) produces a score based on othe amount of false positives, missed detections, and identity switches [5].

Our approach has been tested for detection and tracking of both visible and hidden objects of interest on the four multi-camera video streams of the CVLAB dataset (see Fig. 3).

Samples of our results are presented in Fig. 4. This scene presents difficult situations such as strong patterns, e.g. the yellow line on the floor in views 2 and 3 or the staircases in views 3 and 4, poor foreground/background contrast, light reflections, or illumination changes. Moreover, some target objects could only be seen in one of the views as per configuration illustrated in Fig. 2. Hence, in Fig. 4, the four persons present in the scene are only visible in two of the four views (views 3 and 4). View 1 shows two of the four persons, whereas only one of them appears in the view 2. Our system copes well with these situations as discussed below.

**Table 1.** Multiple Object Detection Accuracy (MODA) and Multiple Object Detection Precision (MODP) in CVLAB *Passageway* video frames, using approches such as ◇[12], □[4], and our.

|      | ◇   | □   | Our   |
|------|-----|-----|-------|
| MODA | 63% | 72% | 96.5% |
| MODP | 66% | 70% | 94.2% |

**Table 2.** Multiple Object Tracking Accuracy (MOTA) and Multiple Object Tracking Precision (MOTP) in CVLAB *Passageway* video streams, using approaches such as □[4] and our.

|      | □   | Our   |
|------|-----|-------|
| MOTA | 73% | 95.8% |
| MOTP | 68% | 94.3% |

In Table 1, we have reported the Multiple Object Detection Accuracy (MODA) and Multiple Object Detection Precision (MODP) rates of our method against the rates achieved by [12] and [4], while in Table 2, we have displayed the Multiple Object Tracking Accuracy (MOTA) and Multiple Object Tracking Precision (MOTP) scores of our method against the rate obtained by [4].

From Tables 1 and 2, we can observe that our system provides reliable detection of objects of interest in multi-camera environment, and that our multiple-object tracking method is also very accurate, outperforming state-of-the-art techniques. Indeed, methods relying, e.g. on detection maps which can get very noisy due to the difficult real-world, outdoor environment conditions, have thus their performance greatly affected [4,12], unlike our approach.

Furthermore, state-of-the-art methods only deal with partial occlusions of the objects, whereas our system allows the detection of hidden objects, i.e. objects of interest fully occluded by either other foreground objects or by background objects. Our system performs the invisible object detection and tracking by means of the conjunction of effective vision techniques with knowledge induction and integration of qualitative spatial and temporal relations. It is worth noting that strong occlusions are an additional difficulty for tracking systems to keep the tracks of the objects of interest.

For all the dataset, the average computational speed of our approach is in the range of milliseconds, thus our developed system could be used in context of real-world, video surveillance.

## 4    Conclusions

Our system to detect and track objects of interest, which could be visible or hidden in a scene captured by multiple, synchronized cameras, is based on both high-level and low-level data. On one hand, visual information are extracted by our system in all of the acquired views. On the other hand, our system uses spatio-temporal symbolic knowledge, and in particular computationally efficient temporal concepts, as well as semantic information in order to perform reasoning about the scene for the automatic generation of a scene description and for the knowledge induction to accurately detect hidden objects within the scene.

## References

1. Albanese, M., Molinaro, C., Persia, F., Picariello, A., Subrahmanian, V.S.: Finding unexplained activities in video. In: Proceedings of the AAAI International Joint Conference on Artificial Intelligence, pp. 1628–1634 (2011)
2. Allen, J.F.: Maintaining knowledge about temporal intervals. Commun. ACM **26**(11), 832–843 (1983)
3. Bai, L., Lao, S., Jones, G.J.F., Smeaton, A.F.: Video semantic content analysis based on ontology. In: Proceedings of the IEEE International Machine Vision and Image Processing Conference, pp. 117–124 (2007)
4. Berclaz, J., Fleuret, F., Tueretken, E., Fua, P.: Multiple object tracking using K-shortest paths optimization. IEEE Trans. Pattern Anal. Mach. Intell. 33(9), 1806–1819 (2011)
5. Bernardin, K., Stiefelhagen, R.: Evaluating multiple object tracking performance: the CLEAR MOT metrics. EURASIP J. Image Video Process. **2008**, 1–10 (2008)
6. Bhat, M., Olszewska, J.I.: DALES: automated tool for detection, annotation, labelling and segmentation of multiple objects in multi-camera video streams. In: Proceedings of the ACL International Conference on Computational Linguistics Workshop, pp. 87–94 (2014)
7. Chen, L., Wei, H., Ferryman, J.: ReadingAct RGB-D action dataset and human action recognition from local features. Pattern Recogn. Lett. **50**, 159–169 (2014)
8. Dai, X., Payandeh, S.: Geometry-based object association and consistent labeling in multi-camera surveillance. IEEE J. Emerg. Sel. Top. Circ. Syst. **3**(2), 175–184 (2013)

9. Evans, M., Osborne, C.J., Ferryman, J.: Multicamera object detection and tracking with object size estimation. In: Proceedings of the IEEE International Conference on Advanced Video and Signal Based Surveillance, pp. 177–182 (2013)

10. Ferrari, V., Tuytelaars, T., Gool, L.V.: Simultaneous object recognition and segmentation from single or multiple model views. Int. J. Comput. Vis. **67**(2), 159–188 (2006)

11. Ferryman, J., Hogg, D., Sochman, J., Behera, A., Rodriguez-Serrano, J.A., Worgan, S., Li, L., Leung, V., Evans, M., Cornic, P., Herbin, S., Schlenger, S., Dose, M.: Robust abandoned object detection integrating wide area visual surveillance and social context. Pattern Recogn. Lett. **34**(7), 789–798 (2013)

12. Fleuret, F., Berclaz, J., Lengagne, R., Fua, P.: Multicamera people tracking with a probabilistic occupancy map. IEEE Trans. Pattern Anal. Mach. Intell. **30**(2), 267–282 (2008)

13. Fookes, C., Denman, S., Lakemond, R., Ryan, D., Sridharan, S., Piccardi, M.: Semi-supervised intelligent surveillance system for secure environments. In: Proceedings of the IEEE International Symposium on Industrial Electronics, pp. 2815–2820 (2010)

14. Gomez-Romero, J., Patricio, M.A., Garcia, J., Molina, J.M.: Ontology-based context representation and reasoning for object tracking and scene interpretation in video. Expert Syst. Appl. **38**(6), 7494–7510 (2011)

15. Jeong, J.W., Hong, H.K., Lee, D.H.: Ontology-based automatic video annotation technique in smart TV environment. IEEE Trans. Consum. Electron. **57**(4), 1830–1836 (2011)

16. Kasturi, R., Goldgof, D., Soundararajan, P., Manohar, V., Garofolo, J., Boonstra, M., Korzhova, V., Zhang, J.: Framework for performance evaluation of face, text, and vehicle detection and tracking in video: data, metrics, and protocol. IEEE Trans. Pattern Anal. Mach. Intell. **31**(2), 319–336 (2009)

17. Kowaslki, R., Sergot, M.: A logic-based calculus of events. New Gener. Comput. **4**, 6795 (1986)

18. Lehmann, J., Neumann, B., Bohlken, W., Hotz, L.: A robot waiter that predicts events by high-level scene interpretation. In: Proceedings of the International Conference on Agents and Artificial Intelligence, pp. I.469–I.476 (2014)

19. Mavrinac, A., Chen, X.: Modeling coverage in camera networks: a survey. Int. J. Comput. Vis. **101**(1), 205–226 (2013)

20. Natarajan, P., Nevatia, R.: EDF: a framework for semantic annotation of video. In: Proceedings of the IEEE International Conference on Computer Vision Workshops (ICCVW 2005) (2005)

21. Olszewska, J.I.: Multi-target parametric active contours to support ontological domain representation. In: Proceedings of the RFIA Conference, pp. 779–784 (2012)

22. Olszewska, J.I.: Multi-scale, multi-feature vector flow active contours for automatic multiple-face detection. In: Proceedings of the International Conference on Bio-Inspired Systems and Signal Processing (2013)

23. Olszewska, J.I.: Multi-camera video object recognition using active contours. In: Proceedings of the International Conference on Bio-Inspired Systems and Signal Processing, pp. 379–384 (2015)

24. Olszewska, J.I., McCluskey, T.L.: Ontology-coupled active contours for dynamic video scene understanding. In: Proceedings of the IEEE International Conference on Intelligent Engineering Systems, pp. 369–374 (2011)

25. Olszewska, J.: Tracking the invisible man - knowledge-based detection of hidden objects for complex visual scene understanding. In: Proceedings of the International Conference on Agents and Artificial Intelligence (ICAART 2016), pp. 223–229 (2016)
26. Park, H.-S., Cho, S.-B.: A fuzzy rule-based system with ontology for summarization of multi-camera event sequences. In: Rutkowski, L., Tadeusiewicz, R., Zadeh, L.A., Zurada, J.M. (eds.) ICAISC 2008. LNCS (LNAI), vol. 5097, pp. 850–860. Springer, Heidelberg (2008). doi:10.1007/978-3-540-69731-2_81
27. Remagnino, P., Shihab, A.I., Jones, G.A.: Distributed intelligence for multi-camera visual surveillance. Pattern Recogn. **37**(4), 675–689 (2004)
28. Riboni, D., Bettini, C.: COSAR: hybrid reasoning for context-aware activity recognition. Pers. Ubiquitous Comput. **15**(3), 271–289 (2011)
29. Ryoo, M.S., Aggarwal, J.K.: Semantic understanding of continued and recursive human activities. In: Proceedings of the IEEE International Conference on Pattern Recognition (ICPR 2006) (2006)
30. Sridhar, M., Cohn, A.G., Hogg, D.C.: Unsupervised learning of event classes from video. In: Proceedings of the AAAI International Conference on Artificial Intelligence, pp. 1631–1638 (2010)
31. Vrusias, B., Makris, D., Renno, J.P., Newbold, N., Ahmad, K., Jones, G.: A framework for ontology enriched semantic annotation of CCTV video. In: Proceedings of the IEEE International Workshop on Image Analysis for Multimedia Interactive Services, p. 5 (2007)
32. Yilmaz, A., Javed, O., Shah, M.: Object tracking: a survey. ACM Comput. Surv. **38**(4), 13 (2006)

# Author Index

Printed in the United States
By Bookmasters